Fascist Spectacle

Studies on the History of Society and Culture
Victoria E. Bonnell and Lynn Hunt, Editors

Fascist Spectacle

The Aesthetics of Power in Mussolini's Italy

SIMONETTA FALASCA-ZAMPONI

University of California Press

BERKELEY   LOS ANGELES   LONDON

University of California Press
Berkeley and Los Angeles, California

University of California Press, Ltd.
London, England

© 1997 by
The Regents of the University of California

Library of Congress Cataloging-in-Publication Data
    Falasca-Zamponi, Simonetta, 1957–
        Fascist spectacle : the aesthetics of power in Mussolini's Italy /
    Simonetta Falasca-Zamponi.
            p.   cm.—(Studies on the history of society and culture ; 28)
        Includes bibliographic references and index.
        ISBN 0–520–20623–1 (alk. paper)
            1. Fascism—Italy.   2. Italy—Politics and government—
    1922–1945.   3. Fascism and culture—Italy.   4. Aesthetics, Italian—
    20th century.   I. Title.   II. Series.
    DG571.F2   1997
    320.5′33′0945—dc20   96–28827
                                                                    CIP

Printed in the United States of America
9   8   7   6   5   4   3   2   1

A Ugo e Marusca

Contents

Illustrations

Acknowledgments

This book is the result of long and often difficult research and theorizing on the relation between fascism and aesthetics. I want to thank the numerous friends and colleagues who have encouraged and supported me in this intellectual enterprise. In particular, I wish to express my gratitude to Victoria Bonnell for her scholarly guidance and Martin Jay for inspiring and enlightening my interest in the topic. Both offered critical readings of the original dissertation manuscript during my graduate studies at the University of California, Berkeley. Jerome Karabel and Giuseppe Di Palma provided insightful suggestions on the original manuscript. Roger Friedland, my colleague at the University of California, Santa Barbara, critically engaged with the argument and presuppositions of my study. Richard Kaplan read, commented on, and discussed the several different versions of this project. I also greatly benefited from reviewers' comments solicited by the University of California Press.

During my research in Italy I enjoyed the helpful assistance of Alberto Maria Arpino, Renzo De Felice, Luigi Goglia, and Neri Scerni. Mario Missori and all the librarians and staff at the Archivio Centrale dello Stato in Rome and the Archivio Storico del Ministero degli Esteri were immensely helpful. At the Istituto Luce, director E. Valerio Marino gave me the opportunity to review rare documentaries and newsreels.

In addition to individuals, several institutions contributed to this project. A John L. Simpson Memorial Research Fellowship provided funds for preliminary research at the dissertation level. A Faculty Career Development Award at the University of California, Santa Barbara, allowed precious time for writing. Finally, research assistance from graduate students was funded by grants from the Academic Senate, Committee on Research, and the Interdisciplinary Humanities Center at the University of California, Santa Barbara.

I would like to thank Richard Kaplan again for being there. I will only add that this project and I owe him more than he might be willing to accept.

This book is dedicated to my parents.

Introduction

At 10:55 on the morning of October 30, 1922, in a sleeping car of the DD17 train coming from Milan, Benito Mussolini arrived at the Termini station in Rome.[1] With him he carried the written proof of the mandate bestowed on him by the king to become the new prime minister of Italy.[2] After a brief stop at the Hotel Savoia, Mussolini headed to the Quirinale for a meeting with King Vittorio Emanuele III. He returned to the Quirinale that same evening with a list, to be approved by the king, of the ministers participating in his "national government." Amidst praises for Mussolini from newspapers, politicians, cultural personalities, and industrial elites, fascism's reign in Italy began.[3]

The circumstances leading to Mussolini's proclamation as prime minister were quite unusual. Only a few days earlier, on October 27, 1922, a group of fascists had mobilized with the plan of marching on Rome and occupying the capital.[4] The leaders of the march held their headquarters in Perugia, a city one hundred miles from Rome, while Mussolini remained in Milan. The core of the fascist forces was located on the outskirts of the capital, from where, according to the scheme, they would all be ready to converge on the city on October 28. Luigi Facta, the prime minister at the time, decided to proclaim martial law in Rome in order to protect the city. And although there were some doubts about the army's behavior in case of a clash with the fascists, from a military point of view Mussolini's Black Shirts were unlikely to be victorious.[5] However, the unexpected happened. The king refused to sign the decree that established the state of siege. Mussolini, who had been negotiating with the government for a nonviolent satisfaction of his power demands, was invited to participate in a coalition dominated by conservatives and nationalists. Mussolini rejected the offer and imposed the condition that he form his own government. The king accepted, and on October 29 Mussolini was summoned to Rome, where he was officially proclaimed prime minister the following day. On October 31 the Black Shirts, who had been waiting for the order to march, reached the capital (many by special trains) and paraded before Mussolini and the king. The violent takeover of Rome thus never took place, and the Black Shirts' march-parade ended up being the choreographic appendix to Mussolini's legal appointment as prime minister.

Though the episode of the march unfolded along these peculiar lines, the fascist regime never accepted this historical account of its ascent to power. On the contrary, it elaborated its own interpretation of the march and always called the events of late October 1922 a "revolution."[6] In his Milan speech of October 4, 1924, Mussolini proclaimed: "Like it or not, in October 1922 there was an insurrectional act, a revolution, even if one can argue over the word. Anyway, a violent take-over of power. To deny this real fact . . . is truly nonsense."[7] A few months earlier he had told the Grand Council gathered at Palazzo Venezia: "Fascism did not come to power through normal means. It arrived there by marching on Rome *armata manu*, with a real insurrectional act."[8] Fascist rhetoric made of the march a mythical event in the history of fascism. October 28 became the date of one of the most important fascist celebrations, the anniversary of the March on Rome, first observed in 1923 in a four-day commemoration.[9] In 1927, the new fascist calendar identified the pseudo-march as the epochal breakthrough of fascism: years were counted beginning with October 29, 1922, year I of the "fascist era." In 1932 the regime remembered the Decennial of the Revolution with great pomp and later established a permanent Exhibit of the Revolution. In sum, although the march never occurred, and although behind the scenes Mussolini had actually tried to avoid an armed insurrection,[10] the regime took the march to mark the beginning of the fascist epoch. By transforming a choreographed rally into a glorious event, fascism made of the March on Rome a symbolic moment in the construction of its own revolutionary identity. The mythicization of the March on Rome became a narrative device in fascism's elaboration of its own historical tale.

Jean-Pierre Faye claims that history, in the process of narrating, produces itself and that discourses, while telling about actions, at the same time generate them.[11] In this book I will look at fascism's official symbolic discourse—manifested through images, rituals, speeches—as a text that narrates fascism's epics, that recounts its story.[12] I will also interpret fascist discourse as producing, through a work of weaving and plotting, its own happening. In this context, the mythicization of the March on Rome appears as the opening prologue to fascism's creation of its own story/history.[13]

NARRATIVE AND REPRESENTATION

This cultural approach to the study of Italian fascism is founded on a notion of narrative as intersubjective discourse that takes place within a social space and a historical time.[14] We resort to narration in our everyday world as a way to describe objects and events. Through these narrative presentations we establish mutual understanding with members of the collectivity to which we belong. A crucial means for social recognition, narratives also provide us with ways to organize reality and construct meanings: we make sense of our experience by telling stories that draw from a common stock of knowledge, a cultural tradition that is intersubjectively shared. In this process we develop personal and social identities as subjects of communication, social actors in the life-world in which we take part. As Habermas explains, people "can develop personal identities only if they recognize that the sequences of their actions form narratively presentable life histories; they can develop social identities only if they recognize that they maintain their membership in social groups by way of participating in interactions, and thus that they are caught up in the narratively presentable histories of collectivities."[15] Following the critique of the traditional view of language as transparent and reflecting an existing reality, Habermas emphasizes the pragmatic dimension of language as communication. He suggests adopting a practical notion of speech acts as mediating and creating social meanings. Within this context, what Austin calls the performative quality of language, its ability to bring about a change, becomes another important feature of narratives. When we speak we indeed do more than describe events. We also produce actions, which then exercise profound consequences on social and historical processes.

The performative character of language draws attention to and dramatizes the relation between power and representation. Not only are there unequal positions from which discourse unfolds, as Habermas warns, but narratives of power are also able to create new categories of understanding, frames of reference, forms of interpretation that naturalize meanings and in turn affect the course of social action.[16] Moreover, if we assume that power cannot subsist without being represented—if representation is the very essence of power, its force—then narratives also produce power while representing it.[17] Because we normally tend to identify sense with reference, content with form, and reality with representation, the fact that events seem to narrate themselves self-referentially doubles the authority of power, whose discourse purportedly tells the truth.[18] Power becomes both the producer and the product of its own discursive formation.[19] The power of narrative and the narrative of power form an explosive combination.

This book takes the power of discourse, including its nonlinguistic forms (rituals, myths, and images), as an essential element in the formation of the fascist regime's self-identity, the construction of its goals and definition of ends, the making of its power.[20] By examining cults, symbols, and speeches, this study looks at the process through which fascism shaped its contours, delineated its purposes, negotiated its meanings, and built its authority. Mussolini's regime unfolded over more than twenty years, and at its foundation on March 23, 1919, the fascist movement had no clear doctrinal boundaries; though rooted in revolutionary socialism, it echoed nationalism's appeal to potency via a struggle between nations, not classes. Following the dictum that the movement was supposed to produce a doctrine, not vice versa, fascism opposed ideological orthodoxy, the party system, and, more generally, bourgeois political life.[21] Although the movement turned into a party (the Fascist National Party) only two years after its foundation, and though it became a governmental force in 1922, it still vowed to maintain the feature of political and ideological flexibility that had characterized the movement's previous experience. Only in 1932 was an official fascist doctrine elaborated.[22]

This is not to say that fascism's identity was always in flux; certainly a core of assumptions and values, although loosely structured, continuously operated within fascism. Indeed, no movement can ever be said to be fixed, an objectified and objectifiable entity. Nor do self-proclamations, such as Mussolini's denial of a permanent political stance, necessarily convey the truth or postulate reality. But the moment proclamations become public and are shared intersubjectively, they acquire a power of their own, they cast and frame prospective actions, and they make the speaker liable to its referent, whether it is to embrace, retract, eradicate, or assail it. Although no locutionary act can be taken at face value, the choice of things to speak of cannot be dismissed either. When fascism chose to define the March on Rome as a "revolution," this decision was not without consequences, both for the internal building of the movement and the determination of its future deeds. Whether or not a fictional trope, the invocation of "revolution," as any form of self-representation, bound and guided fascism's claims to political rule and channeled its demands for change. The new meanings created by representations affected fascism's self-definition, the developmental trajectory of Mussolini's regime, and the formation of its public identity.[23] More than mere means of political legitimation, rituals, myths, cults, and speeches were fundamental to the construction of fascist power, its specific physiognomy, its political vision.[24]

The importance of cultural forms in the history of the fascist regime is increasingly recognized, although studies rarely address the relation of mutual influence between fascism and its symbolic practices. Systematic analyses of the creative impact that cultural elements exercised on the evolution of fascist power are wanting. One notable exception is the work of the Italian historian Emilio Gentile,[25] who, following George Mosse's pioneering study of the cultural roots of Nazi Germany, has examined the fascist regime's symbolic aspects under the category of the sacralization of politics.[26] Both Gentile and Mosse situate the origins of fascism's political style within the historical context of nineteenth-century Europe. At this time, and in the wake of the French revolution, the traditional embodiment of the sacred and its institutions (church and monarchy) were defeated, the myth of Christendom was shattered, and the hierarchical model of social relations had been liquidated. The modern, secular notion of politics, which was co-extensive with parliamentary representation, became the target of critical appraisals about its ability to unify the polity around common goals, particularly in view of the new social groups and classes asserting their political voice. In his discussion of the German case, Mosse connects the appeal of political symbolism to increasing elite and middle-class fears about formlessness in society.[27] Mass democracy seemed to engender anarchy in political life: the recourse to rituals and myths would help establish an orderly social world. The possibility of unifying around national symbols ensured the cohesion of otherwise inchoate "masses," their shaping into a homogeneous political body. Participation in public festivals refurbished national spirit, whereas rituals and ceremonies cemented the unity of the nation. Under the impulse of nationalistic sentiments, and thanks to the new political style, life could resume a form, an order.

In Italy, the critique of parliament and democracy, from which fascism originated, was rooted in the historical reality of the post-Risorgimento. The unification of the state in 1861 had not been followed by a genuine integration of the country's diverse population, and over the years the liberal political class had failed to heal the division between state and civil society despite various attempts at forging a civil and national spirit.[28] At the beginning of the twentieth century, disillusionment over the liberal system and its inability to create a national consciousness among Italians fostered the demand for new forms of political style and government. Organizational questions on how to control and channel the political participation of workers associations, socialist parties, and unions paralleled the search for novel values that would endow Italy with the spiritual unity it had been lacking. Some voiced the need for spiritual ideals and moral renewal; others made more aggressive requests for expansionism and military strength.

The clamoring for new models of political rule became more strident in Italy at the end of World War I, after the experience of the trenches and the collective mobilization of human and material resources seemed to have unified the Italians in their common sacrifice for the nation. The heroic sense generated by the war needed to be preserved in a form of politics that would raise itself above the traditional opportunistic games of petty politicking, then identified with the liberal government of Giovanni Giolitti.[29] Politics of the piazza (open-air meetings), popular during interventionist rallies, became a legacy of the war years, and many invoked it in opposition to the democratic process of public debate and representation of interests as staged in parliamentary discussion.[30] Speakers and protagonists of the piazza developed their own specific rhetoric and adopted new forms of symbolism to reach people's emotions directly. They addressed massive, "oceanic" assemblies within open urban spaces.[31] The poet and writer Gabriele D'Annunzio offered a tangible example of this technique in his short-lived regency in Fiume.[32] In this contested city on the Adriatic, from September 1919 to December 1920, D'Annunzio created a unique experiment in political rule that stood as a model of antiliberal politics. Based on a dialogue with the crowd and drawing on his oratorical mastery, D'Annunzio's regency in Fiume exalted idealism and heroism, spiritual values and aesthetic gestures, social renewal and political rebirth. The poet delivered speeches that superseded the traditional division between religion, art, and politics and encouraged the audience to take up a heroic role. Songs, processions, meetings, military celebrations, and other ritualistic occasions dominated life at Fiume, where the general atmosphere was charged with enthusiasm, excitement, and gaiety.[33]

With the aim of giving "style" back to Italy, Mussolini's movement appropriated many of D'Annunzio's invented myths, cults, and ceremonies.[34] Since the fascist movement's beginning in 1919, reliance on symbols and rites had been its driving motif, connecting its search for a different style in politics to a repudiation of democratic political forms.[35] The call for a renewed model that would counteract democracy's formal procedures and parliamentary institutions became one of the identifying features of a movement that claimed to "represent a synthesis of all negations and all affirmations."[36] In his speeches and writings, Mussolini expressed discomfort with the traditional categories of politics. He invoked symbolic means and forms that would excite emotions in the people. He underplayed traditional and rational laws in favor of a more direct involvement of the polity in public life. Thus, in its twenty long years in power, the fascist regime, after dispensing with democratic procedures and establishing a dictatorship in 1925, tirelessly invented symbols, myths, cults, and rituals. Italian fascism, well before German Nazism, revolved around the myth and cult of the leader; Mussolini—the Duce—occupied a central role in the fascist regime's symbolic world. Over the years the regime rewrote the history of ancient Rome and made of it a myth, which it celebrated yearly. War, as potentially regenerative and also expressing the virility of the country, became another cultural myth of fascism. In general, violence signified rebirth and renewal for the fascists; thus, they mythicized the March on Rome as a "revolution," a bloody event with a purifying effect. Rituals of dressing, speaking, and behaving also entered the domain of everyday life and of private individual bodies. These rituals assumed a prominent role, especially in the second decade of the regime, when rules of conduct were supposed to shape the Italians into fascist men.

Emilio Gentile argues that festivals, symbols, rituals, and cults were the necessary instruments of fascism's sacralized version of politics. For Gentile, the festivals of the nation, the anniversaries of the regime, the cult of the Duce, and the consecration of symbols all participated in creating fascism's lay religion. The erection of buildings and the remaking of the urban landscape, as well as the invention of new rituals and the establishment of pageant celebrations, were intended to contribute to the sacralization of the state under the aegis of the fascist government. The existence of the state depended on people's faith in it. Faith in the state was assured by a mass liturgy whose function was to educate the Italians, making them new citizens and imparting a higher morality. At the same time, the image of fascism as national religion helped shape the characteristics of the regime by stressing values such as faith, belief, and obedience. Gentile emphasizes the link between fascism's symbolic politics and national sentiments, and he interprets this link as part of a more general phenomenon characterizing political modernity.[37]

I share Gentile's cultural-political analysis of the historical context in which fascism's appeal to symbols took place; however, I believe the analytical category of "politics as religion" does not exhaustively convey the nature of Italian fascism, its peculiar cultural content. Although Mussolini's implementation of symbolic politics unfolded in an era that witnessed a common impulse toward nation-building, references to "lay religion" alone cannot explicate fascism's unique turn, its original totalitarian culture. The sacralization of politics does not account for Mussolini's singular approach to governing, his ambiguous sense of morality, his idiosyncratic relation to the polarized concepts of spirit and body, reason and emotion, active and passive, public and private, masculine and feminine. As we shall see, Mussolini's pursuit of a beautiful, harmonious society coexisted with the indictment of stasis and the exaltation of struggle as the fundamental rule of life; his conception of the "masses" as a passive material for the leader-artist

to carve was counterpoised by his belief in people's active, symbolic participation in politics. Mussolini displayed contempt for the "masses'" female,
emotional irrationality and sensitivity yet also expressed scorn for democratic, dry, rational discussion. His solicitation to popular, public involvement in fascism was coextensive and simultaneous with an operation to deny
the private while politicizing it. His negation of the individual in favor of
the state envisaged an exception for the self-referential, self-creating subject: the manly artist-politician.

How can we interpret the apparent contradictions at the core of fascism's
cultural and political identity, these hybrid couplings, this nondescript coexistence? Gentile's sacralization of politics recognizes some of Italian fascism's
discrete dimensions but fails to explain the logic of their interconnectedness
and to exhaust adequately their significance within fascist cosmology. In this
book I propose that the notion of aesthetic politics will further illuminate
the shady links between fascism's belief in the leader's omnipotence and its
conception of the "masses" as object, between the artistic ideal of harmonic
relations and the auratic embracement of war, between the construction of
"new men" and the focus on style, between the reliance on spectacle and the
attack on consumption, between claims to the spiritual functions of the state
and the affirmation of totalitarianism. In his 1937 account of the "essence
and origin" of fascism, Giuseppe Antonio Borgese addressed the aesthetic
disposition present in Mussolini's regime.[38] Borgese specifically underscored
Mussolini's identification of the statesman with the artist and his idea of the
state as a work of art. He emphasized the implosion of means and ends in
the regime's pursuit of its political project and warned of the surrender of
ethical values implicit in fascism's ill-defined aesthetic vision. Despite this
beginning, however, the aesthetic character of fascist politics has been subsequently marginalized and reduced to a corollary position, whereas considerations of aesthetics and politics have enjoyed a legitimate status in scholarly accounts of German Nazism.[39] National Socialism indeed differed from
Italian fascism in several ways, if only because of the centrality of the racial
question in Nazi doctrine. Yet Italian fascism developed much in advance of
National Socialism and provided a model for Hitler's own elaboration of political style. Within this context, the significance of Italian fascism's aesthetic
approach to politics is all the more compelling.

But what characterized fascism's aesthetic politics? And how does the reference to aesthetic politics contribute to our understanding of Mussolini's
movement? Walter Benjamin's philosophical-cultural analysis of art and
mechanization in the modern era provides a theoretical platform on which
to formulate an answer to these questions.

AESTHETICS AND POLITICS

Benjamin considered fascism's aestheticization of politics at the end of his 1936 essay "The Work of Art in the Age of Mechanical Reproduction."[40] In this essay, Benjamin was interested in establishing the consequences of the loss of "aura" in modern artworks. Aura, intended as a quasi-religious halo, characterized traditional works of art, which, being nonreproducible, unique, and authentic, created an aesthetic distance between the public and themselves and led the audience to a general state of passivity.[41] With the development of technological means of reproduction, Benjamin believed, the work of art had lost its distancing aura and its status of cultic object. Deprived of its mystical halo, the work of art enhanced an active attitude in the public[42] and became a potential tool in social struggle.[43]

The political function of the artistic work motivated Benjamin to tie art to fascism's politics. Benjamin noted that in the case of fascism technology, paradoxically, was not leading to the complete decline of aura and cultic values. On the contrary, he thought fascism was able to utilize the remnants of auratic symbols and their mystical authority both to keep the "masses" from pursuing their own interests and to give them a means to express themselves. With fascism, politics was "pressed into the production of ritual values" and became a cultic experience.[44] The logical result of this process, claimed Benjamin, was the introduction of aesthetics into political life. Fascism's meshing of aesthetics and politics had, then, two consequences. First, it culminated in war, because only war could give the "masses" a goal while diverting them from challenging the "traditional property system." Second, and most important, it gave preeminence to the pursuit of total aims without any limits from laws, tradition, or ethical values. As in the "art for art's sake" (*l'art pour l'art*) movement, which defined art as an enclosed space completely separated from the rest of the value spheres, aesthetic politics was involved in the creation of a work of art and thus claimed absolute autonomy. In the fascist case, said Benjamin, *fiat ars-pereat mundus* (let art be created even though the world shall perish) had become fascism's creed and influenced its actions. Art was not a means but rather an end, as the futurist Filippo Tommaso Marinetti demonstrated in his exaltation of war:

> War is beautiful because it establishes man's dominion over the subjugated machinery by means of gas masks, terrifying megaphones, flame throwers, and small tanks. War is beautiful because it initiates the dreamt-of metalization of the human body. War is beautiful because it enriches a flowering meadow with the fiery orchids of machine guns. War is beautiful because it combines the gunfire, the cannonades, the cease-fire, the scents, and the

stench of putrefaction into a symphony. War is beautiful because it creates new architecture, like that of the big tanks, the geometrical formation flights, the smoke spirals from burning villages, and many others.[45]

Benjamin, not unlike theorists of political religion, argued that the loss of tradition and the decline of religious authority constituted critical elements in the "auraticization" of fascism. In contrast to those theorists, however, Benjamin added another crucial element to the understanding of fascism's approach to politics, an element that links fascism closely to the *l'art pour l'art* movement: the prevalence of form over ethical norms. It is the presence of this element, I will argue, that characterizes Italian fascism's aestheticized politics; and it is the emphasis on form (intended as appearance, effects, orderly arrangement) that helps to explain fascism's cultural-political development. This does not mean that the difference between theories of fascism as political religion and as aestheticized politics resides in the assertion of, respectively, the presence or absence of ethics in Mussolini's movement.[46] Attention to the formal aspects of fascist politics does not imply that fascism rejected ethics and spirituality. Rather, the emphasis on form underscores the fate of fascism's claims to ethics, the place of these claims within fascist culture. No doubt fascism presented itself as auratic in opposition to "disenchanted" democratic governments in the same way that the *l'art pour l'art* movement was driven by spiritual aims against the commercialization of art. But the *l'art pour l'art* movement's reaction to the commodification of art under the conditions of capitalism entailed the cutting of any links of art to social life. As Richard Wolin writes: "*L'art pour l'art* seeks *a restoration of the aura though within* the frame of aesthetic autonomy."[47] Similarly, fascism's aim to respiritualize politics unfolded from a position of absolute self-referentiality that inevitably led the regime to privilege in its actions the value of aesthetic worth over claims of any other nature. Within this perspective, then, one needs to reevaluate the trajectory and role of spirit in fascism. Fascism's pretensions to spirituality and religion require testing against the equally fascist invocations of artistic bravura.

Aesthetic considerations were indeed central to the construction of fascism's project, and they reached deep into the heart of fascism's identity, its self-definition, its envisioning of goals. But lest we conflate aestheticized politics with fascism and Nazism or interpret any application of aesthetics to the political realm as unequivocally negative,[48] we need to spell out the peculiarities and implications of fascism's relation to aesthetics. In particular, we ought to begin questioning the meaning of aesthetics and its identification with art, an equation that is itself the result of a specific historical shift.

Aesthetics, in fact, originally applied to nature; its etymological source, the Greek term *aisthitikos,* refers to what is perceived by feeling.[49] As the realm of sensation through smell, hearing, taste, touch, and sight, aesthetics concerned our ability to experience and know the world through the body. It represented a mode of cognition founded on the material dimension of the human.[50] When in the eighteenth century it developed into an autonomous discipline within Western philosophy, aesthetics still maintained its primary link to the body, the material. However, in a complex operation at the height of the Enlightenment process, modern aesthetics began to be concerned increasingly with cultural artifacts (then available on the market as commodities) and was subsumed in the artistic field. Nature was displaced by human-made objects as the realm of application for aesthetics' cognitive functions. Art and aesthetics overlapped. Although art still involved sensory experience and feelings, aesthetics' original meaning of bodily perception underwent continuous challenges. On the one hand, once art developed into an autonomous discipline and was raised to the status of theory, it suffered from abstraction and formalization under the aegis of aesthetics. Born as a discourse of the body that would complement the philosophy of mind, aesthetics turned the natural into its opposite—an intellectual object.[51] On the other hand, art's self-proclaimed role of representing the expressive dimensions and communal desires of humans—against the purposive rationality of the bourgeois, capitalist world—led art to pursue autonomy from the functionalization of everyday life. With the *l'art pour l'art* movement, this move culminated in the attempt to reduce the sensual and impose form. One strand of modern art thus cut loose the senses, and avant-garde artists declared their independence from nature through the fable of autogenesis—the belief in *homo autotelus,* who creates ex nihilo and self-referentially.

Cornelia Klinger argues that the fable of autogenesis reproposes the myth of man's irreducibility to the serfdom and yoke of the senses, and it is a typically modern response to the critical dualism between culture and nature.[52] This dualism constitutes the matrix for a whole string of binary oppositions characterizing Western thought: mind and body, reason and emotion, active and passive, public and private. Furthermore, says Klinger, such polarized concepts ultimately incorporate the dualism of gender, in which the rational, spiritual, "cultural" man confronts the irrational, sensual, "natural" woman. In order to realize his aspirations to boundless creativity but also to freedom, man needs to overcome the feared laws of nature, with their impositions of limits and closures. Interestingly, Klinger also shows that the cultural tensions inscribed in Western thought are reasserted in modern aesthetics' concepts of the sublime and the beautiful as they have been developed from Kant's *Critique of Judgment,* beginning in the second half of the eighteenth century.[53] The dilemma of man's "sublime," limitless struggle with feminine, "beautiful" nature reappeared then in full extension.[54] Stretched to its extremes, this dilemma gives way to, among others, the modern artist's God-like claims to creation and the consequent displacement of the body's relationship to the world, the negation of the senses, the emotions, the feminine.

I suggest that in order to explain fascism's version of aestheticized politics, we need to focus on this split between aesthetics and the senses. More specifically, I contend that if we want to understand the idiosyncrasies at the center of fascism's identity, we need to interpret fascist aesthetics as founded on the sublimation of the body and the alienation of sensual life. Mussolini's aspirations to transform Italy and create it anew was yet another variation on the theme of the God-like artist-creator. And although fascism relied on people's feelings and sentiments (much as art came to appear as the refuge from instrumental-rational society), it still strove to neutralize the senses, to knock them out.

In his discussion of the spectacle of war valorized by Marinetti, Benjamin mentioned fascism's sensory alienation.[55] He interpreted this alienation within his general theory of the loss of experience and the transformation of sense perception characterizing modernity.[56] According to Benjamin, in the age of crowds and automatons,[57] bombarded by images and noises, overwhelmed with chance encounters and glances, we need to put up a "protective shield" against the excess of daily shocks hitting us. In this process, our system of perception ends up repressing our senses, deadening them as in an "anaesthetic" procedure,[58] and we lose the capacity for shared meaning. For Benjamin, this alienation of the senses was a condition of modernity, not a creation of fascism. However, he believed that fascism took advantage of modernity's contradictions by filling the absence of meaning left by the loss of experience, thus enforcing the crisis in perception.

I would like to stress Benjamin's point further and add that fascism actively strove to impel and actuate sensory alienation. In a time of new technologies, filmic panoramas, dioramas, and world exhibitions, fascism offered a phantasmagoria of rituals and symbols—"big tanks," "flights," and "burning villages"—flooding the senses.[59] With photographic images and newsreels, appearances on airplanes and motorbikes, and speeches from balconies and extravagant podiums, Mussolini dominated the fascist spectacle. Festivals, rituals, and ceremonies punctuated the fascist year, and permanent and ephemeral art celebrated the regime's accomplishments. Iconographic symbols in several forms and shapes filled public spaces, from walls and buildings to coins and stamps. Radio and cinema constantly recorded fascism's deeds and periodically reported Mussolini's speeches, thoughts, slogans, and proclamations.[60] With fascism the senses were truly excited, although also fundamentally denied. Though posters of Mussolini looked down on people from every corner, the regime rejected the dreamworlds of mass consumption as the receptacle of wants and desires; celebrations united people in a common cult, yet materialism and happiness became the main targets of fascism's antidemocratic stance. Fascism turned sensory alienation into the negation of human nature, the depersonalization of the "masses," the deindividualization of the body politic, as evidenced in Mussolini's identification of the "masses" with dead matter, a block of marble to be shaped. In this apotheosis of the senses' denial, the conception of the "masses" as raw material meant that one could smash the "masses," hit them, mold them: there would be no pain, no scream, no protest, for there were no senses involved. In fascism's representation, people were disembodied and became alive only under the hands of the sculptor-leader, who then channeled popular enthusiasm toward communal rituals. The figure of the artist implied by this metaphor presents the alter ego of the mass object: the omnipotent, manly creator who, as the fable of autogenesis suggests, self-creates himself.[61] Fascism's artist-politician, not unlike the independent nineteenth-century exponent of *l'art pour l'art,* claims full autonomy to his creative will and substitutes his artistic vision for the disenchanted world of democratic governments.[62] Guided by an aesthetic, desensitized approach to politics, Mussolini conceived the world as a canvas upon which to create a work of art, a masterpiece completely neglectful of human values. I would argue that fascism's conception of aesthetic politics here reveals its truly totalitarian nature.

Claude Lefort claims that at the heart of totalitarian politics lies the idea of creation.[63] The world-transformer, the artist-politician of a totalitarian state, aims at founding a new society on fresh ground and free of limits from laws, tradition, or ethical values.[64] This new creation is built upon the suppression of any division between state and civil society. It eliminates the existence of autonomous social spheres and turns out to be, in the intention of its producers, a unitary whole. In order to maintain the unity of the whole, parts need to be sacrificed. Any possibility of conflict dissolves within this context, because differences are denied in the name of a state of harmony that appears to constitute the core of the totalitarian idea of a beautiful society.

Mussolini strove to fulfill this model of the totalitarian artist in order to forge fascist men. In accordance with his belief in struggle, however, he ensured internal uniformity and harmony by establishing difference through an external war. Imperialistic drives subtended fascism's historical unfolding. But fascism's pursuit of war was not connected to the need to divert the "masses," as Benjamin suggested. Rather, fascism's raison d'être, its understanding of social relations, and its view of the world were founded on the worship of action, the exaltation of conflict, the continuous assertion of man's ability to control and transform reality and impose his will without limits. Fully entrenched in the modernist dilemma of creation/destruction,[65] fascism offered its own ambiguous response to the contradictions of cultural modernity by coalescing the incongruous and reconciling the incompatible. The hybrid offspring of turn-of-the-century political events and culture, the fascist movement reflected its protagonists' struggle to imagine and establish a novel form of government that would redefine life, rejuvenate politics, reinvent social relations, and revive cults and traditions. Thus, fascism burst open Italian society in order to mold it. It exploded the humus of everyday life by imposing new practices. It crushed individual freedom in the pursuit of a collective whole. It bent people's will to engage in military enterprises. It assaulted democratic procedures and exalted one man's rule. It destroyed in order to construct a totalitarian state and a totalitarian society. Spurred by an aesthetic vision of the world, fascism wanted to remake Italy and the Italians. In the process, as we are going to see, it made itself.[66]

1 Mussolini's Aesthetic Politics

THE POLITICIAN AS ARTIST

In a speech delivered in 1926, on the occasion of the *Novecento* art exhibit, Mussolini confessed that the question of the relationship between art and politics was challenging and certainly troubled his thoughts.[1] However, Mussolini affirmed, he was certain of one thing: strong points of contact united politicians to artists:

> That politics is an art there is no doubt. Certainly it is not a science, nor is it empiricism. It is thus art. Also because in politics there is a lot of intuition. "Political" like artistic creation is a slow elaboration and a sudden divination. At a certain moment the artist creates with inspiration, the politician with decision. Both work the material and the spirit. . . . In order to give wise laws to a people it is also necessary to be something of an artist.[2]

In this address Mussolini identified the political with artistic creation, and he asserted that the politician's task consisted in working the material and the spirit, just as artists do. Politics constituted a form of art, and the politician needed an artistic soul in order to perform his role.

In raising the relationship between art and politics, Mussolini revealed openly in the *Novecento* speech the importance that aesthetics played in his conception of politics.[3] The tight connection Mussolini envisaged between politics and art in that speech[4] was not merely the product of a picturesque literary pretension. Nor would Mussolini only display that attitude on rare occasions. To the contrary, the link between politics and art constituted the central element of Mussolini's political vision; it guided his notion of the politician's role and informed his conception of the leader's relation to the populace. For Mussolini, aesthetics represented a major category in the interpretation of human existence. Life itself was a white canvas, a coarse block of marble that needed to be turned into an artwork; and he often declared his Nietzschean will to "make a masterpiece" out of his life.[5] However, and in view of his own leadership position, Mussolini interpreted life mainly in political terms. Hence, when the journalist Emil Ludwig asked him how he could reconcile statements such as "I want to dramatize my life" with the political affirmation "My higher goal is public interest," Mussolini not surprisingly answered he did not see any contrast between the two. The connection appeared entirely logical to him: "The interest of the populace is a dramatic thing. Since I serve it, I multiply my life."[6] Mussolini did not find any contradiction between aesthetic aspirations and political practice, personal ideals and general well-being. He rejected the bureaucratic concept of politics and turned to aesthetics in order to revitalize the politician's role.[7] Accordingly, whether he was conducting his life as a romantic drama or accomplishing more immediate and strategic tasks, Mussolini considered his decisions as political leader in terms of the production of a final masterpiece. For him, reality could be artistically formed according to one's will; and he believed in the omnipotence of the artist-politician. In effect, his reliance on aesthetics had provided him with an absolute notion of the politician's power. "[T]he world is how we want to make it, it is our creation," he claimed in an almost God-like spirit.[8] The politician built a world anew through the force of his will; he constructed a different political order through his decisions.[9]

Following this interpretation of the politician's role, Mussolini presented himself as the artist of fascism, the artificer of a "beautiful" system and a "beautiful" doctrine. In his Milan speech of October 28, 1923, Mussolini proclaimed: "[T]hose who say fascism, say first of all beauty."[10] And in his January 28, 1924, address to the Fascist Party, he defined fascism as a "doctrine of force, of beauty."[11] It was in relation to fascism that Mussolini foresaw the possibility of fully attaining his role as artist-politician. It was within fascism that he could realize his aesthetic masterpiece. Thus, when Ludwig asked him with reference to the March on Rome episode, "In your trip to Rome, did you feel like an artist who starts his work of art or a prophet who follows his own vision?" Mussolini not by chance answered: "Artist."[12] And when Ludwig told him, "You sound to me . . . like the men I studied in history; too much of a poet not to act completely intuitively in decisive moments, as under an inspiration," Mussolini replied: "The March on Rome was absolutely an inspiration."[13] Since the beginning of his leadership role, Mussolini considered himself the creative soul of the nation, the guide to a future renewal of the country, the propeller of new ways of living. In sum, Mussolini concretely established a correspondence between artist and politician through reference to his own case, and he identified his artistic work with the realization of the political project of fascism.[14]

Mussolini's aesthetic conception of politics was founded on an elitist vision of social relations. This vision characterized turn-of-the-century mass-psychology theories, elite theories, and theories of the crowd as elaborated by, among others, Gaetano Mosca, Vilfredo Pareto, Gabriel Tarde, Gustave

Le Bon, and Robert Michels. Le Bon's conceptualization of the crowd and his call for a strong leader particularly inspired Mussolini's interpretation of his own role as artist-politician and influenced his opinion of the "masses."

The Feminine Crowd

At the end of the 1800s, there developed in France a "scientific" interest in the crowd.[15] Social theorists focused on mass movements in order to establish the scientific laws of human behavior, and new interpretations of people's conduct were thus produced. These theories arose in a climate of anxiety among intellectual elites over the fast development of an industrial-urban society.[16] But they also reflected growing perceptions about societal crisis in the wake of France's large military defeat in 1870 and the violent social upheavals that characterized the end of the Commune in 1871.[17] Suddenly, the old, familiar order seemed to be breaking into pieces, and the intellectual and scientific community began to doubt the primacy of France's civilizational role and the value of French culture. Modern discoveries and industries, and the new conditions of existence deriving from them, created uncertainties among members of the upper class, who worried about the continuity of a political and economic system that had privileged the individual against egalitarian tendencies. The specter of the crowd, with its disruptive potential and violent energy, came to haunt the imagination of France's privileged classes.[18]

To be sure, the number of strikes had risen in France by the end of the nineteenth century, and workers' movements acquired unprecedented visibility. Yet research has shown that violent episodes occurred in only 3.6 percent of all labor protests, and only in one case had there been a murder. This notwithstanding, the public presence of the "masses" was increasingly interpreted as a social rupture, an internal disturbance.[19] Social psychologists reflected these perceptions by dedicating their attention to the study of the crowd. Under their pen, mass violence became magnified, and crowds came to embody the source and mirror of social problems.

This new wave of psychologists seemingly continued the historical and literary tradition initiated by Hippolyte Taine and Émile Zola, who just a few years earlier had offered in their fiction suggestive and negative descriptions of crowds' behavior.[20] But whereas Taine and Zola had merely portrayed what they believed was the irrational nature of the crowds, the new social theorists tried to transform descriptive observations into general explanatory laws that would account for collective behavior in modern social relations. Gabriel Tarde, Henri Fournial, Alfred Espinas, Gustave Le Bon, and the Italian Scipio Sighele were the major representatives of the new science, and all shared a common premise: they believed that a gathering of people would cause the blinding of the individual minds participating. Accordingly, a collective mentality would dominate the group and turn it into an unpredictable and uncontrollable force. For Tarde and the others, the result of collective interaction was doubtlessly negative, and they identified the melding of minds with the suspension of reason—that is, with the necessary condition for the perpetration of crimes.[21] The first elaboration of crowd theories thus issued from a direct interest in determining the criminal responsibility of crowds.[22] Drawn on contemporary medical studies of nonrational processes in people's conduct, these theories extended the discussion of crowds' crimes to a general assessment of crowd behavior. Hence, Sighele believed that mass revolts, strikes, and riots made urgent a solution to the question of collective actions' general causes and consequences.[23] Though he proposed a differentiation between two kinds of collective crimes, premeditated and spontaneous, he still maintained that all kinds of crowds were susceptible to evil and tended to commit antisocial acts.[24] People, whenever grouped in a crowd, formed an irrational whole, an irresponsible acting subject. Following this trend, Le Bon stressed the element of irrationality in the "masses." For him, crowds were characterized by illogical spirit, instinctive character, and a propensity to be governed by feelings. "Little adapted to reasoning, crowds, on the contrary, are quick to act," Le Bon stated in the introduction to his popular text *La psychologie des foules*.[25] The book proceeded to list other distinctive attributes of the crowd: "impulsiveness, irritability, incapacity to reason, the absence of judgment and of the critical spirit, the exaggeration of the sentiments."[26] Le Bon affirmed that the qualities one could find in the crowd were the same as the ones in "beings belonging to inferior forms of evolution"—that is, women, savages, and children.[27] Crowds were instinctual and emotional, and feelings dominated them. Le Bon ultimately offered a portrayal of the "masses" as unable to participate responsibly in political processes.

One of the main arguments social theorists used to support their negative judgment of the "masses" was the identification of crowds with women. Women, along with drunkards, had indeed become the object of strict pathological analyses in the Third Republic because of the belief in their potential power to undermine civilization.[28] Physicians, criminologists, and other social scientists dedicated their efforts to examining the female gender's pathologies and deranged behavior.[29] Having established women's biological impurity and consequent predisposition to insanity and hysteria, some scientists concluded that public life would aggravate this condition. It was then necessary to limit women's participation in society, especially because female insanity was considered transmissible.[30]

The analogy between women and crowds reinforced the deeply negative judgment of the "masses" that social scientists of the time were popularizing.[31] It also aggravated the belief in the dangerous potentiality of crowds. All the critical attitudes that fundamentally stated women's unfitness for public life applied to the crowd; the crowd was definitely depicted as a threat to civilization. For these reasons, and for the sake of society's survival, solutions concerning the crowd needed to be found. Le Bon provided some of these solutions by referring to the same scientific theories that had proposed the permanent exclusion of crowds from political responsibilities: the theory of cells.[32] The latest developments in physiology had shown that the passage from monocellular to pluricellular organisms, from simplicity to complexity, from homogeneity to heterogeneity, necessarily implied risks caused by the multiplication of cells and the question of coordinating them in a new state of equilibrium. Theories claimed that, if uncoordinated, cells would provoke the decomposition of the organism by going back to primitive forms of aggregates. When applied to the explanation of social phenomena, this theory of evolution replaced the optimistic belief in the idea of progress with a theory of historical cycles punctuated by periods of decadence and regression. Social scientists suggested that the same risk of decomposition characterizing the development of organisms also affected society. Within this context, they castigated crowds as a heterogeneous element that disrupted equilibrium. If society did not provide a solution to the problem of the crowd and its relation to the social order, these theorists concluded, society risked stagnation and collapse.

The theory of cells had proved that the successful passage from monocellular to pluricellular organisms took place through a process of coordination among different groups of cells. It had also explained that this process was guided by a centralized power. Now the same hypotheses concerning cells were applied to crowds and the female gender, with society's survival at stake. In the case of women, the scientific explanation of their inferiority and tendency to dissolution (insanity) resulted in the affirmation of men's natural superiority and the legitimation of male social control and leadership.[33] In the case of crowds, too, the scientific interpretation of their behavior as deranged gave birth to the suggestion that a limited elite should lead the process of civilization's evolution. When women's most important personality disorder, hysteria, was created, along with its method of treatment, hypnosis, so was the political leader—anticipated by the crowd psychologists—conceived as a doctor-hypnotist.[34] Le Bon's prescriptions to the leader on how to control crowds heavily relied on the French research on hypnotism of the late 1800s. Through reference to this new psychological science, Le Bon provided political leaders with devices to neutralize the danger of crowds.[35]

The challenge that the "masses," as new political subjects, presented to society was diagnosed as a pathological case. Hence, its solution did not imply the widening of the crowd's participation in decision-making processes or the widening of popular representation. On the contrary, the crowd, because of its inner characteristics, needed to be kept in a prepolitical (or pseudo-political) stage by a leader.[36] Because the "masses" were dominated by emotions, social theorists argued, the creation of myths would become the leader's means to excite and subordinate them. Le Bon advised the leader to know "the art of impressing the imagination of crowds," because that knowledge would endow him with the ability to govern them.[37] According to Le Bon, the art of government relied on the leader's clear understanding of the rules guiding the "masses'" mentality. One of these rules was that "crowds being only capable of thinking in images are only to be impressed by images. It is only images that terrify or attract them and become motives of action."[38] Le Bon encouraged leaders to play on the power of representation and to adopt theatrical modes.[39] He equally directed attention to the use of words and language in combination with images. In the same way that representations, if "handled with art," can turn magic, so words and formulas could become "supernatural powers." No matter what their meaning, the power of words was relevant, Le Bon claimed. "Words whose sense is the most ill-defined are sometimes those that possess the most influence." Words had a "truly magical power."[40]

By emphasizing magic in the leader's relation to crowds, Le Bon instituted a doctrine of mystification.[41] Since he believed he had scientifically proven crowds' irrational nature, Le Bon in effect advised the orators to appeal to their "sentiments, and never to their reason."[42] He suggested that in order to convince the crowd, it was necessary to know more than the feelings that animated it. One also needed to "pretend to share these sentiments" and possibly to "divine from instant to instant the sentiments to which one's discourse is giving birth."[43] No doubt Le Bon was founding and propagandizing a subtle art of political manipulation.[44] Although he formulated his theories as advice to democratic leaders, Le Bon was in a way anticipating the coming of a new Machiavellian prince. His influence on politicians such as Roosevelt, Clemenceau, Briand, and others was remarkable.[45] As a matter of fact, Le Bon became Mussolini's own mentor. On the one hand, he himself sent his books to Mussolini;[46] on the other hand, Mussolini affirmed being influenced by Le Bon: "I have read all the work of Gustave Le Bon; and I don't know how many times I have re-read his *Psychologie des foules*. It is a capital work to which, to this day, I frequently refer."[47] Le Bon's influence on the Duce emerges from Mussolini's own perspective on the crowd. Mussolini's aesthetic notion of the "masses" relied on the derogation of the crowd elaborated by Le Bon and complemented it perfectly.

The "Masses" as an Artistic Object

Mussolini's conception of the politician's work as an aesthetic enterprise influenced the way Mussolini related to the "masses"—the subject of his rule—and determined the way he understood power. In fact, all the metaphors that identified politics and politicians with art and artists, metaphors that abounded in Mussolini's political speeches and writings (especially until 1932), conveyed more than just a suggestive rhetorical message. Those metaphors portrayed the theoretical framework underlying Mussolini's public-political actions, and they implied a negative vision of the "masses," now an inert object at the mercy of the politician. Through those metaphors, Mussolini identified the "masses" with the working matter of the artist— a powerless and passive whole:

> When I feel the masses in my hands, since they believe in me, or when I mingle with them, and they almost crush me, then I feel like one with the masses. However there is at the same time a little aversion, much as the poet feels towards the material he works with. Doesn't the sculptor sometimes break the marble out of rage, because it does not precisely mold in his hands according to his vision? . . . Everything depends on that, to dominate the masses as an artist.[48]

The figure of the artist-politician that Mussolini evokes here worked the "masses" into a coherent object; he gave them a shape.[49] As Mussolini proclaimed in a speech of September 20, 1922: "[T]he task of fascism is to make of it [the mass] an organic whole with the Nation in order to have it tomorrow, when the Nation needs the masses, much as the artist needs raw material in order to forge his masterpieces."[50] For Mussolini, the "masses" only constituted the expressive medium of the politician's artistic and creative genius, and he theorized a model of government that fundamentally affirmed the politician's superiority over the populace. Even Lenin represented an example of aesthetic rule, as Mussolini claimed in an article of July 14, 1920: "Lenin is an artist who has worked with human beings as other artists work with marble or metals."[51] Lenin, according to Mussolini's interpretation, was using the masses-object in order to forge them and create a final work of art. Unfortunately, in his case, the results had not kept up with the artistic promise: "But human beings are harder than rock and less malleable than iron. There is no masterpiece. The artist has failed. The task was beyond his power."[52] Lenin as a political leader fit Mussolini's category of the artist-politician, although he represented a failed one.

Mussolini's contempt for the "masses," which emerges from his aesthetic conception of politics, was undoubtedly quite remarkable. In the years immediately preceding the March on Rome, at a time when he wanted to affirm himself as the opponent of the rising socialist movement, Mussolini had pragmatic reasons to reject the "masses." The latter, Mussolini asserted, represented the "fetish" of socialists and democrats, whereas fascism fundamentally opposed socialism and democracy.[53] Besides, fascism's program was to endow Italians with a national identity via the elimination of internal divisions and the creation of a classless society ideology.[54] Because "masses" at the time often referred to the proletariat, the fascist movement refused to consider them an independent political subject. Yet, even taking into account such an ideologically charged context, Mussolini's negative opinion of the "masses" did not only derive from a strategic attitude. He specifically admitted: "In me two Mussolinis fight: one who is individualist and does not love the masses, the other absolutely disciplined."[55] Only when he forced himself could Mussolini appreciate the "masses." Nevertheless, for him the "masses" formed no more than the politician's forging material, and he still denied them any responsible role within his government. As he told Milan workers on December 5, 1922:

> [M]y father was a blacksmith who bent the red-hot iron on the anvil. Sometimes as a child I helped my father in his hard, humble job; and now I have the much harsher and harder job of bending the souls.[56]

Mussolini certainly realized that people were not dead matter, as his comments on Lenin hinted. On January 3, 1924, in response to a salute of ministers visiting him, Mussolini reiterated that "politics is not an easy art . . . for it works the most elusive, the most fluctuating and uncertain matter . . . the human spirit."[57] The politician's work differed from that of the artist's because the masses constituted the "most refractory of matters"—living people.[58] This is why it was so difficult to shape them and "bend their souls." Mussolini also perceived that, in an era of mass politics, the politician could not exercise his function without establishing a relation with the populace. Yet, according to his vision, that relationship was one of producer and product: the "masses" represented an object that the artist-politician could shape and mold with his hands. They lived through the leader; they acquired a form thanks to his creative genius: "What would the masses do if they did not have their own interpreter who was expressed by the spirit of the populace, and what would the poet do if he did not have the material to forge?"[59] Mussolini recognized the role of the "masses" in providing the context from which a leader would emerge as an emanation of their spirit. However, his appreciation of the "masses'" active stance ended there. For Mussolini the artist-politician was supposed to establish order and subject the "masses" to his talent. The artist created himself; and the "masses" were only a malleable object in his hands.

Mussolini's aesthetic-political vision of the "masses" as raw matter combined well with his identification of the "masses" as female. And as much as the metaphor implied the preeminence of the sculptor's role in the relationship between the artist and matter (politician and "masses"), so the conception of the "masses" as female legitimized the guiding role of the political leader, the man. Mussolini never entered openly the question of whether he considered women inferior or superior to men. However, he did believe that women and men were not equal. "[L]et's confirm that she is different," he once stated. Then he continued: "I am rather pessimistic . . . I believe, for example, that a woman does not have a large power of synthesis, and that she is thus unfit for great spiritual creations."[60] Women were not able to create a work of art, within Mussolini's frame. Therefore, they could not build a sublime political form.

Mussolini's pessimistic judgment of women contributed to the widening of the distance between the leader's government and the people's participation, although at the same time it established the criteria for the relationship between politician and "masses." On the one hand, Mussolini used his negative appreciation of women's qualities in order to affirm his nondemocratic vision of the world. Within that vision fascism dominated not only the "masses" but also liberalism and democracy, for they were both weak, peaceful, irresolute—that is, they embodied female characters. On the other hand, by rejecting women's feebleness, fascism defined itself, in opposition, as manly, and in this guise affirmed its rule as necessary for guiding the nation and the "masses."[61] To the old liberal system, Mussolini presented the alternative of a new, "very strong," and "virile" fascist state.[62] Fascism was aggressive, intrepid, and courageous. The political opposition was accused of wanting fascism to be less "virile."[63] Anything fascist became "virile" in Mussolini's rhetoric, from his own speeches to fascism's politics of peace.[64] Thanks to its manly characteristics, fascism could look after the populace and establish a domineering relationship with "her." As Mussolini told his biographer: "The multitude is female."[65] In this sense, fascism and Mussolini represented the male pole of the union between fascism and the "masses," between Mussolini and the Italian people (the female pole). "What drives me more," Mussolini declared, " . . . is . . . the love of the Italian people! Because I do love the Italian people, I love it in my way. Mine is the armed love, not the tearful and unwarlike love, but severe and virile."[66] Through reference to gender identity, Mussolini defined his attitude toward the "masses" and conceived his relationship to them as founded not on empathy and equality but rather on paternalistic dominance. Mussolini's love for the people followed the model of the patriarchal family structure. Mussolini was first of all the father, the leader, the Duce of what theories of the time defined as an illogical, moody, and variable woman: the "masses." Therefore, he himself emphasized his function as *duce*. "I am your Leader," he cried from the balcony of Palazzo Venezia in his first speech for the Decennial of the Revolution.[67] Mussolini was the governing patriarch, the strong man. The "masses" needed him, because, as he affirmed with Nietzschean tones: "[T]he mass . . . is nothing other than a flock of sheep, until it is organized."[68] In order to attain a form, the "masses" needed a leader, a strong *dux*, who could artistically mold them into a beautiful shape.[69]

The ideal of artistic creation and the political necessity of a dictatorial one-man rule, the reality of which Mussolini never denied, certainly fit well with Mussolini's negative conception of the "masses" as female. Once transferred to the "masses," women's allegedly negative attributes—their illogicality, sensuality, and wildness—justified Mussolini's rejection of any power demand from the part of the populace and his claim that subordination to the will of the leader was vital to fascism. The belief that the "masses" had female features reinforced Mussolini's aesthetic conception of politics, which entailed the dependency of the mass-matter upon the politician-artist. In addition, the "masses," as female, asked to be dominated by "virile" leaders. Whereas the manly, rational politician approached the "masses" as a spiritually superior patriarch, the female, irrational "masses" longed for a strong man, or so Mussolini claimed. "[C]an a dictator be loved?" asked Ludwig to Mussolini. "Yes," he replied, "when the mass is at the same time afraid of him. The mass loves strong men. The mass is female."[70]

Susan Buck-Morss suggests that the narcissistic myth of total control, connected to the idea of the *manly* creator and the motif of autogenesis, constitutes "one of the most persistent myths in the whole history of modernity (and of Western *political* thought before then . . .). Doing one better than Virgin birth, modern man, *homo autotelus*, literally produces himself."[71] For Buck-Morss, the myth of autotelic genesis expresses a fear of the biological power of women. The self-creating male subject avoids external control by giving up sex. He is thus wholly self-contained and sensedead.[72] Mussolini's conception of the mass-object's feminine status reflected the Duce's subscription to the myth of autotelic creation. It also provided the basis on which Mussolini constructed his model of rule. Because the "masses" were not rational, they needed to be governed with enthusiasm more than pragmatic interest. The mystical side needed to be taken into account,[73] because the hope of serving a "beautiful" cause would hold even those who were not connected by any interest to the fascist movement.[74] Following Le Bon's view on the means to address and conquer the "collective consciousness" of the "masses," Mussolini resorted to myths and aesthetic images on the premise that they were able to influence the crowd, its behavior and beliefs.

To be sure, the participation of the "masses" in politics was an integral part of the fascist regimes, as Benjamin suggested.[75] The "masses" were at the same time part of the fascist spectacle and fascism's spectatorship; they were acted upon and actors. Slogans, rallies, and images excited people's senses, though as an object of power people were also denied their senses. Benjamin's notion of aestheticized politics indicates that fascism, by resorting to symbols, rituals, and spectacle, was able to offer the "masses" a chance to express themselves and be part of a movement, even if their participation was based on a cultic experience. By beautifying politics, fascism created the auratic distance between the regime and the governed necessary to channel people's involvement in politics through faith, myths, and cults. By beautifying politics, fascism reaffirmed the value of tradition—a tradition founded on hierarchy and respect for authority and drawing its aura from faith. Indeed, Mussolini insisted, the identity between fascist and Italian was not meant to derive from constraint or, even less, from interest. Fascism, Mussolini wrote in 1932, "is a religious conception, in which man is seen in his immanent relationship with a superior law, with an objective Will that transcends the particular individual and elevates him to a conscious member of a spiritual society."[76] The existence of an "objective will" obliterated the role of individual, independent judgment and declared its obsolescence. Whereas Le Bon encouraged the birth of a new Caesar who could stop the deleterious consequences of crowds' appearance on the political scene, Mussolini developed the deep conviction that he represented the alternative to Italy's defective parliamentary system. He could dominate and control the "masses'" natural irrationality. He would be the one to enhance progress and avoid stagnation. The idea that faith bound the population to fascism and that the "masses" could be moved by images, words, and feelings led Mussolini to adopt a political style that privileged the symbolic aspects of power relations, the mystical side.

FROM ART TO VIOLENCE

In a speech in Milan on October 4, 1922, Mussolini stated:

> Democracy has deprived people's lives of "style." Fascism brings back "style" in people's lives: that is a line of conduct, that is the color, the strength, the picturesque, the unexpected, the mystical; in sum, all that counts in the soul of the multitudes. We play the lyre on all the strings, from violence to religion, from art to politics.[77]

Three years after this speech, in the aftermath of the special laws of 1925–1926, when fascism liquidated the opposition and moved to become the only governing party, Mussolini's call for "bringing style" to people's lives turned into a rhetoric envisaging the birth of a "new man." This man would be "serious, intrepid, tenacious."[78] The artistic metaphor linking the politician to the sculptor who smashes and carves the marble led Mussolini to declare the need for "reshaping the Italians," "making the Italians' character," "creating a new generation of Italians."[79] Like the artist who molded his material in order to realize his inspiration, Mussolini aimed at forging the Italians' character into a work of art to carry out his political vision. By building a new, fascist Italian and by establishing new, fascist ways of living, Mussolini would create his final masterpiece: a long-lasting fascist Italy. For this purpose, he required the total involvement of every person; he demanded people's full participation.

Indeed, "to give style," the aesthetic expression that reflected Mussolini's political aim to transform the populace, had as a pragmatic counterpart the expression "to fascistize." The regime started to adopt this expression at the same time it began to utilize the term "totalitarian"—the term that most successfully conveys the regime's aim to exercise full authority. Mussolini first used the term "totalitarian" in a speech delivered at the conclusion of the Fascist Party's fourth national congress, on June 22, 1925.[80] On that occasion Mussolini, after declaring "all power to all fascism" (*tutto il potere a tutto il fascismo*), talked about fascism's "totalitarian will" and hinted that others had previously characterized his fascist movement in this manner ("that goal that is defined as our ferocious totalitarian will will be pursued with even greater ferociousness").[81] As a matter of fact, the origins of the word "totalitarian" can be found slightly earlier in the political discourse of the antifascist opposition, whose leader, Giovanni Amendola, first employed the term in a May 12, 1923, article. In this writing, Amendola discussed the electoral maneuvering pursued by Mussolini's government, and in this context he referred to fascism as a "totalitarian system." After this first, very technical use, the word was imbued with another meaning. In November Amendola wrote about the "totalitarian spirit" of fascism and interpreted it as the inner characteristic of fascism's attempt to constitute a new, all-encompassing order, an authoritarian state structure.[82] In this larger sense, the word continued to be invoked by the opposition during the following two years, especially in concomitance with the 1924 parliamentary elections. On January 2, 1925, the noun "totalitarianism" appeared for the first time, in an article in *La Rivoluzione Liberale* by the socialist Lelio Basso. Only one day later, on January 3, Mussolini delivered the famous speech that marked a turn in the history of fascism. With that speech Mussolini asserted the role of force and the obsolescence of the constitutional state, and he sanctioned the beginning of a formal dictatorship. Then, on June 15, 1925, Amendola gave a political speech in which he referred to fascism's "totalitarian will."[83] A week later Mussolini would repeat those words in his first use of the term "totalitarian."

The attempt to understand the new political phenomenon of fascism had pushed the opposition to discover new explanatory notions in order to come to terms with a reality that escaped existing categories of political discourse. Mussolini and his movement appropriated those words to define themselves,[84] and in so doing they elaborated a vision for the future organization of state and society in the new, fascist-dominated Italy.[85] "Totalitarian" came to coincide with *fascistizzare* ("to fascistize").

> [T]hat goal that is defined as our ferocious *totalitarian* will will be pursued with even greater ferociousness: it will truly become the dominant thought and preoccupation of our activity. We want, finally, *to fascistize* the nation.[86]

The regime's aesthetic-political operation of "giving style" to the Italians and constructing a beautiful whole ran parallel to fascism's realpolitik attempt to organize a totalitarian state.[87] The two projects depended on each other. The population's homogeneity not only provided the state with full power but also allowed the creation of a harmonious artwork. Only through the identification of the individual with the state, only when the new fascist man was totally submitted to and coincided with the fascist state, could the beauty of the whole emerge.[88] Consider this interesting passage from Simmel's discussion of symmetry in aesthetics:

> Quite apart from its consequences for the individual, the rational organiza-
> tion of society has a high aesthetic attraction. It aims to make the totality of
> lives in the whole organization into a work of art. . . . Consider, for example,
> the aesthetic appeal of machines. . . . The organization of a factory and the
> plan of a socialistic society only repeats this beauty on larger scales. This
> peculiar interest in harmony and symmetry by which socialism demon-
> strates its rationalistic character, and by which it aims to stylize social life,
> is expressed purely externally by the fact that socialistic utopias are always
> set up according to principles of symmetry. . . . This general trait of social-
> istic plans attests to the deep power of attraction in the idea of an harmonic,
> internally balanced organization of human activity overcoming all resistance
> of irrational individuality.[89]

Simmel was referring to socialism, yet his observations can as well apply to Mussolini's aesthetic design.[90] The "irrationality" of the "masses,"
which Mussolini posited as a fact, could not be tolerated by a system that
aimed at the harmonious organization of the whole and the "stylization of
social life" within a totalitarian state. Therefore, the leader was in charge of
building an "internally balanced organization of human activity"—a work
of art—by overturning the irrationality of the "masses." The identification
of the individual with the state allowed for the development of the fascist
reality that Mussolini was pursuing.

Fascism's aesthetic-totalitarian project and its ideal of harmony were
founded on violence, although the regime denied it at the level of representation. In fascism's discourse, as a matter of fact, violence turned out to
be a rhetorical trope and a mystique. Through a series of mythical transformations and discursive reconfigurations, fascist representations of violence glorified force and identified it with renewal and rebirth.

Violence as Regeneration

Mussolini's aesthetic vision of politics, his identification of the politician with
the artist, and his conception of the women-masses as passive material combined to form Mussolini's negative judgment of the populace. Mussolini despised the "masses," although he was also attracted by them, and Le Bon
offered him the "scientific" justification for such contempt. However, Mussolini was not the only one to cultivate such feelings toward the population.
Distrust for the "masses" emerged in the current of antidemocratism that,
by the end of the 1800s, had fully developed in Europe and even in the United

States.[91] Parliament, as the fundamental institution of "bourgeois" representative democracy, especially attracted criticism from the whole political spectrum.[92] For the left, parliament failed to fulfill the democratic principles of egalitarianism, popular sovereignty, and pacifism.[93] For a large part of the radical right wing, parliament epitomized the regressive and decadent aspects of democracy, as it upheld the principles of egalitarianism, pacifism, and representation. The liberal-conservatives, in their turn, attacked parliament for allowing the advent of a new political elite to replace their own leadership. The liberal-conservatives opposed the new politicians, who were supposedly defending particular interests, and against them they strenuously upheld the legitimacy of their own claims to power.[94]

Crowd psychologists had elaborated their theories of mass behavior in part as a critique of the widening of parliamentary representation.[95] Although claiming to be defending democratic principles, these social scientists actually held a peculiar notion of democracy: democracy was valuable as long as it maintained the existing social order.[96] In effect, crowd theorists forcefully attacked the egalitarian doctrines that threatened to upset traditional class divisions.[97] Within an interpretive framework concerned with the danger of stagnation and dissolution, crowd theorists considered parliamentary representation an element of risk, for it eliminated differences in social relations. Democracy amounted to a negative balancing of interests, and crowd theorists attacked it for its tendency to smooth over conflicts and create leveling compromises.[98] Following the same logic, the intellectuals of the nationalist radical right criticized the resolution of conflicts via parliament, a body they considered a basic mystification. The representative system allowed for the coexistence of oppositions. In so doing, however, it substituted for division its fictional representation.[99] For the nationalists, parliament turned out to constitute the theatrical staging of violence—the institutionalization of conflicts through the suppression of violence. Parliament deprived struggle of its role in the evolution of society, with the risk of exposing the latter to decadence and regression.

The rightist radicals shared with a large part of the contemporary political culture a belief in the important role of violence as the engine of history, the element that would fight mediocrity and lack of differentiation.[100] In effect, the opposition in Europe to representative democracy inserted itself in a general climate that praised violence and emphasized its dynamic function within society.[101] The publication in 1906 of Georges Sorel's *Réflexions sur la violence* played an enormous role in creating this atmosphere.[102] Sorel interpreted the crisis of the bourgeois world as embedded in a lack of appeals to violence. The growing bureaucratization of modern society and the "cowardice" of the middle class impeded, in Sorel's opinion, the manifestation of the "energy" that was necessary for the continuation of life in Europe and the creation of moral values in the public sphere. Transferring Bergson's idea of *élan vital* to the sociopolitical arena, Sorel believed that new social formations would be born through a creative spur in the manner of a violent catastrophe.[103] Civilization, as Le Bon had predicted, risked sinking into decadence. Violence, by destroying materialism, utilitarianism, liberalism, and democracy, could prevent stagnation and save the world from barbarism and degeneration. For Sorel, permanent struggle became the solution to society's decline, a response to the threat of democracy. Against parliamentary debates, Sorel proposed the general strike; against the bourgeois compromise he suggested proletarian violence: "Proletarian violence, carried on as a pure and simple manifestation of the sentiment of the class war, appears thus as a very fine and very heroic thing; it is at the service of the immemorial interests of civilization; it is not perhaps the most appropriate method of obtaining immediate material advantages, but it may save the world from barbarism."[104]

Adopting a revisionist interpretation of Marx, Sorel argued that violence was not so much a means to obtain gains as a purposeless effort to overcome the barbarism caused by peacefulness and humanitarianism.[105] The continuous application of violence via the general strike would ensure civilization's survival because history only makes progress through violence. Furthermore, violence turned people into creative protagonists of history. Whereas for Marx struggle was determined by the contradictions inherent in the economic structure of society at a historical time, for Sorel, on the contrary, violence derived from the contrast between historical reality and the world of fantasy. Sorel presented an antiutilitarian vision of violence in which myth played a special role. According to him, important ideas were able to triumph in the world thanks to the mythical power they exercised over the people. Myths such as those of Christianity or the French revolution were able to carry crowds to battle, inspire them, and give them the strength to fight. Likewise, the myth of the general strike would push people to engage in action and give them the determination "to enter on a decisive struggle."[106] For Sorel, the most distinctive characteristic of the myth, as opposed to utopia, was that myths cannot be refuted: a myth is neither right nor wrong, and it does not promise an immediate reward. Myth is a motivating force expressing a determination to act, a demonstrable example of "sublimity," to which socialism subscribes.[107] As Sorel concluded: "It is to violence that Socialism owes those high ethical values by means of which it brings *salvation* to the modern world."[108]

In its double meaning of regeneration and antiparliamentarism, Sorel's theory of violence exercised wide influence at the turn of the century, especially among revolutionary syndicalist circles.[109] Mussolini, proclaiming himself a revolutionary syndicalist,[110] called Sorel "nôtre maître" in a review article of Prezzolini's *La teoria sindacalista* (Syndicalist Theory).[111] He also praised *Réflexions sur la violence* in another review article, published June 25, 1909, in *Il Popolo d'Italia*.[112] Sorel, wrote Mussolini, taught people that "life is struggle, sacrifice, conquest, a continuous 'overcoming of one's self.'"[113] Furthermore, Sorel showed that the permanent struggle between bourgeoisie and proletariat would generate "new energy" and "new moral values."[114] Other cultural and political groups in Italy, besides the revolutionary syndicalists, were inclined to support violence in the name of regeneration. Futurists, the intellectuals gathered around the Florentine reviews *Leonardo* (1903–1907) and *La Voce* (1908–1916), and nationalists all invoked the thaumaturgical power of violence, though in different ways. They feared that Italy, yoked to the power of the liberal class and Prime Minister Giovanni Giolitti, had become utterly idealless and prone to decline.

In his first futurist manifesto, dated February 20, 1909, Filippo Tommaso Marinetti wrote: "There is no more beauty if not in struggle." Then, in the manifesto of April 1909, he "screamed": "War? . . . Well, yes: it is our only hope, our reason for living, our only will."[115] The critical appraisal of contemporary Italian politics inspired Marinetti and the futurists to look for a new model of existence as a substitute for tradition. Movement and dynamism became the central principles of their conception, in which war turned out to be the implementation of political action for the transformation of life. For the futurists, to be human in the modern world of machines meant to be moving; they rejected everything leveling or static. Because the futurists stressed action and glorified the future, only war could respond to their ideal of a never-ending movement. War embodied the perennial necessity of fighting: it was a festival in which the expenditure of energies, almost in an ethnological sense, emphasized life's fullness. As "the only hygiene of the world," war granted the expansion of human potentialities. It was a purifying bath from which a new person, who perceived the world through categories of action, speed, and confrontation, would be born. War could thus clean Italy from *passatismo* and open the way to future renewal.

For the young generation of intellectuals who founded the journals *Leonardo* and *La Voce,* violence and war also constituted the elements necessary for the regeneration of Italian society.[116] Although, unlike the futurists, they adopted a moral tone, the Leonardiani's rhetoric of rebirth, renewal, and resurgence was connected to a call for virility that entailed violence and war. In his "Elegy on Violence," published in *Leonardo* in June 1904, Prezzolini wrote that "so-called gentility, silence, politeness are very often just synonyms for cowardice, lack of argument, weakness of mind. . . . The violence that we employ has to do not with hatred for others but with love of ourselves. . . . Violence is, then, a moral cure, an exercise that strengthens, a categorical imperative for all those who love themselves."[117] Italy could show love for herself only by being active and aggressive. A few years later, writing from the columns of *La Voce*, Prezzolini identified war with the values of discipline and faith. War revealed the healthy components of one's country and indicted the decadent, rotten sides.[118] When World War I finally approached, the Vociani rallied together in favor of intervention. The world conflict appeared as the opportunity, not to be missed, to reshape Italian life and endow it with the spiritual direction it was presently lacking.

The praise for violence and war equally characterized the nationalist movement, which developed around the review *Il Regno* at the turn of the century.[119] This time, however, war was intimately connected to expansion. The nationalists, headed by Enrico Corradini, believed it necessary to fight democracy and socialism in order to establish a nation founded on expansionist goals. Corradini and his collaborators despised Italy's political stasis of the time. The glorification of heroic life, war, and action against the policy of domesticity, cowardice, and pacifism was constant in their speeches. Thus, the nationalists violently attacked the government led by Giovanni Giolitti. They accused the prime minister of suffocating the courageous, enterprising, young, and dynamic Italy and of impeding its growth. In 1910, when the nationalist movement called its first congress in Florence (December 3–5), the program emphasized foreign policy along with the idea of war as an instrument of power. In opposition to the political class, appeals of heroism resounded in the hall where the nationalists assembled. In that same congress, which marked the foundation of the Nationalist Association, Corradini proclaimed his theory of Italy as a "proletarian" nation that needed to fight and redeem itself from plutocratic countries such as France and Britain.[120] The nationalists aspired to convert heroic actions into the conquest of new territories, for Italy needed to share the "bourgeois" nations' colonial wealth.

The Italian fascist movement, which Mussolini founded on March 23, 1919, as Fasci Italiani di Combattimento (Italian Fasces of Combat), represented an expression of the cultural-political attack on parliamentary institutions and the idealization of violence.[121] The fascist movement defined itself as an anti-party,[122] refused any fixed ideological identity,[123] and affirmed the concept of struggle as its primary characteristic. As Mussolini told the people of Trieste on September 20, 1920: "Struggle is at the origin of everything because life is full of contrasts: there is love and hatred, black and white, day and night, good and evil . . . the day when there is no fight will be a day of sadness, it will be the end, the ruin."[124] In that same speech he also affirmed: "We call our Fasces Fasces of Combat, and the word combat does not leave any doubt. [We intend] to combat with peaceful arms, but also with war arms."[125]

Violence granted movement and dynamism and brought about change; struggle constituted the fascist movement's life warranty. Mussolini compared the vitality and spontaneity of the "young" fascists to the staleness and stagnation of the "old" parties: "Our movement is a continuous elaboration and transformation: it undergoes a work of unceasing revision, the only means to make of it an element of life and not a dead remain."[126] Pure politics, a politics of action, opposed the decadence of parliamentary debates, which Mussolini once defined as "a boring masturbation."[127] Within this context, violence acquired a positive role, and the discourse on violence, woven in with a critique of democracy, became one of the fascist movement's foremost means of self-representation, to be later adopted and further developed by the regime.

The Representation of Violence

On December 13, 1914, Mussolini made a speech in Parma protesting Italy's neutrality in World War I, concluding: "We must act, move, fight and, if it is necessary, die. . . . It is blood that moves history's wheel!" (*E' il sangue che da' movimento alla ruota sonante della storia.*)[128] Mussolini accused the pacifist socialists of "sacred egoism" and of offering only words to a France victimized by Germany's attack. To the contrary, Mussolini called for a "solidarity of blood," and he encouraged the Italians, especially "proletarian Italians," to oppose neutrality and join the fighters "with courage and dignity."[129] Although initially siding with his fellow socialists in supporting neutrality at the outbreak of the war, Mussolini had later reached the conclusion that intervention was a national duty.[130] Against socialist formulas of immobilism, Mussolini proposed action: "Do we want to be as men and as socialists the inert spectators of this grandiose drama? Or don't we want to be in one way or another its protagonists?"[131] Expelled from the Socialist Party for his interventionist stance on November 24,[132] Mussolini incited Italy to war from the columns of his newly founded paper, *Il Popolo d'Italia.*[133] War, he claimed, allowed the socialists to participate in the creation of history.[134] Not surprisingly, Mussolini joined the army on September 2, 1915, once Italy finally entered the world conflict.

At the end of the war, the experience of the trenches (*trincerismo*) became the basis for Mussolini's new vision of politics. The violence and death experienced by the soldiers—the sacrifice of blood—called out for social changes that would bring along a new order. The war cataclysm could only be redeemed by a rejuvenated society. As a journalist of *Il Popolo d'Italia* wrote in 1918: "We are all sure that a radical, deep, unforeseeable transformation awaits us. Everybody feels that millions and millions of men cannot die without incredible renewals ensuing from the tremendous slaughter."[135] The survivors brought with them at the end of the conflict a "culture of war" that sought an outlet in civilian life.[136] Mussolini took charge of this responsibility, and in 1919, when he founded the Fasci Italiani di Combattimento, he conceived of them as a logical continuation of the war years and the battle for renewal.[137] The hostility between neutralists (mainly socialists) and interventionists, which had divided the Italians during World War I, was thus continued after the war by Mussolini's adepts. The fascists affirmed their will to fight the institutions of the past, and they accused the neutralists of belonging to the "old" Italy. They claimed that by virtue of their "revolutionary" stance they had gained the right to shape Italy's future.[138] Hence, the war became for the fascists the prelude to an internal revolution that would mend Italy's moral crisis—a crisis that before the war had already been diagnosed and dissected by the critics of Giolitti's government. The tension and difference between the "two Italies" grew after the war. It eventually resolved into a violent conflict, of which Mussolini's movement became the main protagonist.[139] On April 15, 1919, fascists—more specifically, ex-Arditi[140] and futurists—burnt down the headquarters of the socialist newspaper *Avanti!* in Milan.[141] Meanwhile, fascist squads were being organized as paramilitary groups. And in the years before the March on Rome, the countryside of Italy's northern and central agrarian regions became the theater of fascist "punitive expeditions," aggressions, and murders.[142] Fascists made recourse to castor oil, the cudgel (*manganello*), devastations, and fires.[143] In 1921 the deaths provoked by fascist violence totaled from 500 to 600 people.[144] Hundreds of socialist headquarters, cooperatives, cultural centers, popular libraries and theaters, peasants leagues, and unions were also destroyed—726 locations in all.[145]

After each violent episode involving fascist squads, Mussolini, with an eye on the possible institutionalization of his movement, justified fascist violence as a reaction or defense against the red menace.[146] And even though fascist violence in the years between the end of the war and Mussolini's takeover of power served the interests of the agrarian class, Mussolini never admitted it.[147] However, although he monitored his language and propagandized a vision of conflict as a means to extirpate "evil," neither did Mussolini refrain from praising violence for its contribution to dynamism, movement, and change. These two representations of violence alternated and coexisted at the same time. Mindful of his prewar ideas, Mussolini actually admitted that the result of the battle was the least important factor in fascism's embracement of fight.[148] He praised the fascist militants' spirit of sacrifice and faith in the fatherland. The fascists' heroic nature, against any utilitarian view of politics, granted them the right of bearing the war legacy. Fascist militants constituted the necessary link between the youth who died in the war and the new, "born again" Italy.[149] It was in the name of the war dead that fascism advocated its right to defend the nation against socialists and other internal "enemies."[150] It was in the name of the movement's own dead that fascism claimed its legitimate role in determining the future of the Italian nation. If sacrifice, blood, and regeneration had been the characteristic features of World War I, they also became the identifying traits of the fascists, thus reaffirming more strongly the ideal link between fascism and the war. Here is how in 1922 Mussolini remembered the squads who had participated in the 1919 assault on the socialist newspaper *Avanti!*:

> [T]he two Fallen that we remember here and all the squads of the Milan *Fascio* assailed the *Avanti!* as they would assail an Austrian trench. They had to pass walls, cut barbed wire, break doors down, face red-hot bullets that the assailed launched with their arms. This is heroism. This is violence. This is the violence of which I approve and which I exalt. This is Milan Fascism's violence. And Italian Fascism—I speak to all Italian fascists—should adopt it.
>
> Not the little, individual, sporadic, often useless, but the great, beautiful, inexorable violence of decisive hours.
>
> It is necessary, when the moment comes, to hit with the maximum decision and inexorability. . . .
>
> Our friends have been heroes! Their gesture has been warlike. Their violence has been saintly and moral. We exalt them.[151]

The violence that Mussolini defined as beautiful turned the fascists who died by it into "martyrs." Mussolini defined their gestures as warriorlike, and he called their violence "saintly and moral." The rhetoric of blood and of fascists' sacrifices sanctified fascism's adoption of violent means and exalted the value of fascism's violence and goals. The dead from violent causes became one more reason to affirm the high value of the movement.[152] As

Mussolini wrote on January 20, 1922: "No party in Italy, no movement in recent Italian history can be compared to Fascism. No ideal has, like the fascist one, been consecrated by the blood of so many youths."[153]

In these terms, the discourse on violence provided fascism with a preliminary source of self-representation. A Janus-faced approach to force—on the one hand seen as "surgical," on the other as "regenerating"—allowed the fascist movement to propose itself as the national savior and in this fashion to complete its ascent to power. Subsequently, in the aftermath of Mussolini's takeover, the blood of the dead continued to be invoked and served to legitimize the regime's actions. To this end, the rhetoric adopted by Mussolini and fascist pamphlets inflated the total of fascist victims. Estimates ranged from 3,000 to 50,000.[154] Speaking to the Neapolitans on September 16, 1924, Mussolini proclaimed that "the ineffable sacrifice of our 3,000 dead" would grant fascism a glorious destiny.[155] According to Petersen, a more correct estimate of fascist dead up to 1926 is 500 or 600.[156]

By magnifying the fascists' blood and sacrifice, the regime sanctified violence as the premise for Italy's renewal, the foundation for a morally regenerated society. In its idealized and exaggerated form, the cult of the fallen, which had played a major role in the liturgy of the movement before Mussolini's governmental appointment, bloomed during the regime. The official statutes of the party reserved important honors for the fallen in fascism.[157] In 1932 the Exhibit of the Revolution dedicated a hall to the martyrs. The Sacrario (Chapel of the Martyrs) was supposed to represent the spiritual origins of the movement in a suggestive atmosphere.[158] Every party branch also kept a shrine where the memory of the dead rested.[159] Pennons of fascist groups were named after the fallen. The regime often dedicated to the memory of single martyrs the inauguration of new works or classrooms in schools.[160] And the Fascist Association of Families of the Fallen, Disabled and Wounded for the Revolution was constantly represented at official fascist festivities.[161] In "Dottrina del Fascismo," published in 1932, Mussolini wrote of his followers:

> The years that preceded the March on Rome were years when the necessity
> of action did not tolerate complete doctrinal elaboration. People were
> fighting in towns and villages. People were discussing, but what was more
> sacred and important, they were dying. They knew how to die.[162]

Violence replaced words and speech, action substituted for theory. More important, fascist discourse in effect melded reality with fiction.

With all its references to the material reality of blood, violence in fascism's rhetoric was fundamentally fictional. This is not to suggest that the violence the fascists inflicted upon their opponents both before and after Mussolini's appointment as prime minister and following the totalitarian turn did not make victims. Nor is it to imply that force and repression were absent under Mussolini's rule. But at the level of representation, fascist violence became a self-absorbed experience. It turned out to be a rhetorical trope and a mystique. The blood that reddened the streets of Italy was first and foremost fascist blood. Martyrs were only the young fascist patriots who immolated themselves in the name of the nation; these youths filled the fascist "book of martyrs" (*libro dei martiri*).[163] Fascism's discourse of fascist victims radically eliminated the victims of fascism. The cult of the fallen and the magnification of figures precipitated the fall into oblivion of the "other" uncounted dead.

In his writings on fascism, Salvemini recalls that the number of victims of fascist violence was absolutely hidden during the regime. At the most, propagandistic publications would claim that the number of fascist victims was close to zero compared to fascist martyrs killed by the "reds."[164] Even newspaper reports of fascist violence, both before and after the March on Rome, when the press had not been subjected yet to the rules of the totalitarian state, were lacking. Major newspapers missed the chance to report several violent activities by the fascists.[165] As the socialist deputy Giacomo Matteotti complained in his speech at the Chamber of Deputies on January 31, 1921, newspapers did not report on socialist victims, nor on dead workers.[166] Only when the victims were fascist would journalists publish the news in large type. Furthermore, Matteotti continued, journalists would exploit the fascist corpses for months in their columns in despicable speculation. Even the official statistics of the liberal government failed to make crucial distinctions in the nature and object of violence during the years of fascist raids. Then, during the fascist regime, the Ministry of Interior's statistics for the years 1925 and the first four months of 1926 and 1927 indicated a larger number of dead on the fascist side than on the opponents' side.[167] Fascism hid and mystified the reality of violence with the help of the liberal government and the liberal press, when they existed.[168]

A similar mystification of violence through the surgical erasure of victims took place in Mussolini's discourse on the violent relation between politician and "masses," the artist and his raw material. In this case, violence does not make any victim, because matter is intrinsically desensitized or, better, senseless, especially as it does not bleed. In fascism's representation, as in a magician's hat, the violated bodies of evidence disappear. As in the solipsistic ideal of the "I" who does not recognize the "other" and turns it into a thing, so objects replace bodies in the creation of a work of art out of fascist Italy.[169] Hence, the body of the antifascist Giacomo Matteotti disappeared after he was kidnapped and assassinated by a recently constituted Fascist Party police squad on June 10, 1924. The worst crisis in Mussolini's governmental career before the dictatorial turn, the abduction of Matteotti produced a frenzied search for the missing politician. Rumors circulated about the corpse's location, placing it as far as 600 kilometers from Rome.[170] The leader of the crime, Amerigo Dumini, was arrested two days later.[171] Circumstances hampered Mussolini's effort to pretend that Matteotti had just disappeared, probably emigrating to Austria.[172] Matteotti's decomposed body was, however, only recovered on August 16. The funeral of the socialist deputy took place on June 23 without the corpse—that is, the victim.[173] When it was eventually found, the body of Matteotti was taken to his hometown, Rovigo.

Within fascist discourse, only auratic violence existed. Only if transfigured by aura (the saintly halo, in the case of the martyrs) could violence take place. Thus, fascist rhetoric invented and mythicized a "revolution" after the fictionalized episode of the March on Rome. Although the march turned out to be more of an appendix to a threatened violent takeover than an actual revolutionary act, the regime always referred to it as "revolution." Mussolini—reminiscent of Le Bon—admitted that the word "revolution" had some magic,[174] and he repeatedly pronounced it. In 1924 Mussolini tried to rationalize the peculiar factors of his movement's power seizure as compared to the more violent classical examples. He preferred to stress the accomplishment of the fascist revolution over time, not just its insurrectional episode. Nevertheless, he still did not renounce the term "revolution," with its implicit meaning of action and movement. Again, the invocation of blood served the goal of making fascist violence real. "If in the insurrectional days of October there was no blood—although there had been tens of glorious dead—much blood—very pure—ran in the previous three years," Mussolini told the Grand Council on July 22, 1924.[175] On October 17, 1932, during the festivities for the Decennial of the Revolution, Mussolini told a crowd of 25,000 *gerarchi* in Piazza Venezia: "[A]mong all the insurrections of modern times, ours has been the bloodiest. . . . The conquest of the Bastille only required a few tens of dead . . . the Russian revolution did not cost more than a few tens of victims. . . . Our revolution during three years has required large sacrifice of young blood."[176]

The Myth of the Nation

In the regime's representation, violence played an important role as a mark of fascist identity, a necessary element in fascism's self-definition. A dilemma, however, faced fascism's evolution as a regime vis-à-vis its fictional image of violence: could movement and innovation still ideally define and distinctively highlight fascism's actions when the regime's work of art was founded on uniformity and unity? Could the idea of relentless violence coexist with the regime's aspiration of imposing order and attaining harmony within Italy? More concretely, the questions the regime needed to solve were: could fights between Italians still take place in a totalized, homogenized state? Yet could fascism renounce its identification with violence as "history's wheel"? In "The Work of Art in the Age of Mechanical Reproduction," Benjamin stated that the result of mythicized and auratic politics could only be war. ("All efforts to render politics aesthetic culminate in one thing: war.")[177] In Mussolini's Italy war became the inevitable conclusion of fascism's apology for violence, via the medium of the myth of the nation. In his pre–March on Rome speech of October 24, 1922, Mussolini told an audience in Naples:

> We have created our myth. Our myth is a faith, a passion. It does not need to be a reality. It is a reality because it is a spur, it is a hope, it is faith, it is courage. Our myth is the Nation, our myth is the grandeur of the Nation! And to this myth, to this grandeur, that we want to translate into a complete reality, we subordinate all the rest.[178]

Myth did not need to be a reality, suggested Mussolini in a Sorelian mode.[179] But it could be turned into a concrete bastion of the affirmation of Italy's strength. Beginning in 1925 the theme of Italy's glory, the myth of a strong Italy, and the rhetoric of a final goal began to constitute recurrent motifs in Mussolini's speeches. At the same time there emerged a discourse on the "new man" within the regime, along with calls for the "fascistization" of Italy and the totalitarian transformation of the state. In the speech in which Mussolini used for the first time the terms "totalitarian" and "to fascistize," he also stated: "[T]he goal is that one: the empire! To found a city, to discover a colony, to found an empire are the wonders of the human spirit."[180]

Although fascism did not launch its imperial campaign until 1935, Mussolini had already anticipated it in 1925, if not earlier.[181] Claims about Italy's achieving its place in the world, or about the Italians' becoming proud of their nation, continually posed the question of Italy's role in foreign policy. Using metaphoric images, Mussolini hinted at the future possibility of Italy's showing her power to the world: "[W]hen the wheel of destiny will pass into our hands, we will be ready to catch it and bend it to our will."[182] In 1932 he told Ludwig that the life of the nation needed to be organized around military necessities, because the power of a nation was mainly dependent on its strength in war.[183] Mussolini wanted to build a powerful, armed Italy, a warriorlike nation, not a peaceful, democratic, womanlike one. Pacifism inherently meant cowardice, renunciation of struggle and heroism. In contrast, war would impress people with a "seal of nobility."[184]

Through reference to war, Mussolini solved the contradiction between his dynamic conception of violence and his view of internal social relations. Politically, fascism could not tolerate violence within Italy, because the regime's goal was to control the country totally. Aesthetically, conflicts could not exist within the Italian borders, because homogeneity was a necessary element in the development of a beautiful fascist state. At the same time, however, fascism's masterpiece could not be achieved by merely accepting and maintaining harmony. Aesthetics' sublime heights were only to be reached through a continuous battle against laws and limits. With the transference of violence to the international level, fascism affirmed its belief in struggle and kept the harmony and order it needed internally by emphasizing differences outside Italy and between countries.[185] The myth of the nation became the crucial link between fascism's aesthetic vision and its realpolitik ends. The aesthetic-political shaping of the "masses," the molding of a new Italian, and the creation of a disciplined fascist man allowed for the establishment of a strong, warriorlike state. Once the appeal to nationalist feelings ensured the internal uniformity of the populace, the country could then, as a whole, conquer an empire. Only imperialism would avoid stagnation. As Mussolini told the Fascist National Congress on November 8, 1921: "Those people [*popoli*] who one day, lacking will, lock themselves inside their homes will be the ones to approach death."[186]

Fascism's critique of mediocrity and egalitarianism found a solution in the affirmation of heterogeneity at a broader level. Conflict was transferred to war among states.[187] And Mussolini fully adopted the nationalists' division between "proletarian" and "plutocratic" nations.[188] Class struggle, which needed to be avoided in domestic politics, became the main category of interpretation of a country's international relations. Whereas the "masses" should not fight within Italy, Mussolini foresaw the possibility of transforming them into "virile" warriors in the world arena.[189]

The differentiation between interior and foreign politics allowed for the revitalization of the populace and the redemption of the "masses" from their negative qualities. Yet the Italians' redemption was only functional to the ends of fascism and did not change the people into men. Only as a whole and under the guidance of the leader did the "masses" show virility; only as a homogeneous army did they participate in fascism's masterpiece. Furthermore, only the politician could transform the female "masses" into warriors. In the end, Mussolini established a violent relationship with the "masses" that allowed for the development of an institution-transcending politics devoid of moral constraints.[190] This situation granted the leader free rein in the development of his artistic-political aims and in the establishment of an aesthetically sublime totalitarian order.

2 Mussolini the Myth

On July 7, 1912, the Italian Socialist Party opened its thirteenth national congress in Reggio Emilia. Participating as an almost unknown delegate from the Forlì province, Mussolini emerged from the congress with a personal success and an appointment to the national leadership of the party. Mussolini had been able, thanks to a series of favorable circumstances, to attract consensus at the congress around his denunciation of the socialist reformists.[1] He had also succeeded in putting forward the sentiments of the revolutionary wing of the party, a group itself internally divided. In his winning address to the fellow socialists on the afternoon of July 8, Mussolini passionately invoked the fighting spirit of socialism and advocated the abandonment of economic struggles in favor of purely political ones. He denied the value of social legislation for the working class and attacked the socialists' participation in government. More specifically, Mussolini, as he had already done in the days preceding the congress, called for an antiparliamentary socialism that would delegitimate the current government in the eyes of the people. Socialists, he argued, needed to aim at the subversion of democratic-representative institutions. By participating in them, the Socialist Party contributed to keeping alive a moribund bourgeois system inevitably bound to decadence and decline. Mussolini directly accused the socialist deputies in parliament of lacking principles, morals, and, even worse, ideals. He then concluded with a specific request to expel from the party parliamentary deputies—traitors of socialism's spirit and tradition.

With a simple and forceful oratory, Mussolini won over the sympathy of the congress. He also became the major protagonist in newspaper reports on the gathering.[2] Even though some journalists considered Mussolini's stress on the revolutionary role of the party "crazy" and "paradoxical,"[3] they still described him as an "original thinker," "the hot-blooded revolutionary," a "rough orator" and "original agitator."[4] Mussolini was saluted as a new figure in the socialist and political panorama.

A few days after the congress, Mussolini expounded on the idealistic, almost religious character with which he conceived socialism and that had attracted so much attention at Reggio Emilia.

The socialist congress of Reggio Emilia must be interpreted instead as an attempt at idealistic rebirth. The religious soul of the Party (ecclesia) collided yet another time with the realistic pragmatism of those who represent the economic organization. The latter is not a community of ideas, but a community of interests. There are the terms for the eternal conflict between idealism and utilitarianism, between faith and necessity. What does the proletariat care for understanding socialism in the way one understands a theorem? And can socialism actually be reduced to a theorem? We want to believe in it, we must believe in it, humanity needs a *credo.* It is faith that moves mountains, because it gives the illusion that mountains move. Illusion is perhaps the only reality in life.[5]

Mussolini's spiritualistic approach to socialism emphasized disinterest, faith, sacrifice, and heroism.[6] At a time when some critics attacked democratic ethics for being fundamentally materialistic and utilitarian and for precipitating the fall of spiritual values, Mussolini's call for high ideals attracted the attention of intellectuals and politicians. An old Italian communard, Amilcare Cipriani, wrote of Mussolini after the socialist congress: "Today, among those who have triumphed in Reggio Emilia, there is a man, Mussolini, whose agenda has triumphed. I like this man very much. His revolutionarism is the same as mine, I should say ours, that is 'classical.'"[7] Although Cipriani lamented Mussolini's failure to be both a socialist and a syndicalist, he still called him *valoroso* (valiant.) A year later Giuseppe Prezzolini, director of the journal *La Voce,* thus described Mussolini's newly founded journal *Utopia:* "[The journal] is trying a desperate enterprise: to bring back to life the theoretical conscience of socialism. It is an enterprise that to us seems even superior to the forces of B[enito] M[ussolini], although he has many. This man is a *man* and stands out even more in a world of half-figures and consciences that are finished like worn-out rubber bands."[8] Prezzolini seemed to recognize in Mussolini exceptional qualities that turned him into a real innovator, a "man." In the same vein, Leda Rafanelli, a young anarchist writer who subsequently had an intimate relationship with Mussolini, wrote after listening for the first time to a speech by Mussolini in March 1913: "Benito Mussolini . . . is the socialist of the heroic times. He still feels, he still believes, with an enthusiasm full of virility and force. He is a Man."[9]

We know very little about the use of "man" (*uomo*) in the political language of the time. It is, however, plausible to infer that in the statements above the term indicated the preoccupation with finding a person who would rejuvenate political life and give new energy to a moribund political system. Typical is the case of *La Voce,* which, although not socialist, admired in Mussolini those qualities that Giolitti and the Liberal Party seemed to be lacking. Compromises, clientelism, and corruption characterized the politics of Giolitti and impeded the actualization of true democracy. Revolutionary idealism and its leader, Mussolini, opposed the degenerate methods of Italian politics. They represented a moral force.[10] Within this interpretive frame the value of Mussolini "the man" magnified and grew over time. The newspaper *L'Unità* wrote on May 1, 1914: "Benito Mussolini has been the man, who was necessary and who could not be missing, to express and represent the need, in this historical moment, for a sincerely revolutionary movement in our country."[11] On November 13, 1914, after Mussolini had quit the Socialist Party and begun the newspaper *Il Popolo d'Italia*, Prezzolini composed a short note for *La Voce:* "Now there is *Il Popolo.* And I am in Rome to help Mussolini. Do you know that he is 'a man'? He has made a newspaper in a week. All 'technical men' are astonished, because they do not know what 'a man' is. They only know what a 'technical man' is."[12]

The admiration for "the man," the mystique of the exceptional personality, almost a deus ex machina, constituted another version of the charismatic leader, the theory of whom Max Weber was formulating at the time as an alternative to the figure of the instrumental, professional politician. This mystique also expressed the belief in the coming of the *capo* in Italy, the *meneur des foules* in France, and the Caesar in Germany.[13] From Le Bon to Sorel and, later, Spengler, the call for a "new man," the future leader of the "masses," was intended as a remedy to the evils of democracy—its materialism and egalitarian principles—by infusing the political process with a new spiritual sense. This ideal leader would establish with the "masses" a novel relationship founded on emotions and the power of myth.[14] He would bring new energy and life into the political arena, thus counteracting the dangers of mass participation in politics. Mussolini, too, expected the arrival of a new man. In 1908 he presented his conception of the superman's role in modern society in a writing on Nietzsche entitled, "The Philosophy of Force." Here, Mussolini, interpreting Nietzsche, connected the superman with the return to the ideal. In order to understand that ideal,

> a new species of "free spirits" will come . . . spirits endowed with some sublime perversity—spirits who will free us from the love for fellow creatures and from willing nothing. They will return her goal to earth and to men their hopes—new, free, very free spirits who will triumph over God and the Nothingness.[15]

The new spirits were needed in a reality that Mussolini believed was dominated by a lack of ideals and spiritual values.

> The Superman is a symbol, the exponent of this anguishing and tragic
> period of crisis that is traversing European consciousness while searching
> for new sources of pleasure, beauty, ideal. He testifies to our weakness, but
> at the same time represents the hope for our redemption. He is dusk and
> dawn. He is above all a hymn to life, to life lived with all the energies in
> a continuous tension toward something higher.[16]

Only the superman could make life heroic. Only the new spirits could upset the egalitarian system that democracy had introduced into social and political life.[17]

As a matter of fact, well before he took the role of *duce* of fascism,[18] and
prior to the mass organization of his myth, Mussolini came to represent the
model of a new generation of politicians. Whether he stood in the forefront
of the battle as leader of the revolutionary socialists or played the role of
spokesman for interventionism in World War I, Mussolini's claims to spiritualism, his activism, and his nonconformist political theories attracted the
attention of many critics of the liberal system who were looking for a "new
man."[19] A few years later, when Mussolini became the central cult figure in
the fascist regime, his myth was made possible by the search for "the man"
in what Warren Susman labels "the culture of personality."[20] The widespread
mystique of the great leader explains as well the extended admiration and
success of the Duce when he was appointed prime minister in 1922.[21]

MUSSOLINI IN THE CULTURE OF PERSONALITY

In the middle of the twentieth century's first decade, a change occurred in
the normative expectations of ideal social behavior for the individual. As
Susman argues for the American case, "the modal type [of self] felt to be
essential for the maintenance of the social order" shifted in the 1910s from
"character" to "personality."[22] The notion of character had responded to the
nineteenth-century preoccupation with elaborating a standard of conduct
in society that would ensure the mastering of the self and its moral development. It also constituted a model for the presentation of the self to others that established the link between the "social" and the "moral." Hundreds of books, pamphlets, and manuals connected to the building of
"character" were published during the century. Other cultural forms, such
as literature and the arts, also testified to the concept's influence upon the
moral spirit of the 1800s.[23] Qualities such as citizenship, duty, democracy,
work, honor, reputation, and integrity were most frequently associated with
the notion of character.[24] Values of work and production, as embodied in Max
Weber's ideal type of the Protestant capitalist, were particularly emphasized.

The Protestant capitalist, representative specimen of the "culture of character," exemplified the construction of the moral self via the disciplined control of impulses and the internalization of moral values.

At the beginning of the twentieth century, however, and in the face of changes in the social order, a new vision of the self emerged, along with a new method of presenting the self in society. The development of psychiatric and psychological studies at this time was symptomatic of the growing awareness of the effects that material transformations were exercising upon individuals.[25] Self-help books appeared with new kinds of advice that responded to novel needs and conditions caused by technological discoveries' effects upon people's sense of time and space.[26] The new American disease, "neurasthenia," spurred the spread of therapies seeking to relieve nervous depressions, or what Victorian England called "shattered nerves."[27] Within this context, therapeutic ideals of self-fulfillment overcame the interest in moral qualities and ascetic self-denial; the notion of expressive "personality" and individual needs began to come to the fore. Manuals for self-improvement suggested ways to build one's personality and referred to qualities such as *"fascinating, stunning, attractive, magnetic, glowing, masterful, creative, dominant, forceful."*[28] This constituted a fundamental shift in the social ideal of the self.[29] Uniqueness became a must in a society dominated by "crowds." Having an identity meant being someone special, unusual. Interestingly, as Susman remarks, self-help guides indicated that individuals needed to be themselves in order to develop a personality. At the same time, guides suggested ways to achieve this end that clearly subordinated spontaneity to the more urgent requirement of being liked, conforming to people's expectations. Hence, on the one hand the individual needed to show uniqueness in order to stand out from the crowd.[30] On the other hand, one's success depended on one's relationship with the crowd, on "making oneself pleasing to others," on acting in order to impress others.[31] The culture of personality emphasized strong individuals who would be able to compel people to like them. Personal charm and fascination, rather than moral attributes, constituted major qualities.

Masterful Personality, published by Orison Swett Marden in 1921, glorified personalities who could achieve supremacy and "sway great masses."[32] Leadership was connected to magnetism. In the same way that Le Bon instructed the leader to adopt a style that would attract people's favor, so self-help guides urged great personalities to present themselves in a likable manner. The road for the development of a dramaturgical self, the self as spectacle, was thus paved. Not by chance, modern motion picture stardom began to take place at around the same time the "culture of personality" replaced the "culture of character." As Christian Metz affirms, "[T]he cinema was born . . . in a period when social life was deeply marked by the notion of the *individual* (or its most elevated version, 'personality')."[33] Movie actors turned into images and were marketed as personalities to be admired. In a society slowly moving from production to consumption, actors and entertainers, along with politicians and businessmen, became the main protagonists of a new popular column in magazines and weeklies: biographies. "[O]ne of the most conspicuous newcomers in the realm of print since the introduction of the short story," says Leo Lowenthal, biographies grew into a standing feature in periodicals immediately after the First World War.[34] Their appearance indicated a growing interest in individual personalities, great figures. In Germany after 1918, political biographies took a major role as "the classical literature of the German middle-brow."[35] In general, popular biographies became a staple of French and English publications— another proof of the fascination with the idea of unusual, unique types in the first twenty years of this century. Personalities, because they were distinctive, deserved admiration and applause and lured public interest.

In Italy, the search for a new leader, a "man," had anticipated the attraction for great personalities. Before the war the quest for leaders often involved nostalgia for traditional kinds of rulers (strong characters à la Bismarck). After World War I, qualities such as "exceptional" appeared to be more appealing.[36] Within this context, once Mussolini became prime minister in the wake of what appeared to be a "revolutionary" March on Rome, his "glowing" personality immediately drew widespread attention. Journalists, writers, intellectuals, and politicians glorified the youngest prime minister in Italian history—even though in his first two years of rule Mussolini formally renounced the revolutionary principles of his movement and surreptitiously governed within the democratic institutions he had previously attacked. As a matter of fact, Mussolini's fame boomed during the two to three years that preceded the dictatorial turn. The quest for a new order and the search for novel political figures who could bring forth changes helped to confer upon Mussolini a symbolic aura.[37] Whereas only a few years earlier a minority of intellectuals had regarded Mussolini as the "new man," suddenly Mussolini came to be considered an exceptional individual by a much larger audience. The man and his personality monopolized attention.[38]

Illustrazione Italiana, a weekly magazine that mainly reported national and international events through photographs, testifies to this trend.[39] Upon his assignment as prime minister on October 1922, Mussolini became a major subject of *Illustrazione*'s photographic stories. Besides making the front page in the aftermath of his appointment (November 5, 1922; the whole

issue was dedicated to this event), Mussolini appeared in almost every issue of the journal in the next three months, then approximately twice a
month from February 1923 to December 1924.[40] *Illustrazione* featured him
on the front cover fifteen times during 1923 and seven times in 1924, the
year of the Matteotti crisis.

The amount of coverage Mussolini received in *Illustrazione* over the first
two years of his prime ministership was quite unusual, even discounting
the extraordinary circumstances surrounding Mussolini's assignment. The
fascist March on Rome had certainly disrupted the normal course of Italian political life, and in this fashion it constituted an important event for
journalists. However, the frequent presence of Mussolini in the news continued well beyond the aftermath of the march and surely exceeded that of
any preceding prime minister. In the year and a half of Giovanni Giolitti's
government, from November 1903 to March 1905, for example, *Illustrazione* published only one photo of Giolitti, on July 3, 1904. Giolitti appeared in the picture amid other people at the inauguration of a monument
to Goethe. In the case of Prime Minister Boselli, who was appointed in June
1916, *Illustrazione* only printed his picture once, at the end of his ministry
in October 1917. Mussolini, by contrast, made the headlines at least twenty
times in the second semester of his government. *Illustrazione* dedicated five
covers to him during that period.

In July 1921, when Bonomi was elected prime minister, *Illustrazione*'s
coverage of the office increased, a sign of a growing tendency in the news
industry to build events around individual figures. Bonomi appeared on the
front page once, on July 10, 1921, and was part of the journal's news six
times in the first semester of his presidency. However, all the photographs
Illustrazione published of Bonomi, besides the classical upper-torso portrait
of July 10, showed him among other people. Furthermore, in two cases
Bonomi appeared almost completely disguised. In the October 16 issue, *Illustrazione* dedicated the front page to the launching of a steamship at
Castellammare, near Naples. Bonomi, who supposedly was part of the picture, appears as a little, unidentifiable figure showing his back. In the issue
of November 13, which was dedicated to the celebration of the Unknown
Soldier, Bonomi is only present in a couple of photos amid other people. The
background role Bonomi played on this occasion is quite surprising considering the enormous importance the Unknown Soldier held for those nations
that participated in World War I. In this highly charged symbolic ritual,
Bonomi did not stand out.

In the case of Mussolini, the exact opposite took place. On November 26,
1922, *Illustrazione*'s front cover announced: "The trip to Lausanne of Hon.

Mussolini. Waiting for the presidential train at a station." The picture portrayed a couple—a woman and a man wearing a black shirt and holding a club in his hands—with each holding a child and a bouquet of flowers. In this picture, the prime minister was not depicted. Yet the photo was built around Mussolini's figure, even if he was physically absent. The woman, the man wearing the symbols of fascism, and the children who were brought to witness the event all testified to the trust the adult couple invested in Mussolini as the Italian representative at a conference in Lausanne.[41] We might say that the choice of the photo testifies to the magazine's trust, too. Mussolini was already becoming an icon.

On December 17, 1922, *Illustrazione* constructed another photographic event around the absence of Mussolini. The caption read: "Paris: photographers waiting for the arrival of Hon. Mussolini." In a curious reversal of roles, photographers became the subject of the photo, although the significance of the event relied on its connection to the physically absent Mussolini. He was the event. The presence of the photographers waiting for him epitomized Mussolini's public role, his star status. On February 4, 1923, *Illustrazione*'s cover page portrayed Mussolini's daily strolling: "The morning walk of the President." The private act of a political figure was featured as a public event.[42] Publicity made visible what used to be invisible; it also created an audience. In this process Mussolini attracted more attention. Visibility, appearance, and performance magnified Mussolini's personality, and interest in his person grew.[43] On the occasion of the April 6, 1924, elections, in a preview of contemporary scoops on celebrities, *Illustrazione Italiana* printed "unpublished photos" of Mussolini (issue of April 13, 1924).

Pictures of Mussolini inundated the postcard market, with Mussolini appearing in different attires, postures, contexts, and situations.[44] The first biography of Mussolini was printed in 1923, and writings on him rapidly multiplied.[45] The descriptions of Mussolini responded to the elements of political novelty he seemed to represent or was believed to represent. In 1922 Emilio Settimelli affirmed that Mussolini's "personal magnetism is enormous" and that "his magnetic glances mean command."[46] He compared Mussolini to the figure of *condottiere*. Ettore Ciccotti, a university professor with a socialist past, wrote in September 1922: "In today's evident scarcity of political *personalities*, Mussolini is the one that more than any other, if not the only one, can deserve this name."[47] A parliamentary deputy concurred: "In order to understand something of Fascism, one must consider the *personality* of its founder and its leader: Benito Mussolini. . . . The leaders of Fascism who surround him express the most bourgeois mediocrity and nothing more. . . . Mussolini emerges above them in a conspicuous, absolute way, not as much for his intellectual vigor, his cultural, technical and concrete preparation, as for the 'insolence' of his *personality*. . . . what counts is his *personality*. . . . the only theory that fascism has is one person: Benito Mussolini."[48] Mussolini was the man that many longed for in order to revitalize a nation that was experiencing a deep crisis of political representation. "Benito Mussolini is not a man: he is *the man*. He is the one the Nation has been waiting for."[49]

Antonio Beltramelli published the first comprehensive biography of Mussolini in 1923, only a few months after the March on Rome.[50] Previously, in 1915, Torquato Nanni had written a short biographical history of his friend Mussolini, defining the Duce as "spirit of steel, at the service of a formidable will."[51] Other writings on Mussolini continued to be published in the years before the fascists took power. These publications were often inspired by Mussolini's own recollections of his youth taken from the war diary he kept during World War I or from the brief account of his life he compiled in prison from 1911 to 1912.[52] These early profiles of the Duce depict him as an exceptional, unique, quasi-romantic character. Mussolini comes across as lonely and poor but also passionate and adventurous, vital and brilliant. Beltramelli's 1923 biography, entitled *The New Man* (*L'Uomo nuovo*), follows this line of interpretation. Beltramelli romantically portrayed every stage of Mussolini's life in terms of the construction of a great personality. Mussolini, as the title of the book clearly stated, was the new man who "sacrificed his youth for the well-being of troubled multitudes."[53] He was the "savior" of a corrupt world, the *homo unus* Italy needed to build a new society. Beltramelli offered an image of the Duce as predestined to a successful future. Anecdotes and witnesses supported the representation of the Duce as an exceptional man, "God's elect." Mussolini, Beltramelli seemed to suggest, was the man Italy had been waiting for.

In 1924 Giuseppe Prezzolini wrote a brief biographical account of Mussolini that, he warned, was not an apologia but a realistic, "impartial" analysis. Still, objectivity did not stop Prezzolini from founding his whole description of the Duce on the idea of Mussolini's exceptional qualities. From the beginning, Prezzolini defined Mussolini as "an exceptional man" and insisted on his "force": "Mussolini is a force who came at the right historical moment. . . . The elements of this force revolve around one quality: will."[54] For Prezzolini, as for most of Mussolini's biographers, the Duce possessed innate qualities, "a natural predisposition" to be the leader.[55] "One cannot acquire certain qualities. One is born with them," Prezzolini insisted.[56] For him, Mussolini clearly exemplified this law. Margherita Sarfatti, in her turn, wrote the first official biography of Mussolini in 1925. *The*

Life of Benito Mussolini was printed in 200,000 copies, with seventeen editions and translations in eighteen languages.[57] Sarfatti began her story lamenting the absence of great, outstanding figures in World War I; she then proceeded to describe Mussolini as an exceptional person. Even Mussolini's childhood showed, according to her, a sign of future greatness: "The childhood of superior men is never really happy. . . . The latent forces on a leash within him prevent him from enjoying things quietly like ordinary children."[58] According to Sarfatti and other early biographers, Mussolini was endowed with exceptional characteristics that made him into a great individual, a personality.[59]

The admiration for Mussolini and his leadership did not remain a local phenomenon. The Duce won acclaim far beyond Italy's borders, conquering fans in more than one continent. Americans, French, British, and Norwegians participated in the chorus of eulogies for Mussolini. Georges Sorel with great foresight declared in 1912: "One does not know it yet, but he is the only energetic man capable of fixing the government's weakness."[60] Maxim Gorki, supposedly citing a quote from Trotsky, told some journalists in 1924: "From Mussolini's governmental actions I have got to know his energy and I admire him, but I prefer Trotsky's opinion: Mussolini has made a revolution, he is our best student."[61] In the aftermath of the March on Rome, appreciations of Mussolini filled foreign newspapers' articles and reports. On November 3, 1922, the *New York Herald* defined Mussolini as the regenerator of Italian nationality, a man who deserved a place in history similar to that of Garibaldi. On October 31, 1922, the *New York Tribune* proposed a question about Mussolini: was he Garibaldi or Caesar?[62] On November 1, 1922, the *New York Times* predicted that Mussolini's chin would become famous for its "squareness and force." According to the paper, Mussolini reflected the description of him given by an American: "A Napoleon turned pugilist." The American newspapers anticipated endless attempts to compare Mussolini to great men, from Cromwell to Napoleon.[63] On November 4, the British *Daily Telegraph* echoed the similitude between Garibaldi and Mussolini. The Swiss newspaper *S. Galler Tageblatt* declared on November 4, 1922, that Mussolini's characteristics were "an extraordinary temperament, an exceptional organizational strength and a marvelous ability to dominate."[64] Henri Bidou in *Le Figaro* of December 1, 1922, referred to Latin qualities in order to praise Mussolini: "We can't but rejoice for the fresh energy that the new party gives the Italian nation. . . . in order not to be alarmed, one needs to give large credit to the Latin wisdom and prudence of Mussolini."[65]

The admiration for Mussolini and the infatuation with strong men continued after Mussolini instituted the dictatorship in 1925. Within a developing culture of personality Mussolini was able to prolong his success as a leading figure well into the 1930s, and the image of the "right" dictator began to circulate. On November 24, 1925, on the occasion of the Locarno Pact, the *National Zeitung* admitted to being surprised at Mussolini's aristocratic manners. After all, Mussolini was the son of lower-class people. The newspaper then proclaimed: "The Duce is of that race that we are used to portray as leaders of men."[66] The fact that Mussolini had "humble" origins supported those theories postulating a direct correlation between democracy and the birth of new leaders.[67] Robert Michels wrote in 1915 that "while monarchy is irreconcilable with the principle of democracy, Caesarism may still claim this name if it is based upon the popular will."[68] In his discussion of charismatic leadership a few years later, Michels again considered the relationship between democracy and the *duce*. On that occasion Michels took Mussolini as his example of a popular leader born from the "masses."[69] This new Caesar constituted the unifying symbol of the "masses." He granted social stability to the nation through the institution of a new political order.[70]

Within this depiction of democracy, Mussolini's dictatorship came to be widely accepted in many countries. His anticommunist stance made him a strongly desirable dictator, unlike the Soviet Union's leaders, Lenin and Stalin. In the United States, for example, the *Saturday Evening Post*'s Will Rogers wrote after his 1926 interview with Mussolini: "Dictator form of government is the greatest form of government: that is, if you have the right Dictator."[71] From 1925 to 1928 more than a hundred articles were published on Mussolini in the United States, only fifteen on Stalin. From 1929 to 1932, at a time when, according to Diggins, Americans were very interested in the Soviet five-year plan, articles on Stalin increased to thirty-five, but Mussolini still counted forty-six.[72] In 1928 a serialized biography of Mussolini, published in eight installments and supposedly signed by Mussolini himself, appeared in the *Saturday Evening Post*.[73] The *Saturday Evening Post* contributed to the creation of an image of Mussolini as respectable. Numerous U.S. daily papers did the same. Mussolini's anticommunist ideology especially carried the American middle class toward the dictator. The fear of socialism helped build Mussolini's positive image in the United States, although other factors and circumstances also favored the acclamation of Mussolini as an estimable leader.[74] All in all, the American press presented Mussolini as a new man and an exceptional personality. In 1932 the renowned journalist Lowell Thomas participated in the production of a Columbia Pictures film on Mussolini supervised by the Duce himself. *Mussolini Speaks!* presented documentary images and speeches of the Duce described and interpreted by

Lowell Thomas (Figure 1).[75] Thomas's commentary appeared to be hyperbolic, admiring, and celebratory, and he emphasized the Italian leader's grandeur. At some point his admiration for "the man I will never forget" reached an apex, and in the scene where Mussolini was going to begin a speech in Naples in October 1931, Lowell exclaimed: "This is his supreme moment. He stands like a modern Caesar!"[76] In the film Mussolini appeared to be the model for a new, ideal ruling style, the center of a new state of harmony between citizens and leader, people and fascism.[77]

The image of Mussolini as an exceptional person and a great leader outlasted the novelty of Mussolini's first years of government. In 1926 an Italian psychologist dedicated a whole study to Mussolini's "psychic individuality." According to the study, Mussolini possessed a perfect balance of the three psychic faculties: intellectual, sentimental, and will. "The exuberance of his conceptual processes," "[t]he elevation of his sentiments," and "[h]is indomitable will" made Mussolini into a marvelous, harmonic personality.[78] Margaret Beavan, mayor of Liverpool, confessed to the *Daily Mail* of May 31, 1928, that she had never seen a man so different from all others, one with such a "magnificent *personality*." She had been moved by his "dominant, magnetic, impressive, immense *personality*."[79] In 1933 Winston Churchill affirmed that Mussolini "was the greatest living legislator."[80] That same year Sigmund Freud sent Mussolini one of his books, *Warum Krieg?* written with Albert Einstein. In the dedication he wrote: "To Benito Mussolini, from an old man who greets in the Ruler the Hero of Culture."[81]

But most significant of all among the eulogies of Mussolini's personality and panegyrics of his activity was the quiet sense of admiration evident in Emil Ludwig's 1932 interview with Mussolini.[82] At the time Ludwig had already written several biographies and had interviewed famous statesmen such as Stalin.[83] In the introduction to the interview, he admitted to having opposed Mussolini until five years earlier. Then, three factors made him change his mind:

> The concepts of democracy and parliamentarism began to fade for me,
> other forms came forward, political life in its traditional forms was de-
> valued, important men began to be lacking. At the same time in Moscow
> and Rome I saw things that were really grandiose, i.e. I recognized
> the positive sides of these two dictatorships. Third, some psychological
> considerations led me to recognize that, despite some of his speeches,
> the Italian statesman did not hide any war aim.[84]

Ludwig's first two reasons reflected a tendency in the political culture of the time to search for new forms of political representation. The third

Figure 1. Advertisement for *Mussolini Speaks!* in *Variety,* March 14, 1933.

element was the fruit of Ludwig's own analysis and later proved to be fundamentally flawed. Yet, the question of war apart, Ludwig specifically admitted that in the end he did not need to believe in those three factors because "[m]ore decisively than all these considerations I was strongly influenced by the question of *personality*. When I thought I recognized in Mussolini some traits that reminded me of Nietzsche's conception, I mentally detached him from the political movement and began to regard him as a phenomenon."[85] Mussolini's personality convinced Ludwig that the Duce's work was positive, although Ludwig was an "individualist *par excellence*" and would never become a fascist.[86]

What encouraged Ludwig with reference to Mussolini was in effect "an artistic interest in an exceptional *personality*."[87] The portrait of Mussolini that emerges from Ludwig's interviews testifies to the attraction Mussolini held for the journalist. In Ludwig's account Mussolini comes across as a *condottiero*, a hero, but also a suave, sophisticated person who is always self-assured, meditative, wise. Ludwig talked of Mussolini's "patience and calm that never oscillated" and that showed "his interior security."[88] He referred to Mussolini's "marvelous mastery of thought and expression" and described the Duce's dialogue style as "metallic . . . a finely tempered steel." Mussolini appeared to him "devilishly Napoleonic," a "lucid man." In a final, quasi-apotheosis, Ludwig saw in Mussolini "the expression of father of the country," "the man-creator."[89] In sum, although he differed from Mussolini on issues of war, individualism, and other questions, Ludwig constructed a romantic, heroic image of the Duce—an admiring portrait of his exceptional personality.

The example of Ludwig shows further the connection between Mussolini's fame and the social context in which it developed. Mussolini's success and the building of his myth were embedded in a political culture that advocated strong leaders and placed growing emphasis on personality.[90] Within this frame, numerous intellectuals and politicians came to view Mussolini as a "glowing," "magnetic," "masterful," "strong" man. The rhetoric of personality, which was not limited to Italy, infiltrated a wide number of cultural forms.[91] In the culmination of this star-making process, by which personalities become actors, Mussolini was featured in a 1938 documentary by Edwin Ware Hullinger entitled *The Private Life of Mussolini*.[92] He thus concluded an "acting" career initiated in 1922 with George Fitzmaurice's film *The Eternal City*. This work showed the fights between communists and fascists and took the latter's side. Mussolini posed for the final scenes.[93]

The admiration for Mussolini as representative of "new men" reinforced his power position in the government of Italy and cast more of an aura over him. In this process of reciprocity between reality and representation, the myth of Mussolini continued to expand, developing independently of the regime. The emphasis on the person of Mussolini created in fact the premises for the popular distinction between Mussolini and fascism, the leader and his movement.[94] People believed in Mussolini more than in the party, and they often differentiated the regime's faults from those of the Duce.[95] Letters were addressed to Mussolini asking for his direct and illuminated assistance and complaining about the local fascists' bad administration.[96] Even when the regime definitely collapsed and the partisans hung the dead body of Mussolini upside-down at a gas station in Milan, a complete rejection of Mussolini did not accompany the condemnation of fascism.[97] The myth of the Duce survived the regime.

This paradoxical situation has led some to interpret the myth of Mussolini as an ad hoc construction, a propagandistic device aimed at fabricating consensus and behind which the harsh reality of the dictatorship hid. Whereas the Italians were not as fond of fascism as they were of Mussolini— the interpretation goes—they ended up accepting the regime because Mussolini represented it. The myth was a manipulative means the regime used in order to persuade the people to embrace the fascist cause. To be sure, Mussolini exploited his own fame and fostered the building of a propaganda machine around his person. Nevertheless, as Mussolini's success in the "culture of personality" shows, the exaltation of Mussolini during the regime's years was more than a work of propaganda. Nor did the cult of the Duce solely derive from Mussolini's inherently "charismatic" qualities. The myth of Mussolini (*Mussolinismo*), in effect, reflected Mussolini's own wish for power. It expressed fascism's identity the way Mussolini conceived of it. In Mussolini's political vision, only if he rebutted internal competition could his leadership go unchallenged.[98] Consequently, and following the March on Rome, Mussolini began to create the conditions for the demise of the Fascist Party and the growth of his own stardom. He envisaged a strategy that would transform the Fascist National Party (PNF) by progressively diminishing its functions.

MUSSOLINI AND THE PARTY

At the beginning of Mussolini's mandate as prime minister, his governmental actions did not exceed the limits of a legal system founded on democratic rule. Mussolini presented himself as the supporter of rational order and technical efficiency, and one of his first actions concerned the reorganization of public administration.[99] Bureaucracy had been a long-standing problem in the Italian state and seemed to be particularly in disarray in the postwar period. Proposed to the Chamber of Deputies on November 17, 1922, the new law delegating full power to the government in the administrative and tax sector passed on December 3 as Law Number 1601. The new ministry presided over by Mussolini thus initiated its legislative action in the tradition of prior governments.

Following his predecessors, Mussolini took a moderate stance in the area of legislation and administrative affairs. However, he also introduced radical political changes in the structure of the liberal parliamentary system vis-à-vis questions of authority and power. One of these changes was the institution of the Gran Consiglio (Grand Council), which officially convened for the first time in the evening of January 12, 1923. The Gran Consiglio, later defined as the "supreme organ" of fascism,[100] was supposed to decide the future politics of the Italian government and sketch the general lines of policies concerning both interior and foreign affairs. With this purpose, the Gran Consiglio would meet once a month under the presidency of Mussolini, with all the most influential fascist members participating.[101] The Gran Consiglio, in its original formulation, constituted a special organism depending on Mussolini and functioning outside the boundaries of parliament. In the guise of an alternative body within the administration of the liberal-democratic state, it contributed to making a regime out of Mussolini's rule from the beginning of his mandate and surreptitiously prepared the terrain for the establishment of a dictatorship.

As many scholars of fascism recognize, the creation of the Gran Consiglio represented the first attack launched by Mussolini's government at the heart of democratic institutions. At the same time, however, the Gran Consiglio also had enormous consequences for the internal organization of the Fascist Party, the most important one being the corrosion of the PNF's effective power. Indeed, the Gran Consiglio had in appearance assigned a crucial role to the highest fascist hierarchies, placing them in charge of drawing up programs on state reforms and foreign policy. But in actuality the Gran Consiglio exclusively played consulting functions within Mussolini's government and did not have any autonomous power. Fascist leaders gathered in an organ with little or no decision-making power—an organ that in fact helped initiate the decline of party members' authority within the fascist government. The institution of the Gran Consiglio hence allowed Mussolini to relegate the party to a secondary position and to decrease the risk of internal challenges to his own power. On December 9, 1928, when fascism had already imposed a dictatorship, the Gran Consiglio became a constitutional apparatus of the state and was given a juridical status and an internal regulation. By then, though, Mussolini's leadership was unquestioned, as was his supremacy over the party. The internal rules of the Gran Consiglio stated this reality very clearly:

> Art. 1: His Excellency the Head of Government, President of the Gran Consiglio of Fascism represents the Gran Consiglio and directs and regulates its activity. He convenes it when he thinks it necessary and establishes its agenda; he nominates the rapporteurs on the single affairs to be discussed in the meeting; he asks questions; he gives the chance to speak; he directs the discussion and synthesizes its outcome. . . .
>
> Art. 2: His Excellency . . . has the right to interrupt at any moment the discussion on any question and to suspend the Gran Consiglio's deliberations.
>
> Art. 14: . . . the Gran Consiglio deliberates with the absolute majority of the voters: in case of tied votes it approves the proposal that obtained the vote of the Head of Government, the President.[102]

The Gran Consiglio greatly enhanced Mussolini's leadership within fascism. The creation of the Milizia produced the same result. On January 14, 1923, Royal Decree Number 31 prescribed "the dissolution of all formations of a political-military kind" and instituted a voluntary militia subordinate to Mussolini.[103] The Milizia per la Sicurezza Nazionale, later called Milizia Volontaria per la Sicurezza Nazionale (MVSN), gathered under one single organization several military fascist squads that once mainly acted on a local basis. These were transformed into a national military corps obeying the direct orders of the prime minister. With the creation of the Milizia, erected on the ashes of *squadrismo*, Mussolini founded a personal armed force he could utilize in case the antifascist opposition seriously threatened his power. Thus, the Milizia, as Mussolini wrote in 1927, constituted an important innovation in terms of governmental activities: "The creation of the Milizia is the fundamental, inexorable fact that put the government on a plane absolutely different from all the previous ones and made of it a Regime."[104] The Milizia, insisted Mussolini, was the harbinger of the totalitarian regime and marked the death of the democratic liberal state.[105]

The Milizia, as Mussolini's statements rightly highlight, had an intrinsically destabilizing effect on liberal institutions, especially considering that it was assigned the specific function of defending fascism and the "October revolution."[106] However, Mussolini failed to acknowledge that the Milizia also granted him a larger hegemonic role within the fascist movement. First, by recruiting its members from the violent fascist squads who used to act on the orders of a local *ras,* the Milizia highly diluted the power of local fascist leaders. The militiamen now responded directly to Mussolini and were supposed to obey him with absolute, blind discipline.[107] Second, through the Milizia Mussolini was able to exercise control over fascist leaders and prevent challenges to his authority. On October 13, 1923, the Gran Consiglio decreed that holding both military and political positions was inadmissible.[108] Those who held posts within the party could not lead the Milizia nor, by implication, have any influence on it. As a matter of fact, the cadres of the Milizia mostly came from the regular Italian army and presumably obeyed the head of government out of a sense of duty.[109] Hence, with the Milizia Mussolini undermined the possibility that any fascist member could ever hold enough power to challenge his own leadership.

The organization of the Milizia constituted a further step in the process of neutralizing the party's role, a process that Mussolini carried out first as prime minister and later as head of the regime. Other measures Mussolini adopted in this direction included the opening of party enrollment immediately after the March on Rome.[110] This opening helped devitalize the identity of the party by allowing people of minimal conviction to become members. The new rule of October 15, 1923, further undermined the political vitality of the party. The rule stated that many appointments within the Fascist Party should be determined from above and no longer through internal elections.[111] In October 1926 the new statute of the PNF definitively proclaimed the system of nominations from above, suppressing the voice from the base and any form of debate within the fascist membership.[112]

The laws on the Gran Consiglio had opened the way to Mussolini's supremacy over the party. From the juridical point of view, and in the face of the Gran Consiglio's transformation into a state organ in 1928, the laws also marked the end of the division between party and state—a division that had already been dissolved in practice with the establishment of the dictatorship.[113] However, in this case the state encapsulated the party, and not vice versa. Since the beginning of his appointment Mussolini had emphasized the difference, in terms of authority, between party and state and had privileged the state over the party. In the first measure of a series aimed at weakening the party's role, on June 13, 1923, Mussolini circulated to the prefects of the provinces a note in which he gave them power over party representatives.[114]

> The Prefect and nobody else is the one and only representative of the
> Government authority in the provinces. . . . The fascist province leaders
> and other party authorities are subordinated to the Prefect. It is intended

that since fascism is the dominant party, the Prefect has to keep contacts with the local fasces in order to avoid dissent and whatever else can disturb public order.[115]

Mussolini conceded that because the Fascist Party was the dominant one, the prefect had to be in touch with local fascist sections, primarily in order to avoid disagreements and violence. Nevertheless, he stated in absolute terms that any illegal act, independent of its origin, needed to be curbed: "Phenomena of illegalism must be inexorably repressed, no matter who practices them."[116] This clause doubtless applied to his own party. On April 3, 1926, Law Number 660 definitely affirmed the power of the prefects. The following year, in the document to the prefects of January 5, 1927, Mussolini wrote that the prefect was the highest authority of the state: "He is the direct representative of the central executive power. All citizens, and first of all those who have the great privilege and highest honor to serve Fascism, must respect and obey the maximum political representative of the Fascist Regime."[117] The party, Mussolini continued, needed to be "a conscious means of the state's will, at the center and at the periphery."[118] Two years later, on September 14, 1929, Mussolini told the party's high hierarchies gathered at the PNF assembly: "The Head of the Province (the *prefetto*) has at his orders all the peripheral forces in which the State and the Regime express themselves; this also includes the Party, and the federal Secretary who plays his function of subordinate collaborator of the Head of the Province, a true functionary of the regal *Prefettura*."[119]

On October 28, 1925, Mussolini inaugurated a formula that became a password of fascism: "Everything within the state, nothing outside the state, nothing against the state."[120] Four years later, on September 26, 1929, Mussolini stated the political terms of the party's subordination to the state: "If in Fascism everything is in the state, also the Party cannot escape this inexorable necessity, and must thus collaborate in a subordinate way with the organs of the state. . . . One cannot confuse the PNF, which is a primordial political force of the Regime, with the Regime that conveys, embraces and harmonizes this political force and all others of various nature."[121] The party statute of December 14, 1929, mirrored Mussolini's philosophy and further limited the role of the PNF, precipitating its transformation into a merely bureaucratic apparatus. The new statute reduced the number of the Gran Consiglio's members and established that the secretary of the party was to be nominated not by the Gran Consiglio but by the head of government via royal decree. At the same time, the Gran Consiglio lost its right to nominate the party's high officials. The government was then in charge.[122]

The diminished role of the party served to highlight the importance of Mussolini's functions within the regime. As Mussolini said on the fifth anniversary of fascism's foundation, on March 24, 1924: "[B]ig historical movements are not only the result of numerical addition, but also the epilogue of a very tenacious will."[123] Mussolini affirmed that fascism was the fruit of one will: his own. In 1925, after the famous speech of January 3, which marked the beginning of the totalitarian regime, Mussolini's leadership became an established fact. Leadership meant complete, absolute power over everybody; and Mussolini—turned dictator—did not have any hesitations claiming it. On May 15, 1925, speaking at the Chamber of Deputies, Mussolini warned: "All force is subordination. . . . Remember that in this subordination of all to the will of a leader. . . . Fascism has found its strength yesterday and will find its strength and glory tomorrow."[124] Mussolini indicated that the leader's supremacy was the element necessary for the victorious march of fascism. Obedience to the leader constituted a duty of the Italian people in general but also of those fascists who had participated "yesterday" in fascism's successful achievement of governmental power. A few months later a law presented to the Chamber on November 18, 1925, juridically sanctioned the head of government as the expression of state sovereignty. The ratification of Mussolini's personal power was then reinforced on January 31, 1926, by Law Number 100, establishing that the executive had the right to issue juridical norms without previous consultation with parliament.[125] On September 26, 1929, Mussolini explicitly told the Assembly of the PNF that he was operating independently of it. At a time when he had again made important changes in government, Mussolini said:

> My words, as always in my twenty years of political battles . . . come after facts. These facts do not originate from assemblies, nor from previous advice or inspirations of individuals, groups or circles. They are decisions that I mature by myself and of which, as is right, nobody can know in advance.[126]

In 1932, in his first speech for the Decennial of the Revolution, Mussolini suggested to the 25,000 *gerarchi* gathered in Piazza Venezia: "We need some main directions in this beginning of the second decennial. I will begin with the one that concerns me personally. I am your leader."[127] That same year the new party statute, promulgated with Royal Decree Number 1456, highlighted Mussolini's leadership position. The document bore the word "Duce" in bold characters in order to differentiate it from the rest. In February 1933 the party secretary, Achille Starace, prescribed that "in official acts the word DUCE has to be written always in all capital letters."[128] Both legally and symbolically, Mussolini acted in ways that made of him an exclusive figure and distinguished him from the members of the party. Within this context, and in view of the depoliticization of the PNF, Mussolini's personal power expanded. This was also the case in connection with the issue of succession.

The continuous political marginalization of the party had hampered it from accomplishing successfully its role of creating fascism's future political class.[129] The party's activity was actually limited to daily administration. Party assemblies became more rare, and state control over the high ranks of the party became tighter.[130] Besides, the early liberalization of party enrollment had indiscriminately opened fascist doors to nonbelievers or weak believers.[131] In this context, as Aquarone writes, "the possibility that the party could represent a fecund center of discussion—although within the rigorous limits of the regime's institutions and ideological rules—and could become the propeller of a strong political life was very dim."[132] The party did not have the capacity nor the means to develop a vital fascist culture. But how would a new worldview and way of life grow and take shape if the party relinquished the task? How could a new fascist political class develop in these conditions? The party was unable to create a viable, active elite, and Mussolini had effectively preempted future possibilities for the party to play a major governmental role. Mussolini's actions ended up reinforcing his own central position and power to a point of quasi-absolutism, whereas the lack of a political class also prejudiced the chances of finding a successor to Mussolini.

The question of Mussolini's successor preoccupied many fascists, who worried about the fate of the regime in case of Mussolini's death. Since it seemed that the whole regime revolved around Mussolini, the problem certainly could not be underestimated. The Fascist Party's difficulties in capturing people's sympathies, and the preponderance of *Mussolinismo*, left little chance for fascism to survive once Mussolini was dead. Some old-guard fascists, at the sudden death of Mussolini's brother Arnaldo in December 1931, wondered: "If the 21st of December a tragic misfortune had painfully hit the nation, and to be clearer, if the 21st of December the Duce had suddenly died, what would have happened?" They urged: "We need to prepare today the ground, the political yeast for tomorrow."[133] On January 22, 1933, former party secretary Roberto Farinacci wrote to Mussolini:

> Is it or is it not true, President, that a succession in twenty, thirty years (I am willing to say: in a century, so that people do not think that I want to shorten your life) would be very difficult, if not impossible? . . . It seems at times that our institutions and laws are on one side, and the men on the other, silent and suspicious. In effect, President, what is the state today?

> Trust in Mussolini. We have not created yet a state that gives force to men.
> There is the man who gives strength to the state. What will happen when
> this man is gone?[134]

Mussolini did not seem interested in answering these questions, and none
of the party statutes ever mentioned the issue of Mussolini's successor. As
a matter of fact, the statutes never discussed a procedure for nominating the
party leader. In truth, the law of December 9, 1928, granted the Gran Consiglio the right to designate the head of government. According to the law,
the Gran Consiglio was to keep a list of names proposed by Mussolini to
present to the king in the event of Mussolini's death. However, as far as
what is known, the Gran Consiglio never participated in a discussion concerning this matter and never possessed any list.[135] Mussolini continuously
reiterated that he was the only leader, not only of the government but also
of the fascist revolution. On October 25, 1925, he told the people of Mantova: "Be sure: I will lead the fascist revolution to its final goal."[136] But if,
as Mussolini proclaimed, the revolution was "permanent," when would
Mussolini's leadership end? In effect, Mussolini pronounced himself to be
the only possible leader of fascism. On May 26, 1927, he told the fascist
deputies: "I am convinced that, despite a ruling class in formation, despite
the fact that people are more consciously disciplined, I need to take the task
of governing the Italian Nation still another ten or fifteen years. It is necessary. My successor is yet to be born."[137] In 1932 Mussolini confessed to
Ludwig: "I truly believe that there will not be a Duce number two."[138] The
following year, on October 28, Mussolini told war-decorated soldiers: "Nor
let people say that perhaps there would have been some other movement
and some other Leader."[139] Mussolini was the legitimate *capo*, the only possible one.

Due to the relationship between party and state, the lack of a political
class, and the absence of a possible successor, Mussolini's leadership constituted a given fact and reflected the Duce's substantial power. Mussolini was
the leader, and he could do without the party.[140] In 1921 Mussolini, elaborating his thoughts on parties, had admitted: "After all, for what does the
content of a party count? What gives it force and life is the 'tonality,' the
will of those constituting it, the soul of the Leader."[141] Now the will of the
party members was reduced to one: Mussolini's. In this sense, Mussolini
anticipated Oswald Spengler's critique of parties, which Spengler, in fact,
constructed with reference to Mussolini:

> What anticipates the future is not the being of Fascism as a party, but
> simply and solely the figure of its creator. Mussolini is no party leader . . .

he is the *lord* of his country. . . . The most difficult victories of a ruler, and the most *essential*, are not those won over enemies, but those won over his own supporters, the praetorians, the "Ras," as they are called in Italy. This is the best of the born ruler. . . . The perfection of Caesarism is dictatorship —not the dictatorship of a party, but that of one man against all parties, and, most of all, above his own. Every revolutionary movement reaches its victory with a vanguard of praetorians—who are henceforth of no more use, but merely dangerous. The *real* master is known by the manner in which he dismisses them, ruthlessly and without thanks, intent only on his goal.[142]

As Spengler wrote, Mussolini, whether he thought of himself as a new Caesar or believed that destiny had assigned him the role of leader, clearly worked his way to primacy and an exclusive monopoly of power.[143] "I came to stay as long as possible," Mussolini told Ludwig in 1932.[144]

The focus on the person of Mussolini and the centralization of power within the Duce's hands greatly weakened the regime; it created a fracture between Mussolini and fascism. The regime suffered from a personalistic ruling style that underplayed the belief in fascist principles and values in favor of the cult of the leader. Faith in Mussolini became the substitute for belief in fascism. Within this context, the myth of Mussolini acquired even more importance. But the myth was not a facade. The actual dominance of the Duce and his attempt to centralize power reinforced the extent and force of his myth—a myth that had allowed Mussolini to achieve power in the first place. Reality and representation fed upon each other.

But what was this myth? How did Mussolini present his leadership role? Louis Marin, in a study of Louis XIV, asked: what is the imagination of absolutism? How does a power that wishes to be absolutist think of itself?[145] Within this frame, and with reference to fascism, we could ask: how did the myth of Mussolini symbolically express the regime's image of power? How did it portray Mussolini's fantasy of supremacy?

THE DEIFICATION OF MUSSOLINI

Omnipotence

During the early years of the fascist regime, a Catholic prayer of faith in God was adapted for use as an expression of belief in Mussolini:

I believe in the high Duce—maker of the Black Shirts.—And in Jesus Christ his only protector—Our Savior was conceived by a good teacher and an industrious blacksmith—He was a valiant soldier, he had some enemies—He came down to Rome; on the third day—he reestablished the state. He ascended into the high office—He is seated at the right hand of our Sovereign—From there he has to come and judge Bolshevism—I believe in the wise laws—The Communion of Citizens—The forgiveness of sins—The resurrection of Italy—The eternal force. Amen.[146]

This oath was taught to pupils of Italian schools in Tunisia.[147] The oration, in the spirit of religion, elevated Mussolini to a quasi-divine state, though it also skillfully stated that Jesus Christ was the Duce's protector; a "real" God overlooked Mussolini's actions. The regime could not afford to be blasphemous in a country dominated by Catholicism. The exaltation of the Duce could not overshadow God's glory. The auratic frame within which the eulogy of the Duce was composed, however, clearly envisioned the transfiguration of Mussolini to a God-like position. "I believe in the high Duce—maker of the Black Shirts," replaced in the original act of faith the phrase, "I believe in one God, the Father, the Almighty, maker of heaven and earth." True, Mussolini had only created fascism, but through it he had been able to "resurrect" Italy, to reestablish the power of the state, to suppress the Bolshevik evil, and to bring back order to the life of the country. Objective results had proved the semidivine character of Mussolini. What "the Man" had been able to accomplish turned him into an almighty figure.

Celestial comparisons and heavenly invocations of the kind this credo suggested often punctuated praises of the Duce, who was variously referred to as "social archangel" and "envoy of God."[148] Religious figures especially put Mussolini in close proximity to the sacred high spheres. On November 2, 1926, after an attempt on Mussolini's life, *Osservatore Romano*, the official newspaper of the Vatican, claimed that God's intervention had saved Mussolini. "The people have recognized in it Heaven's hand," read the article. According to the Vatican, Mussolini was being protected by superior forces who, in their clairvoyance, recognized that the Duce's life was necessary to the well-being of the nation. Heavenly powers were aware that Mussolini had saved Italy from chaos (bolshevism) and had endowed the country with a peaceful and ordered existence. They also expected the Duce to ensure Italy's bright future and to continue his work of "resurrection." A priest pushed his admiration and awe for Mussolini to the point of drawing a comparison between the Duce and St. Francis. In a book published in 1926, father Paolo Ardali provided a saintly image of Mussolini, one of the several hagiographic profiles of the Duce published during the regime. For the father, Mussolini, like St. Francis, had suffered and sacrificed himself for others. Like St. Francis, he was guided by the "high vision of a superior end," and "all his good qualities harmonized in an intimate, superior, calm, serene and luminous atmosphere."[149]

On February 13, 1929, Pope Pius XI, in the aftermath of the Lateran Pacts, which solved the historical question of the relationship between the Vatican and Italy, called Mussolini "the man of Providence": "Maybe we needed a man like the one Providence had us meet."[150] Mussolini had been able to realize finally the moral unity of Italians, which had been at stake since the annexation of Rome to Italy and the retreat of the Pope to the Vatican in 1870. At that time Pope Pius IX did not acknowledge the existence of the post-Risorgimento Italian kingdom and forbade Catholics from participating in Italian political life. With the Lateran Pacts, promoted by Mussolini, the dialogue was reestablished between church and state, and the Catholic religion came to play a more legitimate role in the country.[151] The Pacts stated that Roman Apostolic Catholicism was the one and only state religion, and Catholic doctrine became part of the obligatory teaching in schools. Pope Pius XI could not but praise these events, yet it was Mussolini who capitalized most on them.[152] The phrase "man of Providence" became one of the most popular characterizations of Mussolini.[153] The deification of Mussolini continued to evolve to the point that, in father Giovanni Semeria's article in *Corriere d'Italia* of February 14, 1929, all the pronouns referring to Mussolini were capitalized, as in "Him" (Lui) and "His" (Suo).[154]

The divinelike interpretations of Mussolini depicted him as the chosen one, an "elected" person who enjoyed the direct assistance of God and gained force and power from his close relation to Him. Most often, however, the regime's characterizations blurred the difference between the Duce and God, and Mussolini himself appeared as an omnipotent being with supernatural powers. Take the example of Mussolini's working abilities. On March 10, 1929, at the quinquennial assembly of the regime, Mussolini presented a summary of his government's accomplishments during the previous seven years. He covered, in his words, "sea, mountains, rivers, cities, country, people."[155] He showed that the regime had transformed Italy through various policies and legislative interventions, from school reform to corporativism, from land reclamation to demography. At the end of a quite long list, Mussolini stated:

> Now, do not think that I want to commit a sin of immodesty if I say that all this work, of which I gave you a stringent and very short summary, has been activated by my spirit. The work of legislation, of beginning, controlling and creating new institutions has only been one part of my labor. There is another not well known part whose entity is given to you by these interesting figures. I presided over 60,000 hearings; I took interest in one million and 887,112 petitions of citizens, which directly reached my secretariat. Every time that individual citizens, even from the most remote villages, turned to me, they received an answer.[156]

Following these numbers, Mussolini granted between November 1922 and March 1929 an average of 26 hearings and took care of 813 petitions per day.[157] The Duce explained that "[i]n order to sustain this effort I put my engine at a regimen, I rationalized my daily work, I reduced any dispersion of time and energy to a minimum."[158] Mussolini gave a rational account of his capabilities and posited them as normal. As he said in a January 12, 1927, interview to the *London Daily Express,* it was natural for him to dedicate long hours to assiduous work.[159] In a June 8, 1923, speech to the Chamber, Mussolini told the deputies that because his ambition was "to make the Italian people strong, prosperous, great and free," he did not mind working fourteen or sixteen hours a day.[160] Still, Mussolini's presumed efficiency looked superhuman. And whether he actually held 60,000 hearings or looked at 1,887,112 petitions in seven years, Mussolini's attitude toward work facilitated popular interpretations of his abilities as quasi-divine. Already in the first months of his government, *Il Popolo d'Italia* reported praises for Mussolini from the English press describing him as a "human dynamo." In these eulogies, Mussolini's "only sorrow and almost grudge towards life is that the day is too short. 24 hours are too few, they should be 34. At the moment the Italian Prime Minister works from 6 a.m. to midnight."[161] And Mussolini, the article continued, never appeared tired.[162]

According to De Felice, Mussolini attempted to intervene personally in every single affair concerning the regime, from the most minimal to the most important. The Duce was fixated on total control. "To be apprised of everything and to control his sources of information, their 'sensibility' and efficiency was a constant preoccupation for Mussolini"[163]—a preoccupation that often reached levels of absurdity. Mussolini continuously intervened in banal questions that attracted his attention. On September 11, 1930, he wrote to the prefect of Milan: "Tell Prof. Franco Coletti to make a correction in his next article and state that the Italian population as of May 31 was 41,710,000 as it results from the Monthly Statistical Bulletin of the month of August, and not 41,340,000 as he says in yesterday's article. This is necessary in order to avoid misunderstandings and inaccuracies."[164] Mussolini's activity "was enormous and, from the quantitative point of view, such that it justified, for once, the exaltation of the fascist propaganda," says De Felice.[165] Mussolini, in sum, effectively cultivated his own political fantasy of total control. The image of omnipotence that the regime propagandized reflected Mussolini's own desire to supervise all decisions and take care of every single question facing the regime.[166] The myth of *homo autotelus,* creator ex nihilo of his own work of art, resurfaces here as the myth of an overpowered superman.

As the mystique of the Duce's omnipotence evolved, many wondered: does he sleep?[167] A light was always left on in Mussolini's office to show that the regime never rested, spurring the myth. An elementary school pupil, evidently impressed by the propagandized image of Mussolini's super powers, wrote: "He always works and never, or almost never, sleeps. He closes his eyes every ten minutes, then he wakes up, washes himself, and goes immediately back to work, fresh like a rose."[168] In children's accounts, Mussolini's actions were close to magic, as another child from Ferrara expressed in his basic Italian: "At the order of Mussolini, as to the touch of a magic wand, they came out in Tuscany warships that he is building."[169]

Mussolini's superhuman abilities also gave birth to the image of the Duce as valiant, fearless, heroic, and able to engage and succeed in several more or less daring activities. From the beginning of his governmental career, Mussolini was portrayed as practicing different kinds of sports, from skiing and fencing to swimming and horse riding. Already in 1923, the riding skills of Mussolini entered the world of fame. "The daily horse riding," "the daily walk," and, later, "the daily car ride" of Mussolini were analyzed in newspapers and magazines to highlight Mussolini's qualities. Mussolini, who had just learned how to ride, rode "under heavy rein," "mastered gallop," and one day had to change horses four times to complete his ride.[170] In a kinder version, Mussolini was seen riding with a rose in his lips.[171] Pictures of Mussolini on a horse, a quasi-Romantic figure, filled the periodical press and became a staple of the postcard market. In the 1930s, photographs marking important political events featured an equestrian, but less gentle, Mussolini. *Illustrazione Italiana*'s cover page of November 6, 1932, portrayed Mussolini on a horse and in military uniform inaugurating *Via dell'Impero* (Avenue of the Empire). In the same fashion Mussolini reappeared on the May 27, 1934, cover page of *Illustrazione Italiana* performing a Roman salute in celebration of May 24, anniversary of Italy's intervention in World War I. The Duce on a horse was again featured for the anniversary of the March on Rome on October 28, 1934, as founder of the empire on November 8, 1936, and as a conquistador of Libya on March 28, 1937. Whether depicted romantically in the 1920s or in military scenes in the 1930s, the horse accompanied the fearless Duce's enormous accomplishments.

Mussolini, whether he conquered lands and people or wild animals, was a hero. In the early 1920s photographs portrayed him as completely at ease visiting cages of lions (Figure 2).[172] In 1923 a circus owner offered Mussolini a lion cub as a gift. The Duce kept the animal for some time with him in his house at Palazzo Tittoni, then donated her to the zoo, where he continued to visit and be photographed with her. Images of Mussolini with the

Figure 2.　Mussolini as lion tamer.

little lioness, "Italia," riding an automobile initiated the vogue of Mussolini as tamer. A postcard sponsored by the Pirelli wheel factory reflected this image, showing Mussolini in a coat and bowler hat, a lion on his lap, being driven in a car. "The daily car ride of His Excellency Mussolini," the caption read, yet another sign of the publicity surrounding the Duce.

Mussolini also came across as the courageous experimenter with new sports and the dominator of modern mechanical media. The image of the Duce wearing large road goggles and driving motorbikes and automobiles became part of the iconography of his myth, especially in the first ten years of his government, and again millions of such photographs were distributed in the postcard market.[173] But most of all, the Duce's presumed skill as an aviator made him a gallant hero. These were times when Charles Lindbergh's transoceanic flight struck people's imagination.[174] Airplanes were symbols of a new era, and aviators, like actors, were saluted as stars. In fact, most major actors sooner or later played the role of a pilot, most often a war pilot, in a film.[175] Fascism, as futurism had done earlier, appropriated the airplane as its own symbol and transformed it into a cult.[176] Airplanes embodied qualities such as dynamism, energy, and courage—attributes that fascism worshipped and claimed as its own. Mussolini as aviator automatically represented and promoted those virtues.[177] He had begun to take flying lessons from the pilot Cesare Redaelli in the summer of 1920. In the words of his teacher, he had been an exceptional, astonishing student with an attention span superior to any other trainee's.[178] On January 3, 1926, Mussolini officially established himself as head of aviation by claiming the leadership of the ministry. (On that occasion, Mussolini, already prime minister, also took over the Ministries of Foreign Affairs, War, and Navy.) The news continuously reported Mussolini's hours of flight on his personal airplane.[179] Official photographs of Mussolini the aviator, semiotically linked to war themes, appeared in the second half of the 1930s, concomitant with the preparation and execution of the Ethiopian conquest and the growing emphasis on military activities.[180] The trend toward militarization was also reflected in the depiction of Mussolini in uniform most of the time.[181]

Mussolini's superhuman attributes emerged in his activity as head of the fascist government. They also surfaced in numerous other situations that revealed the exceptionality of Mussolini, an individual above all others. During his 1932 interview with Ludwig, for instance, Mussolini was asked about his wounds as a soldier in World War I. Mussolini first emphasized the gravity of his condition. Then, to Ludwig's question, "Is it true . . . that you did not let them give you anesthetics during surgery?"—Mussolini answered with nonchalance: "I wanted to see how doctors were scoring."[182] Mussolini's strength supposedly allowed him to bear undergoing a delicate operation without the support of pain relievers.[183] This image of Mussolini followed the model of Sarfatti's biographical panegyric of the Duce. With reference to the same episode of World War I, Sarfatti reported: "When he was taken to the operating theater and felt the knife enter his flesh, he met the spasm of pain by closing his lips with a smothered curse, but immediately relaxed and smiled quietly at those around. . . . He refused to have chloroform, saying that the mind should be able to rise above pain."[184] The mystique of Mussolini as an exceptionally gifted person finds its most telling characterization in the attribution of miraculous powers to the Duce, as during Mussolini's visit to Sicily in June 1923. At the time the volcano Etna was erupting. The moment Mussolini arrived, however, the lava stopped its flow, and, according to journalists' reports, a whole village was saved from destruction. In this instance, Mussolini allegedly performed a superhuman act even without a magic wand. As a newspaper wrote in the aftermath of the episode: "The river of flowing lava had to stop in the face of the fire, much more ardent, of the Duce's eyes."[185] A few years later, in August 1932, *Il Popolo d'Italia* printed an incredible account that suggested the miraculous:

> Six months ago one Aurelia Giaccani married to the porter Riccardo Maiolini, gave birth to a girl. . . . On the left side of the newborn the mark of a *fascio littorio* was visible. . . . the explanation of this phenomenon seems to originate from the impression that the mother of the girl received one night in Piazza Roma facing a shining *fascio littorio*. It seems that Giaccani, who was pregnant at the time, simply expressed the desire to give birth to a child with a *fascio littorio*. . . . A photo of the girl was sent to the Duce.[186]

The woman's admiration for the *fascio littorio* constituted the transposition of her admiration for Mussolini and his fascist creation, as symbolized by the *fascio*. Hence, the miracle was a direct work of Mussolini, a reward for the woman's faith in him.

In 1937 newspapers reported the news that rains had finally begun to ease the long drought in Tripolitania and Libya. Incidentally, the rain had come at the time of Mussolini's visit to the area in March 1937. The journalists immediately related the timely weather relief to Mussolini: "The largely diffused hope among the Arab and Berber population that the Duce with his visit to the colony would propitiate beneficial rain has not been deceived. From the 29th to the 31st of March abundant rain fell all over Northern Tripolitania. On April 2, it also rained abundantly in Cyrenaica."[187] Mussolini had again performed a miracle. His power overcame human limits.

This image of omnipotence was advertised in one of the most popular fascist slogans: "The Duce is always right." The slogan was created by a young fascist, Leo Longanesi, in a book published in 1926 as *The Vademecum of the Perfect Fascist.* The regime appropriated the slogan and made it into its own narrative device to present Mussolini as the oracle, the indubitable carrier of the official truth. In his memoirs to De Begnac, Mussolini thus patronized the slogan and erased its origins: "I was the one who gave the order to say that I was never wrong. My office translated this concept into the formula: 'The Duce is always right.'"[188]

Youth and Immortality

Mussolini's supernatural qualities and his proximity to the sacred favored the diffusion of the myth of Mussolini as immortal. The idealization of Mussolini as the embodiment of youth, both in a spiritual and biological sense, helped create this image of immortality. In fascism's symbolic world, youth constituted a metaphor of action. It epitomized fascism's novelty as a political movement in contrast to the stasis of the liberal government.[189] In 1921, in an article written for *Il Popolo d'Italia* of March 23, second anniversary of the *fasci* foundation, Mussolini defined his movement as a "superb creature, full of all the impetuousness and ardor of a youth overflowing with life."[190] In his first speech to the Senate as head of government, on November 16, 1922, Mussolini reiterated this definition, telling the senators that he interpreted and represented Italian youth.[191] A few years later, on May 24, 1926, he affirmed to the people of Genova that fascism had succeeded in making the nation young. "Yesterday's Italy is not recognizable in today's Italy. The whole nation is twenty years old and as such it has the courage, the spirit, the intrepidity."[192] *Giovinezza* (*Youth*), the hymn that the Arditi chanted in World War I and that later reappeared in Fiume during D'Annunzio's regency, became the official song of the fascist movement. During the regime, *Giovinezza*, with music by maestro Giuseppe Blanc, was sung along with the traditional hymn of the kingdom, the *Marcia Reale.*[193] Indeed, it became the new national anthem, with Mussolini as the central hero (the refrain acclaimed Mussolini with the fascist hurrah *"Eia, Eia, Alalà!"*). Youth spiritually infused fascism and gave Mussolini, as representative of youth, the right to lead Italy. When he took office, Mussolini became the youngest prime minister in Italian history and probably the youngest in Europe. His physical appearance, sporting activities, dynamism, and efficiency proved that he was full of energy and life. Mussolini insisted that this image of the young Duce persist during the regime. Thus, the government's communications to the press, via Ufficio Stampa (the government press office), forbade journalists from publicizing Mussolini's birthdays.[194] He did not want to give the impression of aging; the fact that he had become a grandfather was never mentioned.[195] Nor could Mussolini's illnesses be made known. Whenever the rumor circulated that Mussolini was sick, the Duce appeared at the balcony of Palazzo Venezia and openly defied those "lies." Berneri tells the story that on the occasion of one of these rumors, Mussolini convoked journalists at his house in Villa Torlonia and performed equestrian exercises for them. Then he defiantly said: "Now go and write that I am sick."[196] In the same vein, a unique photograph of the Duce as skier was circulated in early 1937 and appeared in *Illustrazione Italiana* on January 24. The picture portrayed Mussolini bare-chested on the snowy slopes of Terminillo, near Rome (Figure 3). Coming this late in Mussolini's career, the picture reaffirmed Mussolini's virility and young spirit at a time when he seemed preoccupied with aging and its effects on his image. Curiously, he chose this sport for his revitalized public persona, when according to some he was unable to ski.[197] Mussolini wanted to appear above human limits.

In 1921 Mussolini survived an airplane disaster. According to the reports of his teacher, Cesare Redaelli, there had been an attempt on his life.[198] At that time some Milanese fascists wrote a song for Mussolini highlighting his power to dominate events: "The airplane and the bomb wanted to oust you. But you know which fate belongs to your male virtue. You answered to Lady Death: come back another time."[199] Mussolini could defy death because of his special attributes. Even his wounding in World War I came to be narrated as a mythical event, not only because it showed Mussolini's incredible courage but also, and more crucially, because it exemplified his power over mortality. Sarfatti wrote in her biography of Mussolini that his life had been seriously endangered during the war. He had forty-two wounds "for more than eighty centimeters in all."[200] His body was burnt, and a multitude of splinters pierced his flesh like the arrows of Saint Sebastian.[201] Mussolini was compared to a saintly figure but fared better than Sebastian. He was able to remain alive and overcome bodily limits.

The legend of Mussolini's ability to escape death became the main narrative device in the fascist regime's stories of the attempts on Mussolini's life. Four failed attempts between the end of 1925 and the end of 1926 contributed to the myth of Mussolini's special powers, in particular his "immortal" qualities, strengthening his own government and legitimating strict antiopposition laws.[202] The first attempt on Mussolini's life was supposed to occur on November 4, 1925. The would-be assassin, Tito Zaniboni,

Figure 3. Mussolini as skier at Terminillo, near Rome (note the absence of skis on his feet).

a former socialist deputy, had rented a hotel room facing the balcony of Palazzo Chigi, from which Mussolini was going to give a speech for the anniversary of victory in World War I. Equipped with a rifle, Zaniboni planned to wait for Mussolini's appearance at the balcony and then to shoot him. Before he could put his plan at work, however, the police arrived and arrested him. The police had known about the criminal plan since its conception. A spy, the journalist Carlo Quaglia, pretended to help Zaniboni but was actually playing a double role, informing the police all along.[203] Instead of immediately arresting Zaniboni, the police decided to wait until the last moment so as to make the plot appear really dangerous, something that might have really happened. This event—the way it was constructed—clearly had the propagandistic goal of emphasizing Mussolini's value. Calls for the institution of the death penalty against would-be assassins multiplied in the fascist press.[204] The day after the attempt, Mussolini exploited the situation by giving a speech to the people of Rome. "You feel that if I was hit at this balcony not a tyrant, but the servant of the Italian people would have been hit," he dramatically declared.[205] The attempt gave the Duce the occasion to emphasize his role. Most important, as the first among other failed threats to Mussolini's life, it helped to build the framework for the deification of Mussolini.[206]

On April 7, 1926, an older Irish woman, Violet Gibson, shot Mussolini while he was leaving Palazzo dei Conservatori. Gibson, standing in the front row among a crowd of people saluting the Duce, had aimed at Mussolini's head but only grazed his nose. Mussolini, this time really miraculously, had again escaped death, and the near miss, following the first, constructed one, contributed symbolically to the legend of his survival.[207] Pictures of the Duce wearing a bandage on his nose testified to the reality of the attempted assassination. At the same time, they showed the slightness of the injury inflicted. Mussolini was again dominating earthly matters. That same day Mussolini told the Assembly of the Direttorio that his motto was Nietzsche's dictum: "to live dangerously."[208] And to the crowd in Rome he said: "I want to let you hear my voice for a few minutes, so as to convince you that its timbre has not changed at all. And I can also assure you that my heart has not accelerated its beats."[209] Danger and courage constituted the essence of Mussolini, and they could not be defeated by crazy gestures. On April 26, referring to the failed attempt on his life, Mussolini told the crowd in Milan: "Bullets pass and Mussolini stays."[210]

Only five months after Gibson's attempt, Mussolini was again the target of a murder plot. While he was driving in a car along the road from his house to Palazzo Chigi, an anarchist emigrant from France, Gino Lucetti, threw a bomb at the automobile. It was September 11, 1926.[211] The device briefly hit the car, then exploded on the ground, wounding eight people. Mussolini remained unhurt. Like the previous attempts, this one failed, but it became the occasion for definitive sanctifying of Mussolini's sacredness. On the one hand, Mussolini proved yet again able to overcome "evil forces" and to master contingencies. On the other hand, and somewhat contradictorily, the regime used the attempts to present a terrible scenario of what could happen in the case of Mussolini's death. The disappearance of such a great figure, a sort of demigod, would topple the nation into trouble and chaos. The death of Mussolini would bring about the end of Italy's well-being. In his speech to the crowd a few hours after the Lucetti's attempt, Mussolini hinted at both these implications. Thus, he invoked the death penalty but maintained the image of a daring, fearless leader, a superhero. "[W]e need to apply other measures. And this I say not for me, because I really like to live in danger. But the Nation, the Italian Nation strenuously working . . . cannot, must not be periodically troubled by a group of criminals. . . . we intend to stop the series of attempts by applying capital punishment. In this way it will become less and less easy to almost threaten the regime's existence and the tranquillity of the Italian people."[212] In this speech Mussolini again presented himself as a valiant man, a heroic character who lived dangerously. But he also stated that if he died the regime would be over and the Italian people would once again experience times of disorder. The regime depended on him. This was evidently what the assassins thought, too.

During Mussolini's speech, when he said he did not want to apply the hard measures for himself, voices from the crowd shouted: "For you! You are the Nation."[213] In that instance Mussolini had succeeded in affirming his large power. As the crowd suggested, he embodied the nation; he had created fascist Italy.[214] After a fourth presumed attempt on Mussolini's life occurred on October 31, 1926, the law of November 25, 1926, finally introduced the death penalty for crimes against the head of government, the king, and some members of the royal family.[215] The decree legally sanctioned the importance of Mussolini's life, even though Mussolini still proclaimed to the Senate that attempts against him were not the reason for the law. The crimes, he stated on November 20,

> leave me perfectly indifferent. If those who make of me the object of their ballistic attention believe to exercise on me even a vague and distant intimidation they delude themselves. I absolutely exclude this, it is totally ridiculous. Whatever happens, I stay at my post, because this is my precise duty.[216]

Mussolini detached himself from earthly matters and seemed to offer an almost spiritual image of himself. He was driven by a superior goal and stood above petty matters.[217] But his attitude reveals that for Mussolini the death penalty, more than punishing those who actually committed the crimes and more than discouraging people from threatening his life, symbolized Mussolini's own sacredness and reaffirmed it.[218] The death penalty testified to

Mussolini's uniqueness, thus adding symbolic value to his authority in the regime. The whole discourse on the Duce's immortality actually constituted a fundamental element in the regime's narration of Mussolini's quasi-absolute power. As a semantically charged master fiction, the myth of Mussolini's immortality accompanied the institutional transformations of the regime—transformations that, via laws and reforms, had contributed to centralizing power in Mussolini's hands and to undermining the creation of a viable fascist political class. Within this context, the image of Mussolini as immortal also conveyed the message that the Duce did not need a successor. The Duce's power was eternal.

Ernst Kantorowicz, in his study of the legal roots of the absolutist state, has examined the immortal character of power in connection to the question of the king's death.[219] According to Kantorowicz, the absolute monarchy was granted its sacred role thanks to the legal distinction the Tudor judges made between the king's two bodies. That distinction, deriving from the ecclesiastical concept of *corpus mysticum,* posited that the king had a natural body similar to that of any other human and naturally subject to death. But the king also had another body, the body politic, of which he provided the head and his subjects constituted the members. The body politic, unlike the body natural, was not exposed to death, "for as to this Body the King never dies."[220] The authority of the king, in fact, lived beyond the person who embodied it. The principle *le roi est mort, vive le roi* affirmed the sacredness of royal authority beyond its representatives.

By contrast, the sacred character of Mussolini's power was indeed connected to his body natural—a body represented as eternally young. Immortality symbolized Mussolini's uniqueness; it was impossible that another person, another body natural, could substitute for him. There could be no successor to replace the Duce in fascism's leadership, because Mussolini was the essence of fascism, its sine qua non. Hence, the sacredness of Mussolini's power doubled in comparison to that of the king of the absolutist state. The king's divinity could never equal God's, because the king's body natural was mortal. In the case of Mussolini, both his bodies were immortal, so he more closely approached divine status than the king.[221]

He ultimately was more sacred than fascism itself. In 1938 the Ministry of Popular Culture thus summarized the image of the Duce circulating in the regime: "Not only the so called educated and cultured people, but also the man in the street have noticed that the Duce's scorn for danger and his audacity are known all over the world, not only in Italy. Twenty years of assiduous, continuous daily practice of the most dangerous sports . . . have created around the Duce the conviction that nothing, literally nothing, is forbidden to him."[222] Mussolini believed himself to be special. Writing about his flight from Ostia to Salerno on July 6, 1935, when lightning struck the plane, he made the following observation: "It must be admitted that not every common mortal gets struck by lightning at ten thousand feet above sea level and escapes unharmed."[223]

Omnipresence

Besides omnipotence and immortality, Mussolini's divine character was conveyed by his omnipresence, his continuous visibility. Through photographs, graffiti, radio, and cinema, Mussolini appeared everywhere and, like God, permeated places and objects of everyday life. Henri Béraud's book *Ce que J'ai vu à Rome* captures the atmosphere that characterized Italy, in particular Rome, in the late 1920s. When he arrived in Rome in 1929, Béraud, a French journalist, noticed an increasing proliferation of the Duce's images, which were filling with their constant presence the daily existence of Italians. "The profusion of the images is truly incredible. The image of the Duce is part of the existence; it directs all circumstances of Italian life."[224] "You enter a hat place, a jewelry, a bakery, a drugstore . . . the image of the dictator, in a funereal shirt, is there and observes you with his arm raised. He dominates the counter, presides over traffic, witnesses the civic activities of the merchant. It is the same at the station, on the bus, or at the dentist's." And more: "Open a newspaper, no matter which: here you will find a commented and celebrated reproduction of a speech of the 'very genial' Duce. . . . A magazine: it shows us the great man framed with flowers and autographs. Wherever you look, wherever you walk, you will find Mussolini, still Mussolini, always Mussolini."[225] Mussolini, Béraud realized, was "everywhere, with his name as well as his effigy, in gestures as well as in words—and more than Kemal in Turkey and even more than Lenin in Moscow."[226]

Mussolini's omnipresence colonized people's lives in different forms and through different means. Millions of postcards and photographs of the Duce, for example, became part of home decor, as in the house of a Sicilian widow who "preserved" his image as a treasure.[227] Every year the fascist party printed a calendar iconographically dominated by Mussolini and encouraged every good citizen to buy it. The calendar was publicized as being both ornamental and symbolic of true "Italianness," and the party made serious efforts to sell and distribute it. In 1934 Giovanni Marinelli, the PNF's administrative secretary, sent letters inviting people to buy the calendar. He affirmed that its purchase would show "enthusiasm" and "gratitude" to the Duce, a sign of the pride with which Italians acclaimed the growing pres-

Figure 4.   Children in fascist uniforms receiving Epiphany gift packages.

tige of fascism.[228] In schools, as well as in other public establishments, every room was adorned with a picture of Mussolini.[229] The unveiling of Mussolini's portrait was an important ceremony. According to the instructions: "Students will all convene in the exercise room and the directors next to the school's flag will present the picture of the Duce and will speak about the great work that he has done for our fatherland." Also, the "national copybook" featured Mussolini on the cover, and schools' walls were imprinted with the phrase: "Mussolini to the children of Italy."[230] Mussolini's photograph was distributed to children who received a gift package for the Epiphany (*Befana fascista*) (Figure 4).[231]

The use of walls and public spaces for political messages was certainly not an invention of the regime.[232] But Mussolini utilized these surfaces in a thorough manner in order to emphasize his own leadership. Béraud

Figure 5.   Monumental living M in honor of Mussolini's visit at Verrès (Valle d'Aosta), May 1939.

observed that old buildings' facades were covered with "placards, posters, tracts, proclamations, 'graffiti.' No place is missed. The walls seem to scream."[233] The walls featured Mussolini's image and sentences from his speeches, famous slogans written with indelible black varnish that can still be found in Italy today.[234] The Duce's words substituted for his image when the icon of Mussolini was not present.[235] In the same way, the signature of Mussolini often replaced his iconographic representation and conveyed his essence, as in the collected works of Mussolini's speeches and writings.[236] The capital letter "M" (Mussolini's initial) or the word *dux* (the Latin version of "duce") also appeared very frequently on monuments and buildings, in gymnastics choreographies during celebratory games, and in groves and gardens (Figures 5 and 6).[237] The "M" of Mussolini also featured on the badges and uniforms of fascist organizations, including the buckle of suspenders for the young Figli della Lupa (Sons of the She-Wolf).[238] In an early example of the celebrity system and consumer culture, one could even find soap bars in the shape of Mussolini,[239] hails of *Duce, Duce* on the scarves of

Figure 6.   Human choreography during a speech of Mussolini in Venice, late 1930s.

massaie rurali (rural homemakers), and swimsuits with the effigy of the Duce (Figure 7). Moreover, new fashion waves proposed Mussolini as a model for the Italian male, and Béraud observed the presence of many Mussolini imitators: "One can see many of them. Because, needless to say, glory has largely diffused the Mussolinian type, and every fascist endowed with an open forehead, a strong jaw, dark eyes, willingly tries on a terrible air and charming looks."[240] Not surprisingly, Béraud concluded by comparing Mussolini to God. He had the impression that Mussolini's eye, like God's, followed people everywhere.

In effect, Mussolini's ability to appear in several different places and under various, multiple forms closely mirrored the divine quality of ubiquity. Another observer, Ludovic Naudeau, thus described his impressions of the Duce in 1927:

> Painted on the wall, at man's height, Mussolini's head fixed me with severe eyes. My God! What did I do wrong? In all Italian cities some zealous patriots have infinitely multiplied, thanks to a stencil, and on all the available surfaces, a portrait of the dictator that resembles Napoleon. It is impossible to find a hidden place, a discreet corner where the severe face of the dictator is not observing you. While you listen to one of your friends' intimate talk, the black head observes you all the time. Be careful! While you exchange anguished words, the face on the wall scrutinizes your thoughts! Silence! Let's speak softer! [Figure 8].[241]

Through his presence Mussolini watched over people: like God, he could see everything.[242] This image of Mussolini as an observant, transcendent being actually recurred in the iconographic narrative of the regime. Employing the technique of photomontage, the regime's official photos presented compositional superimpositions in which the image of Mussolini, hanging over figures, emerged in the background as if blended with the sky. The graphic device of blending in Mussolini's face with the background occurred in particular during the early years of fascism, but it underwent a revival at the time of the Ethiopian conquest in the second half of the 1930s.[243] The celestial location of Mussolini conferred an extrahuman character on him. The eye of Mussolini resembled God's eye.

Mussolini's overwhelming presence and the constancy of his visibility also took place through noniconographic means, including audio-visual combinations. Newspapers regularly reported his speeches and writings and endlessly cited him.[244] Mussolini's speeches for the empire were collected in a volume set of fifteen phonograph records in 1938.[245] Quotes from the Duce's speeches also appeared in a series of sixteen stamps printed to celebrate the

Figure 7. Woman in a swimsuit featuring Mussolini.

Figure 8.   Walls with the stenciled head of Mussolini ("Origins," by Piero Maria Bardi, 1933).

proclamation of the empire and to illustrate different events of Italian history.[246] The radio, starting in 1925, broadcast live the Duce's main speeches.[247] Through this new mass medium, Mussolini enhanced his ability to reach people. He obtained the same result with another mass medium: cinema. In 1926 a royal decree established that all feature films in every single theater had to be preceded by the Luce Institute's newsreels and documentaries portraying the Duce's activities.[248]

Mussolini's speeches constituted an example of spectacular communication through multiple means. Mussolini, in contrast to his predecessors, traveled all over Italy to deliver speeches, and he often returned to the same city more than once.[249] In the first year of his appointment, from November 1922 to October 1923, Mussolini visited almost three-fourths of Italy's regions. Neither Giolitti nor Bonomi ever toured the country or harangued the people to communicate their messages. They belonged to a traditional political class that fought its battles within parliament and through electoral maneuvers. In fact, for most Italians the only contact with the government occurred via tax agents or local police. They had never seen a head of government until Mussolini paid a visit. Yet the novel character of Mussolini's speech-making activity was not just a quantitative question. Beginning with his political engagement in the socialist ranks, Mussolini commanded the attention of intellectual elites and of his socialist comrades thanks to his new style.[250] The name of "new man," or "Man," came to him also in connection with his new approach to political communication.[251] Prezzolini remembered the first time he heard Mussolini: "Nobody interrupted him. Nobody breathed. Some kind of 'heavy silence' fell over the audience which was fascinated with 'the new kind' of dry, tight, decisive, pricking eloquence."[252] Prezzolini compared Mussolini's style to that of other politicians and found major differences between them. Whereas traditional politicians used solemn tones and "ornamental eloquence," Mussolini spoke directly, in a functional way. Moreover, Mussolini did not use high language: his words were plebeian, his sentences short and essential, his syntax simple.[253] Mussolini, unlike traditional politicians, rejected rhetorical statements. He aimed at "schematic" eloquence.[254] Rhythm and tone were more important than learned expressions.[255]

Thanks to this oratorical technique, Mussolini's speeches could reach many people. Besides, Mussolini used the piazza to deliver his messages. His audience was, therefore, potentially large and diverse; high attendance was ensured via the *cartolina-precetto*, a postcard ordering people to show up at events. In his addresses to the public, Mussolini engaged in a dialogue with the crowd, the technique that D'Annunzio adopted during his prowar rallies and his regency in Fiume.[256] He wanted his speeches to be neatly distinguished from the model of democratic debates, which he had always opposed. Thus, on September 20, 1922, he told his audience in Udine: "Oh, if it would be possible to strangle, as a poet advised, the wordy, prolix, inconclusive, democratic eloquence that has spoiled us for such a long time. I am sure, or at least I have this hope, that you do not expect from me a speech that is not truly fascist, i.e. skeletal, harsh, frank and hard."[257] Mussolini invented "fascist speeches" whose foundation was action.[258] Throughout his rule, he reiterated his hate for long, prolix speeches.[259] At some point he even thought that fascism should abolish speeches.[260] Yet Mussolini continued to give them. As he told the people of Mantova on October 25, 1925: "Somebody might say that I again give a speech. I answer that mine are not speeches in the traditional sense of the word. They are elocutions, a touch between my soul and yours, my heart and your hearts."[261]

Emotional appeals and direct communication helped Mussolini to enlarge his own audience. But his oratorical style also attracted people's attention. First of all, Mussolini had a phonetic repertoire that enriched his verbal presentation. He talked with tight teeth; words were assembled in groups and distanced by pauses; each unit of words was pronounced with a measured rhythmical style. His face was a spectacle in itself, appropriately coordinated with Mussolini's oratorical tone and body movements. His head leaned halfway back, his eyes almost out of their sockets, his chin and mouth forward, Mussolini underlined with his exaggerated facial expressions the word units he uttered.[262] At the same time, by moving his head down and striking his classical posture of hands at the waist, waving his right hand with a rotary movement, Mussolini communicated hardness and firmness.[263] In sum, the speech gave Mussolini the opportunity to increase his visibility.[264] Mussolini's mimicry, his bodily postures and gestures, constituted impressive imagery that circulated through pictures, films, and other means. The speech became one of the main elements through which the spectacle of Mussolini's power unfolded. With sentences from his declarations reproduced in graffiti, his words aired through the radio, his oratorical moments portrayed in newsreels that reached to the countryside, Mussolini's visibility was undoubtedly very large.[265]

The ubiquity of Mussolini's image, words, and actions, along with the heroicization of his person and the myth of his power, contributed to the deification of the Duce. These elements constituted the main narrative device of the fascist regime's discourse about its leader. Within this discourse, Mussolini occupied all the visible realms of politics; he monopolized public space. Fascism presented the people with a model of centralized power that rotated around the mythical and spectacular authority of one person. The image of Mussolini as omnipotent, valiant, and heroic invested the Duce with a magical, mystical aura that placed him above common people—or, better, above mortals. In addition, Mussolini's constant presence in people's everyday life, his supervising gaze that looked over pupils in schools, workers in factories, families at home, even passersby in the street, exercised a continuous authority over Italians (Figure 9; also see Figure 17, Chapter 3).

Figure 9.   "Passersby," by Vincenzo Balocchi, 1942.

Like God, Mussolini followed ordinary citizens in the fulfillment of their tasks and controlled them.[266] At the symbolic level Mussolini proposed himself as the supreme leader, the invincible "Man." How effective this program was, we hardly know. But through the myth of the Duce, the regime and Mussolini created their own political fantasy about one man's power.[267]

Mussolini's understanding of life and his elitist conception of politics fore-saw the coming of a Nietzschean superman who would dominate over the common people; his vision of the politician as artist-creator placed the su-perman in a near-divine condition. From these beliefs, Mussolini did not have to journey far to interpret himself as a God-like figure. His efforts to de-politicize and subordinate the party, his personalistic approach to politics, and his centralization of authority testify to the Duce's desire of being the one and only leader of fascist Italy. This desire to achieve an absolute posi-tion within the regime gave way to Mussolini's fantasy of God-like power. The myth of *homo autotelus* found in Mussolini its perfect embodiment.

3 The Politics of Symbols
From Content to Form

The myth of Mussolini dominated the fascist regime's symbolic world and shaped its cosmogony. The Duce was the savior of the Italian nation. He led the party, the government, and the people, and through his charismatic power he would create a beautiful fascist society. Under Mussolini's leadership, the regime was going to produce a homogenized and unified polity that would then be ready for combat. A new order would be established in which fascist Italians, in the name of the nation and its *duce*, followed their duty as citizen-soldiers. Mussolini thus invited his subjects to fulfill their role:

> Each of you must consider himself a soldier: a soldier also when you are not wearing the uniform, a soldier also when you work, in the office, in factories, in yards or in the fields: a soldier tied to all the rest of the army, a molecule that feels and beats with the entire organism.[1]

The regime required total control over its governed in order to accomplish fascism's masterpiece: an expansionist Italy. To this end, as Mussolini proclaimed in the concluding speech to the fascist congress on June 22, 1925, fascism aimed at remodeling the Italians' style, their way of living, attitudes, habits, and character:

> Today Fascism is a party, is a militia, is a corporation. This is not enough: it must become a way of life! There must be the Italians of Fascism. . . . Only by creating a way of life, i.e. a way of living, will we be able to mark some pages in history, and not merely in the chronicle. And what is this way of life? Courage, first of all; intrepidity, love of risk, repugnance for peace-loving. . . . we will create, through a work of obstinate and tenacious selection, the new generation, and in the new generation each one will have a defined task. Sometimes I like the idea of laboratory generations: to create, that means, the class of warriors, who is always ready to die; the class of inventors, who pursues the secret of mystery; the class of judges, the class of big captains of industry, of big explorers, of big governors. And it is through this methodical selection that one creates the big categories that,

in their turn, will create the empire. Certainly this dream is superb, but I see that it is gradually becoming a reality.[2]

Fascism dreamed of empire. And the new style that fascism invoked sought to transform the people into warriors. For this purpose, and in order to inspire the Italians to share its expansionist fantasies, the regime resorted to other myths and rituals in addition to those surrounding the God-like figure of Mussolini. In its twenty-year existence, the regime drew from several historical, mythological, religious, and psychological sources to portray symbolically its ideals and values. New fascist traditions, ways of behaving, forms, and gestures were invented to replace old customs and to convey novel meanings. In this search for avenues and modalities of representation, the regime cultivated the terms for its own self-definition. Changes in rites and festivals expressed and at the same time reflected fascism's concepts and beliefs. The spectacle of fascism's newly construed symbolic world illuminated the internal journey of the regime's construction, its *Bildung*.

THE MYTH OF ROME

Since the Middle Ages, governments, intellectual movements, and artists in Europe have frequently invoked the Roman past and appropriated it as a source of political and cultural legitimation. Medieval emperors praised Rome's political power and aimed to emulate it. In the Enlightenment and Romantic periods, by contrast, intellectuals and politicians connected Rome's history to the ideal of a universal "mission." In Italy during the Risorgimento, the idea of a national mission was elaborated by the liberal patriot Giuseppe Mazzini, who pointed to Rome as a civilization that could find new life on Italian soil.[3] In Mazzini's lay vision, Rome served as a leading force in the Italians' struggle for unity; and he foresaw the possibility that Italy might found a united Europe on the premises of Rome's universal values. Following Mazzini, the tendency to regard Rome as the antecedent to some sort of Italian mission in the world prevailed in postunification Italy.[4] The spiritual and humanistic aims that had underpinned Mazzini's vision of a united Europe, however, slowly turned into an ideology of supremacy. Indeed, in 1848 the Catholic Vincenzo Gioberti had already provided an interpretation of Roman Christian glory as the basis on which to claim the "moral and civil supremacy" of Italians.[5]

By the end of the nineteenth century, the image of Rome's political grandeur definitively triumphed in Italy over the belief in Rome's universal cultural mission. An international politics fed by the rhetoric of power and oriented toward imperialistic and colonial enterprises favored this outcome. Roman military glories indicated to Italians the path to follow.[6] The evocation of a shared history conveyed a new sense of the fatherland and reinforced national consciousness. When the call to make Rome capital of the newly created Italian nation became urgent, patriots invoked the Roman tradition as the basis for national renewal.[7] This supposed affinity between the country and ancient Rome ended up constituting a common belief in the Italian polity, so much so that Gramsci in his *Prison Notebooks* lamented: "[T]he rhetorical prejudice (of literary origin) that the Italian nation has always existed, from ancient Rome to the present . . . although 'useful' politically at the time of national struggle as a motif to raise enthusiasm and concentrate forces . . . become[s] an element of weakness. . . . [It does not] allow one to appreciate correctly the effort of those generations who really fought to constitute modern Italy, and lead[s] to a sort of fatalism and passive expectation of a future which would be completely predetermined by the past."[8]

On the spur of this Roman "prejudice," and in view of the new imperial and colonial mentality characterizing Europe, Italy's 1911 militaristic enterprise in Libya was saluted by, among others, nationalists, futurists, and followers of D'Annunzio as the beginning of a bright future for the young nation. After World War I, expansionist sentiments and the aspiration to create a more aggressive country accompanied criticisms of the liberal government, which was variously accused of pacifism and of lacking a heroic attitude. In the name of war, with its sacrifices and spiritual aims, critics of liberalism called for a new political organization to lead Italy and pursue national glory and domination. They favored the exceptional as opposed to everyday normality; struggle as opposed to peace; conquest to comfort; action to parliamentary debate; supremacy to equality.[9] At the time of its founding in 1919, the fascist movement responded to this call for a new political trend with an emphasis on heroism. The movement's elaboration of its own version of the Roman myth served to define fascism as the repository of a universal mission, the carrier of a tradition that exalted Italy's superior values.[10]

On April 3, 1921, a few months before the transformation of the fascist movement into a party, Mussolini delivered a speech in Bologna in which he proclaimed April 21, the anniversary of the founding of Rome, an official fascist holiday.[11] On April 19, 1923, six months after the fascists' seizure of power and well before the implementation of the dictatorship, the Birth of Rome became the first celebration instituted by Mussolini's government.[12] Mussolini intended the holiday to be more than a commemoration or a mere fascist festivity. According to his proposed decree, the Birth of Rome marked the new Labor Day in fascist-dominated Italy and replaced the socialists' major symbolic event, May Day, which was thus suppressed.[13] For Mussolini, as he had suggested on the 1922 anniversary of the Birth of Rome, a logical relation connected the Roman values of "work" and "discipline."[14] Through submission to the leader and soldierly obedience to him, these values would ensure the making of a great Roman Italy.

As Gramsci feared, by claiming Roman origins, fascism naturalized its role within Italian history.[15] Through this symbolic reconnection to Rome, which took place in a cultural climate already sensitive to symbolic solicitations of historically grounded patriotism and nationalism, fascism stressed the need to reach higher ends and to reactualize the grandeur of the past.[16] Indeed, fascism's own appreciation of the future was envisioned in a dialogic relation with the past. For Mussolini, the glorious tradition of Rome represented a model of action, an inspiration for fascism's ideals of renewal. Thus, references to Rome did not imply static admiration or nostalgia. Instead, Rome constituted the foundation on which to build a bright fascist tomorrow. As Mussolini wrote on the occasion of the 1922 Birth of Rome:

> The Rome that we honor . . . is not nostalgic contemplation of the past, but hard preparation for the future.
>   Rome is our departure and reference point: it is our symbol or, if you wish, our Myth. We dream of Roman Italy, i.e. wise and strong, disciplined and imperial.[17]

The Roman tradition constituted a firm and necessary point of reference in fascism's attempt to build Italy's identity as an aggressive and forward-looking country.[18]

Fascism's identification with Rome rested above all on Rome's triumphs and supremacy. Thus, citations of Roman history varied, although they especially exalted Rome's role in establishing Christianity as a universal religion and in founding the Roman Empire. The diversity of Roman thematics that the fascist government utilized in the production of postage stamps testifies to this trend.[19] During the 1920s, views of modern Rome (as in the 1926 series printed for the militia, then repeated in 1928 and 1930) alternated with scenes of Roman legionnaires (1923), portraits of Julius Caesar and Caesar Augustus, and the mythical scene of the she-wolf nursing Romulus and Remus in the 1929 series. The theme of the empire began to surface and found several expressions in stamps printed in the 1930s, as in the series celebrating the second millennium of Virgil's birth (1930), the second millennium of Horatius (1936), and the second millennium of Titus

Livius (1941). Also, the 1932 series commemorating the second decade of the fascist revolution, as well as the one on the proclamation of the empire in 1938, emphasized Rome's imperial and warlike virtues. In 1937 the link between Rome and Christianity was highlighted in a 25-cent stamp for the second millennium of Augustus. The stamp showed the city of Bethlehem with the comet star framed between Roman *labari*, and it was dominated by a cross and the inscription from Virgil's *Eclogue* prophesizing the birth of Christ. The caption read, *"Censum populi regi"* (Census of the people for the king), which referred to the census Augustus ordered at the time.[20] Rome's glorious past, in both its spiritual and material aspects, was unfailingly interpreted by the regime as the sign of Italy's future glory under Mussolini, the herald of fascist Italy's high destiny and imperialistic expansion. A postage stamp issued in 1932 for the anniversary of the March on Rome and captioned "Returning where we already were" (*Ritornando dove già fummo*) showed a worker shoveling amid Roman ruins and against the background of an African landscape. The appeal of the past was an incentive to a successful future.

Within this rhetorical context, fascism developed a selective interpretation of the Roman tradition, excluding what was believed to be decadent and highlighting the great accomplishments of the Roman civilization—i.e., its superior power. In the name of an ideal past, the regime commissioned archeological digs in search of the ruins of "its" Rome.[21] During the excavations, buildings belonging to the Middle Ages were found and immediately destroyed in order to let ancient Rome predominate as the original witness of fascism's glorious destiny.[22] Nothing was supposed to undermine the image of Rome that the regime had construed and that it wanted to convey, since the image of fascism lived in symbiosis with the myth of Rome.

Not surprisingly, the regime more strongly affirmed its linkage with ancient Rome in the wake of the proclamation of the empire in 1936. At this time, the production of historical films focusing on Rome boomed.[23] In September 1937 the regime opened the "Mostra Augustea della Romanita'" as part of the celebrations for the second millennium of Augustus's birth. The exhibit had actually been organized well before the conquest of the empire to link fascism's imperial spirit with that of Augustus's Rome.[24] Mussolini's words—"Italians, you must ensure that the glories of the past are surpassed by the glories of the future"—dominated the entrance to the exhibit, and a special section entitled "Fascismo e Romanita'" concluded the revisitation of Augustus's Rome. In this proclaimed connection between the Augustean era and fascism, the emphasis on Caesarean leadership in turn stressed the importance of the Duce's role in fascist Italy. In the aftermath of its successful expansionist campaign in Ethiopia, the regime even seemed to believe that fascism now overshadowed its legendary Roman past. In 1937, the series of ten stamps produced on Italian history featured a 10-cent stamp with Romulus working the furrow. A sentence by Mussolini captioned the vignette: "The sign of the infallible destiny." The history of Rome was mythologically interpreted as the antecedent of fascism, the harbinger of an inescapable fate. In the regime's self-representation, Rome teleologically announced the coming of fascism and its empire.[25]

With the myth of Rome, Mussolini keenly deployed a symbolic tradition that had a long-lasting and meaningful presence in the Italian polity. The evocation of the Roman mission had prefaced the patriots' struggle for independence and unification during the nineteenth century; the glories of the empire had fed the colonial aspirations of the post-Risorgimento ruling coalitions; Roman history was abundantly taught in school to those middle-class individuals who later became the strongest supporters of the regime;[26] and colossal historical films produced between 1912 and 1915 on imperial Rome circulated a phantasmatic image of an exalted era. In general the myth of Rome reconnected the country to a common past, a shared rootedness. The invention of historical memory spurred collective identity. Within an environment highly imbued with Roman rhetoric, it was easy for fascism to reach out to people by means of the myth of Rome. Furthermore, the recourse to the Roman tradition legitimated fascism's leadership role by asserting a continuity between fascism and Italian history. The regime was thus able to frame the existing interpretations of the myth of Rome within its own hegemonic discourse and to propose its version of the Roman past as the truthful one, the historically grounded account of Italians' immemorial roots. If, as Barthes claims, the function of mythologies is to normalize and naturalize meanings and to contain them within a space that appears permanent, then, via the myth of Rome, fascism presented its own values as inherently right and natural.[27] The myth contributed to establishing the regime as the legitimate representative of the Italian nation.

The long-standing familiarity of Italians with the myth of Rome eased fascism's efforts to historicize its own political role and to affirm itself as the expression of a national tradition. One could speculate in addition that the ambiguities in the regime's reconstruction and representation of ancient Rome also increased the naturalizing effect of the Roman myth. Christian motifs intertwined with militaristic and aggressive themes, especially in the representations of Caesar Augustus, and nationalistic stances alternated with pleas for peace and universalism. In the end, the rhetoric of superiority doubtless underlay all fascist characterizations of Rome and subsumed them under a unified ideological discourse. The ambivalent nature of the regime's references to Rome, however, permitted different interpretations of the myth to coexist, thus enlarging the chances of popular identification with fascism. Ambiguity paved the way for the normalization of fascism's values as represented in the regime's version of the semantically rich Roman myth.

The Ax and the Bundle

The regime drew extensively from the Roman myth as a source for the elaboration of its official symbolic discourse and the building of its public image. The name *fascismo* in itself demonstrated the fascists' linkage to Roman civilization. The term derived from the Latin *fascis*—a bundle of equal rods tied together and to an ax. In ancient Rome *fasces* represented authority and were carried by minor Roman officials, *lictores,* who preceded the high magistrates in the procession.

To be sure, Mussolini had not been the first one to use the Roman term. In 1919, when he founded the original nucleus of fascism as Fasci Italiani di Combattimento, *fascio* constituted a common political expression meaning "group" or "association." In this manner, it was especially used by the left.[28] In the early 1890s *fasci dei lavoratori* (workers' fasces) were formed in Sicily by peasants and workers wanting to protest their miserable social conditions both at home and at work. And in 1914–1915 interventionist groups founded the Fasci di Azione Rivoluzionaria (Fasces of Revolutionary Action) with the goal of promoting Italian intervention in World War I. Mussolini's Fasci Italiani di Combattimento, however, monopolized the term *fascio,* in both its meanings (unity and authority), by turning into a party in 1921 with the name of Partito Fascista Italiano (Italian Fascist Party).[29] "Fascist" at that point unequivocally referred to Mussolini's organization, whereas members of the movement were already called "fascists."[30]

The *fascio littorio,* as an iconographic symbol, was also patronized by the rising fascist movement through systematic and persistent use. With its rods and ax signifying unity and authority, the *fascio* had already been adopted by many countries and appeared in different contexts. *Fasces* constituted an important element in the radical imagery of the French revolution and were featured in the seal of the republic.[31] The image of the Roman *fascio* was adopted by the U.S. government in a copper coin at the turn of the century and in a quarter coined in 1932.[32] *Fasci* also appeared on American buildings, statues, and monuments, such as the Lincoln Memorial in Washington, D.C. Yet the fascist regime appropriated the *fascio* as its main identifying feature, its signifier. The *fascio* represented a new movement of spiritual renewal, an organization founded on discipline and authority and whose unity and force was granted by obedience. Thus Mussolini affirmed in his 1932 "Dottrina del Fascismo":

> [Fascism] wants to remake not only the forms of human life, but the content, man, character, faith. To this end it requires discipline, and an authority that would impress the spirits and dominate them fully. Its sign is thus the *fascio littorio*, symbol of unity, force and justice.[33]

The *fascio littorio* embodied Mussolini's desire to forge fascist Italians and employ his totalitarian power as artist-politician to create an undifferentiated, harmonious, and disciplined whole. The *fascio*, in which rods were fastened together into a bundle and became indistinguishable, iconographically portrayed the desired unity of Italians under the leadership of Mussolini.[34]

On January 21, 1923, a royal decree-law established the production of coins amounting to 100 million lire in value in celebration of fascism's advent to power. The coins, with the nominal value of 1 and 2 lire, were supposed to feature the effigy of the king on one side and the *fascio littorio* on the other. The art critic Margherita Sarfatti encouraged the government to take particular care in the artistic representation of the *fascio* in this instance, especially in view of the coins' large circulation. Mussolini charged an eminent archaeologist with the task of researching the original details of the design and its historical transformations. In the end, Mussolini decided to adopt for the coins the iconography of the *fascio* typical of Roman symbolism. This version differed from the one the fascist organization had been using, wherein the ax appeared at the center of the bundle in the fashion of the French revolution and the Italian Risorgimento. In the Roman tradition, the ax was definitively moved to the side of the rods.[35] Historical and aesthetic motives guided fascism's adoption of its iconographic symbol, and over time these reasons inspired a plethora of specific rules governing the symbol. Hence, whereas until 1926 the *fascio* still appeared in two designs, with the ax either at the center or on the side, after the decree-law of December 12, 1926, which made the *fascio* an emblem of the state, the Roman version officially prevailed.[36] In this guise the *fascio*, like Mussolini's image, was ubiquitous. With its connotations of order, discipline, and unity, the *fascio* became the regime's main form of visual representation.

The Roman *fascio* appeared in innumerable official and unofficial objects: banners, government documents, publications, and envelopes and stationery of clubs, associations, and cultural groups. *Fasci littori* framed the windows of the governmental building from which Mussolini delivered his speeches

Figure 10.   Mussolini saluting from the balcony of Palazzo Venezia (with Starace on the far right).

(Figure 10); formed the facade of the 1932 Exhibit of the Revolution at Rome's Palazzo delle Esposizioni; constituted the stage from which Mussolini addressed the crowds in his tours of Italian cities; and opened the Luce documentary films. Medals featured the symbol of the *littorio*,[37] as did the calendars produced by the PNF. Even toys and other objects the regime distributed to children for the Epiphany festivity were imprinted with the *fascio*.[38] *Fasci* also appeared in monuments, such as the one dedicated to the

Figure 11. A sewer plaque in Littoria featuring a *fascio littorio*.

Marinaio d'Italia (Sailor of Italy) in Brindisi. The sailors were represented with an enormous helm accompanied by an equally enormous *fascio*.[39] *Fasci littori* decorated uniforms of party members. The official badge of the party, for instance, featured a *fascio*, and in 1926 the badge became an obligatory accessory to be worn on civilian clothes. At the same time, the make and sale of nonauthorized badges was forbidden.[40] *Fasci* also appeared on the belt dividing the pants from the black shirt; on the special beret, the *fez*; on the service cap; and on the epaulets of official fascist uniforms.[41] At a less elevated level, *fasci* were also imprinted on sewer plaques and even invaded the language. Thus, the Agip brand of gas was called *Littoria*; a coach train was named *Littorina*; and a town was founded in 1932 with the name of Littoria (Figure 11).

Through its overwhelming presence in the daily reality of Italian society, the *fascio* dominated public life and testified to the regime's authority; it officially represented the regime. In 1923 three special postage stamps of 10 cents, 1 lira, and 5 lire were issued to celebrate fascism's advent to power, and they all portrayed *fasci littori*. In the 10-cent stamp, designed by Duilio Cambellotti, *fasci* appeared on both the left and right sides, and a third one filled the center, intertwined with flowered branches symbolizing spring.[42] The 1-lira stamp, designed by the futurist artist Giacomo Balla, featured the word *Italia* and an eagle with open wings standing on a *fascio*. The 5-lire stamp, also designed by Balla, featured the word *Italia*, a star, and three airplanes flying over smoking chimneys, with *fasci littori* on the left and right sides.[43] On a stamp for the militia issued on October 29, 1923, a *fascio littorio* appeared in an uncommon horizontal position.[44] Beginning in 1926, *fasci* were displayed regularly on Italian stamps on one or both sides, framing the scenes portrayed in the central part. In 1929 the stamp with the effigy of King Vittorio Emanuele III featured two small *fasci* at the sides of the lower half. Furthermore, the few stamps that were not imprinted with *fasci* still portrayed the Roman symbol in the Italian coat of arms that most often appeared on stamps.

The royal decree of December 12, 1926, had declared the *fascio littorio* emblem of the state, "given that the *fascio littorio* has become by now and through a very long practice an emblem of the state, [and] given the absolute and urgent necessity of protecting such an emblem."[45] On March 27, 1927, a new decree described the rules connected to the use of the *fascio littorio* by state administrations. The decree ordered that the administrations allowed to use the state coat of arms should post the *fascio littorio* on the left side of the state emblem.[46] On April 11, 1929, another decree modified the state coat of arms. The *fascio* no longer stood at the side; instead, two *fasci* replaced the lions in the traditional design, featuring the royal emblem of the Savoy House.[47] This new coat of arms became in a subsequent decree the one adopted by state administrations and notaries and was also featured in official seals of state.[48] In this guise, the coat of arms also appeared on stamps. State and fascism were represented as a single entity.

After the dictatorial turn in 1925, fascism increased its claim of expressing Italy's spirit. In the same way, the *fascio littorio* could no longer merely symbolize the Fascist Party. It needed to constitute the iconographic representation of Italy's new values and principles under the spiritual guidance of the regime. Although the *fascio* was not an original discovery, through a capillary use and widespread diffusion it became, after Mussolini, the fascist dictatorship's second main symbol, its visual form of self-representation.[49] As such, the Roman *fascio* gradually established the connection between fascism and Italy and signified Italy's new existence under Mussolini's regime.

THE DISCOURSE ON STYLE

The myth of Rome and its symbolic corollaries provided the fascist regime with a solid basis upon which to create those new traditions, rituals, and festivals that Mussolini's conception of politics envisaged as necessary in modern political rule. Symbolic forms were supposed to convey the values and principles of the fascist movement, and through their communicative function they aimed to solicit and channel popular participation in political life. Mussolini's regime also considered symbols and rituals elements through which fascism could affect the Italians' style and turn the inchoate "masses" into "new men." Mussolini invoked the coming of "citizen-soldiers" in the guise of courageous and valiant individuals. The "new men" would contribute, through disciplined behavior, to a harmonic and beautiful order; they would supply Italy with renovated grandeur and future glory.[50]

Mussolini's aesthetic-political yearning exuded high ambitions. But how was the regime's symbolic lexicon and ritualistic constellation supposed to bring forth "new men"? What was the relation between symbolic practices and fascist behavior? Mussolini and the regime believed that style was a visible sign of internal characteristics, and, in a peculiar logical reasoning, they also seemed to think a change in style could produce a transformation in character. Hence, whereas Mussolini claimed to be concerned with the content and substance of the people, he dedicated most of his attention to the formal aspects of the Italians' way of living. The word "style," in addition to its artistic meaning, etymologically connotes external appearance. The stylistic and aesthetic elements of rituals attracted the regime's scrutinizing eye.

Attention to the external aspects of Italians' conduct especially characterized the regime's life after Achille Starace became the new party secretary on December 7, 1931. At this time the rhetoric of style underwent a major turn. With the establishment of the dictatorial regime, Mussolini more strongly emphasized the need to give Italian society a new shape. In a speech to doctors published in *Il Popolo d'Italia* of January 29, 1932, Mussolini declared: "I am deeply convinced that our way of eating, dressing, working and sleeping, the entire complex of our daily habits must be reformed."[51] In Mussolini's vision this transformation had an immense scope. It was foremost supposed to affect people's habits, but it was also meant to modify people's physical characteristics in the near future. The notorious lassitude of Italians needed to be replaced by dynamic qualities, both from the internal point of view of moral strength and sturdy character and from the external perspective of physical appearance. A robust and trim body shape reflected inner force and energetic power. A body trained by physical activity gave the impression of vigor, movement, and tenacity—i.e., fascist virtues.

Mussolini's preoccupation with appearance brought a peculiar scrutiny of people's modes of behavior and ways of dressing. Because they constituted the most visible signs of the desired change in style, everyday practices became the most insisted-upon elements in the regime's rhetoric and the target of extremely petty rulings and orders. Starace's injunctions to party members and fascist associations multiplied, touching the lives of millions.[52] Fascist rituals, conceived as norms regulating people's daily conduct, invaded the private sphere.

Dress, Behave

In the early stages of Mussolini's movement, members of the squads who engaged in violent attacks against socialist and leftist organizations wore black shirts and metonymically came to be called Black Shirts.[53] When Mussolini became prime minister in 1922, he dismantled the squads and created the Milizia. The black shirt, however, symbolically remained a fascist outfit, a reminder of the movement's historical exordium. As such, the black shirt constituted the basic piece of party members' uniforms and a constant of fascist attire spanning more than twenty years of variations in fashion.[54] All participants in the numerous fascist organizations, from women's *fasces* and children's groups to school associations and sport clubs, also wore the black shirt.[55] In November 1934 even infants and children up to eight years old were organized under the umbrella name of "Sons and Daughters of the She-Wolf" (*Figli e Figlie della Lupa*) and outfitted in miniature black shirts (Figure 12). Store advertisements for the black shirt and other fascist clothes punctuated papers and magazines.

During the 1920s, use of the black shirt did not follow precise rules. Mussolini himself wore it on random occasions, even though he claimed that the black shirt had a sacred value and should not be spoiled by mundane usage. Thus, in a speech to parliament of September 12, 1924, Mussolini proclaimed that the black shirt could not be worn every day, only in particular circumstances. He even ordered the arrest of those who wore it "improperly."[56] Almost a year later, on June 22, 1925, he reiterated his thoughts to the fascist congress:

> The black shirt is not the everyday shirt, and is not a uniform either. It is a combat outfit and can only be worn by those who harbor a pure soul in their heart.[57]

Figure 12. *Figlio della Lupa* (son of the she-wolf) posing next to a portrait of Mussolini (note the *M* on the buckle).

Mussolini's high-sounding rhetoric, which identified the black shirt with all the regime's cherished values—courage, struggle, and spiritual superiority —soon turned into a series of precepts that defined the proper employment of the shirt. The black shirt became the object of rigid orders aimed at eliminating any sign of confusion and disunity. One of the ten fascist commandments stated: "He who is not ready to sacrifice body and soul to Italy and to serve Mussolini without question is unworthy to wear the black shirt, symbol of Fascism."[58]

In 1932 the statute of the Fascist Party for the first time included an article on the black shirt: "The black shirt constitutes the fascist uniform and must be worn only when it is prescribed."[59] Besides giving instructions on the occasions upon which it was appropriate to dress in a black shirt, party secretary Starace also began to specify the proper combination of accessories for the black shirt. When it was required, the black shirt needed to be complemented with care in all details. Injunction 93 of March 22, 1933, discussed the young fascist's summer outfit; youth were allowed to wear the black shirt without the tie and with the open collar, but they were absolutely forbidden to roll up the sleeves.[60] On August 7, 1933, Starace reiterated that a fluttering tie was not allowed. On May 23, 1934, he "absolutely forbade" wearing the black shirt with a starched collar. A September 13, 1937, *disposizione* ordered party members not to wear decorations on their uniforms at the Exhibit of the Revolution.[61]

In March 1937, *disposizioni* provided instructions on uniforms in the territories of the empire and included a detailed description of hat, jacket, pants, and belt.[62] A special belt was designed for gala events in 1939 to complement the gala uniform designed in 1938.[63] On April 21, 1939, a new accoutrement was added to the already large paraphernalia of the fascist outfit: the *sciarpa littorio*.[64] The scarf, with the Roman colors yellow and red, had supposedly been worn by Mussolini on the occasion of the March on Rome. The Duce instituted it on the twentieth anniversary of the founding of the *fasci* and ordered that only selected fascists, such as those who had participated in the march, could wear it. The *sciarpa* was a sign of recognition, and it showed the hierarchical structure of the regime. Accessories, ornaments, and medals demonstrated a person's position in the regime's organization.[65] Children, youth associations, and women's groups had their own particular variations in outfit. Each group occupied a place in the whole, and the sense of discipline and order emanating from their uniforms produced an aesthetic effect that reflected fascist inner qualities and expressed spiritual attributes. Thus, when the regime, on the model of the military, instituted uniforms with relative degrees for the personnel of state civil administrations, newspapers were ordered to publish the event with great pomp and to comment on it, according to the Duce's words, as "a new step towards the spiritual mobilization of the Nation, also in its external aspects."[66] Uniforms came to epitomize change and differentiated fascist spirit from bourgeois values. Thus, university professors, compelled in 1931 to take a fascist oath and later to become fascist members, wore black shirts, "at least on graduation days."[67] In 1933 rectors and deans were ordered to dress in black shirts during important university ceremonies.[68] Beginning in late 1934, elementary school teachers, who normally were required to participate in official parades wearing the black shirt, also were obliged to dress in the party uniform during school hours.[69] On July 5, 1938, journalists and photographers covering news of ceremonies presided over by the Duce were told to dress in a black shirt.[70] The uniform, along with the other daily rituals the regime imposed, were intended to wipe out bourgeois mentality and habits. Failure to wear the fascist outfit revealed one's bourgeois spirit. In his *disposizioni* of April 25, 1936, Starace lamented what he called "a common reluctance" to wear the fascist uniform at prescribed events. He defined those attitudes as "emanating from a bourgeois spirit that is absolutely in contrast with the fascist mentality."[71]

The bourgeoisie, intended as a moral category, was the main concept in opposition to which fascism built itself as a movement. Bourgeois clothes thus constituted only one of Starace's targets. He issued several other *disposizioni* indicating how fascists needed to demonstrate spiritual and material contrast with the bourgeois individual. The supposed utilitarian and materialistic values of the bourgeoisie—its ideals of well-being, the quiet life, and maintaining the status quo—naturally went against the fascist characteristics of dynamism, courage, discipline, and self-sacrifice. With the ascendance of Achille Starace to the secretariat of the Fascist Party, the hunt for the bourgeois became a high priority in the regime. Starace's daily *disposizioni* tirelessly and endlessly aimed to cure Italians of their bourgeois habits.

In one of his first *disposizioni,* on August 23, 1932, Starace warned against participating in banquets. He defined them as "typical of other times."[72] In February of that same year, Starace already had forbidden gala shows and what he called *ranci d'onore* (gala rations). They reminded one of an "old style, perfectly in contrast to the fascist style."[73] Amusements also needed to have a fascist character in order not to undermine the seriousness of the regime. Hence, dances could not take place in connection with fascist events.[74] On November 8, 1938, Starace attacked New Year's Eve celebrations and especially the "Happy New Year" wishes that people exchanged.[75] The habit was particularly odious because the regime had actually changed the calendar standard: starting in 1927, the fascist year began on October 29, the day after the anniversary of the March on Rome. Years were counted from 1922 according to a Roman numeral and belonged to the *era fascista.*[76] Evidently the Italian people had not fully converted to this new custom, and Starace strongly reprimanded "the attachment to these habits which are scrupulously observed even when it would not be inconvenient to abandon them." Starace considered this attachment "the sign of a conservative mentality, which is typically bourgeois and thus not fascist."[77] On December 13, 1939, the orders to the press forbade writing about New Year's Day.[78] The new Italian was supposed to change his style, to follow new values, to transform his way of living. The persistence of old, bourgeois practices denoted an unfulfilled *fascistizzazione*.

Starace's diligence in fighting nonfascist conduct culminated in the organization of an Anti-Bourgeois Exhibit, which he announced in the *disposizione* of November 29, 1938.[79] The exhibit, to be displayed in a special pavilion at the Autarchic Exhibit of the Italian Mineral (Mostra Autarchica del Minerale Italiano), aimed at "denouncing the typical aspects of bourgeois mentality." Starace invited Italian artists to prepare caricatures and drawings that would ridicule typical bourgeois attitudes and forms. Among the subjects to be covered, he listed: handshakes; suits and top hats (what he called "stove pipes," *tubi di stufa*); courtesies of reverence; raising of one's hat; social games; afternoon tea; and inaugural ceremonies.[80] Following Mussolini's vision, Starace wanted to change the Italians' way of life, their style. The targets of his attention were daily practices and gestures.

Speaking Fascist

Language, as an exemplification of people's character, became another target of the secretary's *disposizioni*. On April 11, 1934, Starace warned that correspondence between fascists should be addressed with the formula: "To the Fascist." He also specified that even if the word "fascist" was an adjective, when used as a substantive it had to be written with an initial capital letter.[81] A few months later, on September 19, 1934, he advised abolishing any form of greetings in office correspondence between party organizations.[82] On December 24, 1936, he asked the federal secretaries to be concise in their reports.[83] On June 21, 1937, Starace issued various *disposizioni* in bold characters in which he condemned prolixity and held up the Duce as an example of perfect conciseness.[84] The secretary identified speaking style with physical characteristics: "The prolix man in writing and speaking is to be compared to the plump man who is uncertain and slow in action and thought, since fat exercises an influence over the muscular and cerebral systems." The fat man was the bourgeois, who led a sedentary and quiet life among comforts and leisure.[85] "Prolixity," insisted Starace, "is a characteristic of sedentary, rhetorical, exhibitionist people and inexorably leads to waste, and makes others waste, time. Anything but 'new men'!" A year later, on October 10, 1938, Starace wrote: "Those who show bureaucratic tendencies end up becoming also physically heavy."[86]

According to Starace's sociobiological interpretation, in order to be a new man one needed to be slim, which was also more appropriate aesthetically.[87] Starace's *disposizioni* on the formal aspects of habits and behavior generally highlighted the aesthetic dimension of change. The use of some linguistic expressions and, in general, exaggerations and amplifications in speaking and writing styles were rejected as less aesthetic—or, more exactly, as ugly.[88] In a *disposizione* of April 13, 1938, Starace wrote that the form of office correspondence should be revised to emphasize dynamism: no "dear such and such"—an address sufficed; nor should there be "cordial greetings" or "fascist greetings" and other bad bourgeois and servile formulas, as he had already suggested in 1934. "Shortness!" he implored. "We still write too much, despite the numerous encouragements to write little. A *gerarca* stuck to his table, constantly dealing with paper, takes away very useful time from the activity he should be engaging in outside the office, and runs the risk of losing that dynamism which must characterize him."[89] In September 1938, Starace condemned the journalists' use of the phrase "the laying of the foundation-stone" (*posa della prima pietra*). For him that formula needed to be replaced with a fascist-style sentence such as "the beginning of works" (*l'inizio dei lavori*) or "the first stroke of the pick" (*il primo colpo di piccone*)—i.e., an announcement that was both "dynamic and concrete." Again he concluded his injunctions with an attack on bourgeois habits: "It is no longer the time of top hats."[90]

Starace's preoccupations with aesthetics and language focused in particular on the use of *lei*, the third person singular, as a formal way to address people. On January 15, 1938, a Tuscan writer, Bruno Cicognani, published an article in the daily *Il Corriere della Sera* in which he suggested that the new fascist Italy, which was reemerging as a great nation, needed to abolish the *lei*. He considered the *lei* form a "witness . . . to the centuries of serfdom and abjection." The *lei* was a "grammatical and syntactic aberration" imported from Spain during the Baroque Era. It was a product of courtier's art, and it signified cultural degeneration. Cicognani called for the use of the *tu*, second person singular, and the *voi*, second person plural, the latter to be used only as a sign of respect to superiors. To support his thesis, the writer referred to the Roman tradition that lay at the basis of fascism's civilization:

> The fascist revolution intends to bring back the spirit of our race to its
> authentic origins, freeing it from any pollution. Then, let us bring forth
> this purification. Also in this, let us go back to the use of Rome, to the
> Christian and Roman *tu* which expresses the universal value of Rome and
> Christianity. Let the *voi* be a sign of respect and of hierarchical recognition.
> But in any other case let the *tu* be the form of communicating, writing or

speaking: the grammatically, logically and spiritually true, immediate, simple, genuine and Italian form.

Cicognani's linguistic polemic was immediately appropriated by the regime. The reference to Rome and spirituality and the critique of the *lei* as a foreign expression corresponded well with the regime's aspirations to establish a new national and fascist style. Thus, the formal *lei* came to be considered a sign of bourgeois behavior, unfit for the new reality fascism had created, and the regime endorsed Cicognani's interpretation of the *tu* and *voi*. In the aftermath of Cicognani's article, Starace issued *disposizioni* that abolished the use of *lei* among members of the party. The *tu* was adopted, and the *voi* was to be used in case of hierarchical relations.[91] The *tu* indicated "intimate camaraderie, the presence of a community of faith"; the *voi* constituted an optimal formula to express the hierarchical nature of the regime.[92] Starace advised extending the linguistic rule to the youth organizations, whose members could effectively be considered to belong to the party only at age twenty-one.[93] In the virtually unanimous condemnation of the *lei* following Cicognani's article, failure to drop this bourgeois habit became the target of Starace's witch hunt. He suggested ignoring any correspondence not written in fascist style—i.e., with the adoption of the *tu*.[94] A women's magazine, unfortunately called *Lei*, vainly tried to make the case that its title simply meant "she," in the sense of woman. (In Italian *lei* is synonymous with *ella* or *essa*, the feminine variant of the third person singular.) Eventually, *Lei* became *Annabella*.[95]

The anti-*lei* campaign was pursued forcefully by the regime. Press orders insisted that newspapers revamp the discussion on the issue by writing articles and by avoiding the use of *lei* in vignettes, tales, and dialogues. The *lei* form was considered foreign, servile, feminine, and against the rules of grammar.[96] In 1939 Starace planned an Anti-*lei* Exhibit (Mostra Anti-lei) that was supposed to ban definitely the use of the *lei*. The poster of the exhibit portrayed a tree whose branches formed the word *voi* and whose roots surrounded a coffin containing the *lei* (Figure 13). Newspapers, writers, and philologists also participated in Starace's battle against the *lei*. That same year the periodical *Antieuropa*, directed by Asvero Gravelli, published a list of intellectuals supporting the new fascist measure. The painter and novelist Alberto Savinio wrote that "[t]he 'lei' is the linguistic tool of those who have something to hide . . . the ideal bridge of hypocrisy. . . . The 'lei' implies humiliation and servility." Savinio concluded by asking who would want to continue in this vice: "Who, if not the incurable 'bourgeois'—'traditional' enemy of the clear and direct expression that Fascism prefers?"[97]

Figure 13.   Poster of the Anti-*lei* Exhibit held in Turin in 1939.

Despite the intellectuals' rhetorical support for the *voi*, however, resistance to the linguistic measure persisted (Figure 14). On August 19, 1939, Starace issued another *disposizione* in which he desperately stated: "It is absurd and deplorable after what has been said and written, also by newspapers, that here and there people find it hard to adopt the '*voi*' and reject

Figure 14. A sobbing bourgeois in a stovepipe hat tries to reanimate the defunct *lei* (caricature drawing, "The Inconsolable," by Angelo Burattini, for the Anti-Bourgeois Exhibit planned by Starace in 1938).

the '*lei*' neatly. . . . Besides any other consideration, all this reveals the absence of that fascist temperament which must be able to carry out in every circumstance the style of Mussolini's time." And, Starace continued: "The federal secretaries must call upon the *gerarchi* and talk clearly to them without omitting to indicate that when the injunctions I have ordered regarding this matter are not followed, it may mean either little sense of discipline or even little fascist faith. This is one of those cases in which form, by definitively affecting customs, expresses its deep content with exactitude."[98]

Starace assigned rituals an important role in the new society organized by fascism. He worked diligently to fulfill Mussolini's aesthetic-political vision through means that corresponded to the regime's own identification of style with character and spirit. Within this frame, the observance of myths, rituals, and symbols signified the people's acknowledgment of their fascist identity, and adoption of new rituals was intended to signify a truly radical change in style. This interpretation is exemplified by the case of the Roman salute, one of the main ritualistic gestures that fascism introduced in daily life.

The Roman Salute

The Roman salute, in which the right arm was raised in a straight and perpendicular manner, had been adopted by D'Annunzio during his regency in Fiume. Like other rituals utilized by D'Annunzio, the salute became part of the rising fascist movement's symbolic patrimony and was inherited by Mussolini's government. On January 31, 1923, the Ministry of Education instituted a ritual honoring the flag in schools. During the ceremony, students paid homage to the flag with fascist songs and a Roman salute (Figure 15).[99] In 1925, when Mussolini began his work of *fascistizzazione* of the state, the salute officially became part of the regime. Mussolini ordered all state civil administrations at the center and the periphery, including schools, to adopt it as of December 1, 1925.[100] The salute was supposed to reflect a sense of discipline, as it addressed a superior as a sign of respect from an inferior in the ranks. But there were also rules concerning the salute between *gerarchi* of equal importance. Mussolini sent telegrams to the several ministers communicating his orders. Amidst requests for clarifications on the modalities and circumstances concerning the salute, the Roman gesture became part of people's everyday existence and experience.

In 1932 the Roman salute was adopted as the substitute for the bourgeois handshake. In his *disposizioni*, Starace wished that "the year XI signs the twilight of shaking hands."[101] The salute was considered "more hygienic, more aesthetic and shorter," in the words of Mussolini,[102] and the regime defined itself as antibourgeois through the Roman salute. Unlike ugly, slow bourgeois culture, fascism was efficient, harmonic, and dynamic. The aesthetics of order and discipline combined with the regime's emphasis on character; the Roman salute represented the physical sign of a truly new man, whose gestures reflected his intimate fascist nature (Figure 16).[103] Thus, on August 28, 1932, Starace hinted that "[t]o salute the Roman way by remaining sitting is . . . little Roman"—that is, little fascist.[104] On June 12, 1933, he suggested that the Roman salute did not imply the necessity of taking off the hat unless one was indoors.[105] And on September 9, 1933, he reprimanded *gerarchi* who in a dispute had used the formula: "[T]hey reconciled with a handshake." They should have adopted instead the sentence: "[T]hey reconciled with a Roman salute."[106]

The symbolic value assigned to the Roman salute grew to such an extent that complaints began to rise about its improper execution. The president of the Ministers' Council, for example, took into serious consideration Professor Wasserman's observations about the malfunctioning of the salute and his scientific description of a perfect execution. According to Wasser-

Figure 15. Schoolchildren saluting the flag ("The Promise to the Fatherland," by Stagnoli).

man, the proper Roman salute had the effect of showing the fascist man's "decisive spirit," which was close to that of ancient Romans.[107] "Habitual gestures, if decisive, especially when following trajectories, which in general express a symbol, reveal firm characters, who always have a clear vision of their intentions, who are conscious of their ability to realize them." Wasserman claimed there was an interdependence between psychic life and

Figure 16. "Degenerate" bourgeois handshake (caricature drawing, "Handshake," by Avondo, for the Anti-Bourgeois Exhibit).

physical life and that gestures revealed psychic idiosyncrasies. Thus, a well-executed salute showed that "in the spirit of those who perform it there is no hesitation, from the subjective point of view." It also offered a "sincere and virile tribute of deference."

For Wasserman, the perfect Roman salute showed the fascist's decisive spirit, firmness, seriousness, and acknowledgment and acceptance of the regime's hierarchical structure. Therefore, the salute was an unfailing proof of fascist character, and Professor Wasserman's observations became the guideline for the party's enforcement of the Roman salute, with the conviction that a correct physical gesture brought forth a change in character.[108] Hence, the Roman salute, which was supposed to be a sign revealing fascist character, suddenly turned out to be the sine qua non of the real fascist, the element without which one could not be considered a fascist. The means had become ends, and the ritual in itself ensured the coming about of the new fascist man. Within this interpretive frame, shaking hands was naturally considered a disgrace, a real betrayal of fascist principles. Starace ordered that a note be put in the personal file of people who continued to shake hands. The note would say, "Devoted to hand shaking," as a sign of a lesser fascist spirit.[109] In 1938 a party *disposizione* stated that hand shaking, along with the use of *lei,* was abolished in films and theatrical representations.[110] The bourgeois gesture was supposed to disappear from the view of Italians and not contaminate their daily life (Figure 17). Even official photographs of visiting dignitaries were touched up so as not to show them shaking hands.[111] On November 21, 1938, the Ministry of Popular Culture issued orders not to "publish photographs showing hand shaking, even if those gestures were performed by very high dignitaries."[112] In contrast, the regime was eager to emphasize the adoption of the Roman salute for important occasions. On March 23, 1939, the daily orders to the press invited journalists to write that during her visit to the Chamber, the queen had saluted with a straight arm and not by reclining her head.[113]

The Passo Romano

The cult of rituals and the belief in their ability to transform people led the regime to institute a new fascist custom in February 1938: the *passo romano,* the Roman step for military parades.[114] The appeal of military-style customs had been present in fascism since its beginnings. On April 3, 1921, Mussolini, proclaiming the Birth of Rome a fascist holiday, suggested adopting the *passo romano* as a way of celebrating the festival. In his vision, "[T]he regional legions will parade with our order which is not militaristic, nor German, but simply Roman."[115] Mussolini proceeded to explain what he meant by Roman order:

> [O]ur march . . . imposes individual control on everyone . . . impresses on everyone order and discipline. Because we want in fact to initiate a solid

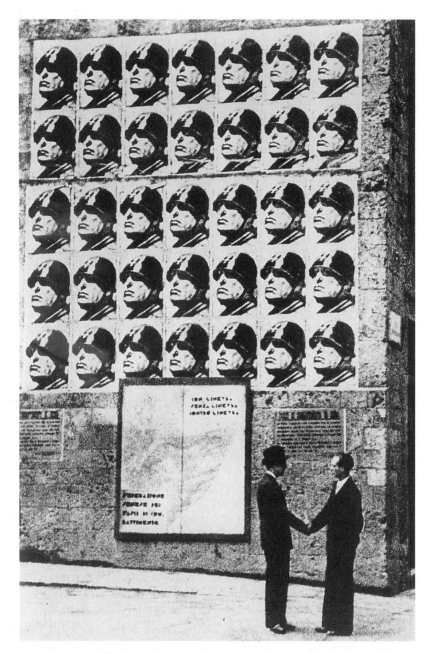

Figure 17.   Handshake under Mussolini's gaze ("Florence," by N. Tim Gidal, 1934).

national discipline, because we think that without this discipline Italy cannot become the Mediterranean and world nation of which we dream. And those who reproach us for marching like the Germans should realize that it is not us who are copying from them but the Germans who copy and have copied from the Romans. Thus it is us who return to our origins, to our Roman, Latin and Mediterranean style.[116]

Mussolini bestowed upon the march the symbolic meaning of embodying discipline and order—values that would ensure Italy's aggrandizement.[117] It is no surprise that the anniversary of the March on Rome, the anniversary of the foundation of the *fasci,* and the Birth of Rome were commemorated with military-style marches in which columns escorted the banners of the party in perfect order. Ludovic Naudeau recounts schoolchildren's participation in the march on the occasion of the 1926 Birth of Rome celebration in Turin: "By superior orders boys and girls were all uniformly dressed as fascists, with the black shirt and, on the head, the fez of the same color. . . . The whole day . . . children of both genders formed long processions and marched militarily, hitting the ground rhythmically with their feet and singing patriotic songs."[118]

Fascism's anniversaries, celebrated in a solemn atmosphere, aimed to reaffirm the hierarchical structure of the party. Uniforms were obligatory on these specific days, along with all the decorations that distinguished one person from the next in the hierarchical scale. In these rallies the fascist regime displayed its difference from liberal governments. People were turned from "flocks" into ordered ranks, thus contributing to the inner beauty of an Italy infused with fascist spirit.[119] As the journalist Mario Apollonio wrote in the January 27, 1935, issue of *Illustrazione Italiana:* "The people believe, obey, fight: and they aesthetically express in their meetings and rituals their faith, their law, their action." The rallies, continued Apollonio, were expressions of a spiritual reality through which the Italians represented their national unity. Thus, the march was something "animate and exactly proportional," and it showed its difference from the German and Russian versions. The march expressed fascist identity: it epitomized the new fascist style.

The implementation of the *passo romano* ideally concluded the regime's attempt to build a new style—a style Mussolini had forecast in his 1921 eulogy of the march. In 1938, in the preface to the *Grand Council of Fascism,* Mussolini wrote: "The Revolution must affect people's 'customs' deeply. In this regard, the innovation of the *passo romano* is exceptionally important."[120] Although many criticized the *passo* and saw it as an imitation of the German goose step, Mussolini strongly supported it.[121] According to him:

> The *passo* symbolizes the force, the will, the energy of the young lictorial generations who are enthusiastic about it.
>
> It is a step that has a difficult and hard style, which requires preparation and training. For this reason we want it.
>
> It is a step that the sedentary, the big-bellied, the half-wit and the so-called shrimps will never be able to perform. For this reason we like it.
>
> Our adversaries proclaim that the *passo* is the most genuine expression of the authentic military spirit. We are happy about it.
>
> For this reason we adopted it and we will soon execute it at perfection, because the Italian people, when they want to, know how to do everything.[122]

The *passo* required a slim physique, supposedly a characteristic of the new fascist man, who was strong and dynamic. The *passo* implied a certain spirit, as one journalist wrote,[123] while a university professor affirmed that the *passo* "exercised a salutary effect on the nervous system."[124] Physiological and psychological motivations turned the *passo romano* into a sign of fascist character. In addition, the aesthetics of order and harmony, which characterized the march, also qualified the *passo* for the fascist altar. The *passo* presented the beautiful image of Italy as a unitary whole, powerful and disciplined. On August 26, 1938, the orders to the press asked that all photos of military parades, youth parades, and *passo romano* be well revised so that only the ones showing "flawless alignments" would be published.[125] From the Milizia, the *passo* soon extended to the fascist youth organizations.[126] In his diary, Giaime Pintor remembered his experience of the *passo romano* as a university student. Despite all his recriminations over the time wasted in parades, Pintor also learned "to disappear in the tens of thousands of men who participated in the reviews . . . and to enjoy the impersonality given by the uniform."[127] In fascism's aesthetically pleasing pageant of marches and Roman salutes, uniforms, and goose steps, military style substituted for military preparation and presided over the shaping of the new fascist man as citizen-soldier.

In general, the way the regime tried to implement new habits among Italians merely addressed the question of the formal acceptance of certain rituals. Having neutralized the cultural-political role of the party, the regime seemed most interested, as Starace's *disposizioni* show, in the execution of gestures, the external tangible proof that people were following the rules and were thus infused with fascist spirit. But could a loyal man become a valiant new Italian simply by adopting the right gestures? Could form really express content as Starace claimed? If, as Mussolini told De Begnac, "the mass must obey and not look for the truth,"[128] then rituals and symbols did not need to convince the people. They just had to be obeyed. The correct performance of rituals ensured the regime of an obedient and disciplined people. Fascism's main value: "to believe" meant to obey the high authority in the hierarchical structure. Within this context, the regime's focus on forms and performance is not surprising. Style was the formal, extrinsic presentation of fascism's substance, and in this sense it had a role in building character.[129] The content was derived from the form, as Mussolini's explanation of the *passo*'s "very great educational importance" tellingly confirms. In his memoirs of 1942–1943, Mussolini recalled the episode of Waterloo and proceeded to affirm: "At one moment during the battle certain Prussian divisions wavered for a moment, surprised by heavy fire from the French artillery. Blücher marched them back to the lines in goose-step, and they then intrepidly resumed the fight."[130] For Mussolini, the adoption of new rituals, which were basically antibourgeois and most often carried the positive imprint of Roman origins, in itself represented the sign of a deep transformation in the Italians' attitude, the proof of a new spirit animating them. Hence, rituals became ends in themselves, at once reality and symbols of transformation.

The insistence on petty rules, and the sustained equation between form and substance, appearance and content, style and spirit, brought the regime to privilege the aesthetic dimension of changes over changes themselves. The principle of *l'art pour l'art* in this case even seemed to conflict with the interests of the fascist government, deluded by its own infatuation with aesthetics. This danger was recognized by some of Mussolini's closest collaborators. Galeazzo Ciano, Mussolini's son-in-law and minister of foreign affairs, felt profoundly skeptical about the regime's stylistic trend. When describing Mussolini's preparations for the 1939 parade of the Milizia, Ciano wrote:

> The Duce is all involved . . . with the preparation of the Milizia for the parade of February 1. He takes care in person of the minutest details. He spends hours at the window of his office hidden behind the blue curtains, spying the movements of the troops. . . . He has ordered the bandmaster to use a baton, and he teaches in person the right movements and corrects the proportions and the style of the club. He more and more believes that form, in the army, also determines the substance. . . . He often accuses the King of having diminished the physical prestige of the army in order to harmonize it to his "unhappy figure."[131]

Following a physiological interpretation of human activities, Mussolini accused the king, who was small and short, of failing to develop rituals and rules that would increase the stature of the army, both in the physical and spiritual sense. In a confusion between reality and the image of reality the way he wished it to be, Mussolini emphasized the external aspects of the transformations he was pursuing. He believed that a change of habits was equivalent to a change in character, that the execution of rituals and gestures also had a positive effect on the body. The body, he thought, adjusted to the new calls for strength and courage, contributing to the formation of the new man as warrior.

This aesthetic vision of a fascist society, whose homogeneity and total submission to the state guaranteed the fulfillment of a future fascist civilization, inspired the regime's adoption of rituals and symbols. The black shirt and the Roman salute, the new calendar and changes in ways of speaking, the march and the *passo romano* were supposed to bring style into people's lives and transform Italy and the Italians. They would contribute to the building of a new, beautiful order, a unitary whole ready for expansion. At the same time, the reinvention of rituals and symbols constituted a source of identity for the regime. The formal execution of gestures and rites became an important value and influenced the regime's own self-understanding, its immediate goals, its elaboration of rules, and the type of relations it established with the subjects of its power. The regime mirrored itself in the symbols and myths it created. In the process of making "new men" and a beautiful Italy, Mussolini's regime refined its political orientations and prioritized its ends. Symbols and myths became fascism's means of self-definition, its main forms of representation, and in this fashion they helped to shape fascism's identity.

4 Bodily Economy
Corporativism and Consumption

The regime's antibourgeois rhetoric of the 1930s exploited themes and myths that had been circulating during the immediate postwar period in many of the countries involved in World War I. War veterans adjusted uneasily to the regular rhythms of daily civilian existence; the banality of normalized behavior was anathema to many of them. Returning soldiers, with their heroicized vision of social relations, denounced the baseness of petty aspirations and utilitarian worldviews. Comfort, egoism, and the pursuit of gain were indicted in the critical representations of the bourgeoisie constructed by the demilitarized youth. An internal enemy, one who failed to be transformed by the sacrifice of the millions dead, substituted for the ones in the muddy battle zones.

As the self-proclaimed voice of the values of *combattentismo,* the early fascist movement glorified the masculine experience of the trenches and exalted struggle as a source of life. History could not unfold without contrasts and conflicts: a social war was now necessary to refurbish spiritual and moral values in Italy and to ensure the country's renewal. Within this vision, the bourgeoisie assumed the role of culprit. "Fascism, interpreter of the healthy majority of the people of the trenches, of sacrifice, and of work cannot tolerate the predominance of conservative bourgeoisie any longer," wrote Piero Gorgolini in 1922, in a book Mussolini praised as "the best publication on fascism" to date.[1] Sacrifice and war did not seem to rhyme with "bourgeois," regardless of the specific semantic approach the fascists applied to the term.[2] Hence, the newly formed Fasci Italiani di Combattimento politically expressed the same contempt for the stillness and conservatism of bourgeois existence that the futurists had displayed artistically beginning on February 20, 1909, when their first manifesto appeared in the Parisian newspaper *Le Figaro.* But whereas the futurists and other modernist movements challenged the pragmatism of the bourgeois world and proposed the domination of fantasy over reality, heroism over habit, difference over "equaling quotidianism,"[3] the fascists concentrated their attack on the bourgeois roots of individualistic stances. The futurist leader Filippo Tommaso Marinetti encouraged the emancipation of all individuals from the tyranny of homogeneous life; Mussolini denigrated the bourgeoisie as the historical formation from which the modern concept of the individual was born.

The combination of individualistic tendencies with peace-loving attitudes and comfort-oriented lifestyles made the bourgeois the natural enemy of fascism, a political system that pursued heroic deeds in the name of the nation and that consigned to a handful—or better, one superior and privileged man—the responsibility of leading. Spiritually, bourgeois conservatism offended fascism's myth of action and its vitalistic conception of life. Politically, fascism reserved the status of individual for the few. With its semantic confusions and overloaded meanings, "bourgeoisie," in effect, constituted a recurrent trope in the fascist movement's attempts to define its own political stance and worldview, its critique of democracy and liberalism. The antibourgeois rhetoric became the discursive context in which to represent an ideal sociopolitical model, an embodied expression of fascism's identity. Thus, when it denied "bourgeois" citizens an active role as individual subjects, fascism declared the obsolescence of democracy. When it assaulted bourgeois egoism, fascism asserted the principles of discipline and obedience. And when it castigated bourgeois spirit and attacked bourgeois style, fascism warned against the evil of a consumption-oriented polity in which hedonism and material pleasure prevailed. The allure of happiness and the economy of desire, typical of an emerging consumer culture, particularly clashed with fascism's effort to combat individualism and homogenize the Italians. Hence, in one of its multiple significations, "bourgeois" came to symbolize in fascist discourse the pursuit of individual happiness and the assertion of one's right to satisfy personal needs—all elements that jolted fascism at its foundations. As such, the war against the bourgeoisie became a mission for fascism's survival. And around this symbolic battle the regime's aesthetic politics took shape via a complex strategy of mimetism, displacement, and incorporation.[4]

DISEMBODYING THE BODY

From 1919 on, Mussolini presented fascism as a movement that, contrary to liberalism, bolshevism, and Catholicism, did not promise "ideal paradises" or universal well-being; did not "trade in miraculous drugs to give 'happiness' to humankind"; and did not come forward with "a recipe for happiness."[5] Fascism opposed false utopias of a future that would provide the definite solution to "primordial needs."[6] In particular, Mussolini attacked the "black" religion of the Vatican and the "red" one of Lenin for preaching the realization of a paradisaical world in which life's problems would be finally resolved, as in the best of fairy tales.[7] Could humankind find its utmost fulfillment through the liberation from needs? asked Mussolini. Or would not this fulfillment bring about the pacification of drives and therefore the end of movement and the decline of civilization? Should life be reduced to the pursuit of salvation and a promised land? Or would not this pursuit deprive existence of its meaning and force? Fascism, as Mussolini later explained, could not but oppose "all theological conceptions according to which at a certain historical time there would be a definitive systematization of humanity."[8] Fascism's opposition was necessary, unless one wanted to "be placing oneself outside of history and life—which are a continuous moving and becoming [*fluire e divenire*]."[9] Against illusory socialist and religious forecasts of the coming of happy times, Mussolini thus proposed a "return to the individual"[10]—an individual who privileged combat, fighting, and activism and who ensured the triumph of spiritualism after a long domination of material values. A mystique of action, freed from any goal, guided Mussolini's vision of a renewed spiritual reality.[11] Within this context, the quest for happiness as a final goal amounted to an undermining of the individual's vitality, his spirituality—the specific notion of historical dynamism to which fascism adhered. Hence, Mussolini's critique of happiness challenged teleological theories of political or religious nature for their inadequacy to express the spiritual essence of human existence.

Over the years, Mussolini's obsessive insistence on spirituality led to a persistent denigration of materialism, defined as the satisfaction of needs. "Economic happiness" became one of the main targets of Mussolini's partisan polemic against socialism's doctrine and liberalism's individualistic principles. "Fascism," claimed Mussolini, "denies the materialistic conception of 'happiness' as possible . . . it denies, that is, the equation 'well-being = happiness,' which would turn men into animals who only think about one thing: to be fed and fattened, reduced, that is, to vegetative life purely and simply."[12] In this graphic depiction, material happiness worked to invalidate fascism's "organic conception of the world,"[13] a conception in which the individual only played a role within the state and in subordination to the state. In fascism, people constituted citizen-soldiers, never private persons. Even heroism was conceived within an ethic of discipline and sacrifice. Particularity needed to disappear within the nation, the whole. Therefore, the idea of personal happiness was to be eliminated. The individual sketched by fascism rejected the material, the body, his/her own physicality. Indeed, the fascist redefinition of the individual took place along the axis of the senses. In an utmost exaltation of the spirit, the regime denied the body as the domain of hedonism and pleasure.

This dimension of fascism's antimaterialism most often goes unrecognized,[14] although scholars widely cite antimaterialism as a crucial element in the making of fascist culture. Zeev Sternhell argues that the revolutionary syndicalists' Marxist revolt against materialism, in combination with the influence of "tribal" nationalism, prepared the soil for the birth of fascist ideology.[15] He refers to fascism's appeal to spiritualism, its supposed invocation of ideal values, and its recourse to disinterested ends to qualify Mussolini's movement as antimaterialist. Sternhell rightly acknowledges that moral preoccupations with social atomism and individualism stimulated fascism's critique of materialism, and he insists that fascism's antimaterialistic attitude involved the discrediting of rationalistic and utilitarian values as responsible for fostering unlimited desires for mere private benefit. In his account, however, Sternhell misses the fascists' repudiation of the natural body as part of their general assault of materialism. This absence is all the more conspicuous if we recognize the centrality of the body in Marx's theory of materialism—a theory around which, after all, the revolutionary syndicalists and the fascists built their cultural revolt. In effect, reference to Marx—in particular, to his conceptualization of the body as the potential locus of a "disinterested" expression of desires, a site of uneconomic aesthetic fulfillment—crucially reveals the spuriousness of fascism's interpretation of materialism. It also directs attention to the link between the body, politics, and the aesthetic. And it challenges the taken-for-granted division between materialism, negatively coupled with "interest" and "utilitarianism," and spiritualism, which supposedly shares the positive meanings of "disinterest" and "ideal." In this war of attributes, Sternhell's and others' interpretations of fascism flounder. They fail to realize that fascism constructed its authoritarian model of aesthetic politics around this controversial definition of the body.

Terry Eagleton's *The Ideology of the Aesthetic* has been most responsible for spurring a reexamination of the role of aesthetics in the Marxist tradition and for inscribing the aesthetic realm around the body and pleasure. In his work, Eagleton situates the emergence of the aesthetic as a theoretical category within the modern process of the differentiation of value spheres, a process in which cultural production ceased to play traditional social roles and became autonomous. In this development, aesthetics assumed an independent function and, beginning with the German philosopher Alexander Baumgarten in the mid-eighteenth century, was specifically born as "a discourse of the body."[16] For Eagleton, aesthetics' originating focus on human perception and sensation created a split between things and thoughts, the material and the immaterial, and it marked "the body's long, inarticulate rebellion against the tyranny of the theoretical."[17] At the same time, however, the opening of the realm of the senses required that new empirical knowledge be applied to a neglected territory that seemed to evade cognition. In Baumgarten's formulation, aesthetics subordinated to reason. An illusory reconciliation occurred between the senses and reason, depriving aesthetics of its radical potential.

Eagleton emphasizes the contradictoriness inherent in the category of the aesthetic. He is fully aware that the autonomous character of aesthetics creates a tendency in modern subjects to separate themselves from the social world: aesthetic autonomy fosters the myth of self-referentiality. Eagleton, however, recognizes that the idea of humanity's self-determining nature also positions the liberatory, radical, and utopian character of the aesthetic as the natural enemy of instrumental reason. If, on the one hand, the aesthetic engenders totalistic beliefs in all-powerful creation and omnipotent domination (as in the realm of art, one could add), on the other hand, by drawing on sensuousness, it also produces creative energies that defy utilitarian ends. Marx's formulation of a materialistic aesthetic can be seen, according to Eagleton, as an attempt to define this second possibility through a theoretical revolution that places the body at the center of all knowledge.

For Marx, sense perception "in the dual form of *sensuous* consciousness and *sensuous* need" represents "the constitutive structure of human practice" and is not mere contemplation.[18] As he writes in the *Economic and Philosophical Manuscripts*: "*Sense perception* must be the basis of all science. . . . The whole of history is a preparation, a development, for '*man*' to become the object of *sensuous* consciousness and for the needs of 'man as man' to become (sensuous) needs."[19]

Marx's project, says Eagleton, is a rethinking of history and society "from the body upwards,"[20] an attempt to construct a science on the basis of the body. Marx believes that humans' goal in life is happiness, not truth. Therefore, he involves himself in establishing the social relations within which happiness can be achieved.[21] Marx's critique of capitalism fits within this search for the causes of an unfulfilled humanity. Under capitalism, he warns, sensory life is being plundered and split into two opposite directions: necessity and narcissism. In the first instance, exemplified by workers, concerns with urgent, basic needs lead individuals to overlook objects' sensuous qualities. In the case of narcissism, in contrast, the social "parasite" is completely self-absorbed, focused entirely on his/her own whims and inflated appetites. Hence, Marx pleads, only a historical transformation can both restore the power of the senses destroyed under capitalist conditions and retrieve human community. Communism responds to this quest by eliminating private property:

> The supersession of private property is therefore the complete *emancipation* of all human senses and attributes; but it is this emancipation because these senses and attributes have become *human*, subjectively as well as objectively. . . . The senses . . . relate to the thing for its own sake, but the thing itself is an *objective human* relation to itself and to man, and vice-versa. Need or enjoyment have therefore lost their *egoistic* nature, and nature has lost its mere *utility* in the sense that its use has become *human* use.[22]

For Marx, sensory emancipation, achieved within specific material conditions, grants the fulfillment of human nature, and human freedom can only be achieved by realizing the senses.[23] Marx maintains that human societies are ends in themselves, divorced from utilitarian purposes. But he argues that the utility of objects renders them pleasurable: what they signify to us makes them close to our senses. Through the concept of use-value, Marx reunites the sensuous and the rational and overcomes the opposition between the practical and the aesthetic. He thus avoids the extremes of what Eagleton calls both "the crude instrumentalism of exchange-value" and "disinterested aesthetic speculation."[24] In the end, Marx's conception of aesthetics as inscribed in the body seems to suggest that social emancipation has to occur before the aesthetic can be realized. The intertwining of aesthetics with politics ensures the radical movement toward the fulfillment of humanity. Human happiness can be achieved only by redefining hedonism as more than mere individual gratification. The senses, says Marx, liberate, but they also concur to establish social relations via the laboring body.[25]

Fascism's critique of materialism and the senses clearly ignores Marx's premises, or at least distorts them to the point that the fascist idea of revolution is totally disconnected from Marxist materialism. Augusto Del Noce suggests that, following early-twentieth-century revolutionary socialism's idealist critique of materialism, Mussolini and the fascist movement overlooked Marx's real position or interpreted it as a contradictory implosion of revolutionary spirit and material human needs.[26] For fascism, these two terms could not coexist. And, unlike Marx, Mussolini thought of revolution not as a class struggle but as a war between nations. The question can be raised whether fascism was simply overlooking Marx's view of materialism or, rather, purposefully discounting it. After all, as Del Noce argues, once it is separated from the social expression of human needs, the idea of revolution becomes irrational; in the case of Mussolini, it gave way to a sort of activism that rejected any end and promoted solipsism. Within this perspective, the will to power becomes the only moral imperative: "I" am the "subject" and must dominate a world that has been reduced to things. Once the "masses" were identified with things, could Mussolini's solipsistic attitude conceive of an emancipation of the "masses"? And was not his denial of the body a sine qua non of his attitude toward the people and their role in politics? Mussolini's attack on materialism in effect paralleled his belief that the "masses'" lack of civilization was a consequence of their privileging of the senses. If civilization meant the repression of physical instincts and the application of norms and rules governing the body, the "masses'" crass vulgarity and their preference for matter over soul and spirit constituted a threat to order.[27] Expressing a sentiment shared by some of Europe's most prestigious cultural representatives, including Nietzsche, Ibsen, Flaubert, and Hamsun, Mussolini could cite the "masses'" material desires and pursuit of primary needs as giving way to an era of barbarism in which ideal, spiritual values were endangered.[28] The "masses'" physicality epitomized their inability to raise themselves from the state of animals: their lustful desires and material instincts testified to their inability to attain civilizational restraints. Their corrupt status canceled out their political rights.

By subscribing to a theory of aesthetics not as bodily senses but as pure form, Mussolini appropriated for himself the role of artist-politician who could give shape to unruly crowds and objectify them while satiating and sedating their chaotic desires. By citing the "masses'" unfitness to reach aesthetic purity—the disinterested sphere of art—fascism aestheticized politics through the establishment of a hierarchical order and the installation of a mythical *dux*. The invocation of spiritual values that transcended the uncivilized status of the "masses" deprived them of their human and political personality. The imaginary and the illusionary substituted for experience. Preoccupation with personal needs was displaced by the alluring representation of a national community destined to bring a brighter future. In sum, the regime's pretense to a spiritualized world was envisaged as a symbolic cage for the repression of more mundane demands. Within this framework, the body became the contested site, an "objective" and "objectified" reason for denying political access to citizens and initiating a regime of disciplined control.

MATERIAL/CONSUMPTION

Fascism's negation of individual happiness and autonomous goals rested upon a sacrificial notion of the polity's immolation on the altars of national glory. Fascism could not tolerate the existence of personal aspirations, the possibility of choosing. The suppression of private desires was necessary to eliminate individual initiatives and conflicting demands. Hence, fascism's attack on the senses led to the totalitarian intrusion into the personal, private sphere—a space that through incessant regulation became politicized at the same moment that it was in principle denied.

In reality, however, the suppression of the senses and the taming of the "masses" was not an easily accomplished task for the regime, especially at a time when a developing consumer culture was beginning to establish itself in many Western countries. Indeed, Mussolini feared consumption's potentially disruptive effects. The multiplication of desires and temptations, as the necessary result of an enlarged spectrum of options, would threaten to reintroduce individualistic principles into a society that was being organized around totalitarian premises. In contrast to social critics who viewed the suppression of individuality and the coming of a "one-dimensional" world as the most negative consequences of mass propaganda and consumerism, the Italian fascists questioned consumption from the perspective of its emancipatory force (although they were also afraid of the leveling effects of mass production). The aesthetic being a "contradictory, double-edged concept," as Eagleton argues,[29] fascism dreaded consumption's appeal to the senses and its potential to provoke a revolt against power.[30] In this fear, however, fascism was not alone. Its worries about consumption and modernity reflected the terms of a moral controversy that took place in many European countries and the United States at the turn of the twentieth century around the question of mass consumption.

Although the development of a consumer public interested in commodities is sometimes situated as far back as the fifteenth century, with the rise of a global trade network,[31] the preoccupation with consumer culture's effects on society became intense at the fin de siècle. It was only then that the growing production of goods gave wide strata of the population access to items previously obtainable only by the upper class. The mass availability of once unreachable products seemed to be encouraging more and more people to possess certain objects in order to achieve a higher social status. The emphasis on luxury, seen as a result of the imitation of superior models, caused economists, social scientists, and philosophers to worry about the consequences on civilization of the democratic revolution.[32] In France, the morality of the desire to consume became an important topic of discussion. The proliferation of unlimited wants solicited an answer to the basic question: "How could the modern economic imperative to multiply needs be reconciled with the moral tradition inherited from Christian and non-Christian antiquity, which counseled self-discipline and restraint of desire?"[33] Economic rationale seemed to dictate that a consumption system was necessary, but consumption appeared to many to be undermining the morality of society. Which should one renounce, morality or progress? And were the two actually incompatible? The debate also addressed the problem of the future of civilization if progress were stopped and the issue of social justice. On the one hand, it was argued, inequality motivates people to work hard in order to attain what others possess, and in this process progress is enhanced. On the other hand, equality establishes social harmony, which grants well-being. Others claimed that consumerism would not necessarily bring inequality.[34] In the end, however, the quest to find happiness through material possessions seemed to many an enslavement of the spirit, a moral degradation. Thus, whether individual consumption was directed toward the acquisition of social status or the achievement of personal self-fulfillment, its deleterious consequences came under attack.[35] Émile Durkheim, for example, wrote that consumption fed "a fevered imagination," which would bring the individual to anomic behavior.[36] For Durkheim, society was possible only if people sacrificed themselves and established social bonds through communal rituals, so he proposed to restrict consumption in order to prevent an objectified and materialistic life. This detachment from the mundane and "profane" world, through what was considered a limited form of asceticism, would allow the individual to enter the sacred—that is, the social. In this process, every person would end up acknowledging society's authority, with rituals sanctifying this recognition.[37]

In Wilhelmine Germany, an ambivalent reaction to consumerism also took place in discussions about luxury's impact on middle- and working-class people and about how to manage the changes brought about by modernity.[38] Between 1900 and 1914 several articles and books of both academic and popular circulation debated the question of whether luxury was harmful or beneficial.[39] Continuing a century-old attack on luxury, which was then limited to the aristocracy, critics of conspicuous consumption targeted all classes who seemingly spent beyond their means. Instead of advocating the widespread banning of luxury, however, these critics set forth a productivist ethos as a way to control spending. "Managing" luxury was the response to a feared loss of vitality and decay among the middle class, whereas the working classes' inclination to emulation was denounced as a possible source of class hatred and social disruption. This eventuality appeared all the more unsettling because the increasingly specialized nature of labor was believed to exacerbate social fragmentation. Educating consumers to discipline their desires offered a viable answer: ethical self-restraint would balance the pleasures of consumption.

In the United States, Robert and Helen Lynd's comparative study of Middletown dramatized the elites' response to the moral conflicts raised by the emerging consumer culture. In *Middletown: A Study in Modern American Culture,* the Lynds presented a striking portrayal of the transformations that Muncie, Indiana, had experienced between the 1890s and the 1920s. In particular, they lamented the loss of genuine social relations and the decline of job satisfaction that seemed to characterize Muncie's transition from the nineteenth century to the twentieth. Alienation and passivity now defined people's lives and their everyday world. Casual relations and deteriorating social values substituted for inclusive participation and deeper human understanding. Within this context, the Lynds were especially concerned with the role of mass leisure activities in the new reality. They concluded that movies, radio, advertising, and the credit system created novel forms of "social illiteracy" that atomized individuals and made them pursue merely subjective needs.[40] Commercial culture circulated an image of money as the solution to people's problems and promoted irrational expenditure. Mass culture, the Lynds estimated, was detrimental to a dignified life and authentic pleasures. Overwhelmed by what they believed was the power of the new leisure ethic, the Lynds advocated limiting the deleterious implications of consumption.[41] In effect, facing the popular classes' need for diversion and compensatory recreation, the Lynds and other 1920s progressive reformers, critics, and ministers advocated a "managerial" approach to mass culture.[42] Managerial liberals resorted to social control in order to channel appetites and wants excited by mass leisure culture.[43]

The disbelief in the possibility of stopping industrial development and halting a fast-growing consumer culture had pushed France, Wilhelmine Germany, and the United States to propose plans for disciplining and managing what could not be eliminated. A politics of control, as theorized by Foucault, became the normal and normalizing means of governing the social in an era of eroding traditions. In fascist Italy, the regime's response to the question of consumption and morality also entailed the restriction of materialistic orientations and emphasized the social over the individual. However, the regime faced conflictual internal demands vis-à-vis the economic issue of mass culture, conflicts that threatened to challenge the existence of the regime itself, its status, nature, and raison d'être. On the one hand, the regime intended to uphold the sacrality of society as dictated by its totalitarian view, which required the suppression of individual stances.

On the other hand, it realized that if it wanted to compete in the international arena, it needed to preserve individual initiative in many fields, especially industry and commerce. Thus, because the regime firmly rested on a capitalist production system, Mussolini needed to circumvent the contradiction of attacking the bourgeoisie on moral grounds while cultivating it as an economic asset. He needed to reconcile the divergent programs of assailing consumption and spurring a market economy. The regime adopted contradictory strategies to answer a challenge that seemed difficult to transcend. One such measure was corporativism, which, through a policy encapsulating the relations between capital and labor, was supposed to contain the denounced materialistic conception of life typical of a modernized society. The regime's corporativism—or, better, its discourse on corporativism—exuded spiritualism through the pores of an industrialized production. It focused on national well-being while displacing consumption. With corporativism, fascism mimetically fought against the denied body's reincarnation, the reincorporation of desire.

MIMETIC ECONOMY

At the end of World War I, currents of revolutionary syndicalism and nationalism converged to elaborate an idea of "national syndicalism" based on the solidarity of all productive classes, from workers to managers to entrepreneurs.[44] Theorists and practitioners of this new form of syndicalism vowed not to renounce proletarian struggle; nevertheless, they believed it was in the interest of the working class to achieve emancipation within a politically and economically strong nation. The "revolutionary event" of the war had shown the importance of capitalists and the capitalist system in upholding the strength and power of a country. If, as the syndicalists believed, the value of the nation overshadowed any other value, then opposing sides in labor disputes should strive toward reconciling their conflicts when these might negatively affect national interests. In contrast to the socialists, who had protested the world conflict in the name of proletarian internationalism, the syndicalists proclaimed their loyalty to the fatherland. In June 1918, as an alternative to the socialist organizations of workers, they founded their own confederation, the Unione Italiana del Lavoro (UIL).

In 1919, when he founded the Fasci Italiani di Combattimento, Mussolini supported UIL, as he had previously done from the columns of *Il Popolo d'Italia*. During the following two years, the relations between the fascists and UIL underwent several problems: some syndicalist leaders refused to align with Mussolini's movement and thus lose autonomy, and the fascists took an increasingly antiworker position.[45] But when on January 1922 fascists and syndicalists promoted the National Confederation of Syndicate Corporations under the auspices of the newly formed Fascist Party, the organization inherited much of the originary impulse at the basis of national syndicalism.[46] Edmondo Rossoni, previously the head of UIL and an opponent of syndicalism's politicization, came to be elected general secretary of the new confederation. Still vowing antisocialism and anti-Catholicism, the organization included five national corporations upon which all provincial sections depended. As in the original formula of the revolutionary syndicalists, the corporations were supposed to bring together all professional activities that identified their own "moral and economic elevation . . . with the indispensable duty of the citizen towards the Nation."[47] Thus, Article 4 of the corporations' principles proclaimed: "The nation—considered a superior synthesis of all material and spiritual values of the race—is above individuals, groups and classes. Individuals, groups and classes are instruments, made use of by the nation to gain a better position. The interests of individuals and of groups acquire legitimacy on condition that they are maintained within the frame of the superior national interests."[48] The corporations rejected class struggle and replaced it with collaboration between producers; labor conflicts needed to be overcome through cooperation. The national solidarity thus established would further the primary goal of the development of production and benefit the whole country, the fatherland. Hence, at the first congress of the National Confederation of Syndicate Corporations, in June 1922, Mussolini affirmed that the fascist syndicates would not replace the socialist workers' organizations.[49] They would not foster hatred and promote conflict, because the resolution of workers' struggles guaranteed the grandeur of the nation through social order, class collaboration, and maximum productivity.[50] National syndicates would still sponsor workers' claims but would do so within the limits set by the primary pursuit of the nation's successful growth.

Between 1922 and 1926, during Mussolini's ascent to power and the regime's totalitarian turn, fascist syndicalism evolved.[51] Through a series of violent acts, laws, pacts, and decrees, it preempted the existence of other syndicates—via the elimination of socialist labor organizations and the marginalization of Catholic ones—and became the exclusive representative of workers. At the same time, relations between the National Confederation of Fascist Syndicates and the Fascist Party became tighter, and Mussolini's government continued a policy that overwhelmingly favored the interests of the industrial classes over those of workers. An important event in this transitional phase was the Pact of Palazzo Vidoni of October 2, 1925, in which delegates of the General Confederation of Industry and of the National Confederation of Fascist Syndicates recognized each other as the only official representatives of, respectively, the industrialists' and the workers' interests.[52] The syndical law of April 3, 1926 (Law Number 563), drafted under the direction of Minister of Justice Alfredo Rocco, legally authorized the fascist syndicates' monopoly over worker representation. The law ruled that only one association of workers and one of employers would be recognized for each branch of production (and such recognition was only extended to fascist organizations), and these associations would be supervised and controlled by the state.[53] The law also eliminated the right to strikes and lockouts, and it instituted labor courts as a system of arbitration in case the involved parties failed to reach agreement. Furthermore, the statute proposed the future creation of provincial corporations that would connect employers, workers, and experts involved in the same field of production.[54] The idea of a fascist corporative system began to take shape.[55] On July 2, 1926, a royal decree established the Ministry of Corporations, charged with overseeing syndicate activity and corporate organizations. On April 21, 1927, the Labor Charter consecrated the main principles upon which the system of corporations was supposed to build. The charter emphasized class collaboration and the preeminence of private initiative over state intervention in the economy,[56] and it reaffirmed the value of the nation and the role of the state as the ultimate guardian of the nation's interests.

In 1928, after the May congress of the National Confederation of Fascist Syndicates, the opinion circulated among fascist elites that the antipathy between opposed class interests, against which national syndicalists supposedly fought, had yet to be overcome in the new regime.[57] Rossoni's syndicates, as the General Confederation of Industry claimed, had not been able to "educate the masses."[58] Within this context, and because of the internal politics of the Fascist Party, which resented Rossoni's autonomous role in the syndicates, and the residual hostility of the labor providers toward workers' organizations, the National Confederation of Fascist Syndicates was dismantled on November 1928. It was fragmented into six associations corresponding to the different branches of production.[59] The original unity of the syndicalist movement definitively collapsed along with what little was left of the principle of class solidarity. In the following years, the corporative structure of the regime continued to grow through a series of laws that contributed to its bureaucratic building and extended corporativism's control from labor relations to economic relations. In 1930 the National Council of Corporations was constituted within the Ministry of Corporations and assigned primarily consulting functions. In 1934 twenty-two corporations were created for agriculture, industry, commerce, and service.[60] Not until 1939, however, one year before Italy's intervention in World War II, did the Chamber of Corporations replace the Chamber of Deputies.

In effect, the corporative system, which the regime seemingly took great pains to organize and plan, never had a real chance to unfold and succeed. Ideally, the corporations were supposed to function as "organs of self-government for issues relating to the specific category as well as the basis for participation with other corporatively organized interests in policy decisions affecting the whole society."[61] However, the centralized and authoritarian system of the regime greatly hampered the production units' ability to govern themselves.[62] The internal composition of the corporations contributed to the elimination of this role. Membership was most often founded on political and clientelistic principles. Workers, in particular, ended up having as spokespersons professors, lawyers, journalists, and other supposedly "technical" people who were unmotivated or unqualified to defend the interests of those they represented. The clash of interests corporativism intended to resolve turned out to be an insurmountable obstacle. Political contrasts underlay the various, apparently coextensive theories of corporativism and resulted in a stalling of substantial transformations. Trends typical of a traditional market economy, rather than any corporative principle, characterized the fascist state's intervention in economic management. Private industries and oligarchies flourished, and the interests of entrepreneurs were favored over those of workers.[63] The corporations ensured class collaboration by annexing to the state all social and political groups that might oppose the fascist organization. Corporative institutions managed to suppress an independent labor movement even while being stripped of their own authority.[64] From the point of view of economic policy, then, the corporations played a very limited, almost decorative, role. The National Council of Corporations mostly discussed matters that had already been decided. By January 1937 the council no longer met.[65]

Though a failed system in its practical applications, corporativism was invoked and exalted in fascist discourse and played an immense role in fascism's self-representation and definition. In a May 1925 article published in *Gerarchia*, Mussolini hailed corporativism as one of the "novelties" of the fascist revolution.[66] On March 11, 1926, he described the newly approved law on the juridical discipline of collective labor relations as "the most courageous, the most audacious, the most innovative, thus the most revolutionary" of laws.[67] On May 7, 1928, on the occasion of the third congress of the National Confederation of Fascist Syndicates, Mussolini forecast the twentieth century as the century in which the corporative economy would substitute for the previous century's capitalist economy.[68] And when the National Council of Corporations was inaugurated on April 22, 1930, Mussolini defined it in his speech as the "thinking brain that prepares and coordinates" the Italian economy.[69] Despite all the contradictions crippling its development, the corporative system produced its own theorists and supporters, economic theorems and philosophical reflections.[70] References to what was defined as a novel approach to political economy abounded in fascism and helped delineate and communicate the principles and ideals to which the regime subscribed. In particular, via the semantics of corporativism, the regime constructed a symbolic representation of the fascist individual, the relations between spiritualism and capitalism, the role of the state and totalitarianism, and the function of discipline. Corporativism ultimately gave fascism yet another opportunity to reformulate the "political" and to redraw the boundaries of the public sphere in the new reality the regime promoted and built. Organic metaphors of economic unity reiterated aesthetic ideals of order.

Fascism's idea of corporativism rose as a phoenix from the ashes of national syndicalism's vision of labor relations—a vision that affirmed capitalism and the harmonic collaboration of classes as positive elements for the fulfillment of national interests. In accordance with such a vision, the fascists upheld the role of capitalism and private property within the new society they wanted to organize. Mussolini defined fascism as antisocialist by acknowledging the "historical function of capital and capitalism."[71] For Mussolini, modern capitalists did not fit the socialists' depiction of them as "vampires." Rather, he thought of them as captains of industry, organizers, men "with a very high sense of civil and economic responsibility."[72] Sketching a quasi-Weberian ideal-type of the ascetic Protestant capitalist, Mussolini argued that entrepreneurs did not merely pursue individual pleasure through their activities, for there is a definite biological limit to the capacity to enjoy one's cumulative fortune. True, Mussolini admitted, the capitalists worked to their own advantage when conducting business, but in the process they also increased general production and benefited the whole community. One needed to consider the broader function of the accumulation of wealth in enhancing the power of the nation. And because, for fascism, the nation "as state is an ethical reality that exists and lives since it develops," the capitalist operated within moral ends and contributed to affirming the values of the spirit.[73] Therefore, when fascism accepted the principle of individual freedom, it did so on the premise that a spirit of initiative was necessary to reach the higher goal of progress.[74] Private property constituted an incentive to engaging entrepreneurs. Lest he be interpreted as a supporter of an economic conception of human existence, Mussolini stressed the more encompassing spiritual frame within which fascism's corporativism situated material wealth. In his formulation, corporativism allowed the overcoming of both liberalism's individualism and socialism's class struggle in a synthesis that purified capitalism of its crass material elements. Fascist corporatist theory reinterpreted capitalism and excised it of its material meaning. It turned the corporation into a moral force that guaranteed the reconciliation of interests between capital and labor and contributed to the production of fascism's spiritual reality.[75] Within this context, some even argued that corporativism marked the beginning of capitalism's end, if one considered capitalism's lack of ideals.[76] The term "capitalism" could be dropped *tout court.*

The spiritualization of capitalism promoted by fascist corporative discourse accompanied the regime's rhetorical effort to moralize economic activity and turn it into an ethical enterprise. This magical transformation occurred through a symbiotic rapprochement between fascism's conception of totalitarianism and its theory of corporations. In both these instances, the state appeared as the dominating component of human coexistence, the element that ensured social unity and, therefore, morality. Thus, fascist theorist Sergio Panunzio, in his 1940 discussion of fascist syndicalism and corporativism, focused on the link between a statist doctrine and ethics.[77] Panunzio resorted to the Latin principle *member sumus corporis magni* to describe the process through which parts return to the whole and submit to it. For Panunzio, all individuals and social organisms, including the syndicates, undergo this process, because parts instinctively tend to rejoin the whole. Members of the social body develop a sentiment of unity because of an awareness of their own insufficiency, their inability to stand alone. Panunzio called this sense of unity "sentiment of the state" and made of it the essence of both fascist syndicalism and corporativism. More than a mere cooperation of classes, corporativism, Panunzio argued, should be understood as the subordination of different categories to the unity of the social body. Corporativism led to national solidarity by teaching people to overcome individual egoism and to develop a "sentiment of the state." The state, continued Panunzio, is point both of departure and of arrival for fascist corporations. Corporations only exist in order to realize the state; therefore, it would be a mistake to talk about them in economic terms. Economics is a liberal science, a science of *homo economicus*, the selfish person. Corporations, however, do not treat humans as egoistic beings. Rather, they represent "the social march and progressive socialization of the I."[78] Corporations foster the individual's identification with and embracement of the state. As such they belong not to economy but to morality.

In a similar flourish of mistaken identity and recognition, another fascist theorist, Carlo Costamagna, warned about the use of the term "corporativism" because of its strong economic connotations.[79] For Costamagna, the use of the formula "corporative state" in reference to fascism diminished and distorted the quintessentially political, and therefore ethical, value of the fascist experiment.[80] Thus, one must refer to the "fascist state," lest there be an excessive and improper emphasis on economic renovation. Costamagna also argued that even when focusing specifically on the economic aspects of the regime, one should not lose sight of the totalitarian essence of fascism. This essence posited the state as a superior moral entity and overcame economistic approaches to the issue of the common good. The state, according to Costamagna, represented the good and transcended all particular interests. The interest of the state was the only interest fascism pursued. Within the context of Costamagna's and Panunzio's discussions, the state transfigured the economic dimensions of the everyday and divorced them of their materiality. The economy imitated the ethical state, mimetically hiding and disappearing within it.

The spiritualization of the economy occurring in fascist discourse allowed the regime both to reaffirm the hierarchical principles and values through which it strove to define itself and to negotiate at an abstract level the contradictory meanings that plagued the regime's identity. Discursive representations of the corporative system reproduced the model of the harmonious whole typical of fascism's totalitarian vision of society. They also depicted corporativism as a subordinate part of the totalitarian state to whose unity it contributed. Supporters of corporativism, although expressing quite diversified positions, reconfirmed the preeminence of the state in fascism and postulated duty as an ethical value of the individual who sacrifices her/himself for the common good. The individual's rights, as Alfredo Rocco argued, only reflected the rights of the disciplining and controlling state.[81] Although the regime encouraged individual initiative in the economic field, corporativism, in Ugo Spirito's words, denied "private activity by recognizing to each individual a public value and function."[82] Fantastic semiphilosophical twists and turns reconciled the irreconcilable in fascism's attempt to build a coherent doctrine that would eliminate the public sphere as the space for free expression. In this process, the regime subjected the terms "private" and "public," "material" and "spiritual," and "economic" and "political" to multiple processes of signification that transcended their common meanings and gave birth to new semantic objects with novel political implications. Fascism's spiritualized reconfiguration of the economy made plausible the proposition that parliament became a merely economic body and only represented producers through the substitution of the Chamber of Deputies with the Chamber of Corporations.[83] Normally a highly politicized field and a site of struggle, the economy was artificially reduced by fascist syndicalism and corporativism to a supposedly disciplined and responsible consideration of the nation's interests. As such the economy became in the regime the symbolic representation of a much-sought-after depoliticized polity—a polity to whom only symbolic forms of participation were made available and whom symbolic forms were ultimately and conveniently supposed to repoliticize. The triumph of the economy took place through a reaffirmation of politics by other means.

The field of economic discourse remained a critical ground of political semantics during the regime, a rehearsal stage for doctrinal stances and principled postures, even when they were embedded in a riddle of contradictions. Thus, as unaccomplished as the corporative system was, claims to a fascist economic "third way" sprouted in the regime's rhetoric. These claims came full circle when capitalism, originally exalted and dematerialized, was put under fire as an expired institution.[84] Hence, on July 7, 1933, *Il Popolo d'Italia* featured an article Mussolini had written for the "Universal Service."[85] In this article Mussolini posed the question he had already asked in his October 17, 1932, speech for the Decennial. Mentioning the crisis plaguing Western economies, Mussolini on that occasion stated theatrically: "Either this is a cyclical crisis *in* the system and will be resolved; or it is a crisis *of* the system. Then we are at the passage from one epoch of civilization to another."[86] On November 14, 1933, Mussolini answered the question in a speech to the National Council of Corporations.[87] He declared the crisis a "constitutional disease," wherein the mode of capitalist production had reached its limits. In a quasi-scientific manner, Mussolini sketched a three-stage history of capitalism: 1) dynamic or heroic capitalism (1830–1870); 2) static capitalism (1870–1914); 3) decadent capitalism or supercapitalism (1914–). Identifying capitalism with industrialism, Mussolini argued that Italy could be considered capitalistic if one referred to its technical progress. Statistically, however, the Italian economy was mixed because of the strong presence of agriculture. He then concluded that in the "current sense of the word" (the third stage, decadent capitalism), Italy was not a capitalist nation because of its agricultural production. Complicating the meaning of capitalism further, Mussolini warned about confusing capitalism, as a mode of production, with bourgeois, as a mode of being that could be either "heroic or philistine."[88] While praising the bourgeoisie as representative of heroic capitalism, Mussolini ultimately condemned decadent capitalism—a "mode of mass production for mass consumption, financed massively through anonymous national and international capital."[89]

By denouncing supercapitalism, Mussolini and the regime did not renounce industrial advances and technical achievements, which according to them Italy had reached. They attacked instead what they claimed were the aberrations of capitalism, its extreme pathological manifestations, its large enterprises, its "utopia of unlimited consumption."[90] Mussolini charged that supercapitalism "would want that all people be born the same height, so that it is possible to make standardized cradles; it would want that all children desire the same toys, that people dress in the same uniform, that all read the same book, that all had the same taste at the cinema."[91] Echoing the moral concern of the turn of the century, Mussolini indicted the "standardization of humankind" produced by supercapitalism.[92] In this process, Mussolini did more than reject the idea of planned mass production. He also attacked (super)capitalism as consumption. In all the rhetoric surrounding corporativism, the fascists had ignored the issue of consumption and concentrated instead on the advantages of production when conducted within the limits of restrained private enterprise. Fascism's attempt to spiritualize the economy made possible and justified the regime's support for capitalist production, captains of industries, modern entrepreneurs. And Mussolini never rescinded his support for private property as long as "it does not confine itself to enjoying wealth, but develops it, increases it, multiplies it."[93] Within this context, Mussolini's polemic against supercapitalism maintained the relevance of heroic capitalism. From the point of view of consumption, however, was there a difference between heroic and decadent capitalism? Could people consume without relying on individual desires and fostering private pleasures? Could consumption ever be redeemed?[94]

Here the Gordian knot of fascism's approach to capitalism reemerges. Mussolini's regime pursued a totalitarian model of obedience and uniformity that needed to arise in the presence of spiritual ideals and respect for hierarchies. Whereas corporative discourse sheltered production under this mantle, consumption hardly fit spiritual aims unless one consumed for the well-being of the nation or limited consumption through self-discipline and sacrifice. In reality, because of the global depression beginning in 1929, the availability of distributive resources to Italians was quite limited in the 1930s. In 1934 wages were reduced by 17 percent compared to 1928, for example, and in 1932 the number of unemployed was over a million.[95] The economic situation certainly worsened following Italy's engagement on the military front in 1935 and the regime's almost simultaneous embracement of autarchy as a policy of economic self-sufficiency and independence.[96] Sacrifices did not constitute a moral or spiritual issue for Italians: they were a constraint. Nor did Mussolini believe the Italians' standard of living had reached new, dangerous, and tempting heights. Summarizing the economic situation in his speech to the Chamber of Deputies of May 26, 1934, Mussolini stated: "We are probably heading towards a time when equalized humanity will rest on a lower standard of living. We should not be alarmed. Such humanity can be very strong, capable of asceticisms and heroisms, such as we cannot even imagine at this moment."[97]

The disjunction between the reality of an ascetic present and future and Mussolini's fear of individual pleasures in a supercapitalist stage suggests that Mussolini's denunciation of consumption was directed not so much against everyone's desiring the same thing but rather, and more radically, against the very act of desiring, which he feared as a politically destabilizing force. The critique of *homo economicus* that fascist corporativism conducted appears here as an unconditional critique of the consumer. In the same speech in which he condemned supercapitalism's standardization, Mussolini recommended three conditions for the success of integral corporativism:

> One only party, so that next to economic discipline also political discipline will act, and above contrasting interests there will be a link that unites all in a common faith.
>
> This is not sufficient. We need, after the one party system, the totalitarian State, that is the State that will absorb, in order to transform and strengthen it, all the energy, all the interests, all the hope of one people.
>
> This is not yet sufficient. Third and last and most important condition: we need to live a time of very high ideal tension.[98]

Mussolini stressed the political elements supporting corporativism's success: one party, totalitarian state, and ideals. He did not include the liquidation of capitalism, from which fascism, he claimed, would inherit vital elements.[99] Indeed, Mussolini glorified the bourgeoisie (whose philistinism Starace attacked in those same years) for its heroic role as producer. Corporativism hailed the function of the bourgeoisie in the new economic mode. The bourgeoisie as producer embodied fascism's *homo corporativus.* One could argue, as a matter of fact, that corporativism envisaged the total disappearance of the consumer. The consumer was directly devoured by the state.[100] An anonymous contributor to the review *Riforma Sociale* lamented in an article on corporativism in March–April 1934:

> What organization . . . will represent the point of view of the consumer? Will there not be a danger that the corporation, inevitably emanating from

the productive classes, workers and traders, will be inclined to shift the center of gravity of the economic world, which has hitherto hinged upon the needs of the consumer, to the interests of the producer? Will it not, little by little, try to discipline, regulate, and control in its own interests the will of the consumer?[101]

In principle, if not in practice, corporativism responded to the threat of "hedonistic" tendencies by eliminating the consumer as a political actor. The contradiction between capitalism and consumption impinging upon fascism's totalitarian identity was overcome through the obliteration of consumption *tout court.*

On a daily basis, however, the Italian people, and in particular the middle classes of urban areas, were pursuing pleasures connected to other cultural and meaningful expressions, not necessarily material consumption. Taking a walk or "just looking" at shop windows could still fever the imagination.[102] Films, and the new Hollywood myths, allowed leaps of fantasy that were hard to discipline, spectacles that constituted counter-altars to spectacular politics. With its totalitarian logic, the fascist regime recognized the unreachable roots of desire and took them as a challenge to its own government of the social. Not being able to eradicate the principle of desire, the regime consistently offered representational solutions in a time of competing representations. Fascism became the target of consumption.

SPECTACLE AND DESIRE

The turn-of-the-century moral preoccupation with consumption rested upon the principle that it was not so much the possession or acquisition of objects that threatened civilization as the desires driving people's dreams. Moralists and politicians in France and the United States worried about the relation between fantasy and social duty, the consequences of a commercial culture that stimulated the imagination. In their eyes amusement parks such as Coney Island, urban cabarets, and jazz clubs cast the same negative spell as did department stores, attracting people through sensory appeals and emotional solicitations.[103] Popular entertainments were attacked for causing the surrender of reason through amusements, the lowering of aesthetic taste, the prevalence of the senses over spirit, self-abandonment, and the release of passion. Critics, reformers, educators, and ministers in the United States indicted mass culture as disruptive of social order. They also maintained that leisure must be edifying and not encourage mere idleness. The "animal" character of human passions could only be overcome through a refined culture that domesticated desires and impulses and publicized the realm of the ideal as the legitimate locus of a modern civilization.

Progressive and conservative reformers alike identified the senses as the pivotal center of their moralizing campaign, and rightly so. Within the context of an emerging consumer society, the senses were indeed the target of commercial entrepreneurs' efforts to lure customers, the basis on which advertisers built their campaigns. Amusement parks, dance halls, and circus shows offered a wide array of sensory attractions that provided aural, visual, and tactile stimuli.[104] In the same way, department stores focused on display as a strategy for exciting people's desires.[105] Visual images in particular constituted the vehicle through which representations, in the vignettelike depiction of familiar and exotic places, domestic and public scenes, mixed reality with fantasy and expanded onlookers' range of wants.[106] The cultivation of desire of objects guided displays at Macy's and Wanamaker's. Commodities were theatrically transformed and magically reinterpreted at Arnold Constable's and Ford and Taylor's. Old goods were given new life as sources of healing and fulfillment in the new shopping centers' enchanting environments. To be sure, the ultimate goal of the strategists of display tended toward increasing sales. But the means they chose contributed to creating new dispositions and behaviors, new private worlds that impinged upon individual identities and affected social roles. The panorama of merchandise circulating within a newly opened public space traversed bodies and excited desires.

According to William Leach, "desire" became part of American discourse in the 1880s, and merchandising techniques formed around it.[107] At this time, because the growth of commodities outpaced people's needs, commercial entrepreneurs increasingly focused on fostering desires and expanding wants in order to enhance the circulation of goods. The use of colors, glass, and light, which Protestant culture had perceived as intrinsically demonic and leading to dangerous appetites, spread widely in commercial displays, initiating a new style of aesthetic representation.[108] Densely visual effects also gained from the revolutionary introduction of artificial light, which made possible stunning nocturnal effects. Originally applied to the whole domain of popular entertainment and consumption, these new techniques were overwhelmingly adopted by 1920 thanks to prosperous times and exploited to the fullest with the help of trained artists and architects. Department stores became aesthetic centers, the fulcrum of a new art, the art of "display."[109] "Desire" and "display" led a parallel existence in the fantastic world created by the producers of aestheticized commodities. Frank Baum, author of *The Wizard of Oz*, believed that an appropriate display of goods would liberate repressed desires and spur a dream life. Baum, who among other things founded *Show Window,* the first magazine on display, encouraged sensual satisfaction.[110] Decorators invested commodities with meanings that went beyond their immediate use or material purpose.[111] A consuming vision gave birth to cultural representations revolving around commodities.[112]

The increasing circulation of goods was driven by displays and desires, fantasies and dreams, images and imagination. Through festivals of color and light, the sale of images became the dominant mode of a new commercial, urban culture comprising department stores, museums, factories, art schools, and motion pictures.[113] This culture found its ideal outlet in movies, where images played at the same time the roles of protagonist, medium, and object of desires and dreams. At its inception, the film industry attracted the kind of criticisms that the "democratization of luxury" had raised with regard to "material" consumption.[114] In the United States, the overture of commercial culture to the previously marginalized publics of working-class people and women provoked worried reactions about movies' appeals to passions and emotions.[115] The unbridling of irrational impulses was always feared when the female gender, laborers, and youth were involved. The resurfacing of animal senses, it was believed, could only come from those in the lower stages of civilization. Thus, middle-class reformers decried what happened on the screen at the same time that they expressed concerns about the consequences of the social mixing taking place in the theater. But they also believed that the power of the medium was tantalizing and threatening regardless of the viewer.[116] Within this context, some American critics proposed an ethics of control to neutralize the negative force of films.[117]

The cultural trends present in more industrialized countries similarly dominated the public realm of urban areas in fascist Italy. Its major cities each possessed a more or less upscale equivalent of a department store, whether it be La Rinascente, Standa, or Upim.[118] In them, new styles and ways of dressing were presented alongside models of behavior, beauty, and femininity. Despite the fact that the Italians' buying power was quite limited, especially in terms of "mass" potential, new commercial products were continuously poured onto the market. As De Grazia argues, although fascist "[p]ropaganda insisted on the sexual puritanism, economic frugality, and austere leisure habits usually associated with early industrialism . . . burgeoning consumer industries, often of foreign, especially American, provenance, publicized ready-made clothing, synthetic fibers, cosmetics, household items, and processed foods, as well as the commodified sexuality typical of a modern consumer economy."[119] Young girls avidly read the increasingly popular fan magazines and women's weeklies and relied upon advice columns to learn about socialization and sexual behavior. Their recreational activities included dancing and window shopping. And whether or not they could afford to adopt them, they followed fashion changes with interest and passion.[120] Images of consumption, indeed, circulated widely during the regime, thanks in part to one of the most accomplished new arts of fin de siècle, graphics and posters—forms of visual consumerism that developed in advance of the consumer economy.[121] The first publicity posters, enhanced by lithographic methods, were produced in Italy between 1884 and 1892.[122] Adopting a new language in the 1910s under the influence of futurism, publicity graphics evolved in the 1920s and 1930s, along with methods of circulation.[123] Under fascism, advertisements were introduced at railroad stations and posted on trains, streetcars, and steamships; newspapers increased their ad sections; publicity made its entry into movie theaters; neon signs began to light up. Material products, tourism, shows, and cultural events were graphically portrayed and lifted to the status of desirability.

As an image of consumption and a consuming vision, cinema also played a role in the modernization of Italian culture and customs. Developed in the early 1900s, the Italian cinema had been very successful up to the early 1920s and was able to export films to foreign markets, including the United States.[124] Spectacular devices and flamboyant use of natural scenes, especially in historical costume dramas, ensured the success of Italian movie production.[125] But other films, such as those of the Dora House in Naples, also contributed to the fame of Italian cinema. Hand-painted strips enhanced the magic of the films Elvira Notari directed, in which scenes were dominated by excess.[126] These works were inscribed in the geography of urban architecture, with its panoramic visions and spectacular spaces. They solicited the "lust of the eyes," be it via an anatomic journey through a corpse or a territorial observation of the city landscape.[127] Despite this positive beginning, however, the Italian cinema underwent a major crisis in the 1920s in terms of both quantity and quality. An invasion of Hollywood films began, and the American cinema ruled practically unchallenged during the first fifteen years of fascism's reign.

Mussolini did not adopt particular measures with regard to cinema until late in the 1930s, although his regime inherited laws and regulations on it established by the liberal government, which first had to face the reality and implications of this new cultural medium.[128] The censorship law of 1910 allowed the minister of interior to forbid films that were offensive to private morality and public decency; that endangered public order; that contained violent, cruel, or perverse scenes; and that offended authorities and public officials.[129] The fascist law of October 24, 1923, on the film industry followed these guidelines and reinforced them by adding a formal prohibition to the depiction of social conflict, suicide, or crime.[130] In general, however, the regime's repressive measures were not accompanied by a direct intervention in the production of films. Between 1920 and 1929 films produced in Italy declined to all-time lows of fewer than ten per year and slowly increased in the 1930s.[131] In contrast, between 1909 and 1919 one of the most important Italian film studios, Cines, alone had produced 1,525 films.[132]

Fascism was slow to discover the cinema as an instrument of political use despite the enormous success of the medium as a private pastime of Italians. Images from films dominated the graphic and publishing industry, with advertisements in posters, magazines, and newspaper stands.[133] Offering a new style of diversion, cinema exercised a strong attraction, especially on youth. In one of the most suggestive and telling accounts of the pivotal role cinema played in socialization at the turn of the century, Emilio Radius remembers spending hours in the movie halls "between blood-red posters" with "juvenile delinquents, female servants, soldiers, some retirees, little artisans."[134] The audience, Radius recounts, was plebeian because moviegoing was considered a vulgar habit.[135] In fact, a guard supervised movie halls, identified as forums of vice, and doctors warned about losing eyesight or developing headaches, palpitations, or even delirium tremens in this abundance of images. After World War I, cinema gained new dignity in Italy. American productions enjoyed high circulation, with an average of 70 percent of the films shown in the whole country. New, more artistic film theaters were built—films became displays within displays. The number of motion picture houses grew steadily in Italy between 1928 and 1937.[136] In 1930 there existed 3,225 theaters (including halls with projection facilities) in Italy, compared to 3,113 in France and 4,426 in Britain.[137] The petty bourgeoisie filled the ranks of the audience. Film criticism began to develop, along with the bourgeois appropriation of cinema as "art."

Between 1928 and 1933 moviegoing grossed half as much as all the other forms of entertainment combined, including theater, sports, and opera. In 1928, 370 million tickets were sold.[138] The commercial success of films increased steadily from 1937 to 1941, at a time when the beloved American films, because of several fascist measures, withdrew from the Italian market.[139] In a 1937 survey conducted by Maria Diaz Gasca, director of Rome's Service for Professional Orientation, young girls of the capital—daughters of petty bourgeois families—preferred dancing and singing to knitting and sewing, and half of them went to the moving pictures at least once a week.[140] All the frills characterizing the nascent "mass culture" also accompanied the rise of the motion picture industry: fan magazines, fashion fads, and stardom.[141] In 1926, touring Italy, Ludovic Naudeau experienced the phenomenon of mythical acclaim surrounding American actors and actresses. He described it with gusto within the frame of the Duce's own mythical persona:

> One evening, on the Corso, a gathering of crowd leads me to think that an extraordinary manifestation is going to take place. . . . The carabinieri are overcome despite all the reinforcements they receive every minute. . . . I expect the arrival of the Duce, when all of a sudden a formidable acclamation rises in between laughs and animal screams. Here they are! Here they are! Douglas Fairbanks and Mary Pickford solemnly get off a taxi. These two magnificent *mastuvus* eclipse the most famous *mastuvu* of politics. Wow! How beautiful they are! Wow! How nice they are! It is a triumph![142]

Cinematic images and commodity spectacles acquired increasing visibility during the regime. The circulation of iconographic representations seemed to outdo the actual availability of the products represented. Although contradictory signs and messages often characterized the development of publicity graphics under fascism, the world of display prospered during the regime.[143] In 1929 the review *Ufficio Moderno* began to dedicate one section to the study and research of issues connected to publicity and advertising. With the subtitle *La Pubblicità*, it valorized commercial graphic art. In 1933 the fourth International Congress of Publicity was held in Rome and Milan; schools and reviews of graphics originated during the 1920s and 1930s; and the cinema, both as an object and a medium of publicity, boomed technically and geographically.[144]

For a regime that opposed consumption not only in its material sense but also as a disease of the body—a site of desire—the high visibility of visual commodities is perplexing. Whether the regime ignored or simply tolerated the dangers deriving from new forms of modern culture, it was evidently aware that it could not eliminate consumption unless it also dispensed with industrialization and technology. Perhaps, as some claim, the regime manipulated the meanings of this new culture to its own benefit or reconciled and fused them with older values.[145] Nevertheless, in elaborating its modern identity the regime both opposed and drew upon commodity culture, with its intersection of display and desire, of the attraction of aesthetics and the aesthetics of attraction, of visual pleasure and the pleasure of vision. Indeed, whereas fascism's discourse of corporativism offered a representational countermeasure to decadent capitalism, the spectacle of fascist politics proposed a countermodel to the commercial spectacle and coexisted with consumption. But in the totalitarian politics of fascism, there was only one focus of desire, only one object of pleasure: the regime, anthropomorphically embodied in the public persona of the Duce, Mussolini. Living in a different constellation than film actors did, but still a star, Mussolini attracted interest and admiration; he projected aura and awe. And the regime seemed to count on the spectacular nature of his political trajectory in order to satisfy the consuming needs of the population. The image of Mussolini sold well, whether in postcards or soap bars or as a model of style. Records and radio diffused his words, the cinema propagated his icon, posters and calendars commemorated his deeds. Political publicity exalted the figure of Mussolini as the link between the people and the nation, the expression of fascist principles. The "gendered mass" was supposed to adhere to the regime and place authority in the hands of the state through its faith in Mussolini, the superior artist, the "man." People's feelings and emotions were channeled toward worshipping Mussolini. The Duce would then be able to capitalize on this love and turn the female mass into a virile army whose spiritual attributes overcame material predispositions. A loving body of admirers was only conceived as a depersonalized and desensitized integration of the body politic.

Spectacular politics was certainly not a fascist invention. In the modern era of production capitalism, visibility, in its many senses, is at the core of new modalities of political rule.[146] One might actually argue that modern visibility is genealogically connected to commerce. The first international exposition, held in 1851 at London's Crystal Palace, launched the display of trade, new technology, and produce as a medium of national expression, the staging of a nation's strength.[147] A monument to consumption via spectacular display, the Crystal Palace exhibit inaugurated a way of seeing things that defined the conditions for the representation of politics as commodity.[148] Politics was supposed to sell, evoke desires, and appeal to the pleasures of private, individual consumption. In addition to transforming ordinary objects into extraordinary things, the exhibit suggested that politics might benefit from a magnified portrayal that spurred the imagination. Politics could be advertised; and, in a game of reciprocity, advertisers thought they could only succeed if they sold ideologies along with objects.[149] The link between politics and consumer culture opened the way to what T. J. Jackson Lears calls "the merchandising of thrills": military adventures and expansionist designs.[150]

The political essence of the commodity form as a system of representation was captured by Mussolini in his revisitation and reinvention of a style of rule. From the exploitation of his own stardom in relation to the people to the visual colonization of public space pursued by the regime, Mussolini's fascism presented a spectacular form of politics that meant to supersede and displace all other representations of spectacle. Caught in the contradiction between economic rationales and cultural demands, the regime opted for an ambiguous coexistence with, and incorporation of, consumer culture—a coexistence it denied, however, at the level of rhetoric. Mussolini dominated the realm of politics through a strategy of display that replaced commercial commodities and was supposed to win over people's favor magically and ensure their participation.[151] Furthermore, the regime adopted measures intended to incorporate other forms of consumption spectacle within fascism's own discourse. Hence, the regime patronized tourism but redefined its goals through an emphasis on health or political history (young married couples were sponsored by the regime if they visited the capital). It presented alternatives to commercial pastimes through leisure organizations under the umbrella of the Organizzazione Nazionale Dopolavoro[152] and through the popularization of sports, again subsumed under the category of health benefits. The "fascist Saturday" introduced in 1935 occupied an entire afternoon every week: all citizens from age six onwards would participate in the fascist organizations' activities. The whole rhetoric of rurality proposed the countryside as the locus of a healthy, genuine, and traditional mentality that opposed the corrupting influence of modernity.[153] Within this context, folklore was invoked as the keeper of people's traditional culture.[154]

A plethora of competing discourses qualified and framed the inevitable presence in Italy of a consumer culture that the regime rejected in principle but felt forced to accept. For example, with reference to women—the officially recognized devil/victim of consumption in most Western countries—the regime's intervention took place at different levels. On the one hand, the fascists campaigned against the thin woman (*la donna crisi*); chastised daring fashion; and limited women's access to an independent life. On the other hand, new roles and duties were assigned to women as the pillars of the newly established totalitarian state. Female models of behavior were propagandized and somewhat enforced within the family.[155]

Through mimetism, displacement, and incorporation, the regime hoped to discount and outdo the inevitable damage caused by the clash between a totalitarian world outlook and the destabilizing, individualistic, and "democratic" tendencies of consumer culture. For fascism, individual desires needed to be public—that is, political. The retreat into privacy conflicted with the regime's vision of a permanent state of mobilization. Mussolini addressed citizens not as private individuals but rather as a mass, a whole. He aimed to incite a collective desire but could only attain this goal through an incursion into the private. The whole division of private/public was at stake in the regime's notion of politics; fascism exploded and reformulated this division in multiple combinations that tended to neutralize and reinvent both terms.[156] Within this vision, the family was a private institution, but its duties became politicized to serve the regime. Women were relegated to the private realm of family life, but they also were asked to support the regime in public rallies and organizations. Privacy was denied as a constituent of the bourgeois individual, but it was also used to deny access to political challenges. The private was, in sum, politicized under fascism, whereas issues of personal and social well-being were depoliticized. Extreme politicization, inextricably tied to a depoliticized orientation, confined individual voices and their claims within the discursive space delineated by the regime. Thus, fascism conducted its main battle for political exclusiveness by attacking the private in all its dimensions. Meanwhile, individuals and their bodies became the object of totalitarian rule. The aestheticization of politics reduced public citizens to the private property of the *dux*.

5 War and Melodrama

The spectacle of fascism exuded war and narratively prefigured the imperialistic outcome of the totalitarian state's aims. A unitary "virile" body was supposed to defeat the danger of "feminine" involutions through the performance of conflictual tasks; the power of a homogenized polity would overcome all obstacles to international epic adventures. In 1935 the fascist regime's "harmonic" whole finally tasted actual war through an energetic discharge in African soil. The parable of symbolic violence, with odes to martyrs and rhetorical erasures, eventually landed on Ethiopian ground.

The threat of war, although ambiguously disguised, always surfaced in the regime's discourse. A Manichean vision of the world, according to which fascism played the role of moral victim and good against evil, underlay the regime's narration of its story and increasingly structured a semantic context that presented war as an inevitable and necessary conclusion. Through mystical accounts and ritualistic tales, Mussolini's regime provided itself with an identity that upheld as just any militaristic effort. This narrative frame endowed fascism with a legitimate "hero" role in the upcoming drama of colonialism. Military preparation, whether fake or real, was deceptively insinuated to counteract the violence of "others."

The mystifying aura of fascism's new political tradition created the presuppositions for a call to patriotic unity—a rallying mass joined in national defiance, during the Ethiopian campaign, against all those international laws that were purported to be unjust. A desensitized, aesthetic outlook on politics turned fascist war into a normalized event. And war was to be fought at all costs and with all means. It began in the cradle, cultivated by demographic policies; it was anticipated in agricultural rituals and in the symbolic discourse of land; it was affirmed in the ostracism of urban existence; and it was embellished in visions of empire. War constituted the ultimate piece of fascism's aesthetic puzzle, the necessary concluding event in the historical project of the regime. Its rhetorical rehearsal took place at the site of agricultural battles.

THE POLITICS OF LAND

Metaphors of War

In an article written on May 25, 1922, Mussolini vaunted the fascist movement's rural membership.[1] Although it had originated in an urban setting (specifically, Milan), fascism, according to Mussolini, soon attracted people from the countryside—in particular the regions around the Po Valley. In these agricultural districts, which registered the highest rural population density, the Fascist Party counted on the support of one hundred thousand regular adepts and another two hundred thousand supporters—consistent figures that sustained fascism's claim to rurality. Country people (*rurali*), Mussolini asserted, rejected socialism's plan of land socialization as extraneous to their culture, which upheld the value of individual ownership. *Rurali* were scared by the threat of becoming "universally poor or without property" through the politics of the socialist movement. For this reason they journeyed toward fascism. From the Black Shirts they could only expect hope, not disaster.

At the time of this article, a few months before the March on Rome, Mussolini was still recruiting sympathizers to his party, and he solicited the support of *rurali* by referring to the very sensitive issue of land. "*La terra ai contadini*" ("Land to the peasants") had been a popular slogan during the Great War as a reward to the soldiers in the trenches, most of whom came from the countryside. Mussolini exploited the themes of both war and land in his discussion of rurality; he defended the peasants' right to land; and he singled out sharecroppers and tenant farmers as the heroes of World War I. Rural people, he wrote, had accepted daily combat with "resignation, patience, discipline,"[2] and, unlike urban soldiers, they did not grunt over bad food and harsh conditions. They only wondered about the reasons for destruction and killing. Furthermore, in the final year of the war, peasants actively participated in the major and more bloody phases of the conflict. They constituted the core of assault battalions, earning decorations and promotions. In those instances, they displayed a potential fascist character with their courage, warlike spirit, patriotism, and sense of duty and obedience.[3] Hence, Mussolini linked fascism to the people of the country. He wished to coopt *rurali* into the fascist movement and make them the active protagonists of a new political course.

In this 1922 article Mussolini laid out some of the major themes characterizing the fascist regime's political and ideological position on the rural question. These included a comparison between city and country, moral condemnation of urban life, and praise for the peasant's spirit of discipline and sacrifice. In the course of the years, these elements were woven into a broader, although often ambivalent, discourse on rurality and its role in the construction of fascist society. Peasant virtues were supposed to grant moral health and well-being to a nation that fascism intended to transform in a totalitarian direction. But rural qualities were also invoked as necessary for the future development of Italy's power. Fascism's ideological investment in rurality was indeed quite complex and far-reaching. In its most overt and straightforward manifestations, it was applied to political and economic initiatives that, via a reevaluation of agriculture and the bettering of peasants' conditions, aimed to facilitate a process of ruralization. Layers of meaning, however, rested underneath the immediate goals launched by these policies. The reading of these meanings is critical for understanding the frame within which fascism contextualized its interest in the countryside. One of the first measures the regime took in the field of agriculture, the campaign for the "Battle of Wheat," provides an example of the regime's ambivalent and polysemic embracement of the rural world.

The Battle of Wheat, officially launched on June 20, 1925, aimed to increase the production of wheat in Italy by adopting intensive forms of cultivation.[4] The government's position on this matter partially derived from Arrigo Serpieri's recommendations on the state of agriculture and its future in Italy. Serpieri, nominated undersecretary in the Ministry of the National Economy in 1923, had emphasized the necessity of improving the conditions of existing agrarian areas in order to enhance their production potential.[5] His legislation encouraged the application of new techniques and methods to augment farm output, especially in the South, where landowners appeared more reluctant to change.[6] Several economic reasons directed the fascist government's efforts toward wheat. To begin with, wheat had traditionally been a liability in the Italian balance of trade, and the increase in grain production would help contain imports and mend the balance of payments. Second, increased wheat cultivation could assure the employment of a labor force in the agricultural sector at a time when, in the wake of the United States' new immigration laws, the escape valve of emigration was coming to an end. Third, the government felt the political pressure of agrarians and representatives of flour-mill industries, who pushed for the introduction of protectionist laws on wheat. Chemical and mechanical industries, with their strong interests in the "industrialization" of agriculture, also brought their political influence to bear on the regime's economic strategies.[7] Last but not least, Mussolini cultivated the ideal of reaching food autarchy through an expanded production of wheat—this cereal being a basic item in the Italians' diet.

The government's decision to focus on wheat was, however, opposed by many experts in the sector, who argued for the development of a more comprehensive plan regarding agriculture and the state of the economy in general. Technicians of the Federazione Italiana dei Consorzi Agrari (Federconsorzi), for example, insisted that the politics of wheat had to be carried out within a policy of productive balance in the agrarian sector.[8] Reform interventions were needed both in terms of the economic imbalance between North and South and in terms of market organization. The Federconsorzi did not exclude the possibility of increasing the wheat harvest, yet it warned against the lack of a more inclusive and radical plan for agriculture. Most economists at the Istituto Nazionale Economia Aziendale (INEA) and at the Ministry of Agriculture also believed that wheat cultivation was even overextended in Italy and that animal husbandry instead needed urgent measures to lift it from the present state of dereliction.[9]

One result of the regime's large emphasis on wheat was to discourage farmers from growing more lucrative crops. Horticulture, truck and dairy farming, and animal husbandry generally declined or did not improve in Italy during the 1920s and 1930s,[10] with malignant consequences particularly affecting the South.[11] Here big landowners, resistant to innovations, simply extended the areas for wheat cultivation and refrained from adopting modern techniques for intensive production, thus failing to develop new and dynamic forms of management in the areas that most needed it.[12] In addition, the lack of facilities for the sectors of truck and dairy farming and animal husbandry discouraged or hampered the efforts of those who invested in them. In this sense, the negative effects of the Battle of Wheat greatly hit agriculture, but they were also felt at the larger social level. First, the government's politics provoked a price increase in wheat, which in turn affected the average consumer of this basic necessity.[13] Second, the Battle of Wheat exercised pernicious long-term effects on the whole economy. As Tannenbaum claims, "much of the savings it brought in purchases of foreign wheat were offset by a decline in foreign sales of some Italian agricultural products."[14] The wheat policy did not create any gains for the general state of agriculture, whereas it further aggravated the disparity between North and South.[15]

Despite all the problems connected to the Battle of Wheat, the regime pursued and ultimately accomplished its goal of increasing the cereal's production. A whole series of initiatives were taken to generate this result, including the financing of experimental research on grains, economic facilitations for farmers, and the enactment of a decree-law (no. 1181, issued July 4, 1925) that established an import duty on wheat; exempted petrol for tractors from custom duty and sales tax; granted awards for improvements; set up provincial and national prize competitions for the best crops; and initiated farm credits.[16] Additionally, the measures were supposed to encourage farmers' productivity by increasing the use of fertilizers, high-quality seeds, and mechanical systems. The regime also established a National Permanent Committee of Wheat (Comitato Nazionale Permanente del Grano) with the task of handling decisions and initiatives dealing with the expansion of wheat production. At the provincial level, Commissions of Wheat Propaganda were instituted.[17]

In general, the regime's propagandistic efforts in the Battle of Wheat were conspicuous, and they concentrated on both divulging new techniques in agriculture and promoting the battle by popularizing its objectives. In 1925, when the Battle of Wheat was initiated, the regime produced a film on fascism's exertions toward increased wheat production. In a year, the film toured the whole country and was shown to thousands.[18] Special journals and magazines began to be printed; for example, the *Collana Agraria*, launched in 1929 by Antonio Maranesi, aimed at improving the "technical and cultural elevation of our farmers."[19] Demonstrations of threshing even took place in Rome's central piazzas, whereas *autotreni del grano* roared into the countryside after being blessed by Mussolini in Piazza Venezia.[20] Often sponsored by producers of fertilizers and seeds, the trucks were escorted by a mobile movie theater that propagandized technical products.[21] The Competition for the Victory of Wheat (Concorso per la Vittoria del Grano) concurred in promoting the campaign, with posters publicizing the contest plastered on walls along roads and at railroad stations. Initially proclaimed in 1922 by the Ministry of National Economy and the Technical Committee for Agriculture, the competition reached full swing in 1925, when it was directly sponsored by the *capo del governo*—that is, Mussolini. The government distributed 1,500,000 awards (a number that was later increased) to the best crops, and Mussolini presided over the annual ceremony in Rome.

Mussolini, as the leading symbolic figure of the regime, played an important role in the propaganda campaign for wheat. Photographs of the Duce meeting in person with the wheat contest winners filled daily papers and weekly magazines.[22] On October 10, 1926, his speech for the first Battle of Wheat awards was broadcast via radio to the entire nation. At this time, photographs of the Duce amid wheat fields began to circulate and advertise the very popular image of Mussolini as farmer, an image that reached its apex during the 1930s reclamation campaign in the Pontine Marshes. The first summer following the launching of the wheat campaign, *Illustrazione Italiana* published a photo of Mussolini amidst tractors and wheat.[23] In October the Duce was shown driving a mechanical sowing machine in Predappio, his hometown.[24] The year after, on June 19, 1927, *Illustrazione Italiana's* cover page presented "The Duce as Farmer." The picture portrayed Mussolini threshing wheat on his own farm. Looking more like a noble gentleman, Mussolini was wearing a formal suit and hat.

On April 25, 1927, Mussolini realized his wish to host in Rome the International Conference of Wheat, an important occasion to propagandize rural aims.[25] (The conference met again in Rome in 1931.) On October 9, 1927, Mussolini opened the first National Exhibit of Wheat at Palazzo delle Esposizioni in Rome. In 1928 special trains for farmers (the regime called them *treni rurali*) were organized to attend the Exhibit of Agriculture.[26] Then, beginning in 1932, the reclaimed lands in the Pontine Ager spurred the "spectacular" rise of wheat production.[27] Deadly swamps were converted into arable fields, thanks to the integral character of the reclamation project.[28] Transformed marshes exemplified the regime's victory over nature and the elements, papers and newsreels indefatigably claimed. The reclamation of the Pontine Ager, one of the most publicized symbols of the fascist era's achievements, epitomized the regime's ability to build life from death. The documentary *Dall'acquitrinio alle giornate di Littoria* (From Marshes to Littoria's Days) opened with images of desolation, marshes, and death. Then, suddenly, an enormous *fascio littorio* shone on the screen. Active work appeared to take place in the whole area: people shoveling and preparing the ground, using machines and tractors. Efficient modern techniques happily married with men's labor as the new town of Littoria gradually took shape, and scenes of wheat dominated the landscape.[29] Fascism granted life and growth. And every year Mussolini made his appearance in the Ager at threshing time, actively contributing to the farmers' work. Often barechested, an image of virility and strength, Mussolini appeared next to big sheaves.[30] Other times, mixing modern and traditional symbols, Mussolini threshed wheat wearing goggles from his automobile ride, an image probably addressed more to the urban audience than to farmers (Figure 18). In a documentary of the Istituto Nazionale Luce shot in July 1938 and entitled *Il Duce inizia la trebbiatura del grano nell'Agro Pontino* (The Duce launches the threshing in the Pontine Ager), the commentary emphasized the 200,000 quintals of wheat threshed in the fields. The camera then tracked Mussolini in his tour of new towns (*comuni rurali*) built from the swamps. In Littoria he was said to have threshed more than 8 quintals of wheat, in Pontinia 11 quintals in just one hour, and finally, in Sabaudia (by then already evening), 8 more quintals in an hour.[31] A whole symbolic and ritualistic apparatus sustained the regime's campaign for the Battle of Wheat—

Figure 18. Mussolini as thresher, July 1934.

a campaign in which the general aim of popularizing agriculture and rurality was pursued more consistently at the aesthetic-political level than at the economic one.

From this perspective, the battle for an increase in wheat did not contribute to the improvement of farmers' and agriculture's conditions. Furthermore, in moments of economic crisis, the government always supported industrial interests over those of farmers.[32] As a matter of fact, agricultural income as a percentage of national income dropped several points during Mussolini's rule, from 45.9 in 1911–1920 to 38.2 in 1921–1930 to 29.8 in 1931–1940.[33] Already in a state of depression before the 1929 crisis, the situation of agriculture worsened in Italy after that date, and Mussolini's ruralization project never accomplished its grandiose goals.[34] Also, the decision to revaluate the lira, the famous "quota 90," negatively affected rural interests.[35] Fascism's intervention in the Battle of Wheat suffered from the limits of the regime's general handling of agrarian politics, a politics that had neglected to reform agrarian credit for small owners despite pressure from the Federconsorzi[36] and that failed to operate concretely for the social elevation of the peasants. Land ownership indeed declined during Mussolini's government.[37] And in the long run the Battle of Wheat did not stop migration to cities, where country workers looked for a better way of life.

In sum, even though the Battle of Wheat reached its goal of increased production, the regime's intervention in agriculture lacked a unitary vision and fell short of establishing the economic and social conditions necessary to realize the process of ruralization touted by Mussolini.

In general, the fascist government's rural politics followed an uneven, inconsistent path that often created a deep chasm between aspirations and realizations, placed disproportionate stress on appearance over substance, suffered from an overlap of objectives and means, and preferred quick and immediate gains over long-term results. The whole rural question raised by the regime underscored the organizational structuring of agriculture, and more than an economic issue became the symbolic locus of competing meanings.[38] Once again, the public representation of politics overwhelmingly eclipsed the content and purposes of fascist policy-making, and the spectacle of fascism illuminated the internal construction of the regime. Caught between contradictory aims, the fascist government chose to follow its path toward spectacular, if not economically wise, achievements and pursued the Battle of Wheat with insistence and perseverance. Although different reasons and motivations intersected in the campaign, through the Battle of Wheat Mussolini formulated and communicated his ultimate vision of fascist Italy. Focusing on wheat offered one of the most symbolically effective means by which Mussolini conveyed interpretation of rurality's role in the virile ascent of fascism. In effect, fascism's investment in wheat, which was disproportionate both to the potential economic gains and the potential impact on ruralization in general, reveals the inherently belligerent nature of Mussolini's regime.

Virility and Fecundity

The main product of wheat, bread has been for centuries the principal sustenance food of the Italian popular classes. However, it also has a more spiritual meaning as Christ's body in Catholic liturgy. During the religious ceremony of Communion, blessing sanctifies the value of bread, and its consumption puts the faithful in a mystical contact with God. Not surprisingly, the regime granted the clergy subsidies to organize annual festivals of wheat seeds' blessing.[39] These religious rituals cast an aura of sacrality on bread by putting it in liminal contact with the celestial sphere. The meshing of the sacred with the profane endowed bread with a plethora of superimposed, ambivalent, and overcharged meanings, which the regime fully exploited. The poster for the VIII National Competition for the Victory of Wheat, for example, portrayed two children holding loaves of bread and sitting amidst wheat that was being threshed by a farmer. The upper caption read: "Give us today our daily bread"—a line from the Catholic prayer *Pater Noster* (Figure 19). For the bread celebration of April 14–15, 1928 (*"Giornate del pane"*), Mussolini prepared a little speech that followed the rhetorical structure of a prayer. In it he defined bread as "the holiest reward of human toil":

> Italians!
> Love bread, heart of the home, fragrance of the board, joy of the hearth. Respect bread, sweat of the brow, pride of work, poetry of sacrifice. Honor bread, glory of the fields, fragrance of the earth, festival of life. Do not waste bread, wealth of the Fatherland, God's sweetest gift, the holiest reward of human toil.[40]

In this instance, Mussolini took bread, product of wheat, to symbolize the land, and he linked it to the rural values of family, hard work, and simple joys. Bread joined people: it was the wealth of the fatherland, the element upon which everybody's life depended. In this highly dramatic vein, the symbolism of bread guided Mussolini's representation of the Battle of Wheat to the public. On July 30, 1925, Mussolini told the representatives of agricultural unions, who were meeting in Rome for the first National Congress of the Battle of Wheat, that the battle meant "to free the Italian people from the enslavement of foreign bread."[41] The Italian nation strove to become self-sufficient and spare its subjects the humiliation of having to look for work abroad: bread signified independence and freedom. In 1928, in his closing remarks at the awards ceremony for the Victory of Wheat of October 14, Mussolini again addressed farmers as crucial providers of Italians' sustenance food.

> Another quintal, and we will have reached what until yesterday seemed like a dream, a prodigy: the Italian land that gives bread to all Italians.[42]

The disadvantaged position into which Italians were forced because of their country's inability to feed them would be overcome by a heroic and united autarchic effort against the odds of nature. Mussolini's rhetoric wove wheat and bread into a discursive plot that postulated Italy's rebirth and Italians' well-being—provided the population struggled in unison not only against nature but also against the tragedy of "foreign enslavement." In this fashion, the Duce's dramatic emphasis on bread served the role of highlighting the value of agriculture—source of bread—while inciting nationalistic spirit. The themes of Italians' enclosure and solidarity complemented the

Figure 19.   Poster for the VIII National Competition for the Victory of Wheat.

regime's vision of a stronger country. Land and bread ominously turned from material tokens for survival into metaphors for the nation's power, in part via a symbolic and material reconnection to demographic growth. The availability of bread would help increase the population; numerically stronger, "proletarian" Italy would then be raised to a position of competitiveness with the more powerful European countries. As Mussolini declared in his Ascension speech of May 26, 1927:

> I affirm that an important, if not fundamental, element of political, and also economical and moral power of Nations, is their demographic power. Let's be clear: what are forty million Italians against 90 million Germans and 200 million Slavs? Let us look to the West: what are 40 million Italians against 40 million French plus 90 millions from the Colonies, or against 46 million British, plus 450 millions in the Colonies? . . .
>
> Gentlemen, Italy, in order to count for something must face the second half of this century with a population not inferior to 60 million.[43]

Mussolini implored people to face reality at a time when Italy's birth rate was lowering. The government issued a tax on celibacy in order to give a "demographic whip to the Nation."[44] Mussolini condemned all those who believed that a large population presented economic and social problems. He rejected Malthusian theories and made a bitter and urgent plea for demographic increase. Population growth created a nation's might and forecast its destiny; the decadence of a country was signaled by low number of births.[45] Mussolini strongly believed that progress and historical development could only occur for those nations that were most populated. As he proclaimed in his Ascension address:

> All nations and all empires have felt the grip of decadence when they have seen their birth numbers go down . . . the destiny of Nations is tied to their demographic power.

Then Mussolini revealingly asserted:

> There is a kind of urban life which is destructive and sterilizes the population. This is industrial, urban life. . . . But do you believe that when I talk of ruralization in Italy I talk for love of fine sentences which I detest? No! . . . If we diminish, gentlemen, we do not build an Empire, we become a colony! . . . you understand now why I help agriculture, why I proclaim myself rural.[46]

In an elucidating passage, Mussolini affirmed that the importance of ruralization in the construction of a powerful Italy went beyond the production of sustenance food. People from the countryside, unlike urbanites, were also and foremost fecund; hence, they could provide the regime with the numerous population it required for building the empire—a continuous outpouring of soldiers to be.[47] The regime's praise for the countryside came to be discursively constructed in opposition to its criticism of industrial cities, where, because of selfish bourgeois motivations, birth rates were conspicuously declining. In his 1928 preface to the Italian translation of Richard Korherr's *Birth Regress, People's Death,* Mussolini clearly stated his thesis on this matter:[48]

> [A]t a certain moment the city grows morbidly, pathologically, that is not by its own virtue, but through others' contribution. The more the city grows and swells into a metropolis, the more it becomes infertile. The progressive infertility of the urban population is directly related to the rapidly monstrous growth of the city. . . . The metropolis grows attracting to it the rural population who, as soon as it settles, becomes, like the preexisting population, infertile. Fields turn into deserts. But when the desert extends its abandoned and burnt regions, the metropolis is taken by the throat; neither its commerce nor its industries, nor its oceans of stones and cement can reestablish the by now irreparably broken equilibrium. It is the catastrophe.[49]

Mussolini supported Korherr's theory of sterile urbanism, noting that in Italian cities deaths overcame births. And since Mussolini agreed with Korherr that birth regression gradually led to a nation's demise, his solution to the problem was to rely on rural people, who procreated at a satisfying rate. The others—the well-to-do, the urbanites—who were contaminated by hedonistic values, only deserved scorn and condemnation. Hence, Mussolini concluded his preface with an appeal to Italians: "Italian fascists: Hegel, the philosopher of the state said: He who is not a father is not a man!"[50]

In a reciprocal causal relation, the regime's discourse connected qualities of might and warriorlike attributes that corresponded to the value of "virility" to the virtues of demographic growth and fertility. Metaphorically, "virility," as the means and expression of supremacy, depended on biological fecundity, but biologically fecundity was contingent upon virile attributes. Thus, in his Ascension speech Mussolini, after indicating that the birth rate in 1927 was 27 per thousand, proclaimed: "The region above this rate is Basilicata, and I pay tribute to it with my sincere praise because it demonstrates its virility and force."[51] The crisscross use of the terms "virility" and "fecundity," both in a metaphorical and biological sense, characterized Mussolini's references to rural people and emphasized his idea of the linkage between the future realization of fascism's "virile" empire and the farm workers' contribution to it. A "fertile" land produced bread, which fed people and allowed an increase in demographic growth. At the same time, rural citizens' biological virility would contribute soldiers to the army and ultimately augment the nation's power and "virility."

In fascism's representation, land was identified with war, and rurality appeared ever more as a condition for strength and supremacy. Incidentally, Italy's countryside became the battleground for semantically charged military metaphors. In his October 10, 1926, broadcast speech to the *veliti* (i.e., soldiers) of the Victory of Wheat, Mussolini defined the farmers, with their will to increase the wheat harvest, as "armed" (as opposed to "unarmed"). He concluded his address to the winning *rurali* by saying:

> Here I am going to award those whom we may call the *veliti* of the Battle,
> those who reached far beyond, those who have realized a conquest, but
> I believe that behind those *veliti* the entire army will slowly march, thus
> following this animating example.[52]

A little earlier Mussolini had defined the Battle of Wheat as a "mobilization" of all rural forces. The very term "battle" carried warlike connotations, as is evident in the language Mussolini adopted in the inaugurating speech for the campaign on April 20, 1925:

> I have made a general commitment to lead the battle of wheat, and I have
> already prepared the General Staff. The General Staff will have to lead
> the cadres . . . and the cadres will have to move the army, the troop of
> farmers.[53]

Three years later, in his October 14 speech to the *veliti*, Mussolini affirmed:

> Armies are perfected when they fight. The same happens with the Italian
> rural army which, after years of battle, now presents itself as bettered in
> the cadres, very compact in its ranks, and determined to march.[54]

Rural people, who occupied the trenches during the war, were united under fascism in a similar task. Like an army, they obeyed and fought at the orders of the leader. Like an army, they were disciplined and followed the Duce in his enterprises. They belonged to that category of the "new" Italian that Mussolini favored.[55]

The juxtaposition of agricultural and military wars continued to fill the regime's rhetoric over the following years. A newsreel entitled "The War We Prefer," produced in 1933, showed "the glorious rebirth of uncultivated lands" in the reclaimed Pontine Ager.[56] The threshing of wheat in this instance epitomized the victorious result of the "war." That same year, a newsreel for the tenth anniversary of the founding of the Milizia posited the unity between bread and war by circulating the message: "The dagger of the Milizia and the plough of the farmer carry the same motto: will to serve."[57] A popular fascist slogan originating in 1934 reproposed the link between land and war: "The plough draws the furrow, but the sword defends it."[58]

The rural army, carrier of positive values, if only because it came from the idealized world of the countryside, created the premises for the "legitimate" heroic role fascist Italy played in the theater of world politics. Toil and fatigue dominated and directed peasants' lives. If, then, peasants looked abroad for new lands to sanctify with their holy labor, theirs were respectful aims. The Italians' survival was at stake. Furthermore, the rural people conducted a "civilizing" mission that relied on millenarian cults of mother earth and fertility. They made fecund the land, our "common source of life, force and happiness."[59] Within this narrative context, the regime framed as malign any obstacle to the fascist rural army's pursuit of a "living space." Because the Italians could not count on endless natural resources, finding new lands abroad appeared a legitimate answer to the problems Italy could not resolve within its own borders. And little mattered if the regime contributed to overpopulation by emphasizing procreation. As Mussolini suggested in his Milan speech of December 4, 1924:

> When a people grows it only has three possibilities: either to devote itself to voluntary sterility, and the Italians are too smart for this; or it goes to war; or it looks for markets where its surplus of human labor can find an outlet.[60]

Italy's role as hero in the drama of war took shape in the aesthetic-political valorization of agriculture. The Battle of Wheat conveyed the regime's fictionalized vision of the world and proposed a melodramatic plot in which fascism played the role of good in the struggle against adversity. This interpretation of reality found its apotheosis in the rhetorical construction of the Ethiopian war, but the trope of an external threat to Italy's future was also alluded to, as a phantasmatic presence, in the regime's rural battle. Thus, from the narrative point of view, the agricultural campaign constituted a prelude to the colonial one. Wheat, via the symbolism of bread, helped lay out the terms of Italy's revenge cry against an unjust outside world. The themes of fertility, unity, and virility surreptitiously drove the regime's discourse of ruralization and disclosed, even as it constructed, fascism's expansionist aims, its intrinsically warlike identity.

THE POLITICS OF WAR

The covert narration of expansionist designs in the agricultural campaign accompanied the regime's similarly ambiguous rhetoric in the more specific discursive context of international relations. Even when Italy's role within world politics constituted the explicit object of Mussolini's official declarations and was not disguised under the symbolism of bread and births, Mussolini still spoke in equivocal terms of foreign affairs and Italy's strategic interests. On the one hand, he invoked the "grandiose future that cannot fail a Nation of forty million people, decided to conquer their legitimate place in the world."[61] And he insisted that "imperial Italy, the Italy of our dreams, will be the reality of our future."[62] On the other hand, he claimed that fascist Italy was only interested in maintaining peace. As he said in his 1923 report to the Senate on the first six months of government: "Italy's foreign politics, while it intends to safeguard national interests, also wants to constitute at the same time an element of equilibrium and peace in Europe. I believe with this politics to interpret the tendencies and needs of the Italian people."[63]

Ensconced within the regime's public discourse were the aspirations to build an empire and to pursue a grandiose destiny. An overproduction of competing meanings on issues connected to military wars incessantly shifted objectives and displaced goals, as in the reshuffling of cards. At the same time, the presentation of imperialism as an "eternal law of life"[64] tended to endow war with a universal status and to deemphasize its material reality, its factual occurrence in time and space, its deadly implications. Hence, fascism's concept of empire as a natural process in the evolution of nations, a necessary component of historical progress, a spiritual principle guiding a vital people's ascent to success, seemed to suggest that war only existed as a philosophical construct. One was led to believe that, as Mussolini wrote in 1932, expansion could indeed occur "without the need to conquer one square kilometer of territory."[65]

The empire's aleatory presence in fascism's spiritual interpretation of modern colonialism allowed the regime to contrast Italy positively against other powerful nations. The discourse of empire became the contentious site of evaluations of countries' rights of conquest, ideological reasons and claims, cultural traditions and styles. In this competition, Italy fared excellently.[66]

A "superior" genius, a high quality of character, and a glorious historical past, as epitomized in the mythical reconstruction of Rome, granted Italy the right to a preeminent position in the world. Spiritual attributes made Italy's expansionist claims morally outstanding, a legitimate demand. As Mussolini declared on the day of the *fasces'* foundation on March 23, 1919: "Imperialism is the fundament of life for every people [*popolo*] who tends to expand economically and spiritually."[67]

Through the proliferation of semantic twists and turns, the regime constructed a virtuous image of Italy, an iconic representation that circulated within the fascist movement from its inception. Mussolini's cry for justice against the Treaty of Versailles at the conclusion of World War I can be retraced as the symbolic origin of this fiction. The treaty, which had offered Italy a minimal share of the winners' dividends, transformed the Italian success into what came to be called a "mutilated victory." Feelings of deception and loss, and a sense of anger toward the major powers and war allies, pervaded the Italian political climate of the time and propelled a wave of popular outrage and reaction. Mussolini called for a revision of the treaty and the affirmation of Italy's territorial rights. His rhetoric pitched Italy as the "great proletarian" against her bourgeois oppressors.[68] "Plutocratic" countries, and in particular Great Britain, "the fattest and most bourgeois nation in the world,"[69] had replenished their colonial booty and were now asking, through the international body of the League of Nations, that other countries not engage in imperialistic enterprises. But, as Mussolini told his adepts on the day of the *fasces'* foundation:

> We say: either everybody is idealist or nobody is. We should all follow our own interests. One cannot understand why those who are doing well preach idealism to those who suffer, because this would be too easy. We want our place in the world for we have the right.[70]

Mussolini then continued his tirade by directly assailing the League:

> [I]f the League of Nations must be a solemn "swindle" of the rich against the proletarian nations to fix forever the actual conditions of world equilibrium, let's look each other well in the eyes. I understand perfectly that arrived nations can establish these awards which ensure their opulence and their actual dominant position. But this is not idealism: this is profit and interest.[71]

A heightened sense of injustice permeated Mussolini's approach to the question of colonial expansion, as did a will to transform the situation. The term "proletarian" conveyed a meaning of inequality and suffering and indicated the presence of a stratifying hierarchy in need of being challenged or balanced. The ideology of the "poor people's imperialism," already coined by the liberal government at the turn of the century, became a formula that happily married with fascism's dramatization of international relations.[72] The "proletarian" trope Mussolini had inherited from the nationalists vehemently preceded and melodramatically introduced the fascist regime's rhetorical depiction of a polarized world—a world in which virtue, identified with good, struggled against evil. A fascist drama of world proportions then began to be staged following the rules of the "romance mode."[73]

The Rhetoric of Virtue

From the early stages of his mandate as head of government, Mussolini directed his oratorical efforts toward the strategic goal of presenting Italy as a victim of other countries' gluttony. And he insisted that "from Italy no initiative will start that might in any way disturb world peace."[74] In all his official discussions of foreign relations the Duce followed a specific narrative scheme that assigned fascist Italy a positive role in world politics and highlighted other nations' wrongdoing. The schema went: peace is desirable, although we fascists do not believe in perennial peace; however, despite Italy's most valiant efforts, all countries are rearming; hence, Italy is forced to prepare for war. A slight variation in the scheme put forward the old question of Italy's rights and the injustices it had suffered because of the plutocracies' egoism. Mussolini wished to achieve equality through peace, but he was hampered in this pursuit by selfish powers, who then provoked Italians into taking an aggressive turn.[75] Mussolini's speech to the war disabled of November 4, 1925, and his address to the Chamber of Deputies on December 9, 1928, constitute examples of the first narrative format:

> [P]eace is certainly a human desire of all individuals and peoples especially after a long war. Well, I strongly declare that, while I believe and hope in a quite long period of peace, I have not reached yet such a high degree of optimism to believe in lasting peace for centuries.
>
> I participate, Italy and the Italian government naturally participate, in all attempts to establish peace, but in the aftermath of the largest peace-oriented event of these last times, the cannon again thundered in Macedonia, it still thunders on the Oriental borders of the Mediterranean, and the day after the event 60,000 soldiers in a big city beyond the border paraded dreaming of revenge.[76]
>
> We are all for peace. We signed the Kellogg Pact. I defined it as sublime. In reality, it is so sublime that it could also be called transcendental. And

if tomorrow there were other pacts, we would hurry to sign them. . . .
But above, under or aside these pacts there is a reality that we should not
ignore, if we do not want to commit a crime of an offended Nation. And
the reality is this, gentlemen: that all the world arms![77]

In these speeches, where peace was at times defined with such high attributes as "sublime" and "transcendental," the contrast between Italy's virtuous position and other nations' threat of war emerged very intensely. The
world was arming, whereas Italy only wished to keep harmonious relations.
But would it be safe for the fascist regime to cultivate such hopes? Mussolini warned Italians about the danger of an armed conflict provoked by
other countries. If he then encouraged the nation "to keep ready," he was
only making the necessary response to a state of threat, for in fact Italy's
interest would be better served by peace.[78] Mussolini could legitimately affirm: "[A]s Islam's paradise, so our safest peace will also be in the shadow
of our swords!"[79] In the same way, in his speeches of October 30, 1927, and
March 10, 1929, which followed the second narrative format, Mussolini affirmed Italy's right to arm:

> We are all vindicating Victory. . . . We are in sum decided to defend at any
> cost the Revolution within and Italy's rights in the world.[80]

> To those who uselessly want to worry the world by representing an Italian
> imperialism, we will remind them yet another time that Italy contains
> its expenses for arms within the limits of the most elementary necessities
> of security and defense. We will remind them that Italy wants to live in
> peace with all people, and in particular with those next to her; that Italy
> has stipulated friendship and trade treaties with many states, and that
> frequently these acts have dispersed fog, thwarted intrigues, reestablished
> equilibrium in the spirits; we will remind them that Italy, since it is engaged
> in the interior in her work of economic and political reconstruction . . . does
> not want to disturb peace, but is ready to defend her interests in any part of
> the world.[81]

Fascism's ambiguous rhetoric gyrated between peaceful proposals and warlike threats. But the latter were presented as consequences; other countries'
malignant behavior determined Italy's military stance. As Mussolini told
the Senate in 1925:

> One cannot think, honorable Senators, that an eventual war tomorrow
> in Europe would spare us the sacrifice. We need to get ready. Nor can one
> think that the war starts and leaves us the time to get ready. War can fall
> on us suddenly.[82]

Mussolini firmly asserted Italy's duty to be militarily prepared, although he cast Italy less as the initiator of any potential conflict than as its victim. The war would "fall" on Italians suddenly, without them knowing it. Whether ready or not, Italy would be involved in the battle. There was no chance that the sacrifice could be avoided.

The frustration over the European nations' unwillingness to help Italy achieve its goals through peaceful means led Mussolini to take a more militant tone in his speeches of the early 1930s. At this time, the regime's discourse on war escalated, though it maintained the familiar narrative format, especially in its second variant. On May 11, 1930, Mussolini thus addressed the people of Livorno:

> I want to tell you, and not only you, but all the Italian people and also the people beyond the borders, that we are not anxious for precipitous adventures, but if anybody made an attempt on our independence and future, they do not know yet at what temperature I would bring all the Italian people![83]

Things had come to a turning point when the regime could legitimately claim its right to respond to other nations' threats. If Italy the virtuous were provoked, then it would defend itself, as Mussolini reiterated in his Milan speech of May 24, 1930, anniversary of Italy's intervention in the Great War. At this event, Mussolini first warned the Italian people not to be deceived by the "bleating of lambs who are authentic wolves."[84] Then he affirmed that the Italian people were armed—i. e., "ready to defend their right under the sign of the *Littorio.*"[85] Then he evoked the injustice of Versailles:

> We left Versailles with a mutilated Victory. But Victory is still in our hands. It was mutilated in the diplomatic protocols, but it is not mutilated in our arms and hearts.[86]

This highly dramatic address asked the whole of Italy to share the same emotions and feel the injustice. In the wake of these sentiments, Mussolini's message for Year IX of the regime (October 27, 1930) responded to the accusations that his recent speeches in Tuscany and Milan were a declaration of war. Mussolini denounced what he called "a state of 'moral' war against us" by a "hypocritical Europe that stutters peace in Geneva and prepares war everywhere."[87] He then accused the League of Nations of being responsible for "perpetually maintaining two categories of states: armed and unarmed ones."[88] What kind of justice was this? Mussolini asked. What judicial and moral equality could exist between armed and unarmed states?

The principles guiding the League were unfair, and Italy as a victim was pay-ing the price. "Some injustices have been committed, also against us, above all against us," Mussolini told the people of Milan on October 25, 1932.[89] He continued: "And nothing is more sad than the task, which sometimes we need to take, of having to defend what has been the magnificent sacrifice of blood of all the Italian people."[90] Debased, wealthy nations were denying Italy the rights it had earned through the sacrifice and blood of millions of soldiers. The rhetoric of blood, which Mussolini had adopted for the cult of fascist martyrs, resurfaced in the regime's representation of Italy's moral stance in world politics. The sanctified blood of war heroes functioned to dramatize further the degree of injustice to which Italy was being subjected. The image of Italy as virtuous victim served Mussolini's attempt to nego-tiate the polyvalent meanings he was attributing to power, war, and empire. This image constituted a constant motif in the regime's discourse. As such, it prepared the ideological and symbolic terrain on which fascism founded its justification for war as the time approached for Italy to initiate its Ethiopian conquest.

The fascist regime's interest in Ethiopia followed a history of Italian ex-pansionist attempts beginning at the end of the nineteenth century, during the governments of Agostino De Pretis and Francesco Crispi. Both prime ministers focused their search for new territories in the African area around the Red Sea; during their regency Italy initiated its penetration of Eritrea, Somalia, and Abyssinia, although amid some unfavorable circumstances. A most significant failure occurred in 1893, during Crispi's second government, when Italy advanced its politics of expansionism in Abyssinia. The emperor Menelik reacted to the Italians' military threat by organizing a strong army, and in 1896 he managed to inflict a large defeat on the Italians at Adowa, where Italy lost six thousand soldiers. The defeat remained vivid in popu-lar memory and became a symbolic moment in Italy's colonial struggle, a humiliation to be revenged. With the beginning of the new century, Italy's colonial politics was still oriented toward the northern African coast. Diplo-matic agreements established between 1902 and 1904 with France, England, and Tunisia acknowledged Italy's interests in Tripolitania (Libya) and Cyre-naica. In 1911, backed by this political support, Giolitti, then prime minis-ter, decided it was time for Italy to actualize its colonial goals. Although Italy had no economic interest in those regions, questions of prestige and the geopolitics of the time[91] encouraged Giolitti's government to declare war on Turkey, on whom Libya depended. Within a month, because of the po-litical and economic crisis of the Ottoman Empire, the Italian army was able to occupy a strategic point in the Tripolitania region, but in the long run the persistence of sporadic warfare created several obstacles to the successful completion of the invasion. Within this context, and because Giolitti's government intended to avoid a compromise peace pact, two months after the first attack, and well before the war was concluded, Italy printed a royal decree establishing its absolute sovereignty over Libya. A year later the Lausanne peace treaty conferred upon Italy the right of sovereignty over Libya, and public opinion acclaimed the country's first colonial success.

With respect to its colonial politics in Ethiopia, Italy's military preparation during the 1900s and 1910s was conceived primarily in terms of a defensive strategy against an eventual Abyssinian invasion of the Italian possession of Eritrea.[92] In the 1920s Mussolini's fascist government continued the policy of the liberal government and even signed a treaty of friendship with Ethiopia in 1928.[93] By the end of the decade, however, the fascist regime called for a politics of force that would pursue the disintegration of the Ethiopian empire.[94] Thus, in 1932, with Mussolini's consent, Minister of Colonies Emilio De Bono officially began the preparation for an aggressive campaign in Abyssinia.

At its inception, the campaign's exact goals were not clear, nor was the beginning date decided. The operation actually underwent several changes over the following year, partly because of the presence of two different centers of power, the military and the politicians, whose opinions on war objectives and strategies differed widely.[95] In February 1934 Mussolini convened the first meeting on the operation and communicated his decision to begin the invasion of Ethiopia in 1935.[96] Military leaders expressed concern about this early date because, according to them, it did not leave adequate time to prepare for what they envisioned as a war of conquest. The course of events, however, contributed to determine this early start to the colonial war. The relations between Italy and Ethiopia having deteriorated drastically at the end of 1934, rumors spread about an Abyssinian mobilization. The rumor proved to be unfounded, but the situation motivated Mussolini—who was convinced for a series of reasons that "time works against us"—to prepare a final plan of aggression in Ethiopia. The invasion, as he wrote in his memorandum to the highest authorities of the regime, was supposed to take place in 1935; and, Mussolini added, it needed to aim at the "total conquest of Ethiopia."

> The problem of the Italo-Abyssinian relations recently moved to a different level: from diplomatic problem it has become a *problem of force*. It is a historical problem that we need to solve with the only means with which such problems have always been solved: with the employment of arms. . . .

> Committed to this war, the objective cannot but be *the destruction of the Abyssinian armed forces and the total conquest of Ethiopia.* The empire cannot be done otherwise.[97]

The history of Italy's colonial interest in Ethiopia thus found its epilogue with Mussolini's plan of total occupation and the submission of the indigenous population to the laws of the regime. The conquest of the African territory began on October 3, 1935 when Italy, without a formal declaration of war, attacked Ethiopia.

While the events unfolded in this manner, the regime told a very different story of the conflict. First of all, pointing to various incidents between Ethiopians and Italians at Ual-Ual and Gondar at the end of 1934, the regime accused the emperor Haile Selassie's government of threatening Italy's colonies. Second, and in order to highlight the situation's dramatic character, the regime emphasized the building up of Ethiopia's military apparatus and the necessity for Italy to be on guard.[98] In his prewar declarations to the Senate on May 14, 1935, Mussolini said:

> For what concerns the diplomatic development of the dispute, it is by now known that we have not refused conversations with the representatives of the Ethiopian government and we have already communicated to Addis Ababa that we are willing on our side to nominate two representatives of Italy in the Committee of Conciliation.
>
> But it is our duty not to cultivate, and even less diffuse, illusions due to the notable Ethiopian armaments, the advanced preparations of Ethiopian mobilization and due above all to the dominant feeling in Addis Ababa, especially among the minor leaders, who are hostile to any agreement with Italy.[99]

And at the Chamber of Deputies he declared:

> The menace at our borders of Oriental Africa is not potential but effective, but in movement, in growing proportions everyday, and such as to pose the Italian-Ethiopian problem in the most crude and radical terms.[100]

The fascist government's responsibilities in the conflict disappeared in Mussolini's recounting of events. He portrayed Italy as the victim of Ethiopia's aggressive behavior—a representation that stood upon the firm ground of Italy's constructed image as a balanced and righteous nation. Furthermore, Italy's willingness to negotiate for peace reconfirmed its role as a paladin of justice in the relations between states. Against this narrative background, the regime told the whole story of the African conquest within a frame that effaced the negative aspects of fascism's warlike attitude; in contrast, it presented Italy as the victim of injustice. The regime's rhetoric of virtue combined with the proletarian trope and the symbolism conveyed in the agricultural campaign. The reality depicted by Mussolini over time became an interpretive model, an explanatory device for the Ethiopian events. The struggle between good and evil defined the central narrative thread around which Mussolini emplotted his representation of the African war to the public.

The regime conceived and constructed the whole Ethiopian episode according to the rules of melodramatic plays. And, following melodrama, it turned its colonial attempt into an ethical conflict of epic proportions. As in the best melodramas, fascism proposed a choice between moral alternatives: light and darkness, salvation and damnation, white and black. As in the best melodramas, which are supposed to unveil the spiritual reality hidden beneath the world of everyday life, the regime transformed the banal cynicism of power relations into a parabolic tale, an exciting context for a highly dramatic epic.[101] Moral life, thus uncovered, became the true story of the African conflict, within which the "dramaturgy of virtue" played its prominent role. Hence, the drama unfolded first by presenting virtue. Then it introduced the forces that worked to undermine virtue. Finally, the drama expressed the liberation of virtue from evil after some kind of spectacular action.[102] The admiration of virtue constitutes the focal point of melodramatic plays, whereas the confrontations and obstacles virtue experiences, and the threats it undergoes, all tend to stress its qualities. That virtue is not recognized at first, and suffers at the hands of villains, helps dramatize the ethical struggle. Thus, evil appears to dominate events and determine the moral laws governing reality. Overcome by the triumph of evil, virtue is eclipsed, fallen, annihilated. But, in the end, the plot resolution leads to the liberation of virtue from evil and to the public's "astonished" recognition of virtue's values. These *coups-de-théâtre* emphasize and characterize the moral issues at stake in melodrama, the dramaturgy of virtue at the center of melodramatic plays.

Mussolini's narration of Italy's international stance strove to assert fascism's morally superior conception of life. Melodramatically presented, this stance involved a strongly characterized antagonism, a battle in which the termination of one ensured the other's salvation. In the Ethiopian case, good and evil came to be redefined according to the logic of imperialism. This distribution of protagonists' roles constituted a *coup-de-théâtre*, an original touch in the writing of the drama.

The Enemy, the Victim, the Other

The regime's discourse on Italy's rightful position in the African conflict was structured around the theme of the Ethiopians' aggression. But in order to legitimize and sanctify fascism's crusade in Ethiopia, the regime especially took advantage of the European reaction to the news of Italy's military preparation. That Great Britain convoked the League of Nations in order to condemn officially Italy's military stance offered Mussolini enormous opportunities for dramatizing the struggle of Italy's unrecognized virtue. Thus, he used the League's chastisement of Italy, and the eventuality of sanctions, to accuse of immoral behavior and bad conscience the greedy and plutocratic nations he had always scorned. Those countries, Mussolini claimed, disguised their evil under the mantle of the League; they dissimulated their villainy by appealing to principles of justice.[103] Furthermore, they were betraying the same moral order—i.e., Western civilizational values—they were supposed to represent. Within this context, the regime found the Europeans, more than the Ethiopians, guilty of immorality and injustice, because the former belonged to a "superior" culture and were not expected to act immorally. The League of Nations' attack on Italy gave the Duce the occasion for some of his most dramatic speeches, in which he voiced the themes of injustice and Italy's victimization. The confrontation between fascist Italy and the Western countries reinforced the drama about Italy's unrecognized virtue and the struggle to affirm it. The "dramaturgy of virtue" in Italy's battle against evil gained, narratively speaking, from the juxtaposition between the fascist regime and the great powers. Hence, the League and its members ended up playing the main enemy in the African drama.

Consider, for instance, the speech Mussolini delivered on October 2, 1935. On this date, the regime organized a rehearsal for general mobilization with the goal of showing the entire world the popular enthusiasm and cohesion that supported Italy on the eve of the armed conflict with Ethiopia. The Italians, Mussolini, and the state (virtue) were a compact unity ready to face any adversary, both in Ethiopia and especially at the League of Nations (evil). The latter, with its bullying attitude, was threatening to cause a European conflict. In solemn tones, Mussolini declared that Italy was doing the impossible in order to prevent a war (affirmation of virtue):

> A solemn hour is going to strike in the history of our fatherland. Twenty million Italians are occupying at this moment the squares of all Italy.
>   Never was seen in the history of humankind a more gigantic spectacle. Twenty million men: one only heart, one only will, one only decision. . . .

It is not only an army aimed at its own objectives, it is a whole people of forty-four million souls against whom they are trying to inflict the worst injustice: that of depriving us of a little place in the sun. . . .

We have patiently waited thirteen years during which the circle of selfishness has become tighter suffocating our vitality. With Ethiopia we have waited patiently forty years! That is enough!

At the League of Nations they talk about sanctions, instead of recognizing our rights. . . .

To the economic sanctions we shall oppose our discipline, our sobriety, our spirit of sacrifice. . . .

To war activities we shall answer with war activities. . . .

But let us say it another time, in the most categorical way . . . that we shall do all we can so that this conflict of colonial character will not assume the character and implications of a European conflict. . . .

And it is against these People to which humanity owes some of its main conquests, and it is against these People of poets, artists, heroes, saints, sailors, transmigrators, it is against these People that they dare to speak of sanctions.

Proletarian and fascist Italy, Italy of Vittorio Veneto and of the Revolution, stand up! . . . a cry of justice, a cry of victory![104]

The themes of proletarian Italy, of injustice and civilization, starkly represented Italy's morality and submerged fascism's motifs and goals in the colonial war. This black-and-white depiction of reality assigned the League, as the "coalition of egoisms and plutocracies,"[105] the role of villain. "Gigantic" Italy, in contrast, was still trying to avoid a world conflict in spite of the injustice imposed upon it. A people of "saints," "artists," and "heroes," Italy was crying for virtue. It represented good in a world of villains.

In the next weeks, Mussolini's speeches continued to assault the image of the League in an attempt to unveil its fundamental immorality. By making recourse to hyperbolic terms, Mussolini defined the eventual sanctions as a "supreme shame" that "all civil people of the world should feel."[106] The League's economic measures constituted "the most costly of injustices."[107] On November 18, 1935, about a month after the beginning of the Italo-Ethiopian war, the League of Nations finally applied sanctions against Italy. This event naturally unchained a strong reaction within the regime. The same day, the party's *Foglio d'Ordini* (Sheet of Orders) communicated that the Gran Consiglio, after deliberating in session, invited Italians "to deck their houses with flags for twenty-four hours on the day of Monday November 18." Moreover, the Gran Consiglio ordered the erection in every town council building of a stone engraved in remembrance of the siege, "so that it will be documented in the centuries the enormous injustice consummated against Italy, to whom the civilization of all continents owes so much."[108] The regime described Italy as being in a state of siege, and all the newspapers and many official documents published a count of the days of siege under the current date. Newsreels also followed that practice; a stentorian voice would announce: "Today, twenty-third day of economic siege. . . . " Thus, the whole of the Italian people were rhetorically involved in the campaign.

In one of his first public speeches after the sanctions, Mussolini, in heightened rhetoric, pointed out the dramatic and immoral character of the siege. His audience being the mothers of the Great War's soldiers, Mussolini managed to touch emotional chords and very sensitive issues as he accused the countries for whose defense these women had donated their sons' lives of training and arming Ethiopians:

> If somebody, in the glorious and tragic years of the World War, when the painful news reached your houses, came and told you that a day would come in which the countries to whom you have offered the youth of your sons would have supplied with explosive guns the enemies who are fighting against Italian troops, you would have rejected this hypothesis as one tries to push back a bad dream.[109]

Mussolini's tone became more dramatic when he quoted World War I hero Filippo Corridoni, a figure exalted by the regime and in whose honor a town had been named: "We go to fight for the martyr Belgium, for the invaded France, for threatened England." Then Mussolini continued:

> Now those we helped, are conspiring against Italy. But what is the crime that Italy supposedly has perpetrated? None, unless it is a crime to bring civilization to backward lands, to build roads and schools, diffuse the hygiene and the progress of our time.[110]

Italy was only accomplishing good, according to Mussolini. But the League of Nations completely disregarded her civilizing mission and, at the zenith of immorality, was even placing Italy on the same plane as Ethiopia.

> It is not the economic side of sanctions that we disdain. . . . What we find disgusting in the sanctions is their moral character. It is this having put on the same level Ethiopia and Italy . . . the People who has given so many contributions to world civilization.[111]

Italy was conducting "a war of civilization and liberation," a "war of poor, disinherited, proletarian people."[112] Its only sin consisted of breaking the shackles of slaves in "barbaric" lands. In spite of this, egoistic and hypocritical countries were disregarding Italy's moral superiority. In his dramatic appeal to students, Mussolini defined European politicians as "bloodthirsty." He warned that the "satanic pressure of imperialist and bloody sects" could cause a world conflict of incredible proportions in which students, not politicians, would be called to fight.[113] Italy did not want a war, Mussolini affirmed, but sanctions would not bring peace either. "That sanctions mean peace in Europe is the mystification of criminals. It is a mephistophelian fraud of sectarians,"[114] Mussolini declared. Hence, he incited the students against the "insatiable imperialists," the "bloody propagandists" with their "diabolical intrigues."[115] In the face of these criminals Italy cried out its innocence and emphasized the moral mission it was leading in Ethiopia—a mission of civilization and liberation from slavery. The antagonism between Italy, the invading country, and the other nations, which condemned the invasion, was framed as a struggle between a victimized country, whose only fault lay in bringing light to backward regions, and superpowers who wanted to deny Italy a piece of their colonial cake—as Mussolini called it, "a little place in the sun." While evil (the League) imposed its rule by discrediting and humiliating virtue (Italy), virtue prepared, in a crescendo, the moment of revelation and triumph.

The dramaturgy of virtue the regime applied to its relationship with the European powers continued in fascism's discourse about the "aggressors" in the Italo-Ethiopian conflict—that is, the Ethiopians themselves. Almost playing a secondary role in Italy's moral drama, the Abyssinians were never considered real and equal interlocutors of Italy on the colonial issue, and Mussolini always maintained a dismissive tone toward them. Colonies, Mussolini claimed, were a right for civilized countries, no matter the reason for initiating their conquest. As a matter of fact, by calling it a colonial question, Mussolini considered Italy's war in Africa a natural outcome, a necessary stage in the expansionist process. There were wars and wars, Mussolini wrote in his appeal to the European students when defending Italy from the accusation that it was provoking a European crisis. Because "the Ethiopian dispute was a colonial question,"[116] it should not have created any protest or opposition from the great powers. A conflict in Europe was a serious matter; a colonial war did not deserve anybody's attention. It involved different, inferior cultures that had not been able to develop a stable and civilized political system. They were thus rightly subjected to other countries' expansionist activities.[117]

From this ideological position, a derogatory and diminished vision of the Ethiopians ensued. Mussolini's government presented the League of Nations with a memorandum that documented the history of Italy's political and diplomatic relations with Ethiopia. Using graphic evidence, the dossier vividly placed the African country at the bottom of civilization. Photos of prisoners in chains, of public whippings, and of men mutilated in the application of a backward justice system advertised Ethiopia's primitive conditions.[118] Images of hangings, violence, plundering, and the eating of raw meat were supposed to inspire feelings of condemnation in the viewers.[119] Italian pamphlets of the time followed the formula of the Geneva memorandum in presenting the Ethiopians. For contrast, they showed pictures of Italy's positive interventions in other African colonies: health care; medical treatments; distribution of food; urban development; and the building of roads, bridges, schools, and hospitals. These were all facts Geneva "refused to see."[120]

Mussolini's official declarations also continuously indicted Ethiopia's savagery and barbarism. The Abyssinians were variously defined as "savage raiders," "slavers," "cutthroats," "barbarians," "bloodthirsty," and "rapacious,"[121] and Ethiopia was called "the land of emperors and ras, of shackles and chains, of slaves' merchants."[122] Ethiopia constituted "a mixture of authentically and irremediably barbarian races."[123] Even though at the beginning of the conflict Mussolini denied that Italy had any interest in Africa other than to guarantee the security of its own territories, the regime made continuous recourse to the rhetoric of civilization during its colonial campaign. Ethiopia's moral inferiority, as depicted in the regime's narration, magnified the value of Italy's civilizing mission.[124] Next to the Ethiopians' cruelties, their lack of morals, their wild customs and brutality, Italy's values would glow; next to Ethiopia's low degree of civilization, Italy's virtue would shine.[125] Thus, on December 18, 1935, Mussolini told farmers at the inauguration of Pontinia: "The war we began in the African land is a war of civilization and liberation."[126] And on March 23, 1936, he told the Assembly of Corporations:

> The sacrifice faced by the Italian People in Africa is an immense service to civilization and world peace. . . . Italy in Africa conquers some territories, but in order to free the populations who for millennia have been at the mercy of few blood-thirsty and rapacious leaders.[127]

According to the regime's narrative, the same indigenous populations welcomed Italy's liberating actions and recognized its superiority. On December 7, 1935, Mussolini told the Chamber of Deputies that the Ethiopians had been waiting a long time for Italy's civilizing intervention.[128] A few months later, in the article to the European students, he wrote that in the Tigrai region Italy was being "waited for and invoked by the tortured populations," who actually joined the Italians in battle against the central government.[129] Newsreels also presented the Italian public with images of

Africans' enthusiasm for Italy's moral mission.[130] Entire villages, according to fascism's propaganda, asked Italy for protection.[131] These first signs of recognition of Italy's virtue were harbingers of her final victory in the conflict. As in melodrama, they forecast the triumph of good over evil, an affirmation of ethical values. Thus, when the Italian troops entered Addis Ababa on May 15, 1936, in the final stage of the war, Mussolini hailed their conquest as a moral success:

> Black Shirts of the Revolution! Men and women of all Italy! Italians and friends of Italy beyond mountains and seas: listen!
> The General Badoglio cables me:
> Today, the fifth of May, at four P.M., at the head of the victorious troops, I entered Addis Ababa.
> During the thirty centuries of her history, Italy lived many memorable hours, but today's is certainly one of the most solemn.
> I announce to the Italian people and the world that the war is over.
> I announce to the Italian people and the world that peace is reestablished.[132]

In this beginning of his important speech on victory, Mussolini emphasized the end of the war and the establishment of peace. Only later did he announce, "Ethiopia is Italian!" And, he immediately added, "rightly Italian, because with the gladius of Rome it is civilization that triumphs over barbarism, that justice triumphs over cruel will, that poor people's redemption triumphs over millenary slavery."[133] Then he ended his speech:

> Today's is an unforgettable date for the Revolution of the Black Shirts. And the Italian people, who resisted, who did not bend to the siege and to the League's hostility, deserves, as a protagonist, to live this great day.
> Black Shirts of the Revolution! Men and women of all Italy!
> One stage of our march has been reached, let us continue to march in peace.[134]

Italy had been mistreated, humiliated, and put under siege and had sacrificed its youth during the conflict. But in the end it had triumphed. Not only had it defeated barbarians and brought them civilization; the "poor" Italians had also shown stamina in front of economic sanctions intended to bend and "starve" them. Through it all, Italy intended to continue and "march in peace." In a sublime way, it represented a new ethical order.

Four days after the speech of victory Mussolini proclaimed the foundation of the empire. In a rare night appearance from the balcony of Palazzo Venezia he told the Italians that the fascist empire was one of peace, because Italy wants peace for herself and for all and decides to war only when commanding, irrepressible necessities force her. Empire of civilization and humanity for all the populations of Ethiopia.[135]

The stress on moral victory and virtue was reasserted in this address, as well as in the one Mussolini delivered when the economic sanctions were finally lifted, on July 15, 1936.

Today, the fifteenth of July of the year XIV, on the ramparts of world sanctionism the white flag has been raised. . . . [In Italy] nobody trembled, nobody bent: all were ready for any sacrifice, though cultivating in their hearts the certainty that at the end civilization and justice would prevail in Africa and Europe.[136]

In the aftermath of the victory, Mussolini continued to present an image of Italy as the defender of justice and ethical order.[137] Nothing and nobody could tarnish the outstanding morality of fascist Italy. Images of tractors illustrated the beneficial effects of the Italian occupation, epitomizing the arrival of technology.[138] Newsreels visually conveyed signs of Italy's recognized virtue. In Addis Ababa roads and buildings suddenly appeared— markers of renewal that dignified the Ethiopian capital of the new Italian empire.[139] At the same time, "enthusiastic" welcomings of the indigenous populations took place during the visits of fascist dignitaries in the "liberated" lands.[140] This reality proved once more that the regime had conducted "one of the most just wars that History remembers."[141]

The Manichean vision of the world, the dramaturgy of virtue, and the emphasis on victimization composed the referential structure within which fascism, through its leader, Mussolini, interpreted its own actions and presented them to the people. As Peter Brooks writes: "At its most ambitious, the melodramatic mode of conception and representation may appear to be the very process of reaching a fundamental drama of the moral life and finding the terms to express it."[142] References to an ongoing ethical struggle that pitched evil against a morally superior order, the representation of fascist Italy as the virtuous victim, and the belief in the final triumph of justice constituted the main narrative units the regime utilized to tell its tale of the Ethiopian conflict.[143] In the process of being woven and plotted, these narrative elements also participated in the making of fascism's history. The regime's refusal to abide by the League's rules, the Italians' struggle against the sanctions, and the submission of the Ethiopians to fascist law, as a proof of Italy's higher value, marked the unfolding of events in the Italo-Ethiopian dispute and determined their course. A melodramatic frame encapsulated the regime's deeds and contained its warlike aims.

The rules of melodrama also governed Mussolini's acting style and diction. The Duce's public appearances during the Ethiopian conquest were characterized by hyperbolic oratory and spectacular excitement. Mussolini's grandiose phraseology and bombastic speeches highlighted a message of virtue, and his presentations relied upon a peculiar repertoire of exaggerated, excessive facial expressions and bodily postures—a range of performance signs that typically belong to melodramatic acting.[144] Indeed, many of his contemporaries recognized in Mussolini theatrical qualities. Aldo Garosci, recalling a live speech of Mussolini in Turin, reports his mother's disappointed conclusions: "a Neapolitan actor." Although this comment in part shows the traditional antisouthern sentiment of Italian northerners, it also highlights Mussolini's magnified expressiveness, which the Turin lady identified with actors of southern provenance (although Mussolini was from the North).[145] Indeed, the macroscopic character of Mussolini's mimicry often led to a depiction of the dictator as an "opera star."[146] In a country whose popular culture was fully rooted in opera—one of the foremost expressions of melodrama—the narrative construction of the Ethiopian conflict contained all elements able to capture people's imagination. The African story, with its moral drama and its repertoire of clichés, including bombastic solemnity, sentimentalism, and noble passions, appealed to what Antonio Gramsci once called the Italians' "melodramatic taste," their operatic conception of life.[147] If, as many affirm, the time of the Ethiopian war witnessed the Italians' utmost support for the regime, some of this support can be explained through reference to the narrative structure of the event.

Melodrama, in its operatic form, was very popular in Italy, and artistic production of operas was quantitatively significant during the regime, both through films[148] and, more notably, through mobile outdoor theaters, the *carri di tespi*.[149] These theaters, which could be assembled and disassembled in less than an hour, were originally assigned the goal of bringing live performances to areas lacking show halls. In 1929 the first *carro teatrale*, which like its successors displayed a *fascio littorio* on its upper front, was inaugurated for theatrical representations. In 1930, a larger *carro* for opera (*carro lirico*) began touring the Italian peninsula with a repertoire that included Verdi, Puccini, Rossini, Mascagni, and Bellini. The *carro lirico* drew much more popular success than the *carro teatrale*; it performed forty-three shows in 1931, eighty-seven in 1932, and in the following years it offered around eighty representations, only to slow down in 1936.[150] In general, the regime's cultural politics favored lyric theaters, and it financed opera in several ways.

The composer and director Pietro Mascagni, for example, was the largest beneficiary of the funds administered by the Ministry of Popular Culture from 1933 to 1943.[151] In 1928, with the aim of establishing a prestigious institution in Rome, the regime preferred opera to theater and created the Teatro Reale dell'Opera.[152] In 1938, during the Italian Musical Summer (EMI) established by the Ministry of Popular Culture, 392 operas were staged, against 52 theatrical shows.[153]

Given this cultural context, one can speculate that the melodramatic narration of the Ethiopian conflict found a receptive audience among Italians. People knew how to decipher the story and how to interpret it. They were endowed with the tools for making sense of the developing events. Hence, they could identify with the victim role the regime attributed to Italy. The regime's narrative benefited from a history in which Italy had already been a "victim" of the Ethiopians. The force of the regime's presentation surpassed that of a mere successful propaganda campaign; it drew its strength from a familiar milieu that the population at large shared and from emotional issues with which people could easily empathize—which they could, as Gramsci would say, feel. As Mussolini told the Chamber of Deputies on March 3, 1936, after Italian soldiers occupied Amba Alagi:

> The occupation of Amba Alagi has made the Italians' heart vibrate. They remember the sacrifice of Toselli and his privates, a sublime sacrifice that is today fully revenged. . . . The Italian people understand and know the historical importance of this effort that the Nation undertakes not only to avenge its dead of 1895–96, but to guarantee the road to the future.[154]

Memory of the dead symbolically sanctioned Italy's righteousness in the conflict and motivated popular support for the regime's actions. After the war, governmental propaganda continued to voice connections to the past. The Luce documentary *From Adowa to Axum* opened with scenes evoking the Adowa battle and concluded with the comment: "Italy is revenged." A newsreel produced in 1937 for the anniversary of the foundation of the empire showed a ceremony in which a simulacrum of the Lion of Juda, symbol of Ethiopia, was placed in Rome at the bottom of the monument to the fallen of Dogali. (In Dogali, Eritrea, 500 Italian soldiers had been killed in 1897.) The commentary defined the lion as symbolic of "a tyranny that Italy humiliates at the feet of the revenged heroes."[155]

The League of Nations' role as enemy also drew Italians closer to the regime, as every citizen purportedly became the target and humiliated victim of the League's "evil" attempt to starve Italy. The whole population was subject to the "injustice" of the European countries, which, according to

Figure 20. Postcard for the Giornata della fede.

Mussolini, intended to destroy Italy's economy and people's lives. The presence of the British Home Fleet, which was sent to the Mediterranean to monitor Italy's activities, deepened the Italians' reaction against the League, thus strengthening the support for Mussolini's government. Even outstanding antifascists declared themselves in favor of the war in a surge of national pride.[156] Within this context, the test of national mobilization, which took place the day before Italy attacked Ethiopia and after the League had threatened to apply sanctions, symbolically prepared the Italians for a joint defense of their rights. On that day, at 3 P.M., sirens, radio bulletins, and church bells informed the population that they were all mobilized. Work was interrupted, and everybody was required to reach a meeting point at which radios would air Mussolini's speech from 6:45 to 7:10 P.M.

In this atmosphere of unity and national mobilization, the Giornata della fede (Day of Faith) was organized as an important symbolic episode, a demonstration of Italy's resistance and of the close relation between the fascist government and its subjects. *Fede* in Italian has both the spiritual meaning of zeal and the material one of wedding ring. On this Day of Faith, proclaimed by the regime on December 18, 1935, a month after the imposition of sanctions, the Italians were asked to donate their golden rings in order to contribute to the country's economy (Figure 20). In Rome, the queen herself provided an example by handing over her own *fede* to the fatherland in a publicized ceremony at the Capitol. In its double meaning, the Giornata della fede aimed to ensure the population's faith in the regime's actions, both materially and symbolically. Thus, Mussolini, celebrating the Day of Faith in the Pontine Ager, told the farmers:

> We inaugurate Pontinia today, day of faith, day in which all fecund Mothers of Italy take to the *Altare della Patria* or around the monuments to the Fallen their nuptial ring. But this is also the Italian people's day of faith in their rights, day of sure and unfailing faith in the destiny of the Fatherland.[157]

The Italians were expected to take their precious metals to the monuments of the fallen—those war heroes who sacrificed their lives for the fatherland and in defense of nations that were now trying to starve their families. Under these heroes' protection, the Italians were fighting against the League. In their name they were uniting against the enemy. In reality, the gold offered by Italians was never melted down.[158] More than anything else, the offer of rings constituted a gesture of national solidarity.

With the conquest of the empire, Italy's power appeared to have reached a milestone. Although the conquest took much longer than one could expect in a duel between countries of such uneven forces and means, the regime celebrated the victory in Ethiopia as a remarkable achievement, the coronation of its political ideals and goals. The evaluation of Italy's success left aside all other issues, including economics, a major factor in modern imperialism. Hence, although the regime had historically portrayed colonial expansion as the answer to problems of limited land, the colonization of Ethiopia did not offer any redress to the country's unemployment or poverty of natural resources. The exalted demographic growth and the amplification of rural themes merely constituted a justification for expansion— numerical strength ensured power.[159] In this sense, the regime looked at the empire as a symbol of fascism's virility. As Mussolini told the farmers of Pontinia on December 15, 1936, the whole Ethiopian dispute constituted a trial for Italian virility:

> It is a test in which we are all engaged, from the first to the last one, but it is a test that proves the virility of the Italian people.[160]

The empire testified to the Italians' combatant spirit in a conflict that had seen them fight not only with arms and guns against Ethiopia but also with sacrifices and economic efforts against fifty-two states. A few months after the war's end, on August 30, 1936, Mussolini told soldiers in Avellino:

[I]t is not in spite of the African war, but because of the African war, that all Italy's armed forces are today more efficient than before.[161]

Whether or not Mussolini was deluded in his belief that Italy had actually achieved the utmost in military preparedness, the theme of virility strongly reemerged in the regime's rhetoric during and after the conquest of the empire, in correspondence with the general effort to transform the Italians in a fascist and military manner (the campaign for style).[162] Despite the fact that at the end of the African war Italians became less and less fond of the regime's expansionist trajectory,[163] fascism's idea of a peace that could only be ensured by military force escalated in the aftermath of the Ethiopian conflict. And Mussolini increasingly insisted on the adjectival side of his formula "virile peace." In that same speech in Avellino he proclaimed:

> The password for the Italians of the fascist time cannot but be this: we must be strong, we must be always stronger, we must be so strong to be able to face all eventualities and to look firmly in the eyes of any destiny. To this supreme categorical imperative all the life of the nation must and will be subordinated.[164]

Then, in his 1939 address for the ventennial of the *fasces,* Mussolini reiterated:

> We need to arm. The password is this: more cannons, more ships, more airplanes. At any cost, with any means, even if we need to make a *tabula rasa* of all that we call civilian life. When one is strong, one is dear to friends and feared by enemies.[165]

Military strength publicly became the regime's priority, the means to realize the virile society Mussolini had envisaged since the beginning of his dictatorial experiment. On the wave of the imperial conquest, fascism's combative conception of life was openly displayed and applied to concrete cases. And even though the Italian army was in dismal condition after the hard-fought conflict in Ethiopia, in the summer of 1936 the Black Shirts joined Franco's troops in the Spanish civil war. In 1939 Italy occupied Albania and annexed it on April 7. A month later, on May 22, the regime signed a military alliance with Germany (the Pact of Steel). Finally, on June 10, 1940, in the military epilogue that also marked the beginning of fascism's end, Mussolini entered World War II on the side of Hitler's Germany, precipitating an unprepared country toward disaster.

Conclusions

In 1934 Giulietto Calabrese published a novel that became one of several texts most recommended to fascist libraries. Titled *Nozze fasciste: Il romanzo fascista* (Fascist Wedding: The Fascist Novel), the book presented the exemplary story of Adamo Adami, a young man whose life seemed to constitute the model of perfect fascist style.[1] A member of the Avanguardisti, the party organization for male youths between fourteen and eighteen years of age, Adamo was a happy laborer at the factory that employed him and a hammering proselytizer for the regime within his family. Not that Adamo's parents could in any way be suspected of disaffection with Mussolini. But Adamo, according to the party's teachings, should not trust his own blood: the regime's interests came first. Adamo considered it his duty to profess the fascist doctrine on a daily basis, and every morning at breakfast he greeted parents and siblings with a Roman salute.

Ambitious and looking forward to the future, in the spirit of fascism's original impulse, Adamo studied at night to become an engineer; according to the regime's dictates, he was engaged to be married and eventually would procreate. His fiancee, Eva Umani, belonged to the Giovani Italiane (Young Italian Women) and responded to the female ideal advocated by the party. Not a thin woman, or *donna crisi*, whose physical characteristics the regime identified with sterility, she had a rounded figure and florid hips: she incarnated fertility and maternity. Adamo respected his girlfriend's virginity; until the wedding day, a few years later, he limited himself to addressing her with a forceful Roman salute.

When the time finally came for Adamo and Eva to be joined in matrimony, the couple, in another manifestation of true fascist spirit, married in fascist uniforms during a party-organized wedding day (*sagra littoria delle nozze*) along with 2,000 other couples. At the end of the ceremony, all the brides and grooms gathered in the headquarters of the fascist leisure organization (Dopolavoro) and in a show of unity and party allegiance sang the fascist hymn *Giovinezza*. After the ceremony, the Adami newlyweds headed to their new, perfectly fascist house, which featured a *fascio littorio* on the main entrance door and, in every room, "Duce style" furniture and paintings with fascist scenes: a symposium of the Grand Council during the

Decennial; a wheat thresher's dinner in the countryside; Mussolini and his family at the table. With the goal of perpetuating the fascist race and ensuring its worldwide success via a virile army, the couple sanctified their legalized relation through intimate encounters. They indeed constituted the ideal fascist subjects.

Bordering on caricature, *Nozze fasciste* summarized and contained all the regime's precepts for a nonbourgeois fascist existence founded on the denial of the private as the realm of the individual and the acclamation of the private as the fulfillment of the political. The new Italian envisaged by fascism belonged to one of the several party organizations; participated in public marches and paramilitary activities; officially paraded in black shirts and other fascist garb; saluted daily in the Roman style; spoke in a fascist manner; and continuously worshipped the Duce. The formal features of the fascist man's behavior were taken to epitomize and aesthetically display the spiritual attributes of faith in Mussolini, obedience to the party, and discipline within the regime. These qualities ensured the military preparedness of the (hopefully) numerically growing citizen-soldiers, who would then be ready to engage in combat in the name of fascism and in order to affirm Italy's superior values. The order and unity of ranks, iconographically portrayed by the symbol of the *fascio*, were a necessary condition for the successful fulfillment of war aims. Imperialistic drives and aspirations counted on a mass molded into a unified warrior society through the visionary talent of the artist-politician.

Fascist representations continuously proposed that the new Italian man's identity depended on the tight observance of aesthetic rules—rules that were conceived as both the signifiers and the signifieds of fascist qualities. A perfect salute and an impeccable march both created the fascist subject and affirmed his presence. In contrast, failure to follow rules on uniforms and language, everyday activities and practices, indicated the lack of a fascist spirit—the inability to host virtues of heroism and sacrifice, without which the Italians could not achieve world supremacy. Over the years Mussolini periodically acknowledged the regime's slow progress in transforming the Italians physically and morally. The picturesque Italy of mandolin players and singers, artists and historical ruins, tourism and nostalgia, indolence and peacefulness haunted like a ghost the regime's worst nightmares, making Mussolini's vision of a courageous, disciplined, and persevering people appear doomed for defeat. The Italians, Mussolini bitterly claimed at the peak of his discomfort, were no marble or precious metal, and any artist would fail with such material. A lasting monument to the glory of the country could not be expected of them.

That the Italians never achieved the aesthetic perfection for which Mussolini strove did not diminish the regime's efforts to pursue the formal transformation of Italian society. Mussolini always envisioned his role of leader in artistic-political terms. And the regime's historical unfolding took place in accordance with the creation and elaboration of spectacular practices and rituals, mythical inventions and cultic constructions. Thus, in narrating the March on Rome, fascism instilled the revolution in its own collective memory; in invoking the martyrs' blood, it sanctified its virtuous role in leading Italy's spiritual rebirth. In the same way, the continuous growth and reinforcement of Mussolini's myth glorified the leader's primary role and reiterated the negative, "object" position of the "masses": the polity was subordinated to the artist-*dux*. Furthermore, the image of Mussolini as omnipresent, immortal, and omnipotent, a type of demigod, fed into Mussolini's actual efforts and will to centralize authority and build an unchallengeable leadership within his own party. The images of power and the power of images enhanced each other and contributed to shape a regime that revolved around one man, sanctified his power, and affirmed his superiority. The auratic mythicization of Mussolini fostered the organization of his cult—a cult that, like a multifaceted mirror, refracted Mussolini's figure a hundredfold and determined the nature and direction of people's relationship to the regime.

The phenomenon of *Mussolinismo* has outlasted fascism. However, in the immediate aftermath of the regime's fall in July 1943, Mussolini's icons were the first to undergo destruction.[2] And in death, Mussolini overlapped with the regime. The gruesome picture of his body hanging upside down from the metal structure of a gas station in Milan, next to his lover Claretta and the faithful Starace, marked the end of an era (Figure 21).[3] The death of the dictator exorcised political phantasms: the image of the Duce turned on his head symbolically reversed and redressed Italy's political path. The miserable spectacle of Mussolini's degraded dead body concluded the spectacular unfolding of fascist power—a power that continuously evoked, and profited from, symbols and rituals, festivals and celebrations, visual pageants and audio productions.

The proliferation of fascist images and sounds and the regime's monopolization of public spaces occurred in an era of new consumption trends and commercialization, an age of a developing market economy and emerging means of technological reproduction. The regime took advantage of the new techniques of audio-visual circulation, although slowly and inefficiently at times. The melodramatic gestures of the dictator mirrored the Hollywoodian mannerisms of film actors and actresses; the metallic voice of Mussolini

Figure 21.   The hanging corpses of Mussolini and other fascists, April 1945.

competed in popularity with those of rising musical stars; the omnipresent icon of the Duce counteracted the just-as-extensive ubiquity of liquor and clothing ads. The entire public persona of Mussolini confronted the publicity of consumer culture. The regime's political apparatus was mobilized in the construction of a fascist spectacle that exploited the principles and drives underlying consumption. At the same time, the regime attempted to displace and overturn the modern principles of consumer publicity on which it built its own spectacle. Within fascism's cultural perspective, the world of desires and dreams promoted by shopping excursions, commodity displays, commercial pastimes, and exotic amusements still cultivated the realm of the private and potentially fostered illicit aspirations to happiness. In the lexicon of fascist doctrine, happiness signified a disease that consumed the person. Material satisfaction was synonymous with betrayal of the common good, national well-being—in sum, the fascist state.

Via economic references and corporativist assumptions, the regime denounced the private body as the site of desire, the locus of utopian visions, the ground of experience. In so doing, it drew the line between fascism's political spectacle and the spectacle of commercial consumption. And although the philistine bourgeois seemed to be the preferred target of the regime's attack on hedonism, the denial of all individuals' autonomy was the base of fascism's creed. Discipline and control needed to be the characterizing features of the new fascist man. The desires consuming shoppers in the world of goods were to be substituted with the desire for the dictator, the absorption of the individual into the body politic, the deadly consummation of one's life in the name of the nation.

A total disregard for its subjects indeed made of fascism a model of totalitarian culture in which symbols and cults became ways to subjugate the people to the rule of a *dux* who enjoyed absolute power, was free of ethical constraints, and claimed full authority in the creation of a political masterpiece. As in Benjamin's model of the *l'art pour l'art* movement, the prevalence of form over other norms characterized fascism's aesthetic approach to politics. The metaphor of the artist working the "masses" as a piece of marble reiterated the passive, "object" status the regime assigned to the people. A sense-deprived polity allowed for a desensitized approach to politics in which human values and life itself were subordinated to the pursuit of aesthetically conceived goals. For the regime, the individual's worth seemed to reside in his or her ability to sacrifice any remnant of autonomous judgment and behavior to the altar of fascism's superior will. People needed to overcome their materialistic dreams and longings for the sake of the spiritual objectives indicated by the leader.[4] Faith and obedience transformed individuals into fascists and ensured the unity of the regime, the legitimacy of its "religion."

The regime self-referentially invoked sacred links.[5] Fascist symbols and rites often echoed Christian and Catholic practices. The cult of martyrs closely resembled the Christian adoration of saints; the ritual of the fascist *leva* had an equivalent in the Catholic rite of confirmation.[6] The regime indeed strove to produce cultic values and hailed spiritual principles as the basis for the regeneration and renewal of Italian society. Born as a countermovement to the "lifeless" politics of liberal governments, fascism claimed its will to create a new world on the premises of a Nietzschean return to the ideal. The rejection of materialistic doctrines and attitudes characterized Mussolini's vision of a renovated spiritualized world. Feelings and emotions were to substitute for reason and discussion. Mussolini's desire to destroy and construct was spurred by an originary cultural impetus toward redrawing the shape and contours of a civilization on the decline.

The "sacralization of politics" doubtless accounts for the regime's recourse to liturgical practices as a means to transform politics and induce the populace to share a panoply of myths and cults. It illuminates the internal organization of the hierarchical order of fascist institutions through reference to the dogmas of faith and belief. And it expresses fascism's reliance on, and appeal to, the superiority of a spiritual conception of reality. Yet there are dimensions of fascism that the formula of sacralization does not adequately contain. The contradictory nature of fascism's attempt to bring forth the changes it was pursuing, the web of ambivalent meanings within which fascism was caught in its search for an identity, especially defined and structured the process of fascism's making. The analysis of such idiosyncrasies, this book has claimed, is crucial in explaining the regime's identity and development. If, on the one hand, the natural, material, bodily beauty of feminine "masses" attracted fascism in its longing for a harmonic social whole, then on the other hand the cultural, formal, spiritual sublimity of masculine battles directed the regime toward total domination and war. Fascism's infatuation with aesthetics previewed the artificial settlement of irreconcilable differences at the same time that it affirmed difference as the principle ensuring a nation's vitality. The history of fascism in Italy testifies to the regime's continuous struggle to master the various meanings that its conception of totalitarian power entailed. Even the regime's simultaneous embracement of capitalism and rurality and its twisted attitude toward the bourgeoisie and consumption indicate this trend. In its multifold narratives, fascism composed and projected a battle for self-definition, an ambiguous, although fatal, overcoming of stasis and homogeneity through virile conquest.

Fascism indeed exuded war. Its originary cult of violence forecast conflictual outcomes; its ideal of a strong state engendered imperialistic suggestions. The combination of nationalism and revolutionary socialism, as well as the solipsistic will to power characterizing Mussolini's aesthetic outlook on politics, concurred in creating the combative essence of fascism, its dehumanized approach to conquest, its absolute notion of supremacy. Whether ensconced behind a narrative of virtue or feigned in a melodramatic plotting, war aims underscored the process of fascism's construction. Metaphors of battle continuously informed fascist discourse and in 1935, in a crescendo of dramatic tones and emphatic oratory, led to the invasion of Ethiopia. In this instance, fascist claims to spiritual supremacy fell short of renouncing territorial acquisitions. Mussolini's notorious plea for a "little place in the sun" epitomized fascism's ambitious search for lands—the most evidential sign of a virile, masculine potency, an irreducible will to power.

Fascism's rush toward war, however, amounted to a declaration of death. Whether or not supportive of the regime, the Italians ultimately rejected its fighting path. After the victorious African campaign, popular discontent over Italy's militaristic involvement and preparation rose to perilous levels. Despite the successful united front in the Ethiopian enterprise, competing factors converged to provoke resistance to the regime's demands at the end of the 1930s. Police reports of the time indicated the increasing presence of dissenting voices among Italians, a sign of impatience and rebelliousness toward the regime's destructive spiral.[7] The extent of these contestatory attitudes, both qualitatively and quantitatively, would be hard to assess. In general, the problem of consensus to the fascist regime remains a thorny issue in Italian historiography.[8] How much did people believe in fascism? What were the terms of people's participation in the regime's practices? And why, if resistance and insubordination occurred in everyday life, did they not evolve into widespread opposition to the government?

Such questions cannot be easily answered, and this book has directed its attention toward the solicitors of consensus, not its targets. Yet the focus on the role self-representations played in the making of fascism encourages us to examine the enigma of consensus, or what we might call the reception of fascism, not only from the viewpoint of the effect of fascist spectacle on people but also from the perspective of the conditions within which people responded to the regime's solicitations. One needs to contextualize the popular reception of fascism by looking specifically at the way the regime conceived its audience and at the implications of that conception on the audience's response. We cannot think of a "public" as an already established entity, an objectified unchanging reality, nor a spontaneous outgrowth. Audiences are a social construction, the product of social processes that situate them within a discursive space characterized by distinctive power relations.

The fascist notion and pursuit of an ideal, unified public defined the limits and constraints within which the Italians answered fascism's appeals. The entire organization of the fascist state was supposed to bring about a society composed of single units, all dependent on a central authority. The presence of plural voices, the reality of class differences, and the impact of geographical divisions were vigorously denied at the orders of the Duce in favor of a unitary, hierarchically structured whole. Political debate was eliminated, both in public and within the party. A system of enforced repression via special tribunals, confinement, and the death penalty helped impose the homogenization of the polity, the neutralization of distinct class or regional solidarity. Guillermo O'Donnell argues that one of the first actions undertaken by repressive and authoritarian regimes is the suppression of "horizontal voices"—that is, the possibility of "addressing others or others . . . addressing me, claiming that we share some relevant characteristics."[9] In the process of addressing others, we recognize ourselves as a "we," and the shaping of a collective identity takes place.

Mussolini's regime suppressed horizontal voices and eliminated the conditions for the formation of collective identities. Once the collective basis of horizontal voices was seriously restrained, resistance to fascism's rule could only take place in individual forms, most often through oblique voices. Luisa Passerini's study of the Turin working class under fascism shows that popular comic tradition and laughter provided means to contest fascism's control; slips of the tongue countered the regime's language policies; graffiti on factories' toilets made fun of fascist rules and leaders.[10] Gianpasquale Santomassimo, in his work on popular antifascism in Florence, also found several expressions of rebellion in official reports on individuals who were caught singing socialist songs or telling discrediting jokes about the Duce and his family.[11] However, instances of collective action hardly ever took place, and although fascism rejected the private, the regime rightly framed the limits of graffiti and songs as forms of "isolated," "individualistic" rebellion. The chief of police of Turin considered subversive graffiti and insults to the Duce "individual in character," the work of "discontented and disheartened elements rather than the expression of a form of planned propaganda."[12] Official police reactions to isolated opinions and gestures categorized rebellious acts as the work of deranged subjects or outcasts. The regime reinterpreted and consequently minimized the nature of popular jokes and laughter on the basis of the same limitations it had placed on the formation of social solidarity.

Certainly, once we have taken into account the boundaries and constraints defining the Italians' response to fascism, questions remain about the meaning of oblique resistance. Though no government, whether democratic or authoritarian, ever succeeds in attracting its subjects' agreement on all policies and decisions, laughter and graffiti do not necessarily undermine the general support for a governing force. Motivations for contesting might not be strictly political and might not involve criticism of the whole system. Furthermore, individual behavior cannot be considered a mere reaction to governmental policies and actions. It must also be interpreted as an assertion of people's own cultural forms, views, and strategies.[13]

In the case of fascism, one could argue, however, that total obedience to and faith in the regime were fundamental requirements for membership in the community. Passive acceptance of Mussolini's rule did not suffice for one to be considered a loyal fascist. Participation was a duty and dictated the inclusion and exclusion of the true believers.[14] The existence of a fascist society relied on the homogeneous subscription to its sacrality. Citizenship was predicated upon blind faith in the dogma; otherwise one risked expulsion to the realm of the profane, an outcast status. Within this context, the presence of oblique voices, however individualistic, signifies fascism's inability to control the Italians totally. Popular response to other policies of fascism, such as the demographic campaign, also indicate more serious problems for the regime's efforts to transform the people.[15] But again, in order to assess the nature of popular resistance to the regime, a rethinking of the category "consensus" is necessary, along with an understanding of the nonrepressive elements that attracted many Italians toward participating in their own immolation as victims/heroes of fascism's totalitarian visions.

The narrative and history of fascism are certainly not unilinear accounts. One should conceptualize the construction of fascism's identity as a multi-faceted phenomenon, from the point of view both of actors and agency and of structures and institutions. At the local level, people's everyday experience of fascism varied substantively from area to area, from the center to the periphery, from class to class, from male to female. Competing discourses, whether they came from party ideologues and intellectuals or from high functionaries and bureaucrats, also traversed the limited space of fascism's public sphere. Although the party's authority was continuously eroded and young fascist members were taught to follow blindly fascist precepts, different voices within the regime still raised advisory or dissenting opinions about official decisions, formulations, and ideas. Diversity, difference, and contradiction testify to the presence of multiple narratives within the regime. But can one therefore assume that a grand narrative was absent in fascist Italy? Can we exclude the idea that fascism possessed a totalizing, unifying tale abolishing the alterity of the other and accomplishing the homogenization of histories in the name of the formula *e pluribus unum?* This book has argued that indeed the fascist regime produced a master fiction via its leader Benito Mussolini—not that fascism can be reduced to the person of Mussolini, nor that Mussolini is identical with fascism, but that Mussolini played the leading role in the official public presentation and representation of the regime. In an era of spectacular commodities, Mussolini offered fascism for communal consumption, and his aestheticized notion of politics governed the organization of the show. Mussolini's solipsism, his aspirations to omnipotence, his moral independence, and his disregard for individuals' values informed fascism's orientations and determined its direction. Through festivals and images, rituals and speeches, Mussolini narrated fascism's story and naturalized the regime's history. These symbolic practices then reflected back and affected the reality Mussolini had articulated in the first place.

No doubt Mussolini often failed to realize the propagandistic potential of some cultural media (such as cinema), or, better, missed the opportunity to exploit these media at an early stage. But if propaganda is a logical corollary of representations, representations cannot be deemed to be pure propaganda. They constitute a model of expression and a source of self-understanding, a means to interpret experience and make sense of reality, a way of connecting to the world. Their analysis leads to an explanation of the fascist regime that does not take the relation between discourses and events to be a process of mere reflection, the mechanical realization of a cause-effect analogy. Rather, it looks at this relation as culturally mediated, structurally bound, and, last but not least, circulatory—that is, not unidirectional.

If we thus recognize the power of culture in politics, what can we conclude about the relation between aesthetics and politics? Do aesthetic visions always produce totalizing ideologies? Or can aesthetics play an emancipatory role? Is aesthetics intrinsically dangerous in politics? Or can we look at aesthetics as a fundamental element for the establishment of an ideal political state? The identification between fascism and aesthetic politics, especially in analyses of German National Socialism and the pernicious character of Nazism, have led many to denounce any kind of mixing between politics and aesthetics.[16] This book's analysis of Italian fascism has, however, evidenced and exposed, as in a photograph's negative, what Susan Buck-Morss calls fascism's *anaesthetics*, in the term's originary and foremost meaning of sensory experience, the absence of aesthetics.[17] If *"Aisthitikos* is the ancient Greek word for that which is 'perceptive by feeling,'" says Buck-Morss, then *"Aisthisis* is the sensory experience of perception. The original field of aesthetics is not art but reality—corporeal, material nature."[18] Italian fascism instead neutralized perception and affirmed the artist's omnipotence and disregard for the human consequences of his creative genius. Although counting on people's emotions, Mussolini's regime assaulted the body and denied the senses. The disregard for the "masses'" flesh and blood and the privileging of form led fascism to embrace artistic ideals that aimed at achieving the heights of "sublimity," a condition of continuous creation-destruction. This aspiration helped shape Italian fascism's peculiar notion of (an)aesthetics and determined the totalitarian character of Mussolini's political vision, its destructive path. Thus, in a paradoxical inversion, I would conclude that the lack of aesthetics, rather than its excess, made fascism totalitarian.

The definition of the term "aesthetic" is in itself controversial. And even the body has not been salvaged from the ruins of a detracted, aestheticized politics. Indeed, Paul De Man constructed part of his critique of aesthetic ideology on the indictment of the body, its seductive and sensual dimensions.[19] Others, however, have emphasized the utopian potential of the senses when they are rooted in an intersubjective notion of happiness. For Jameson, this utopian potential can be fulfilled by projecting pleasure toward the transformation of social relations—that is, by turning local, individual issues of pleasure into allegorical figures for utopia in general.[20]

Aesthetics, to be sure, remains a double-edged concept, at the same time potentially conservative and radical, with its modern claims to autonomy and its opposition to instrumental reason, its subscription to autotelic self-referentiality and its attention to individual needs and desires, its compensatory role away from the utilitarian world of bourgeois individualism and its function of challenging that world through notions of play and pleasure.[21] Yet in its multifarious meanings and inherent contradictions, aesthetics still constitutes a core issue for political theory, an indispensable element for the analysis of politics, be it authoritarian or democratic. One needs to disentangle aesthetics' meanings and contradictions in order to avoid falling victim to fascism's version of aesthetics and to abstain from categorizing aesthetics as irremediably fascist. Indeed, fascism presented an astonishing example of aestheticized politics. And, although manipulated, forced, and violated, many people responded to fascism's aesthetic appeals. However, beyond the complicated and more specific issue of the extent and degree of consensus to fascism, the question is still valid today of what accounts for aesthetics' attraction and what we can learn from the past. A reconceptualization and reevaluation of the political is in order at a time when disaffection with "politics as usual" continuously challenges forms and modalities of governing and when resurgent nationalisms and fundamentalisms seek to unify people through sacrificial and heroic losses of lives. Though the case of fascism alerts us to aesthetics' crucial role in politics, we also need to reassess the essence of the political and the nature of democratic participation in order to distinguish totalitarianism's homogenized wholes from democratic models of social unity, totalitarianism's aesthetics from a democratic, radical one.[22]

Lest we forget, fascist politics inflicted deep wounds to representative governments. Whether aestheticized or anaesthetized, fascism hit at the heart of democratic principles; it annulled the force of people's will. Fascism's version of (an)aesthetic politics was unremittingly and unrestrictedly antidemocratic. It was founded on violence and the obliteration of individuals' rights. No doubt historical fascism died in Italy in 1945, with Mussolini's dead body marking the collapse of the body politic. In the frenzied purge of fascist signs, little was spared: some of Mussolini's indelible sentences on the walls of Lipari and Montefiore; *fasci littori* imprinted on the manholes of the EUR neighborhood in Rome—ruins, fragments. But fascist discourse is not a fossil. And it reemerges every time the critique of the status quo involves challenges to representative institutions, every time intolerance and dogmatism foster antipolitical swings. Although Italian fascism developed in peculiar and specific circumstances, and even though impulses to modify traditional ways of doing politics are more than legitimate—in fact, they are necessary—when institutional changes take place on the corpse of democracy, then we risk losing more than lifeless, utilitarian, and greedy politics. The disturbing tendency in the collective imaginary to merge a critique of established power with the rejection of politics *tout court*, and the ensuing perilous move to withdraw from participating in the public realm, also create a space for authoritarian movements.[23]

Unfortunately, public-popular discussions of Italian fascism tend to suppress fascism's antidemocratic roots. On a regular basis, sensational news about the presumed discovery of Mussolini's late diary, with the dictator's allegedly negative reflections on his relationship with Hitler, provoke revisionist interpretations of the Duce and his movement. Hitler becomes the culprit of Italian fascism's degenerating path into World War II, as if the regime's only guilt lay in entering the war. In the same naturalizing operation, the figure of Mussolini only awaits his redemption, as in the distorted memory of those Italians who still separate him from the regime's wrongdoing.[24] Even foreign assessments of the neofascist party's success in contemporary Italian politics are often only measured against antiracial attitudes. The absence of an organized holocaust has turned Mussolini's regime into a model of "friendly fascism," an innocuous, sometimes even desirable, form of government, despite what is considered its "ridiculous" mise-en-scène, its overdramatized, "comic" histrionics—"typical Italian," some would say. But the low number of dead cannot absolve Italian fascism from denying citizens their rights, freedom, independent judgment, and human dignity. If we consider the assault on democracy an insignificant crime, we have all yet to master our past.

Notes

INTRODUCTION

1. For what follows, see Antonino Repaci, *La Marcia su Roma* (Milan: Rizzoli, 1972), Chapter 28.

2. Mussolini required a written proof of his mandate. Only after receiving a telegram with the mandate did he leave Milan.

3. See Repaci, op. cit., Chapter 30 and Appendix A for telegrams, letters, and articles documenting approval for Mussolini.

4. On the march, see Repaci, op. cit.; Angelo Tasca, *The Rise of Italian Fascism, 1918–1922* (London: Methuen, 1938); Nino Valeri, *Da Giolitti a Mussolini: Momenti della crisi del liberalismo* (Florence: Parenti, 1956); Renzo De Felice, *Mussolini il fascista*, I (Turin: Einaudi, 1966); Adrian Lyttelton, *The Seizure of Power: Fascism in Italy 1919–1929* (London: Scribner, 1973); Luigi Salvatorelli and Giovanni Mira, *Storia d'Italia nel periodo fascista* (Turin: Einaudi, 1957); and Giorgio Alberto Chiurco, *Storia della rivoluzione fascista,* 2 vols. (Milan: Chiurco, 1972).

5. To this day the number of people that constituted the fascist columns has not been established precisely. They certainly did not exceed 26,000 participants, most of them badly equipped. They were to face 28,000 soldiers of the Italian Army. See Repaci, op. cit., Chapter 24.

6. One can trace the origins of this trope to the day Mussolini arrived in Rome from Milan on October 30, 1922. Apparently, Mussolini went to see the king wearing a black shirt. He told the king: "Please accept my apologies if I am forced to introduce myself while still wearing a black shirt. I just came from the battle which was luckily bloodless." Cited in Luigi Salvatorelli and Giovanni Mira, *Storia del fascismo: L'Italia dal 1919 al 1945* (Rome: Edizioni di Novissima, 1952), p. 153. Mussolini's version would change later on, when blood was also invoked as part of the fascists' revolution.

7. Benito Mussolini, *Scritti e discorsi,* 12 vols. (Milan: Hoepli, 1934–1939), vol. IV, p. 293 (all translations are mine).

8. *Scritti e discorsi,* op. cit., vol. IV, p. 223.

9. For a history of the celebration, see Emilio Gentile, *Il culto del Littorio: La sacralizzazione della politica nell'Italia fascista* (Rome-Bari: Laterza, 1993), pp. 90–98.

10. See Repaci, op. cit.

11. Jean-Pierre Faye, *Théorie du récit: Introduction aux "langages totalitaires." Critique de la raison, l'économie narrative* (Paris: Hermann, 1972), p. 9.

12. See Paul Ricoeur, "The Model of the Text: Meaningful Action Considered as a Text," in Fred R. Dallmayr and Thomas A. McCarthy, eds., *Understanding and Social Inquiry* (Notre Dame: University of Notre Dame Press, 1977).

13. For the purposes of my study, I borrow Martin Jay's definition of "discourse" as derived from the Latin *discurrere,* meaning "running around in all directions" (*Downcast Eyes: The Denigration of Vision in Twentieth-Century French Thought* [Berkeley: University of California Press, 1993], p. 16). Jay's definition emphasizes both the loose nature of what the term "discourse" contains and the presence in discourse of contradictions and inconsistencies. "Discourse" constitutes the best term for dealing with the nonsystematic aspects of fascism's "text," especially because I study *non consequitur* cultural forms such as rituals, images, and speeches.

14. See Jürgen Habermas, *The Theory of Communicative Action.* Vol. II: *Lifeworld and System: A Critique of Functionalist Reason* (Boston: Beacon Press, 1987), trans. Thomas McCarthy, first published in German in 1981. Theories of narrative have developed in the last thirty years in concomitance with an attempt to probe the role of narrative in historical explanation. In 1964, in the wake of a "scientific revolution" that subverted the formal, empirical logic of the natural sciences and seemed to annex them to the humanistic enterprise of interpretation, Arthur Danto reaffirmed the autonomy of history, more specifically of its narrative approach. Danto claimed that the way we think and talk about the world is deeply historical, as an analysis of our linguistic vocabulary, grammar, and syntax demonstrates (*Analytical History of Philosophy,* now included in *Narration and Knowledge* [New York: Columbia University Press, 1985]). The question of historical knowledge and its relation to narrativity has continued to dominate the philosophical debate on the nature of cultural interpretation. See *Critical Inquiry,* vol. 7, no. 1 (1987), with essays by, among others, Roy Schafter, Jacques Derrida, Hayden White, Paul Ricoeur. The hermeneutic tradition in Germany has fueled and enlivened the debate. On the exchange between Habermas and Gadamer, see Martin Jay, "Should Intellectual History Take a Linguistic Turn? Reflections on the Habermas-Gadamer Debate," in Dominick LaCapra and Steven L. Kaplan, eds., *Modern European Intellectual History: Reappraisals and New Perspectives* (Ithaca: Cornell University Press, 1982). The identification of narrativity with real representation and the complete break between the form of the account—that is, narrative—and the content of the representation have especially provoked questions about the presumed reification of objectivity in historical explanation. See Hayden White, *The Content of the Form: Narrative Discourse and Historical Representation* (Baltimore: Johns Hopkins University Press, 1987).

15. Habermas, op. cit., p. 136.

16. On the naturalization of meaning, see Roland Barthes, *Mythologies* (New York: Paladin, 1972), trans. Annette Lavers, first published in French in 1957. For Barthes, narrative is a universally available means to represent and structure the world.

17. See Louis Marin, *Portrait of the King* (Minneapolis: University of Minnesota Press, 1987), trans. Martha Houle (first published in French in 1981), and "The Narrative Trap: The Conquest of Power" in Mike Gane, ed., *Ideological Representation and Power in Social Relations* (London: Routledge, 1989). Marin goes to the extreme of affirming that because power has no reality beyond its representation, therefore representation is the very essence of power: "Power is therefore exercised but it does not exist" (ibid., p. 108). Power needs discourse to be represented, and power can only sustain itself through its signs. But because power is the exercise of force,

discourse is also a product of force, and it does establish power by representing it. Marin, however, also suggests that the power of discourse, its performative nature, can oppose through irony and mockery the discourse of power. Although confined to tricks, the weak can challenge power by using power's own force, its discourse.

18. Marin resorts to the Eucharist ceremony of transubstantiation to show the theological illusion that states the coincidence between sense and reference ("The Narrative Trap," op. cit.).

19. I borrow this expression from Peter De Bolla, *The Discourse of the Sublime: Readings in History, Aesthetics and the Subject* (Oxford: Basil Blackwell, 1989), p. 6.

20. On the symbolics of politics, see Clifford Geertz, "Centers, Kings, and Charisma: Reflections on the Symbolics of Power," in Joseph Ben-David and Terry Nichols Clark, eds., *Culture and its Creators* (Chicago: University of Chicago Press, 1977); Lynn Hunt, *Politics, Culture, and Class in the French Revolution* (Berkeley: University of California Press, 1984); Ernst Kantorowicz, *The King's Two Bodies: A Study in Medieval Political Theology* (Princeton: Princeton University Press, 1957); Maurice Agulhon, *Marianne into Battle: Republican Imagery and Symbolism in France, 1789–1880* (Cambridge: Cambridge University Press, 1981), trans. Janet Lloyd (first published in French in 1979); Christopher Pye, "The Sovereign, the Theater, and the Kingdome of Darknesse: Hobbes and the Spectacle of Power" *Representations*, no. 8 (Fall 1984), pp. 85–106; and Stephen Greenblatt, "Invisible Bullets: Renaissance Authority and its Subversion" *Glyph*, no. 8 (1981), pp. 40–61; Roy Strong, *Art and Power: Renaissance Festivals, 1450–1650* (Berkeley: University of California Press, 1984); Jean-Marie Apostolidès, *Le roi-machine: Spectacle et politique au temps de Louis XIV* (Paris: Editions de Minuit, 1981).

21. See Mussolini's speeches and writings from 1919 to 1922; and Emilio Gentile, *Storia del Partito Fascista (1919–1922). Movimento e milizia* (Rome-Bari: Laterza, 1989). See also Cesare Rossi's 1922 "La critica alla critica del fascismo," in which he stated: "Fascism has substantially overturned the schema of traditional politics; it is not anymore the doctrine that guides or imprisons a movement, but it is the movement that produces and animates the doctrine." Cited in Alberto Aquarone, *L'organizzazione dello stato totalitario* (Turin: Einaudi, 1965), p. 5.

22. In *Il problema dell'ateismo: Il concetto di ateismo e la storia della filosofia come problema* (Bologna: Il Mulino, 1964), Augusto Del Noce ascribes fascism's ideological instability to what he calls the two souls of fascism: "traditionalist and revolutionary." Del Noce concludes that "fascist consciousness is traveling consciousness" (p. cli). He borrows this image from Ruggero Zangrandi's *Il lungo viaggio attraverso il fascismo* (*The Long Voyage Through Fascism*). For an opposite view, see Zeev Sternhell with Mario Sznajder and Maia Asheri, *The Birth of Fascist Ideology: From Cultural Rebellion to Political Revolution* (Princeton: Princeton University Press, 1994), trans. David Maisel, first published in French in 1989.

23. On the important role that rituals and symbols play in politics, see Lynn Hunt's pivotal work (op. cit.); also see David Kertzer, *Ritual, Politics, and Power* (New Haven: Yale University Press, 1988).

24. I am using here a working concept of power that is in part rooted in Foucault's culturally founded notion of power as "productive" rather than negating.

25. See Gentile, *Il culto del Littorio*, op. cit. Also see his "Fascism as Political Religion" *Journal of Contemporary History*, vol. 25, nos. 2/3 (1990), pp. 229–251.

26. George Mosse, *The Nationalization of the Masses: Political Symbolism and Mass Movements in Germany from the Napoleonic Wars Through the Third Reich* (New York: Howard Fertig, 1975).

27. George Mosse, "Caesarism, Circuses, and Monuments," in *Masses and Man: Nationalist and Fascist Perceptions of Reality* (New York: Howard Fertig, 1980).

28. Emilio Gentile, *Il mito dello stato nuovo: Dall'antigiolittismo al fascismo* (Rome-Bari: Laterza, 1982); A. William Salomone, *Italian Democracy in the Making: The Political Scene in the Giolittian Era, 1900–1914* (Philadelphia: University of Pennsylvania Press, 1945); Alberto Caracciolo, *Stato e societa' civile: Problemi dell'unificazione italiana* (Turin: Einaudi, 1960); and Guido Dorso, *La rivoluzione meridionale* (Turin: Einaudi, 1925).

29. Gaetano Salvemini, *Il ministro della malavita* (Rome, 1919).

30. Remo Bodei, "Dal parlamento alla piazza. Rappresentanza emotiva e miti politici nei teorici della psicologia delle folle," *Rivista di storia contemporanea*, no. 3 (1986), pp. 313–321.

31. Nino Valeri, op. cit.

32. On Fiume and D'Annunzio, see Michael A. Ledeen, *The First Duce: D'Annunzio at Fiume* (Baltimore: Johns Hopkins University Press, 1977); Anthony Rhodes, *The Poet as Superman: A Life of Gabriele D'Annunzio* (London: Weidenfeld and Nicolson, 1959); Renzo De Felice, *D'Annunzio politico (1918–1938)* (Rome-Bari: Laterza, 1978); Gabriele D'Annunzio, *La penultima ventura: Scritti e discorsi fiumani* (Milan: Mondadori, 1974), ed. Renzo De Felice; Ferdinando Gerra, *L'impresa di Fiume nelle parole e nell'azione di Gabriele D'Annunzio* (Milan: Longanesi, 1966); George Mosse, "The Poet and the Exercise of Political Power: Gabriele D'Annunzio," in *Masses and Man*, op. cit.; Ferdinando Cordova, *Arditi e legionari dannunziani* (Padua: Marsilio, 1969); Umberto Foscanelli, *D'Annunzio e il fascismo* (Milan: Audace, no date); and Paolo Alatri, *Gabriele D'Annunzio* (Turin: Utet, 1983).

33. Although the Fiume enterprise was started on nationalist premises, later D'Annunzio also had contacts with elements of socialist and anarchist groups. Alceste De Ambris, his secretary, was a revolutionary syndicalist, and one of D'Annunzio's projects during his regency was to constitute an alliance of oppressed people against the League of Nations.

The question of classifying the Fiume events as rightist or leftist as a means of assessing D'Annunzio's influence on fascism has generated different opinions. According to Ledeen, the Fiume enterprise defies any attempt at classification. De Felice, by contrast, emphasizes the development of D'Annunzio's ruling in a syndicalist direction, while Alatri has no doubts about the fundamentally conservative roots of D'Annunzio's ideology. See Ledeen, op. cit.; De Felice, *Sindacalismo rivoluzionario e fiumanesimo nel carteggio De Ambris–D'Annunzio 1912–1922* (Brescia: Morcelliana, 1966); and Alatri, op. cit.

34. Mussolini acclaimed the Fiume enterprise. See his speeches and writings on Fiume in *Scritti e discorsi*, vol. II.

35. On the fascist scorn for parliament, see Benito Mussolini, *Opera Omnia*, 36 vols. (Florence: La Fenice, 1951–1963), vol. XIV.

36. Ibid., p. 44, article in *Il Popolo d'Italia* of October 6, 1919, "The First Fascist Adunata."

37. *Il culto del Littorio,* op. cit. Gentile follows Albert Mathiez's 1904 work, *Les origines des cultes révolutionnaires 1789–1792.*

38. *Goliath: The March of Fascism* (New York: Viking, 1937), published in Italian in 1946 with the title *Golia, marcia del fascismo.*

39. Joachim Fest, *Hitler* (New York: Harcourt Brace Jovanovich, 1974), trans. Richard and Clara Winston, first published in German in 1973; Fritz Stern, "The Political Consequences of the Unpolitical German," in *History. A Meridian Periodical,* no. 3 (September 1960), pp. 104–134; Thomas Mann, *Reflections of a Nonpolitical Man* (New York: T. Ungar, 1983), trans. with introduction by Walter D. Morris, first published in German in 1918; Bill Kinser and Neil Kleinman, *The Dream that Was No More a Dream: A Search for Aesthetic Reality in Germany, 1890–1945* (New York: Harper and Row, 1969); Saul Friedländer, *Reflections of Nazism: An Essay on Kitsch and Death* (New York: Harper and Row, 1984), trans. Thomas Weyr, first published in French in 1982; Anson Rabinbach, "The Aesthetics of Production in the Third Reich," *Journal of Contemporary History,* vol. 11, no. 4 (1976), pp. 43–74; Rainer Stollman, "Fascist Politics as a Total Work of Art: Tendencies of the Aesthetization of Political Life in National Socialism," *New German Critique,* no. 14 (Spring 1978), pp. 41–60; and Susan Sontag, "Fascinating Fascism," in *Under the Sign of Saturn* (New York: Farrar, Straus and Giroux, 1980). Also see T. W. Mason, "The Primacy of Politics: Politics and Economics in National Socialist Germany," in S. J. Woolf, *The Nature of Fascism* (New York: Random House, 1968).

Aestheticized politics is often analyzed as a legacy and outcome of Germany's peculiar history. The singular circumstance of Hitler's biographical trajectory as *artiste manqué* has led some to examine Nazism's relation to art.

40. Walter Benjamin, "The Work of Art in the Age of Mechanical Reproduction," in *Illuminations* (New York: Schocken Books, 1973), ed. with introduction by Hannah Arendt, trans. Harry Zohn. This essay was first published in French in 1936.

41. See ibid., note 5, p. 243. Benjamin's conception of aura in this essay is modified in other writings of his. See "The Storyteller: Reflections on the Works of Nicolai Leskov" (1936) and "On Some Motifs in Baudelaire" (1939) in *Illuminations,* op. cit. For discussions of Benjamin's different conceptions of aura, see Andrew Arato, "The Antinomies of the Neo-Marxian Theory of Culture," in *International Journal of Sociology,* vol. 7, no. 1 (Spring 1977), pp. 3–24; Heinz Paetzoldt, "Walter Benjamin's Theory of the End of Art," ibid., pp. 25–75; and Richard Wolin, *Walter Benjamin: An Aesthetic of Redemption* (New York: Columbia University Press, 1982).

42. Benjamin makes a distinction between being absorbed by a work of art (passive attitude) and absorbing it (active attitude). This distinction also involves two polar opposites: concentration and distraction. "A man who concentrates before a work of art is absorbed by it. . . . In contrast, the distracted mass absorbs the work of art" ("The Work of Art," op. cit., p. 239).

43. Benjamin writes that in the age of mechanical reproduction, "the total function of art is reversed. Instead of being based on ritual, it begins to be based on another practice—politics" (ibid., p. 224).

44. Ibid., p. 241.

45. Cited in ibid., pp. 241–242. On the spectacle of war, also see Benjamin's review essay of Ernst Jünger, ed., *Krieg und Krieger,* "Theories of German Fascism:

On the Collection of Essays *War and Warriors* edited by Ernst Jünger," *New German Critique*, no. 17 (Spring 1979), pp. 120–128.

Here are Mussolini's own reactions to the spectacle of war during the First World War: "Late at night . . . the shelling of shrapnels began again. A fantastic spectacle, grand-style symphony" (Letter to De Falco, July 18, 1916, in *Scritti e discorsi*, vol. I, p. 56). Another "futurist" description appears in his Diary of War, Saturday 18, 1915: "At ten action started. Here is the dry and noisy *tam* of Italian rifles. Austrian rifles respond with their *ta-pum*. The 'motorbikes of death' begin to gallop. Their *ta-ta-ta-ta* has a fantastic speed. Six hundred blows a minute. Hand grenades cut the air . . ." (ibid., p. 81). In another entry (December 1, 1915), Mussolini described his first day in the Carso trenches: "Here war presents itself in its grandiose aspect of human cataclysm" (ibid., p. 193). And on December 6: "Very big projectiles pass by high, slow, almost panting and whining, going very far. I, all by myself, outside my hole, to my own risk, enjoy the audio and visual spectacle" (ibid., p. 197). On December 27 Mussolini described a shelling exchange between Italians and Austrians: "With my binoculars, I stood in the ditch of the trench to enjoy the spectacle" (ibid., p. 221).

46. For an interpretation of the affinities and tensions between religion and the aesthetic sphere, see Max Weber, "Religious Rejections of the World and their Directions," in *From Max Weber: Essays in Sociology* (New York: Oxford University Press, 1980), ed. and trans. Hans Gerth and C. Wright Mills, pp. 340–343, section on "The Esthetic Sphere." (This essay was first published in 1915.) According to Weber, both religion and aesthetic are against purposive-rational conduct. Furthermore, religion has historically been a source of artistic creation. But with the rationalization of life, art becomes independent and assumes the function of a "this-worldly salvation," in direct competition with salvation religion, while art also rejects any ethical norm as the basis for judgment in favor of form.

47. Op. cit., p. 188 (italicized in the text).

48. See Alice Yaeger Kaplan, *Reproductions of Banality: Fascism, Literature and French Intellectual Life* (Minneapolis: University of Minnesota Press, 1986) for this position. For an opposite interpretation, see Joseph Chytry, *The Aesthetic State: A Quest in Modern German Thought* (Berkeley: University of California Press, 1989). For an analysis of the debate on aesthetic politics, see Martin Jay, "'The Aesthetic Ideology' as Ideology; Or What Does it Mean to Aestheticize Politics?" *Cultural Critique*, no. 21 (Spring 1992), pp. 41–62.

49. Susan Buck-Morss, "Aesthetics and Anaesthetics: Walter Benjamin's Artwork Essay Reconsidered," *New Formations*, issue on *The Actuality of Walter Benjamin*, no. 20 (Summer 1993), p. 125. My interpretation of aesthetic politics is strongly indebted to this essay.

50. Terry Eagleton, *The Ideology of the Aesthetic* (Oxford: Basil Blackwell, 1990), p. 13.

51. Ibid., p. 2.

52. Cornelia Klinger, "The Concepts of the Sublime and the Beautiful in Kant and Lyotard," *Constellations*, vol. 2, no. 2 (October 1995), pp. 207–223.

53. Ibid. Klinger presents the moral presuppositions guiding Kant's discussion of the sublime and the beautiful.

54. In 1764, prior to the *Critique of Judgment*, written in 1790, Kant had also

written an essay entitled "The Distinction of the Beautiful and the Sublime in the Interrelations of the Two Sexes." In this essay Kant began to discuss the aesthetic categories of the beautiful and the sublime and their difference in terms of gender. He wrote: "The fair sex has just as much understanding as the male, but it is a *beautiful understanding*, whereas ours should be a *deep understanding*, an expression that signifies identity with the sublime." Cited in Klinger, ibid., pp. 209–210 (italicized in the text).

55. The relation between numbed senses and the First World War is explored by Modris Eksteins, *Rites of Spring: The Great War and the Birth of the Modern Age* (Boston: Houghton Mifflin, 1989), Chapter 5. Eksteins describes the soldiers' state as approaching narcosis, what came to be defined as shell shock or neurasthenia.

56. Benjamin writes: "The greater the share of the shock factor in particular impressions, the more constantly consciousness has to be alert as a screen against stimuli; the more efficiently it does so, the less do these impressions enter experience (Erfahrung), tending to remain in the sphere of a certain hour in one's life (Erlebnis)" ("On Some Motifs in Baudelaire," op. cit., p. 163). The distinction between *Erfahrung* and *Erlebnis* is important in understanding Benjamin's concept of authentic experience. On Benjamin and experience, see Martin Jay, "Experience Without a Subject: Walter Benjamin and the Novel," *New Formations*, no. 20 (Summer 1993), pp. 145–156.

Benjamin also connects the destruction of genuine experience to the dissolution of communities and the loss of tradition. Discussing Bergson, Benjamin states: "Experience is indeed a matter of tradition, in collective existence as well as private life. It is less the product of facts firmly anchored in memory than of a convergence in memory of accumulated and frequently unconscious data" ("On Some Motifs in Baudelaire," op. cit., p. 157).

57. Following a discussion of Marx, Benjamin writes: "The shock experience which the passer-by has in the crowd corresponds to what the worker 'experiences' at his machine" (ibid., p. 176).

58. Citing Janet Oppenheim, *"Shattered Nerves:" Doctors, Patients and Depression in Victorian England* (New York: Oxford University Press, 1991), Buck-Morss writes: "Anaesthetic techniques were prescribed by doctors against the disease of 'neurasthenia,' identified in 1869 as a pathological construct. Striking in nineteenth-century descriptions of the effects of neurasthenia is the disintegration of the capacity for experience—precisely as in Benjamin's account of shock. The dominant metaphors for the disease reflect this: 'shattered' nerves, nervous 'breakdown,' 'going to pieces,' 'fragmentation' of the psyche. The disorder was caused by 'excess of stimulation' (*sthenia*), and the 'incapacity to react to same' (*asthenia*). Neurasthenia could be brought about by 'overwork,' the 'wear and tear' of modern life, the physical trauma of a railroad accident, modern civilization's 'ever-growing tax upon the brain and its tributaries,' the 'morbid ill effects attributed . . . to the prevalence of the factory system'" (Aesthetics and Anaesthetics," op. cit., p. 132).

59. Buck-Morss writes that phantasmagorias have "the effect of anaesthetizing the organism, not through numbing, but through flooding the senses" (ibid., p. 134). On panoramas and world exhibitions, see especially Benjamin, "Paris, Capital of the Nineteenth Century," in *Reflections: Essays, Aphorisms, Autobiographical Writings* (New York:Harcourt Brace Jovanovich, 1978), ed. with introduction by Peter Demetz,

trans. Edmund Jephcott, and Susan Buck-Morss, *The Dialectics of Seeing: Walter Benjamin and the Arcades Project* (Boston: MIT Press, 1989). For the use of panorama in early twentieth-century films, see the case of Elvira Notari in Giuliana Bruno, *Streetwalking on a Ruined Map: Cultural Theory and the City Films of Elvira Notari* (Princeton: Princeton University Press, 1993).

60. Fascism fulfilled the role of "society of the spectacle." According to Guy Debord's *Society of the Spectacle* (Detroit: Black and Red, 1983), the spectacle, intended as an overwhelmingly public display, is a context linking people, a social relation that is mediated and hidden by images and that plays the role of a *Weltanschauung.* (The book was first published in French in 1967.)

With the expansion of a new phase of commodity production, the evolution of the market economy, the emergence of commercialization and consumption, and the perfecting of new means of technological reproduction (radio, television, etc.), the role of the spectacle has grown during the twentieth century, and it has also implicated the political realm. Politics has been affected by a more or less open struggle for the monopolization of public spaces. The development of mass media has certainly complicated the issue of politics' relation to spectacle and, convergently, to the public. The fact that fascism had recourse to films and radio broadcasts involves it in this new set of problems.

On the emergence of the quest for high visibility in public space that characterized Western culture at the end of the nineteenth century, see Philip Fisher, "Appearing and Disappearing in Public: Social Space in Late-Nineteenth-Century Literature and Culture," in Sacvan Bercovitch, ed., *Reconstructing American Literary History* (Cambridge, Mass.: Harvard University Press, 1986). The use of images cannot be intended as excluding the spoken word. Although many critics of the spectacle assume that silent images work toward the annihilation of reason, others argue that those with spectacular power drive profits from "a large organization of perceptual consumption." See Jonathan Crary, "Spectacle, Attention, Counter-Memory" *October*, no. 50 (Fall 1989), p. 102.

61. The philosopher Augusto Del Noce recognized "lived solipsism" as the alter ego of fascism's activism. According to Del Noce (op. cit.), a tendency toward goalless action defined fascism's attempt at transforming reality. But in view of action's lack of rationality, the values that would normally give moral meaning to action become tools for promoting action. Furthermore, once value is conferred only to pure action, reality merely exists through "my" action, and other subjects are only obstacles to the affirmation of "my" personality through action. Thus, moral duties toward other subjects become obsolete, because subjects are reduced to objects. "I" am the only subject and dominate the world of things. For Del Noce, Giovanni Gentile's actualist philosophy met Mussolini's revolutionary irrationalism. Actualism and fascism in many ways coincided, although they were by no means the same, nor was actualist philosophy necessarily a source of fascism. For Del Noce, Gentile needed fascism to give legitimacy to his theory of the connection between thought and action. Mussolini needed Gentile to provide fascism with a cultural legitimation.

62. In "Paris, Capital of the Nineteenth Century," Benjamin wrote: "Nonconformists rebel against the handing over of art to the market. They gather around the banner of '*l'art pour l'art.*' This slogan springs from the conception of the total

artwork, which attempts to isolate art from the development of technology. The solemnity with which it is celebrated is the corollary to the frivolity that glorifies the commodity. Both abstract from the social existence of man" (see *Reflections*, op. cit., p. 158).

63. Claude Lefort, *The Political Forms of Modern Society: Bureaucracy, Democracy, Totalitarianism* (Cambridge: MIT Press, 1986), ed. with introduction John Thompson.

64. Peter Murphy, in his review article of Lefort: "Between Romanticism and Republicanism: The Political Theory of Claude Lefort," *Thesis Eleven*, no. 23 (1989), cites the sublime aspect of totalitarian politics. He claims that "[w]hat the romantic idea of the sublime did for aesthetics, totalitarianism did for politics" (ibid., p. 138).

65. See, for example, David Harvey's discussion in *The Condition of Postmodernity: An Enquiry into the Origins of Cultural Change* (Oxford: Basil Blackwell, 1989). Harvey evokes the fictional figure of Faust as a hero who was bound to destroy in order to construct a new world.

66. As will become clear in the course of the reading, my research relies heavily on the analysis of Mussolini's speeches and writings. Filling more than 10,000 pages in a 36-volume set of collected works published posthumously, Mussolini's speeches and writings constitute an irreplaceable source for assessing his political path and theoretical development. They signal his cultural influences and mark his intellectual and political shifts. Contextualized within the specific circumstances of their occurrence, Mussolini's speeches and writings offer primary material for the analysis of his understanding of politics, his conception of fascism, and his vision of the world, but also his more mundane and immediate goals.

In analyzing Mussolini's speeches and writings, I have looked for specific tropes. My primary task has been to probe the presence, intensity, and distribution of references to aesthetics. In view of aesthetics' multiple dimensions, however, my search has widened also to include tropes that were not immediately or directly linked to aesthetics. These tropes include violence, blood, and martyrs; rurality, fertility, and virility; happiness, the material, and consumption; decadence, regression, and the bourgeois; and other tropes not necessarily combined in triads. My analysis of Mussolini's speeches and writings has also served the goal of tracing his narrative construction of his own role within fascism, his interpretation of power, the relation of the leader to the party. In addition, I have used Mussolini's speeches and writings as supporting evidence in discussions of specific historical issues in the course of the book.

It will be useful to keep in mind that both before and after the establishment of fascism, Mussolini visited most Italian regions and took every public appearance as the occasion for a speech. Furthermore, even if delivered in remote places, Mussolini's speeches at the height of the regime were published on page one of all newspapers. In 1925 Mussolini's speeches began to be transmitted via radio. Later on, cinema also became a vehicle for propagating Mussolini's words. (See Chapter 2.)

Although the *Opera Omnia*, published after the fall of fascism, is the definitive and most accurate collection of Mussolini's writings and speeches, I have also relied on *Scritti e discorsi* for my research. As a document of the fascist regime, *Scritti e discorsi* in itself tells a story. Every volume opens with a photo of Mussolini, and every page of every volume features a watermark alternating Mussolini's signature with the symbol of the *fascio*. Whenever possible, I have compared the versions of the speeches and writings in both *Scritti e discorsi* and *Opera Omnia*. *Scritti e discorsi* only collected Mussolini's speeches and writings beginning with November 15, 1914. On the publication of *Scritti e discorsi* during the regime, see Benito Mussolini, *Opera Omnia*, vol. XXVI, pp. 83–84.

CHAPTER 1. MUSSOLINI'S AESTHETIC POLITICS

1. *Novecento Italiano* was the umbrella name for a group of artists who in 1922 gathered to form a movement. Margherita Sarfatti, art critic and Mussolini's lover, inspired the movement and became its sponsor. The group soon dissolved and did not re-form until 1925, again under the aegis of Sarfatti. See Philip V. Cannistraro and Brian R. Sullivan, *Il Duce's Other Woman* (New York: Morrow, 1993), Chapter 18, "*Novecento Italiano*," and Chapter 21, "A New Aspect of Tradition." On *Novecento*, see Rossana Bossaglia, *Il Novecento italiano: Storia, documenti, iconografia* (Milan: Feltrinelli, 1979). *Novecento* generally prescribed a return to classical forms and order.

2. Benito Mussolini, *Scritti e discorsi*, 12 vols. (Milan: Hoepli, 1934–1939), vol. V, p. 279.

3. Mussolini, however, left unclear the issue of how art, in its turn, was affected by politics. According to him, the question of establishing a hierarchy between art and politics in terms of their reciprocal influence was actually quite complex. For this reason, he decided not to engage in a discussion of the topic, saying that it "seduced" him but would take him too far afield. Yet, by suspending his judgment on the question, Mussolini reasserted his aesthetically informed vision of politics. For him, art and politics were so inextricably tied that he could not even exclude the possibility of art's exercising a prior and determinant effect on politics.

4. The definition of politics as art was not original to Mussolini nor to the cultural political movements at the beginning of the twentieth century. Machiavelli had already referred to politics as the art of governing people. However, in the etymological sense of the word at Machiavelli's time, "art" embodied the idea of skill and did not have an aesthetic connotation.

5. See Margherita Sarfatti's biography of Mussolini, *Dux* (Milan: Mondadori, 1926), p. 49. The biography was first published in English under the title, *The Life of Benito Mussolini* (London: Thornton Butterworth, 1925). It is not clear how influential Sarfatti's theories of art were on Mussolini's conception of politics. Cannistraro and Sullivan (op. cit.) claim that Sarfatti's influence was remarkable.

6. Emil Ludwig, *Colloqui con Mussolini* (Milan: Mondadori, 1932), pp. 119–120. Ludwig, a renowned German journalist, interviewed Mussolini for approximately one hour a day between March 23 and April 4, 1932. These conversations were reported in *Colloqui con Mussolini*, published in English as *Talks with Mussolini*.

7. For an analysis of Mussolini as an aesthete, see Giuseppe Antonio Borgese, *Goliath: The March of Fascism* (New York: Viking, 1937).

8. Ludwig, op. cit., p. 206. Mussolini pronounced these words while discussing Pirandello's theater. For him, Pirandello's theater was fascist because it was founded on the idea that life could be radically transformed.

9. We could also define Mussolini's attitude as "aesthetic decisionism." Accord-

ing to Richard Wolin, decisionism, in political terms, "implies that imperatives of efficacy outweigh any and every normative consideration." In its aesthetic form, decisionism can be compared to Nietzsche's aestheticism, within which "the aesthetic attitude toward the world must transgress the boundaries of the aesthetic sphere *per se*, and pursue a cause of conscious world-mastery." See Wolin, "Foucault's Aesthetic Decisionism," *Telos*, no. 67 (Spring 1986), pp. 71, 73.

10. *Scritti e discorsi*, vol. III, p. 229 (speech for the first anniversary of the March on Rome).

11. *Scritti e discorsi*, vol. IV, p. 45.

12. Ludwig, op. cit., p. 96. It is also true that a whole aura surrounded Mussolini's figure, and many writers and journalists tended to give a description of Mussolini as a fascinating character. See Chapter 2.

13. Ibid., pp. 181–182.

14. The connection between artist and politician was also idealized by cultural figures of the turn of the century. In fin-de-siècle Vienna, Arthur Schnitzler and Hugo von Hofmannstahl proposed an art-inspired form of social order that revolved around the idea of harmony and the concept of wholeness. See Carl Schorske, *Fin-de-Siècle Vienna: Politics and Culture* (New York: Knopf, 1980). Hofmannstahl perceived reality as an ensemble of heterogeneous parts, which clearly imprinted a character of indeterminacy on reality itself. Modern society seemed to him to lack in cohesion, with new, "irrational" masses of nonhomogeneous people asserting their voices. For Hofmannstahl, the solution to this situation could come not from reason but from the work of the poet. It was the poet's task to bind together the different parts of society into a unified, harmonic whole, a "dynamic form." Form being the domain of the artist, only art could respond to the presence of the irrational in modern politics. See Hugo von Hofmannstahl, "Der Dichter und diese Zeit," in *Selected Essays* (Oxford: Basil Blackwell, 1955), ed. Mary Gilbert, pp. 120–143. On the cultural critique of politics, also see Peter Gay, *Weimar Culture: The Outsider as Insider* (New York: Harper and Row, 1968), in particular Chapter 4, "The Hunger for Wholeness: Trials of Modernity." In Germany, Julius Langbehn (1851–1907) referred to art as *Kunstpolitik*, or aesthetic politics, where politics follows art's interests and does not concern itself with parties or the military. On Langbehn and the German critique of politics at the turn of the century, see Fritz Stern, *The Politics of Cultural Despair: A Study in the Rise of the Germanic Ideology* (Berkeley: University of California Press, 1961).

15. On the general perception of crowds in nineteenth-century France, see Susanna Barrows, *Distorting Mirrors: Visions of the Crowd in Late Nineteenth-Century France* (New Haven: Yale University Press, 1981).

16. On France's transition to the twentieth century, see Eugene Weber, *France: Fin de Siècle* (Cambridge, Mass.: Belknap Press, 1986).

17. See Robert A. Nye, *The Origins of Crowd Psychology: Gustave Le Bon and the Crisis of Mass Democracy in the Third Republic* (London: Sage Publications, 1975).

18. Roger L. Geiger, "Democracy and the Crowd: The Social History of an Idea in France and Italy, 1880–1914," in *Societas*, vol. 7, no. 1 (Winter 1977), pp. 47–71.

19. Barrows, op. cit., pp. 18–21.

20. Ibid., p. 47.

21. See Geiger, op. cit., and Barrows, op. cit., Chapters 5 and 6.

22. In 1890 Gabriel Tarde published *La philosophie pénale*.

23. Scipio Sighele, *La folla delinquente* (1891) (*The Criminal Crowd*), Chapter 2. On the influence of Sighele's work in France, see Barrows, op. cit., Chapter 5.

24. Michel Foucault noted the problem of public gatherings at executions. The fantastic solution elaborated in 1800–1830 of the panopticon prison was supposed to substitute private, isolated discipline for the contamination of crowds. See *Discipline and Punish: The Birth of the Prison* (New York: Vintage, 1979), trans. Alan Sheridan (first published in French in 1975).

25. *La psychologie des foules* was published in 1895. See the English translation of Gustave Le Bon, *The Crowd: A Study of the Popular Mind* (New York: Viking, 1960), p. xvi. Le Bon popularized the new science. His book has been defined as one of the most influential in social psychology. See Barrows, quoting Gordon Allport, in op. cit., p. 4.

26. Le Bon, op. cit., pp. 35–36.

27. Ibid., p. 36.

28. Barrows, op. cit., Chapter 2.

29. A whole repertoire of women's images as violent creatures (castrators, warriors, sadists, etc.) also developed and typically characterized French art of the time. The most violent mobs were constituted by women: women were inclined to criminal acts. And, more than men, women were susceptible to insanity. See Barrows, op. cit., pp. 57, 59.

30. According to Barrows, women constituted both a concrete source and a metaphor of anxiety in Third Republic France. On the one hand, women effectively threatened traditional social order by forming associations and challenging laws that affirmed gender inequalities. On the other hand, women also represented a metaphor of fear in a milieu characterized by perceptions of social change. The extremely negative depiction of them derived from the same source as the pessimistic appreciation of the crowd. This was a period in which groups and movements were voicing their own rights to participate in the government of society. They were questioning the status quo by demanding political and economic power (ibid., Chapter 2).

31. On the identification of women with mass culture and its negative connotations, see Andreas Huyssen, "Mass Culture as Woman: Modernism's Other," in *After the Great Divide: Modernism, Mass Culture, Postmodernism* (Bloomington: Indiana University Press, 1986), pp. 44–62.

32. An excellent discussion of the relationship between physiology and crowd psychology can be found in Remo Bodei, "Dal parlamento alla piazza. Rappresentanza emotiva e miti politici nei teorici della psicologia delle folle," *Rivista di storia contemporanea*, no. 3 (1986), pp. 313–321. On natural knowledge, organic metaphors, and social relations, see Roger Cooter, "The Power of the Body: The Early Nineteenth Century," in Barry Barnes and Steven Shapin, eds., *The Natural Order: Historical Studies of Scientific Culture* (Beverly Hills: Sage Publications, 1979), pp. 73–92.

33. Barrows, op. cit., Chapter 2.

34. See Bodei, op. cit., p. 316.

35. On hypnotism, also see Barrows, op. cit., Chapter 7.

36. Bodei, op. cit.

37. Le Bon, op. cit., p. 71.

38. Ibid., p. 68.

39. "[T]heatrical representations . . . always have an enormous influence on crowds" (ibid).

40. Ibid., pp. 102, 103.

41. "[W]hen crowds have come . . . to acquire a profound antipathy for the images evoked by certain words, the first duty of the statesman is to change words without, of course, laying hands on the things themselves, the latter being too intimately bound up with the inherited constitution to be transformed." And more: "The power of words is so great that it suffices to designate in well-chosen terms the most odious things to make them acceptable to crowds" (ibid., pp. 106–107). Le Bon warned that the art of words was very difficult, and he suggested that those who govern consider how words often hold different meanings for different social classes.

42. Ibid., p. 112.

43. Ibid., p. 113.

44. This art basically aimed at hypnotizing the crowd. While positing the crowd's instinctive need to obey a leader, Le Bon also indicated the "means of persuasion" available to the leader: affirmation, repetition, contagion. Those elements well responded to the irrational, though mystical and unconscious, process of hypnosis (ibid., p. 124).

45. Barrows, op. cit., Chapter 7.

46. Ibid., p. 179. "After World War I, Le Bon sent Mussolini at least four of his books. . . . "

47. *Opera Omnia*, 36 vols. (Florence: La Fenice, 1951–1963), vol. XXII, p. 156 (interview with the Paris review *La Science et la Vie* of June 1926). In *My Autobiography* (London: Hutchinson and Co., 1928), Mussolini wrote: "One of the books that interested me most was the 'Psychology of the Crowd,' by Gustave Lebon" (sic), p. 25.

48. Ludwig, op. cit., p. 125.

49. The image of the relationship between artist and object actually derives from Michelangelo's theory of sculpture, according to which the artist is supposed to liberate the work of art from the constriction of the marble block.

50. *Scritti e discorsi*, vol. II, p. 313. The speech was delivered in Udine. An amazingly similar statement was made by Nazi propaganda minister Joseph Goebbels in 1933: "We who shape modern German politics feel ourselves to be artistic people, entrusted with the great responsibility of forming out of the raw material of the masses a solid, well-wrought structure of a *Volk*" (cited in Susan Buck-Morss, "Aesthetics and Anaesthetics: Walter Benjamin's Artwork Essay Reconsidered," *New Formations*, no. 20 [Summer 1993], issue on *The Actuality of Walter Benjamin*, p. 141). Also see Rainer Stollman, "Fascist Politics as a Total Work of Art: Tendencies of the Aesthetization of Political Life in National Socialism," *New German Critique*, no. 14 (Spring 1978), pp. 41–60.

51. *Opera Omnia*, vol. XV, p. 93. The article was published in *Il Popolo d'Italia* and entitled "The Artificer and the Material."

52. Ibid. On June 21, 1921, in his first speech as representative at the Chamber of Deputies following the 1921 elections, Mussolini again referred to Lenin as the "artist." While talking about communism, he said: "[T]hat great, that formidable

artist (besides legislator) whose name is Vladimir Ulianoff Lenin, when he had to forge the human material, realized that that material is more refractory than brass and marble." See *Scritti e discorsi*, vol. II, p. 179.

53. See among others Mussolini's article "Adagio" in *Il Popolo d'Italia* (September 17, 1922), *Opera Omnia*, vol. XVIII, p. 410: "Fascism has banned and dispersed the socialist imbecile ideology according to which the mass, only because mass, has become some kind of mysterious divinity. . . . We need to cast down the mass's sanctity from the altars erected by *demos*."

54. See especially Mussolini's speeches and writings between 1919 and 1922.

55. See Mussolini's speech to the Fascist Congress on November 7, 1921, in *Scritti e discorsi*, vol. II, p. 205. Sarfatti wrote in her biography of Mussolini: "But how could he love humans? He sees them as they are with pitiless clairvoyance" (*Dux*, op. cit., p. 313).

56. *Scritti e discorsi*, vol. III, p. 38. The speech was delivered at the steel factory *Acciaierie Lombarde*. Mussolini's references to blacksmiths became an acceptable staple in the regime. See, for example, this interesting passage from a letter Dino Grandi sent to Mussolini in 1940: "To become ever more one of the new Italians whom you are hammering into shape; that is the aim of my life, my faith and my soul, which have been yours for twenty-five years, my Duce." Cited by Mussolini in Raymond Klibansky, ed., *Benito Mussolini's Memoirs 1942–1943*, trans. Frances Lobb (New York: Howard Fertig, 1975), p. 144.

57. *Scritti e discorsi*, vol. IV, p. 8.

58. In an article of October 14, 1920, published in *Il Popolo d'Italia*, Mussolini wrote: "[P]olitics is the highest art, the art of arts, the divine of all arts, because it works with the most difficult material, because it is alive: the human being" (*Opera Omnia*, vol. XV, p. 258). Then, in an article of March 1923 published in *Gerarchia*, Mussolini reiterated: "The Aristotelian unity of time, space and action does not exist in the art of politics. The latter is a difficult and delicate art that works the most refractory and movable matter because it works on the living and not on the dead" (see *Scritti e discorsi*, vol. III, p. 77).

59. *Scritti e discorsi*, vol. II, p. 204 (speech of the Augusteo delivered to the Assembly of the fascist party on November 9, 1921). This interpretation probably reflects Mussolini's own story. He also came from a lower-class family and, in this sense, originated from the people.

60. See his speech on women and the vote at the Chamber of Deputies (May 15, 1925) in *Scritti e discorsi*, vol. V, p. 61.

61. An anti-women "cultural masculinism" and the use of gender metaphors in politics also characterized the Florentine avant-garde artists who participated in the publication of *Leonardo*. In the case of Giuseppe Prezzolini, Walter Adamson cites the influence of Otto Weininger's *Sex and Character* (1903)—a discussion of female and male features wherein feminine becomes synonymous with mediocrity, vulgarity, passivity, etc. See Walter Adamson, *Avant-Garde Florence: From Modernism to Fascism* (Cambridge, Mass.: Harvard University Press, 1993). Mussolini refers to Weininger when talking about women with Ludwig, op. cit., p. 181.

The Futurists showed a similar contempt for female characteristics. See Barbara Spackman's discussion of "virile" attitudes in D'Annunzio and Marinetti in "The Fascist Rhetoric of Virility," *Stanford Italian Review*, vol. 8, nos. 1–2 (1990), pp. 81–101. For an assessment of masculinism in European art at the turn of the century, see Bram Dijkstra, *Idols of Perversity: Fantasies of Feminine Evil in Fin-de-Siècle Culture* (New York: Oxford University Press, 1986). On feminine and masculine values in late Victorian America and their connection to Catholic art, see T. J. Jackson Lears, *No Place of Grace: Antimodernism and the Transformation of American Culture 1880–1920* (New York: Pantheon, 1981), Chapter 6, "From Patriarchy to Nirvana: Patterns of Ambivalence." On women as evil, also see Nina Auerbach, *Woman and the Demon: The Life of a Victorian Myth* (Cambridge, Mass.: Harvard University Press, 1982). On the crisis of masculine identity in fin-de-siècle Vienna, see Jacques Le Rider, *Modernité viennoise et crise de l'identité* (Paris: Presses Universitaires de France, 1990).

62. See Mussolini's June 8, 1923, speech to the Senate in *Scritti e discorsi,* vol. III, p. 137. Here Mussolini defined the liberal state as a state "emptied of all attributes of its virility." I discuss fascism's discourse on virility in Chapter 5.

63. Speech of January 28, 1924 to the Assembly of the Fascist Party, in *Scritti e discorsi,* vol. IV, p. 38.

64. See speech of November 4, 1925, to the National Association of War Disabled, in which Mussolini said: "[Y]ou expect from me a virile speech" (*Scritti e discorsi,* vol. V, p. 184). Also see speech of June 26, 1934, delivered to the people of Venice after Mussolini met with Hitler: "[W]e have become a strong people. Our peace is thus virile because peace avoids weak people and accompanies strong ones" (*Scritti e discorsi,* vol. IX, p. 101).

65. Yvon De Begnac, *Palazzo Venezia: Storia di un regime* (Roma: La Rocca, 1950), p. 295. De Begnac's was supposed to be the official biography of Mussolini.

66. See Mussolini's speech of September 24, 1925, delivered to a fascist audience at the Teatro Alfieri in Asti (*Scritti e discorsi,* vol. V, p. 131).

67. *Scritti e discorsi,* vol. VIII, p. 120 (speech of October 17, 1932).

68. Ludwig, op. cit., p. 119.

69. Mussolini's artistic project is infused with purposeless "activism." According to Augusto Del Noce, *Il problema dell'ateismo: Il concetto di ateismo e la storia della filosofia come problema* (Bologna: Il Mulino, 1964), activism implies the lack of a finalized goal and a misrecognition of the "other" as "I." The others become objects so that no moral duties toward them are implied. Activism identified with solipsism reduces the world to things. "I" am the only "subject," and the world becomes my object of domination. The will to power is an imperative unless "I" want to become an object myself (Del Noce, op. cit., introduction, pp. cxlix–cliii). In Gentile's actualist philosophy, for example, all categories are reduced to one: the act of the thinking thought. Reality is but the thinking thought that makes it; it is reduced to the "I," and the "I" constitutes the perennial actualization of the spirit that creates itself. For Gentile, the spirit's act of self-creation takes place through three dialectical moments: pure subjectivity (the thinking "I"), pure objectivity (the thought "I"), and the synthesis of the two (self-consciousness). To these three moments correspond the three absolute forms of the spirit: art, religion, and philosophy. The subjectivized "I" befits art as one form of the spirit. Of Giovanni Gentile, see *L'atto del pensare come atto puro* (1912); *Riforma della dialettica hegeliana* (1913); *Teoria generale dello spirito come atto puro* (1916).

70. Ludwig, op. cit., p. 65.

71. Susan Buck-Morss, op. cit., p. 126. As for political theory, Buck-Morss refers to the Greek polis and Machiavelli. Also see Cornelia Klinger, "The Concepts of the Sublime and the Beautiful in Kant and Lyotard," *Constellations*, vol. 2, no. 2, pp. 207–223.

72. The idea that modernity tends toward omnipotent domination is typical of Heidegger's philosophy. Heidegger identifies subjectivity with the will to power. For a discussion of some of these issues in relation to democracy, see Joel Whitebook, "Hypostatizing Thanatos: Lacan's Analysis of the Ego," *Constellations*, vol. 1, no. 2 (October 1994), pp. 214–230.

The fantasy of all male creation ex nihilo appears in what Heidegger calls Nietzsche's *Mannesaesthetik* (literally, male aesthetics). According to Buck-Morss, *Mannesaesthetik* "is to replace . . . 'female aesthetics' of receptivity to sensations from the outside" (ibid., p. 128).

73. Mussolini told Ludwig: "The populace is . . . more open to glory. Because glory you cannot understand it logically; it belongs to feelings" (Ludwig, op. cit., p.64; see also p. 124).

74. Ibid., p. 120.

75. Walter Benjamin, "The Work of Art in the Age of Mechanical Reproduction," in *Illuminations* (New York: Schocken Books, 1973), ed. with introduction by Hannah Arendt, trans. Harry Zohn, pp. 217–251.

76. See "Dottrina del Fascismo" in *Scritti e discorsi*, vol. VIII, pp. 69–70. This essay, written in collaboration with Gentile, was Mussolini's first theoretical piece on fascism.

77. *Scritti e discorsi*, vol. II, p. 335.

78. *Scritti e discorsi*, vol. V, p. 197. The idea of the new man had already appeared in the Futurists' longing for a "new" or "very new" Italian. Marinetti foretold the coming of a unique type, a heroic character who was always in motion and always changing. Fascism, however, could not tolerate unique, heterogeneous individuals.

The construction of a "new man" was also part of the socialist project in the Soviet Union and in Nazi Germany.

79. *Scritti e discorsi*, vol. V, pp. 321, 302, 454. The rhetoric of producing was characteristic of fascism. Since it presented itself in opposition to the old status quo—the wordy system of parliamentarism—the fascist regime aimed at presenting an image of itself as concretely working toward the establishment of fascist Italy, as concretely "remodeling Italy's face." Inaugurations of works, for instance, always punctuated the celebration of the new fascist year. Whether it was the reclamation of swamplands, the opening of a highway, the restoration of historical monuments, or the starting of a new railway track, the regime showed it was always moving and was always involved in frenetic activities.

80. For what follows, see Jens Petersen, "La nascita del concetto di 'Stato totalitario' in Italia," *Annali dell' Istituto storico italo-germanico in Trento*, vol. 1 (1975), pp. 143–168. Petersen analyzes the concept of "totalitarian state" by following the method developed in Germany by Reinhart Koselleck: the *Begriffsgeschichte*.

81. *Opera Omnia*, vol. XXI, p. 362. There are slightly different versions of this sentence. See Jean-Pierre Faye, *Théorie du récit: Introduction aux langages totalitaires. Critique de la raison, l'économie narrative* (Paris: Hermann, 1972), p. 59.

82. "Truly, the most salient characteristic of the fascist movement will be for

those who will study it in the future, the 'totalitarian' spirit of fascism, a spirit which does not allow the future to have dawns that will not be saluted with the Roman gesture, and does not allow the present to feed souls that are not bent to the confession: 'I believe'" (cited in Petersen, op. cit., p. 157, from an article in *Il Mondo* of November 2, 1923).

83. Ibid., p. 162.

84. Roberto Forges Davanzati, a high official of the party, affirmed in a 1926 speech: "If the adversaries tell us that we are totalitarian . . . do not panic. . . . Yes, we are totalitarian! . . . We want to be such from morning to evening" (ibid., p. 163).

85. In the first attempt to give fascism a sort of doctrinaire status, the official philosopher of fascism, Giovanni Gentile, elaborated on the concept of totalitarianism in order to explain the fundamental characteristics of fascism. For the development of the concept of *total Staat* in German political culture, see Faye, op. cit. Faye analyzes Carl Schmitt's elaboration of the term *"total"* by referring to the Italian origins of the word "totalitarian."

86. *Opera Omnia*, vol. XXI, p. 362 (June 22, 1925) (my emphasis).

87. On the organization of the totalitarian state, see Alberto Aquarone, *L'organizzazione dello stato totalitario* (Turin: Einaudi, 1965); and Renzo De Felice, *Mussolini il fascista*, vol. II (Turin: Einaudi, 1968). After his appointment as prime minister, Mussolini began to reorganize the state institutions and to reform offices and organs of the public administration. During the years 1925–1926 the pace of reform increased. The fascist regime eliminated from the governmental bureaucracy those it did not consider fervid fascists and expelled from the party undesirable members. Subsequently the regime formulated a law that limited the right of association, thus protecting the fascist state from the danger of internal divisions, and it issued reforms aimed at suppressing local autonomies. Other means of control that the government adopted included the regimentation of the legal and journalistic professions, new police norms concerning political confinement, and, more generally, penal sanctions for political crimes. At the end of 1926, the journal *Critica fascista* proclaimed the death of liberalism and democracy and the birth of a new era: "We consider the pre-fascist political world *finished*. Its men, its doctrines, its ways of life are finished" (cited in Aquarone, op. cit., p. 109).

88. The state, affirmed Mussolini, was not the sum of the people. On the contrary, it represented "the highest and most powerful personality; it is force, but spiritual force." See "Dottrina del Fascismo" in *Scritti e discorsi*, vol. VIII, p. 73. Mussolini applied to the state the principle of hierarchy. In an article published in the fascist journal *Gerarchia (Hierarchy)*, Mussolini defined the state as a "system of hierarchies." He also affirmed that "the state must express itself through the most selected parts of a society, and must be the guide of the other minor classes." See *Scritti e discorsi*, vol. II, pp. 292, 293. Emilio Gentile connects Mussolini's hierarchical vision of the state to Pareto's theory. See Gentile, *Le origini dell'ideologia fascista (1918–1925)* (Rome-Bari: Laterza, 1975). The totalitarian conception of the fascist state was also theorized by other ideologues of the regime, especially Alfredo Rocco and Giuseppe Bottai.

89. Georg Simmel, "Sociological Aesthetics," in *The Conflict in Modern Culture and Other Essays* (New York: Teachers College Press, 1968), trans. K. Peter Etzkorn, p. 74. In his discussion of the new politics in the nineteenth century, George

Mosse connects the emergence of a new political style to elite and middle-class fears about the lack of form in society. See Mosse, "Caesarism, Circuses, and Monuments," in *Masses and Man: Nationalist and Fascist Perceptions of Reality* (New York: Howard Fertig, 1980), pp. 104–118. According to Philippe Lacoue-Labarthe and Jean-Luc Nancy, the exigency of harmony and stability had created the longing for an organic politics—along with an absolute, holistic notion of literature—in the philosophical and literary circles of the Jena Romantics. See *The Literary Absolute: The Theory of Literature in German Romanticism* (Albany: State University of New York Press, 1988), trans. Philip Barnard and Cheryl Lester (first published in French in 1978). On fascism's ambiguous relation to "rationality," see the case of Nazi Germany in Jeffrey Herf, *Reactionary Modernism: Technology, Culture, and Politics in Weimar and the Third Reich* (Cambridge: Cambridge University Press, 1984).

90. For an analysis of Stalin's politics as an artistic project see Boris Groys, *Lo stalinismo ovvero l'opera d'arte totale* (Milan: Garzanti, 1992).

91. See John Carey, "Revolted by the Masses," *Times Literary Supplement* (January 12–18, 1990), pp. 34–36. Also see Giorgio Galli, "Il fascismo e la violenza come strumento di azione politica," in Costanzo Casucci, ed., *Il fascismo: Antologia di scritti critici* (Bologna: Il Mulino, 1982), pp. 591–598.

92. For an analysis of the critiques of democracy, see Norberto Bobbio, "L'ideologia del fascismo," in Casucci, op. cit., pp. 598–624. Bobbio considers five different perspectives covering the reactionary critique of democracy: philosophical, historical, ethical, sociological, and political.

93. The history of how the left considered the masses at the turn of the century is yet to be written.

94. For a critique of professional politicians, see Max Weber's famous lecture, "Politics as Vocation," in *From Max Weber: Essays in Sociology* (New York: Oxford University Press, 1946), ed. and trans. Hans Gerth and C. Wright Mills. The lecture was delivered in 1918 and first published in 1919.

95. Bodei, op. cit.

96. Geiger writes: "When the tenets of crowd psychology were first formulated they declared, with some reservations, that crowds and democracy were basically compatible. Subsequently they reversed themselves, but without being able to establish a more appropriate alternative. Only much later was this incompatibility theoretically resolved, when nationalism was added to their political calculations" (op. cit., p. 47).

97. Within this context, race also became a means to institute divisions.

98. Bodei, op. cit.

99. According to Giorgio Galli, the rejection of democracy involves the rejection of parliamentary representation as a medium that turns conflicts into fiction. As a matter of fact, democratic "representativity" has a common etymological root with theatrical "representation." They were born in the same political and cultural context, sixteenth-century England, at a time when both Elizabethan theater and parliament developed (Galli, op. cit., pp. 592–593).

100. On the question of violence see Hannah Arendt, *On Violence* (San Diego: Harcourt, Brace and World, 1970).

101. Weber's theory also can be understood within this climate. According to Mommsen, "[T]he principle of struggle as an essential element of all voluntary po-

litical 'business' is accepted [by Weber] together with the concept of 'dominance' or 'mastery.'" See Mommsen, "Max Weber's Political Sociology and His Philosophy of World History," in Dennis Wrong, ed., *Max Weber* (Englewood Cliffs: Prentice-Hall, 1970), p. 188.

102. On the influence of Sorel's theory of violence at the time, see H. Stuart Hughes, *Consciousness and Society: The Reorientation of European Social Thought 1800–1930* (New York: Vintage, 1958).

103. Henri Bergson, *L'évolution créatrice* (Paris: F. Alcan, 1907). On Sorel's relation to Bergson, see H. Stuart Hughes, op. cit., pp. 121–123.

104. Goerges Sorel, *Reflections on Violence* (London: Allen and Unwin, 1916), trans. T. E. Hulme, p. 99 (first published in English in 1914).

105. On this issue, see Sorel's distinction between force and violence, ibid., Chapter V, "The Political General Strike." For Sorel, force imposes a social order; violence destroys a social order.

106. Ibid., p. 32. On Sorel's myth also see Michael Tager, "Myth and Politics in Sorel and Barthes," *Journal of the History of Ideas,* vol. XLVII, no. 4 (October–December 1986), pp. 625–639.

107. Sorel's theory of myth also influenced the political theorist Carl Schmitt. In the chapter entitled "Irrational Theories of the Direct Use of Force," in *The Crisis of Parliamentary Democracy* (Cambridge, Mass.: MIT Press, 1985), trans. Ellen Kennedy (originally published in German in 1923), Schmitt praises Sorel's theory of myth. For Schmitt, it is not important what the strike means today or what it can accomplish. Its value resides in its ability to generate enthusiasm.

108. Sorel, op. cit., p. 295.

109. See Zeev Sternhell with Mario Sznajder and Maia Asheri, *The Birth of Fascist Ideology: From Cultural Rebellion to Political Revolution* (Princeton: Princeton University Press, 1994), for Sorel's influence on revolutionary syndicalism. Sternhell affirms: "Sorel's writings represented the conceptual space in which the theoreticians of revolutionary syndicalism evolved" (op. cit., p. 20). On Sorel's syndicalism also see J. R. Jennings, *Georges Sorel: The Character and Development of His Thought* (New York: St. Martin's, 1985). On Sorel's influence on Gramsci see Walter Adamson, *Hegemony and Revolution: A Study of Antonio Gramsci's Political and Cultural Theory* (Berkeley: University of California Press, 1980). On syndicalism also see David D. Roberts, *The Syndicalist Tradition and Italian Fascism* (Chapel Hill: University of North Carolina Press, 1979).

110. According to Renzo De Felice, author of a voluminous biography of Mussolini, the most important influence on Mussolini's formation was revolutionary syndicalism. See his *Mussolini il rivoluzionario, 1883–1920* (Turin: Einaudi, 1965), p. 40.

111. Mussolini's review was published in *Il Popolo* on May 27, 1909, now in *Opera Omnia,* vol. II, p. 126. Mussolini wrote: "I do not think much of Bergson's influence on the formation of syndicalist theories, whereas Sorel is truly *nôtre maître.*" A year earlier Mussolini had subscribed to Sorel's "Apology for Violence." See *Opera Omnia,* vol. I, p. 147.

112. *Opera Omnia,* vol. II, pp. 163–168. It seems that Mussolini first read Sorel during his sojourn in Switzerland. See De Felice, *Mussolini il rivoluzionario,* op. cit., p. 40, footnote 4. Mussolini resided in Switzerland from July 1902 to November 1904.

Also his first encounter with Pareto's theories took place during his stay in Lausanne. See De Felice, ibid., p. 38.

113. *Opera Omnia*, vol. II, p. 164.

114. Ibid., p. 168. Later, in 1910, Mussolini criticized Sorel for sponsoring the monarchy. See Sergio Romano, "Sorel e Mussolini," *Storia Contemporanea*, vol. XV, no. 1 (February 1984), pp. 123–131.

115. English translations of some manifestoes and other writings of Marinetti can be found in Filippo Tommaso Marinetti, *Marinetti: Selected Writings* (New York: Farrar, Straus and Giroux, 1971), ed. with introduction by R. W. Flint, trans. R. W. Flint and Arthur Coppotelli.

116. See Adamson, *Avant-Garde Florence*, op. cit.; Emilio Gentile, ed., *Mussolini e "La Voce"* (Florence: Sansoni, 1976); and Gentile, *"La Voce" e l'eta' giolittiana* (Milan: Pan, 1972). An important influence on the generation of 1880 was Alfredo Oriani's *La rivolta ideale* (*The Ideal Revolt*) (1908), which called for the spiritual rebirth of Italy. Mussolini honored Oriani as a spiritual precursor of fascism. See *Scritti e discorsi*, vol. IV, p. 101 (speech of April 27, 1924, which became the preface to Oriani's *Opera Omnia*).

117. Cited in Adamson, *Avant-Garde Florence*, op. cit., p. 88.

118. Ibid., p. 146. "War is the *general examination* to which people are called every so often by history. When this occurs, everything that is healthy, even if hidden, is revealed; and what is rotten is also revealed."

119. *Il Regno* was founded in 1903.

120. Enrico Corradini, *Discorsi politici (1902–1923)* (Florence: Vallecchi, 1923). Also see Alexander De Grand, *The Italian Nationalist Association and the Rise of Fascism in Italy* (Lincoln: University of Nebraska Press, 1978).

121. See for example Mussolini's May 30, 1920, article in *Il Popolo d'Italia* on the crisis of parliamentarism. The article was entitled "La montagna e i topi" (The Mountain and the Rats), now in *Opera Omnia*, vol. XV, pp. 9–11.

122. "The Fasces are not, do not want, cannot be, cannot become a party," Mussolini wrote in *Il Popolo d'Italia* on July 3, 1919. See *Opera Omnia*, vol. XIII, p. 219.

123. See Mussolini's article in *Il Popolo d'Italia* of October 6, 1919: "It is hard to define the fascists. They are neither republican, nor socialist, democratic, conservative, nationalist. They represent a synthesis of all negations and affirmations. . . . In fascism and its lack of statutes and transcendental programs one can find the liberty and autonomy missing from the rigidly cast organizations [*organizzazioni rigidamente inquadrate e tesserate*]" (*Opera Omnia*, vol. XIV, p. 44). According to Franz Neumann, National Socialism also lacked a specific program: "The ideology of National Socialism contains elements of idealism, positivism, pragmatism, vitalism, universalism, institutionalism—in short, of every conceivable philosophy." See *Behemoth: The Structure and Practice of National Socialism 1933–1944* (New York: Harper and Row, 1966), p. 462. The book was first published in 1942. A revised version was published in 1944.

124. *Opera Omnia*, vol. XV, pp. 216–217. Compare with the German novelist Ernst Jünger's statement as singled out by Benjamin in his review of the collection *Krieg und Krieger*, edited by Jünger: "[I]t is of secondary importance in which century, for which ideas, and with which weapons the fighting is done" ("Theories of German Fascism: On the Collection of Essays *War and Warriors*, edited by Ernst

Jünger," *New German Critique,* no. 17 [Spring 1979], p. 120). The essay was originally published in 1930. See also this quote from Ernst Jünger's *Kampf als inneres Erlebnis* as cited by Jeffrey Herf, op. cit., p. 76: "[P]erhaps we are sacrificing ourselves for something inessential. But no one can take away our worth. What is essential is not what we fight for but how we fight. The quality of fighting, the engagement of the person, even if it be for the most insignificant idea, counts for more than brooding over good and evil." On turn-of-the-century stress on vitalism and motion, see Modris Eksteins, *Rites of Spring: The Great War and the Birth of the Modern Age* (Boston: Houghton Mifflin, 1989).

125. *Opera Omnia,* vol. XV, p. 221.

126. Cited in Emilio Gentile, *Storia del Partito Fascista (1919–1922): Movimento e milizia* (Rome-Bari: Laterza, 1989), p. 400.

127. *Opera Omnia,* vol. XIV, p. 196. In his *Political Theology: Four Chapters on the Concept of Sovereignty* (Cambridge, Mass.: MIT Press, 1985), trans. George Schwab (first published in German in 1922), p. 80, Carl Schmitt followed the reactionary critic Donoso Cortes's characterization of the bourgeoisie as the *clasa discutidora.* Schmitt considered public discussion as a means to escape responsibility and femininize politics by removing oneself from the necessity of taking a stance.

128. *Scritti e discorsi,* vol. I, p. 24.

129. Ibid., pp. 22, 23.

130. On Mussolini's equivocation between neutrality and intervention, see De Felice, *Mussolini il rivoluzionario,* op. cit., Chapter 9, "The War Crisis."

131. See article of October 18, 1914, published in *Avanti!,* in *Opera Omnia,* vol. VI, pp. 402–403.

132. See Mussolini's reaction to the expulsion in *Scritti e discorsi,* vol. I, pp. 11–13 (speech of November 25, 1914, to the assembly of the Milan socialist section).

133. At the time of his expulsion Mussolini was the director of the socialist newspaper *Avanti!* (He had been nominated director in 1912.) He then proceeded to lead *Il Popolo d'Italia,* which first appeared on November 15, 1914.

134. See his article "Audacia" (Audacity), written for *Il Popolo d'Italia* on November 15, 1914, in *Scritti e discorsi,* vol. I, p. 8.

135. Quoted in Gentile, *Le origini dell'ideologia fascista,* op. cit., p. 57. On the history of the war, see Piero Melograni, *Storia politica della grande guerra, 1915/1918* (Bari: Laterza, 1969). On the war myth in Italy, also see Mario Isnenghi, *Il mito della grande guerra da Marinetti a Malaparte* (Bari: Laterza, 1970). In Germany, Ernst Jünger in his novel *Storm of Steel,* published two years after the end of the war, celebrated death and danger as revitalizing moments. On war as redemption also see Roland Stromberg, *Redemption by War: The Intellectuals and 1914* (Lawrence: Regents Press of Kansas, 1982). On the war generation see Robert Wohl, *The Generation of 1914* (Cambridge, Mass.: Harvard University Press, 1979), and Paul Fussel, *The Great War and Modern Memory* (New York: Oxford University Press, 1975).

136. For how some of the survivors merged into the fascist movement see Paolo Nello, *L'avanguardismo giovanile dalle origini al fascismo* (Rome-Bari: Laterza, 1978). For a similar situation in Germany see Robert George Leeson Waite, *Vanguard of Nazism: The Free Corps Movement in Post-War Germany, 1918–1923* (Cambridge, Mass.: Harvard University Press, 1952). The Freikorps were groups of soldiers who believed in the necessity of continuing the battle after the war ended.

They created Volunteer Civic Guards in postwar Germany and affirmed, paraphrasing von Clausewitz, that "politics is the extension of war by other means" (Waite, op. cit., p. 269, footnote 17). On the Freikorps also see Klaus Theweleit, *Male Fantasies*, 2 vols. (Minneapolis: University of Minnesota Press, 1987–1989), trans. Stephen Conway with Erica Carter and Chris Turner. Theweleit analyzes the Freikorps' fantasies concerning women. For Theweleit, the dread of women that the Freikorps expressed was the actual fear of being "engulfed," of "being sucked in" by women.

137. In his speech of March 28, 1926—seventh anniversary of the Fasces—when recalling the foundation of his movement, Mussolini also affirmed: "I could have called the Fasces 'Fasces of reconstruction,' 'of reorganization,' of 'elevation' and with other similar words that end in 'ion.' I called instead this organization : 'Italian Fasces of Combat.' In this hard and metallic word there was all the program of fascism, the way I dreamt of it, the way I wanted it, the way I have made it" (*Scritti e discorsi*, vol. V, p. 297).

138. *Scritti e discorsi*, vol. II, pp. 7–10 (article published in *Il Popolo d'Italia* on March 28, 1919).

139. On the question of violence in the early fascist movement see Emilio Gentile, *Storia del partito fascista*, op. cit., pp. 494–505. On the "young" and "old" Italies see Adamson, *Avant-Garde Florence*, op. cit., pp. 86–87, 282. The distinction between the "young" and "old" Italy accompanied another distinction in the political culture of the time: the "legal" and the "real" Italy. This conceptual opposition was not only typical of Italy. Eric Hobsbawm writes that the logical French in Louis Philippe's era had made the distinction between "the legal country" and "the real country." See Hobsbawm, *The Age of Empire 1875–1914* (New York: Pantheon, 1987), p. 85.

140. Arditi had been the Italian Army's "daring" assault battalion in World War I.

141. Two days later Mussolini defined the episode as "spontaneous, absolutely spontaneous" (*Opera Omnia*, vol. XIII, p. 62). The Milanese headquarters of *Avanti!* were again destroyed after the March on Rome. Damages were estimated at 4 million lire. See Valerio Castronovo, *La stampa italiana dall'unita' al fascismo* (Bari: Laterza, 1970), p. 343.

142. On agrarian terrorism as a solution to social conflicts, see Adrian Lyttelton, "Fascismo e violenza: conflitto sociale e azione politica nel primo dopoguerra," *Storia contemporanea*, vol. XIII, no. 6 (December 1982), pp. 965–983. Also see Lyttelton, *The Seizure of Power: Fascism in Italy 1919–1929* (New York: Scribner, 1973). For Lyttelton, fascist violence was particularly strong in areas where social conflicts were tense. It was more prevalent in agrarian regions than in industrial ones.

143. For some description of the violence, see Gaetano Salvemini, *Scritti sul fascismo* (Milan: Feltrinelli, 1961), vol. I. The *manganello* (club or cudgel), symbol of fascism's violence, was justified by Mussolini as a tool with which to impose fascism's ideas (*Scritti e discorsi*, vol. II, p. 159). The philosopher Giovanni Gentile defined the *manganello* as an "instrument of persuasion" (cited in Salvemini, op. cit., p. 624). A popular song of the fascist movement praised the *manganello* as a saint; see A. V. Savona and M. L. Straniero, eds., *Canti dell'Italia fascista (1919–45)* (Milan: Mondadori, 1979), p. 104.

144. Lyttelton, "Fascismo e violenza," op. cit., p. 971. Lyttelton writes that fas-

cist violence was episodic between 1919 and 1920 (p. 966). The issue of violence in numerical terms is controversial. For example, Gramsci talked about 1,500 Italians dead and 40,000 others beaten and wounded. Cited in Jens Petersen, "Il problema della violenza nel fascismo italiano," *Storia contemporanea*, vol. XIII, no. 6 (December 1982), p. 987.

145. Ibid., p. 1000. For a personal account of fascism's violent surge in Sardinia, see Emilio Lussu, *Marcia su Roma e dintorni* (Turin: Einaudi, 1965). On the rituals that accompanied fascist violence, see Emilio Gentile, *Il culto del Littorio: La sacralizzazione della politica nell'Italia fascista* (Rome-Bari: Laterza, 1993), pp. 46–50.

146. See, among others, Mussolini's article in *Il Popolo d'Italia* November 24, 1920, after a deadly fight between fascists and communists in Bologna; speech of April 3, 1921; speech of July 21, 1921, after the fight between fascists and communists at Sarzana had resulted in several dead and wounded; December 1, 1921, speech at the Chamber, after fascist violence in Rome; and article of January 19, 1922. The title of this article was "Vincolo di sangue" (Blood Tie). *Opera Omnia*, vols. XVI, XVII, XVIII. For a rational-choice approach to the relationship between fascist ideal and the red menace, see William Brustein, "The 'Red Menace' and the Rise of Italian Fascism," *American Sociological Review*, vol. 56 (October 1991), pp. 652–664.

147. See, for example, his maladroit response in his speech of April 3, 1921, delivered in Bologna, to the socialists' accusation that he sold out to the agrarians (*Opera Omnia*, vol. XVI, pp. 239–246). Lyttelton argues that fascism was "a movement founded on an irrational ideology which nonetheless pursued a strategy of calculated, planned, and unusually effective violence" ("Fascismo e violenza," op. cit., p. 981).

148. *Scritti e discorsi*, vol. II, p. 54. At times, Mussolini also resorted to rough, coarse language that metaphorically conveyed threats of violence against adversaries.

149. See Emilio Gentile, *Il culto del Littorio*, op. cit., on violence and fascism in the years between World War I and fascism's takeover of power.

150. The rhetoric of internal enemies had been typical of *La Voce*. See Adamson, *Avant-Garde Florence*, op. cit., pp. 87, 261.

151. *Scritti e discorsi*, vol. II, p. 328 (speech to the fascist group Sciesa in Milan of October 4, 1922).

152. Ibid., p. 233, article of January 20, 1922, published in *Il Popolo d'Italia*. Also see Mussolini's ascetic and heroic portrayal of fascist violence in *My Autobiography*, op. cit., pp. 126–127.

153. *Scritti e discorsi*, vol. II, p. 233.

154. Petersen, "Il problema della violenza," op. cit., p. 998.

155. *Scritti e discorsi*, vol. IV, p. 263.

156. Only in 1942 was a less inflated statistic published by the regime, estimating 672 fascist dead. See Petersen, "Il problema della violenza," op. cit., p. 1006.

157. For the statutes, see Mario Missori, *Gerarchie e statuti del P.N.F.: Gran Consiglio, Direttorio Nazionale, Federazioni provinciali: Quadri e biografie* (Roma, 1986).

158. Marla Stone, "Staging Fascism: The Exhibition of the Fascist Revolution," *Journal of Contemporary History*, vol. 28, nos. 2/3 (1993), pp. 215–243; Jeffrey Schnapp, "Epic Demonstrations: Fascist Modernity and the 1932 Exhibition of the

Fascist Revolution," in Richard J. Golsan, ed., *Fascism, Aesthetics, and Culture* (Hanover: University Press of New England, 1992).

159. Emilio Gentile, "Fascism as Political Religion," *Journal of Contemporary History,* vol. 25 (1990), p. 243. Also see his *Il culto del Littorio,* op. cit., pp. 53–54, 130–135, for the rituals of fascist funerals.

160. Ibid., p. 132.

161. The association was founded in 1924.

162. *Scritti e discorsi,* vol. VIII, p. 76. In a similar way the party Statute of 1938 proclaimed the fascists' ability to die (Missori, op. cit., p. 395).

163. Salvemini, op. cit., p. 201.

164. Ibid., p. 63.

165. Mario Borsa thus wrote in 1925: "The Italian press, especially the liberal and democratic press, has been silent on too many matters and for too long. One can say that the public had just a vague and very imperfect idea of all that happened in 1921 and 1922" (cited in Valerio Castronovo, op. cit., p. 322). Many papers were afraid of fascist violent reactions and destructive expeditions; see Salvemini, op. cit., p. 104.

166. Giacomo Matteotti, *Scritti e discorsi* (Parma: Guanda, 1974), pp. 113–137.

167. See Petersen, "Il problema della violenza," op. cit., pp. 1005–1008.

168. On the liberal press's embracing of fascism, see Castronovo, op. cit., Chapter 4.

169. This idea is closely connected to Nietzsche's image of warriors. See Terry Eagleton's discussion of this issue, in which he cites Nietzsche: "Their work is an instinctive creation and imposition of forms; they are the most involuntary, unconscious artists there are. . . . They do not know what guilt, responsibility, or consideration are, these born organizers; they exemplify that terrible artists' egoism that has the look of bronze and knows itself justified to all eternity in its 'work,' like a mother in her child" (Eagleton, *The Ideology of the Aesthetic* [Oxford: Basil Blackwell, 1990], p. 237).

In his work on National Socialism, Saul Friedländer argues that the Nazi worldview was founded on the fascination with death and destruction. He thinks that with Nazism one can see the degradation of death, almost a trivialization. Death becomes an image and is not understood for its human, existential aspects. Death is objectified. More specifically, for Friedländer death is identified with "kitsch," where kitsch means, among other things, the "pinnacle of good taste in the absence of taste, of art in ugliness." See Friedländer, *Reflections of Nazism: An Essay on Kitsch and Death* (New York: Harper and Row, 1984), trans. Thomas Weyr, p. 25.

170. Cesare Rossi, ed., *Il delitto Matteotti nei procedimenti giudiziari e nelle polemiche giornalistiche* (Milan: Ceschina, 1965). Rossi, head of Mussolini's press office (Ufficio Stampa), was accused of being involved in Matteotti's abduction. He wrote a *Memoriale* after the facts accusing Mussolini of complicity in the murder.

171. In *Diciassette colpi* (Milan: Longanesi, 1958), Dumini presents his version of the kidnapping and murder of Matteotti.

172. See Salvemini, op. cit., on this pretense.

173. De Felice, *Mussolini il fascista,* vol. I, op. cit., p. 619.

174. "That word makes a mystic impression on the masses . . . it gives the common man the impression of participating in an exceptional movement." See Mussolini's conversation with Ludwig, op. cit., p. 106. Also see Mussolini's speech of

March 24, 1924, fifth anniversary of the fasces, in *Scritti e discorsi*, vol. IV, in which he said: "And why do I insist on proclaiming the revolution of October a historical revolution? Because words have their own tremendous magic" (p. 66).

175. *Scritti e discorsi*, vol. IV, pp. 223–224.

176. Speech for the Decennial, *Scritti e discorsi*, vol. VIII, p. 120.

177. Walter Benjamin, "The Work of Art in the Age of Mechanical Reproduction," op. cit., p. 241.

178. *Scritti e discorsi*, vol. II, p. 345. In *The Crisis of Parliamentary Democracy*, op. cit., p. 76, Carl Schmitt cites this quote from Mussolini as an example of the power of myth as theorized by Sorel. Although Schmitt criticizes Sorel for keeping the economic foundation of Marxist theory in his definition of the proletariat, Schmitt sincerely believes in the importance of myth, especially the national myth.

179. As a socialist, Mussolini, in the years preceding World War I, thus described Sorel's theory of myth: "Sorel presented us with a socialism that was decidedly antiintellectual, in fact religious. The myth of the general strike in Sorel's terrible, grave, sublime Socialism . . . is a myth, i.e. a fable, something nondemonstrable . . . that must be an act of faith. . . . One needs to believe in the general strike like the first Christians believed in the Apocalypse. Do not inquire, do not submit the myth to your rationalist critique. Do not break the sublime spell. Socialism . . . is a faith." See *Opera Omnia*, vol. IV, p. 173 (article "From Guicciardini to . . . Sorel" published in *Avanti!* on July 18, 1912).

180. *Scritti e discorsi*, vol. V, p. 118.

181. See Chapter 5.

182. Speech of March 28, 1926, in *Scritti e discorsi*, vol. V, p. 302.

183. See Ludwig, op. cit., p. 62.

184. *Scritti e discorsi*, vol. VIII, p. 77.

185. See, for example, Mussolini's speech to the army at the end of army maneuvers in 1934: "[M]ilitary forces represent the essential element of the hierarchy among Nations. They have not found anything yet that can replace what is the clearest, most tangible and most determinant expression of the total force of an entire people; that is, the volume, the prestige, the power of its arms, in land, at sea and in the air" (*Scritti e discorsi*, vol. IX, p. 115).

186. *Opera Omnia*, vol. XVII, p. 219. Other critics of parliament and democracy resorted to nationalist themes in order to find a solution to the problem of the "masses" and the question of stagnation. The stress on nationalism allowed crowd theorists to fulfill their aspiration to form a disciplined and ordered populace and to avoid internal conflicts. Sighele claimed that nationalist faith could be the means to unite all Italians in the pursuit of a common goal: expansion. Le Bon, in turn, saw in nationalism the occasion to revitalize French civilization. In *La psychologie politique et la défense sociale*, he advised rulers to build a strong state. Internal crises could be resolved by instilling in the masses love for their country and by convincing them that the Fatherland came first. Individual desires could be subordinated to the disciplined community fighting for higher ideals.

187. For Bobbio, antiparliamentary attitudes are at the origin of imperialism: "Antiparliamentarism in domestic politics goes hand in hand with exasperated nationalism, with an 'expansionist' program . . . with imperialism, that is with the refusal of the democratic principle in the relations between states" (Bobbio, op. cit., p. 610).

188. Mussolini borrowed this distinction from the leader of the nationalists, Corradini. However, Augusto Del Noce argues that fascism's replacement of class struggle with struggle between nations takes place through a rethinking of revolutionary socialism's categories, not through nationalism. Nationalism, he claims, was an aristocratic phenomenon. See Del Noce, op. cit., p. cl.

189. George Mosse suggest that the ideal of manliness is closely related to nationalist aspirations. See his *Nationalism and Sexuality: Respectability and Abnormal Sexuality in Modern Europe* (New York: Howard Fertig, 1985).

190. See Jürgen Habermas' analysis of Georges Bataille: "The French Path to Postmodernity: Bataille between Eroticism and General Economics" *New German Critique*, no. 33 (Fall 1984), pp. 79–102.

CHAPTER 2. MUSSOLINI THE MYTH

1. According to De Felice, Mussolini went to the Congress with a specific agenda and did some behind-the-scenes work (*Mussolini il rivoluzionario, 1883–1920* [Turin: Einaudi, 1965], "Il Congresso di Reggio Emilia").

2. See Appendix to Benito Mussolini, *Opera Omnia*, 36 vols. (Florence: La Fenice, 1951–1963), vol. IV, pp. 292–296.

3. See ibid., pp. 292, 294, and comments in *Il Nuovo Giornale* and *Il Messaggero*.

4. See *Il Nuovo Giornale, Il Messaggero, Corriere della Sera, Il Secolo* in *Opera Omnia*, vol. IV, pp. 292–293.

5. *Opera Omnia*, vol. IV, pp. 173–174 (article "From Guicciardini to . . . Sorel" published on June 18, 1912, in *Avanti!*). The piece was a critical response to Sorel's negative opinion of the Congress and its outcome.

6. Ibid., p. 182 (article "Socialist Allowances").

7. Ibid., p. 207 (note). These comments appeared in *Humanité* of August 26, 1912.

8. From *La Voce* of December 4, 1913, cited in Emilio Gentile, ed., *Mussolini e "La Voce,"* (Florence: Sansoni, 1976), p. 18.

9. Article in *La liberté* of April 1913, now in Renzo De Felice and Luigi Goglia, *Mussolini: Il mito* (Rome-Bari: Laterza, 1983), p. 94.

10. The editors of *La Voce* stated on March 27, 1913: "We are not socialists, but we can't refrain from praising, as Italians, the present direction of the (socialist) party." Cited in Gentile, ed., *Mussolini e "La Voce,"* op. cit., p. 17.

11. Cited in ibid., p. 19.

12. Ibid., p. 24. According to Wolfgang Mommsen, Max Weber too "was afraid lest the historical development of man might lead to . . . the total victory of 'technical man' over 'cultured man'"—the cultured man being a "creative individual[s] animated by spiritual ideals." See Mommsen, "Max Weber's Political Sociology and His Philosophy of World History," in Dennis Wrong, ed., *Max Weber* (Englewood Cliffs: Prentice-Hall, 1970), p. 186.

13. For Mommsen, Weber recognized the negative aspects of pure Caesarism. Within his theory, the charismatic leader of modern societies is connected to a system of plebiscitary democracy. This notwithstanding, Weber presented a model of leader who is only responsible to himself. See Mommsen, "Max Weber's Political Sociology," op. cit.

14. In 1911 Luigi Einaudi wished for the coming of "wild leaders" (*capi selvaggi*).

See Renzo De Felice and Luigi Goglia, op. cit., p. 6. According to De Felice and Goglia, however, Einaudi's models of leader were still liberal politicians.

15. *Opera Omnia*, vol. I, p. 181.

16. Ibid., p. 184.

17. In 1917 Mussolini wrote: "The Italian people is a mass of precious mineral. One needs to mold it, to smelt it, to work it. A work of art is still possible. One needs a government, a man, a man who has, when it is necessary, the delicate touch of the artist, the hard hand of the warrior." Cited in Dino Alfieri and Luigi Freddi, eds., *Mostra della Rivoluzione Fascista: Guida storica, I Decennale della Marcia su Roma* (Rome: Partito Nazionale Fascista, 1933), p. 13.

18. The name of Duce was first given to Mussolini by a fellow socialist in 1904. See De Felice and Goglia, op. cit., p. 7.

19. Croce, the Italian idealist philosopher, wrote: "[A]t that time a man with a real revolutionary temperament was emerging . . . Mussolini, who . . . tried to infuse a new soul [to socialism] by using Sorel's theory of violence, Bergson's intuitionism, pragmatism, the mysticism of action, all the voluntarism that had been in the intellectual air for years and that seemed to many idealism, so that he called himself and was called 'idealist.' The effects of his logic and oratory was not little . . . and more than a few intellectuals [listened to him]" (*Storia d'Italia dal 1871 al 1915* [Bari: Laterza, 1966], p. 290 [first published in 1928]).

20. Warren Susman, "'Personality' and the Making of Twentieth-Century Culture," in *Culture as History: The Transformation of American Society in the Twentieth Century* (New York: Pantheon, 1984).

21. Mussolini also made recourse to the rhetoric of "the man" in the case of D'Annunzio (*Scritti e discorsi* [Milan: Hoepli, 1934–1939], vol. II, p. 92 [article for *Il Popolo d'Italia* of September 11, 1920 anniversary of the March on Fiume]): "Luckily for Italy, luckily, we can add, for the world, a Man arose, who was even ready to face the supreme risk, as long as he could save Fiume."

22. Susman, op. cit., p. 273. For Susman, "[W]e can best understand modern cultural developments in all forms if we see and define the particular vision of the self basic to each cultural order" (ibid., p. 274).

23. Susman, citing Emerson, writes that the most popular definition of character at the time was: "Moral order through the medium of individual nature" (ibid., p. 274).

24. Ibid., pp. 273–274. Susman examined more than two hundred books, pamphlets, etc.

25. In Italy, *La coscienza di Zeno*, the novel written by Italo Svevo and first published in 1923, represents an expression of the interest in the psychological makeup of the individual.

26. See Stephen Kern, *The Culture of Time and Space 1880–1918* (Cambridge, Mass.: Harvard University Press, 1983), for an account of how Americans and Europeans experienced time and space at the turn of the century.

27. T. J. Jackson Lears, *No Place of Grace: Antimodernism and the Transformation of American Culture 1880–1920* (New York: Pantheon, 1981), p. 47. On neurasthenia as a new diagnostic category at the turn of the century, see Janet Oppenheim, *"Shattered Nerves:" Doctors, Patients, and Depression in Victorian England* (New York: Oxford University Press, 1991).

28. Susman, op. cit., p. 277.

29. The culture of character did not die suddenly, admits Susman. And books on character are actually still being published. But the culture of character appeared to be inadequate in a changing cultural and social order.

30. The question of individuality is a typical problematic of modernity, as Simmel's work indicates. On the development of the self and modernity see Alessandro Ferrara, "Autonomy and Authenticity," Ph.D. dissertation, University of California, Berkeley, 1984.

31. Susman, op. cit., p. 281.

32. Susman, op. cit., p. 279. In 1899 Marden had published *Character. The Greatest Thing in the World,* in which he emphasized "mental and moral traits" and "high ideals" (ibid).

33. Christian Metz, *The Imaginary Signifier: Psychoanalysis and the Cinema* (Bloomington: Indiana University Press, 1982), trans. Celia Britton, Annwyl Williams, Ben Brewster, Alfred Guzzetti, p. 95. For Susman, the connection of films to the culture of personality is evident in D. W. Griffith shots of the masses and the closeups on the individual apart from the mass (Susman, op. cit., p. 282).

34. Leo Lowenthal, "The Triumph of Mass Idols," in *Literature, Popular Culture, and Society* (Palo Alto: Pacific Books, 1961), p. 109. Lowenthal analyzes American biographies in relation to the question of consumption and singles out the transition in types that are written about: from production (and political) spheres to consumption.

35. Leo Lowenthal, "German Popular Biographies: Culture's Bargain Counter," in Kurt Wolff and Barrington Moore Jr., eds., *The Critical Spirit: Essays in Honor of Herbert Marcuse* (Boston: Beacon Press, 1967), p. 268.

36. See De Felice and Goglia, op. cit., p. 7.

37. As Giustino Fortunato wrote at the time: "[E]verybody is invoking, as it happens in the moments of extreme danger, the providential intervention of a Man, with capital M, who finally knows how to bring back the country to order and legality." Cited in Leo Longanesi, *In piedi e seduti 1919–1943* (Milan: Longanesi, 1980), p. 61.

38. Woodrow Wilson and Lenin were part of the same phenomenon. On Wilson see Jeffrey Tulis, *The Rhetorical Presidency* (Princeton: Princeton University Press, 1987).

39. *Illustrazione Italiana* was first published on November 1, 1875, by the Milanese Emilio Treves on the model of the French *Illustration.* When it began its publication, *Illustrazione's* images were drawn by the *pittore-cronista* (the painter-chronicler). See Enzo Cassoni, *Il cartellonismo e l'illustrazione in Italia dal 1875 al 1950* (Rome: Nuova Editrice Spada, 1984).

40. I am not counting the times that Mussolini appeared more than once in the same issue. This instance occurred in fifteen cases.

41. The conference of ex-allies focused on the "oriental" question and according to De Felice was unimportant from the point of view of foreign politics (*Mussolini il fascista,* vol. I, [Turin: Einaudi, 1966], p. 485).

42. On this question, see Leo Lowenthal, "The Triumph of Mass Idols," op. cit.

43. Here is how Mussolini viewed his public role: "I have sometimes meditated upon the fate, grotesque and sublime, of the public man. But I have not arrived at any conclusions, just because it is Fate we have to deal with. The public man is born

'public'—he bears the stigma from his birth. . . . I am perfectly resigned to my lot as a public man. In fact, I am enthusiastic about it . . . it is the thought, the realization, that I no longer belong merely to myself, that I belong to all—loved by all, hated by all—that I am an essential element in the lives of others: this feeling has on me a kind of intoxicating effect." See Mussolini's preface to Margherita Sarfatti, *The Life of Benito Mussolini* (London: Thornton Butterworth, 1929), originally published in 1925, pp. 9–10.

44. Estimates are that from 3 million to 18 million postcards circulated during the regime. See Luisa Passerini, *Mussolini immaginario: Storia di una biografia 1915–1939* (Rome-Bari: Laterza, 1991), p. 202.

45. According to Biondi, *La fabbrica del Duce* (Florence: Vallecchi, 1967), writings on Mussolini numbered five thousand by 1929. In 1932, during the Exhibit of the Fascist Revolution, a special hall was dedicated to the writings on Mussolini and fascism. The volumes presented more than three thousand writings. See Alfieri and Freddi, eds., *Guida alla Mostra della Rivoluzione Fascista* (Florence: Vallecchi, 1932), Sala D.

46. Cited in Oreste Del Buono, ed., *Eja, Eja, Eja, La stampa italiana sotto il fascismo 1919/1943* (Milan: Feltrinelli, 1971), p. 40.

47. From "Il fascismo: origini, sviluppo e finalita'" (1922) in De Felice and Goglia, op. cit., p. 103. (My emphasis.)

48. Ibid., pp. 104–105. (My emphasis.)

49. Guido Podrecca, *Il fascismo* (1923), in ibid., p. 110 (my emphasis). Podrecca, ex-socialist become fascist, had been the victim of Mussolini's speech at the Reggio Emilia socialist congress in 1912, at which it was decided to expel Podrecca and other socialist deputies from the party.

50. According to Gaudens Megaro, *Mussolini in the Making* (London: Allen and Unwin, 1938), this was the first in a long list of apologetic descriptions of Mussolini's personality. For a discussion of major biographies and writings on Mussolini from 1915 to 1939, see Luisa Passerini, op. cit. Passerini shows how biographies contributed to the creation of several images of Mussolini in people's fantasy and how at the same time they reflected a fascination with the new figure of politician represented by Mussolini.

51. Torquato Nanni, *Benito Mussolini* (Florence: Libreria Della Voce, 1915), now in Gentile, ed., op. cit., p. 163.

52. Benito Mussolini, "Il mio diario di guerra (1915–1917);" "La mia vita dal 29 luglio 1883 al 23 novembre 1911 (1911–1912)," in *Opera Omnia* vols. XXXIV, XXXIII.

53. Antonio Beltramelli, *L'Uomo nuovo* (Milan: Mondadori, 1940), p. 218. "Uomo" was capitalized.

54. Giuseppe Prezzolini, "Benito Mussolini," in Gentile, ed., op. cit., pp. 192, 197.

55. Ibid., p. 194.

56. Ibid. On this naturalistic interpretation of personalities, see Lowenthal, "The Triumph of Mass Idols," op. cit.

57. These figures have been collected by Luisa Passerini, *Mussolini immaginario,* op. cit., p. 43. On the history of the book, see Philip Cannistraro and Brian R. Sullivan, *Il Duce's Other Woman* (New York: Morrow, 1993). The authors claim there have been nineteen translations of the book.

58. Sarfatti, op. cit., p. 37. The 1934 Italian version reports: "The children who are predestined to great things ignore the natural and pleasant equilibrium of mediocre men" (*Dux* [Milan: Mondadori, 1934], p. 22). Sarfatti's book first appeared in English in 1925 and in Italian in 1926. The two versions are not identical, nor are the different editions of the Italian version.

59. See among others Omero Petri, *L'italiano nuovissimo (il Messia)* (The Very New Italian, The Messiah) (Turin: Bocca, 1928); and Guglielmo Policastro, *Homo novus* (The New Man) (Catania: Minerva, 1923). The large number of biographies of Mussolini is particularly relevant if we consider the lack of this literary genre in Italy. In Notebook 6, Gramsci lamented this absence: "In Italy, we lack memorialists, and biographers and autobiographers are rare" (Antonio Gramsci, *Letteratura e vita nazionale* [Rome: Editori Riuniti, 1977], p. 77).

60. Cited in Dino Biondi, op. cit., p. 20.

61. Cited in Longanesi, op. cit., p. 104. According to Sarfatti, Lenin also said: "Mussolini? A great pity he is lost to us! He is a strong man, who would have led our party to victory" (*The Life of Benito Mussolini*, op. cit., p. 278). However, according to De Felice, these declarations have never been documented (*Mussolini il rivoluzionario*, op. cit., p. 427).

62. John Diggins, *Mussolini and Fascism: The View from America* (Princeton: Princeton University Press, 1972), p. 30. In the United States, popular weeklies and monthly magazines welcomed Mussolini's coup d'état. According to Diggins, "the only general periodicals consistently critical were those of a *high-brow* tone, like the two monthlies—the *Atlantic* and *Harper's*" (ibid., p. 25). On the relationship of the Hearst cartel to Mussolini in later years, see Cannistraro and Sullivan, op. cit. Sarfatti wrote a series of articles about fascism and Mussolini for the Hearst chain.

63. Hitler, when his myth began to develop at the beginning of the 1920s, also was compared to Napoleon. See Ian Kershaw, *The Hitler Myth: Image and Reality in the Third Reich* (Oxford: Clarendon Press, 1987), p. 23.

64. Biondi, op. cit., p. 89.

65. Ibid., p. 88. On the French press and fascism see Pierre Milza, *Le fascisme italien et la presse française (1920–1940)* (Bruxelles: Complexe, 1987); on the British press and fascism see Aldo Berselli, *L'opinione pubblica inglese e l'avvento del fascismo (1919–1925)* (Milan: Franco Angeli, 1971).

66. Cited in Biondi, op. cit., p. 154. The representation of Mussolini as an "aristocratic" figure in the spiritual sense appears in Beltramelli's biography.

67. The image of the Duce as "man of the people," the "son of a blacksmith," was quite popular in biographical accounts and popular literature. See Passerini, op. cit. Mussolini himself always insisted that he had "humble" origins.

68. Robert Michels, *Political Parties: A Sociological Study of the Oligarchical Tendencies of Modern Democracy* (New York: Collier Books, 1962), trans. Eden and Cedar Paul, p. 50.

69. Michels, *First Lectures in Political Sociology* (Minneapolis: University of Minnesota Press, 1949), trans. Alfred De Grazia, in particular "The Sociological Character of Political Parties." This book was first published in Italian with the title *Corso di sociologia politica*.

70. See George Mosse's discussion of Caesarism, "Caesarism, Circuses, and Mon-

uments," in *Masses and Man: Nationalist and Fascist Perceptions of Reality* (New York: Howard Fertig, 1980).

71. Diggins, op. cit., p. 27.

72. Ibid., p. 28.

73. This is a controversial issue. Mussolini appeared as the author, but according to some the American ambassador to Italy, Richard Washburn Child, actually wrote it in collaboration with Mussolini's brother Arnaldo. Child officially appeared as the editor of *My Autobiography,* which was published in English in 1928. In the foreword to the book, Child defines Mussolini's government as "superstatemanship." For him Mussolini expressed "greatness." According to Diggins, op. cit., p. 27: "Child became infatuated with the Italian dictator and frequently conferred with him on the state of American opinion." On this issue also see Cannistraro and Sullivan, op. cit., p. 358.

74. According to Diggins, since Americans had lost faith in their economic model at the end of 1929, they began to look for alternatives in Europe. For the American left, Stalin's Russia presented a viable example. The right was instead interested in the corporativist experiment in Italy.

75. The ad for the film described *Mussolini Speaks!* as "A Hit . . . because it might be the answer to Americans' needs" (*Variety,* Tuesday, March 14 ,1933, p. 16). On April 4, 1933, another ad appeared in *Variety* thanking journalist Arthur Brisbane "for telling 14,000,000 readers in hundreds of newspapers what we have been trying to get across to thousands of exhibitors" (p. 20). Brisbane's review read: "The picture shows Mussolini and his work before you. You see and hear him addressing crowds such as never gathered to hear any other man on earth. You study with amazement the physical power that makes it possible for his mental strength to do its work. In the faces of the crowds, and in their frenzied applause you see Mussolini's absolute hold on the people of Italy."

76. Library of Congress, Washington, D.C.

77. According to Gian Piero Brunetta, "Il sogno a stelle e strisce di Mussolini," in Maurizio Vaudagna, ed., *L'estetica della politica* (Rome-Bari: Laterza, 1989), Thomas's film borrowed, and almost copied from, a screenplay by Ferruccio Cerio presented at a 1932 contest for best celebratory film on the fascist revolution. Ezra Pound had collaborated with Cerio on the part to be shown abroad. Pound's description of the subject is in itself the document of an intellectual's admiration for Mussolini (Brunetta, op. cit., pp. 181–182).

78. Giovanni Fabrizi, cited in De Felice and Goglia, op. cit., p. 120.

79. Cited in Biondi, op. cit., p. 227. (My emphasis.)

80. Speech for the twenty-fifth anniversary of the Anti-Socialist League delivered at Queen's Hall, cited in Del Buono, op. cit., p. 201.

81. An account of Freud's gesture can be found in Arnaldo Novelletto, ed., *L'Italia nella psicoanalisi (Italy in Psychoanalysis)* (Rome: Istituto Della Enciclopedia Italiana, 1989). Freud wrote those words in specific circumstances. His friend Edoardo Weiss speculates that Freud did not have any sympathy for Mussolini (ibid., p. 52). Spengler also sent several of his books to Mussolini. See De Felice, *Mussolini il duce,* vol. I, (Turin: Einaudi, 1974), p. 39, note 1.

82. Ludwig's *Colloqui con Mussolini* (Milan: Mondadori, 1932) was published

with Mussolini's approval. Mussolini later tried to disavow the text. On this question see De Felice, *Mussolini il duce,* vol. I, op. cit., pp. 45–47.

83. Leo Lowenthal takes Emil Ludwig as an example of biographies' writers on leaders in his essay "German Popular Biographies," op. cit.

84. Ludwig, op. cit., p. 14.

85. Ibid. (My emphasis.)

86. Ibid., p. 15.

87. Ibid., p. 16. (My emphasis.)

88. Ibid., p. 31.

89. Ibid., pp. 31, 31, 32, 33, 61, 83, 116, 133.

90. Hitler's myth, too, was a creation of his followers, according to Kershaw, op. cit.

91. For the intellectuals' fascination with fascism in Italy, Germany, France, and England, see Alastair Hamilton, *The Appeal of Fascism: A Study of Intellectuals and Fascism, 1919–1945* (New York: Macmillan, 1971).

92. Hullinger published a chronicle of this filming experience in *Photoplay:* "Benito Mussolini is a movie star. He has just completed his first picture, taking the part of himself in a feature pictorializing his private life. To his already widely diversified roles of dictator of Italy, holder of many cabinet portfolios, journalist, playwright and aviator, he has now added that of leading man of the screen. Along with Clark Gable and William Powell, he is an attraction among the flickering marquee lights above the box office. I have just returned from Italy and from producing this picture, the first screen biography, I believe, ever made of a living world statesman." Cited in Brunetta, op. cit., p. 173.

93. Brunetta, op. cit., p. 174.

94. The distinction was not only popular. In his biography of Mussolini, Prezzolini wrote: "The fascist movement has had such an importance in Italy that few, not only among its adversaries, but even among its leaders, could have hoped for and anticipated. . . . But we can affirm one thing: that it would have never had the historical importance it has demonstrated without the will, the energy, the power of organization and the charm, the finesse and the political intuition of Mussolini. . . . Fascism owes Mussolini almost everything. Mussolini owes Fascism almost nothing, because without it he would have certainly led some other movement." See Giuseppe Prezzolini, "Benito Mussolini," in Emilio Gentile, ed., op. cit., p. 191.

95. See Piero Melograni, "The Cult of the Duce in Mussolini's Italy," *Journal of Contemporary History,* vol. 11, no. 4 (1976), pp. 221–237. According to Kershaw, Hitler's rising popularity also developed at the expense of the party and the movement. There was the belief that whatever went wrong in the regime occurred without Hitler's knowledge and that if he only knew, things would get better (op. cit., Chapter 3).

96. See Archivio Centrale dello Stato, Segreteria Particolare del Duce, Carteggio Ordinario.

97. Luisa Passerini, *Fascism in Popular Memory: The Cultural Experience of the Turin Working Class* (Cambridge: Cambridge University Press, 1987). Passerini gathered oral histories from Turin workers who had lived under fascism.

98. Mussolini had experienced some challenges to his leadership within fascism in 1921 when he proposed to institutionalize the movement into a party. At that time, to some, such as Dino Grandi, Mussolini did not represent the revolutionary

spirit of fascism any longer. See Emilio Gentile, *Storia del Partito Fascista (1912–1922): Movimento e milizia* (Rome-Bari: Laterza, 1989).

99. See Alberto Aquarone, *L'organizzazione dello stato totalitario* (Turin: Einaudi, 1965), pp. 5–6.

100. Article 1 of the law on the Gran Consiglio of December 9, 1928, stated: "The *Gran Consiglio* of Fascism is the supreme organ that coordinates and integrates all the activities of the Regime."

101. Aquarone, op. cit., p. 16. On the members of the Gran Consiglio, see Mario Missori, *Gerarchie e statuti del P.N.F.: Gran Consiglio, Direttorio Nazionale, Federazioni provinciali: Quadri e biografie* (Rome: Bonacci, 1986).

102. Aquarone, op. cit., p. 160, note 1.

103. Ibid., op. cit., p. 19.

104. *Opera Omnia*, vol. XXIII, p. 12. These lines were part of Mussolini's preface to the volume published on the first five years of the Gran Consiglio.

105. "The Armed Party leads to the totalitarian Regime. The night of January 1923, during which the Milizia was created, marked the death of the old demo-liberal state and of its institutional game" (ibid).

106. See Aquarone, op. cit., p. 19 (Grand Council's declaration of January 12, 1923).

107. See Article 4 of the regulation of discipline for the MVSN of March 1923 (De Felice, *Mussolini il fascista*, vol. I, op. cit., p. 432).

108. The Gran Consiglio stated: "The unity of political and military offices is not admitted. . . . The Milizia must be preserved from the political escalation of the Party." Cited in Aquarone, op. cit., p. 20, note 2.

109. Ibid., p. 20. See Mussolini's information and statistics on the cadres in the speech he delivered to the Senate on June 8, 1923, after six months of his government (*Scritti e discorsi*, vol. III, pp. 141–142).

110. According to De Felice, enrollment increased from 300,000 to 782,979 by the end of 1923 (De Felice, *Mussolini il fascista*, vol. I, op. cit., p. 407).

111. Aquarone, op. cit., p. 33.

112. Ibid., p. 67.

113. Ibid., p. 162.

114. The prefect was "the central government's direct agent and representative in the province." See Cannistraro, ed., *Historical Dictionary of Fascist Italy* (Westport: Greenwood, 1982), p. 434.

115. De Felice, *Mussolini il fascista*, vol. I, op. cit., p. 440.

116. Ibid.

117. *Opera Omnia*, vol. XXII, p. 467.

118. Ibid.

119. *Scritti e discorsi*, vol. VII, p. 141. On May 26, 1927, Mussolini told the Chamber: "I will never give the head of a prefect to any federal secretary" (*Scritti e discorsi*, vol. VI, p. 65).

120. *Opera Omnia*, vol. XXI, p. 425 (speech at La Scala in Milan).

121. Speech to the Assembly of the Fascist Party, September 14, 1929, in *Scritti e discorsi*, vol. VII, pp. 142–143.

122. According to De Felice, on the question of the party Mussolini differed from both Nazi Germany and the Soviet Union. Whereas those regimes emphasized the

role of the party and subordinated the state to it, in Italian fascism the state became the predominant apparatus. De Felice explains this difference through two factors. First, the presence of the monarchy in Italy prevented the party from prevailing over the state. Second, Mussolini learned from the events in the Soviet Union. After the death of Lenin, the Communist Party had not been able to maintain unity. This internal division threatened the survival of the party-regime, although the Soviet party seemed much more strongly established than the fascist one in Italy (*Mussolini il fascista*, vol. II, op. cit., pp. 297–300). On this question also see Paolo Pombeni, *Demagogia e tirannide: Uno studio sulla forma-partito del fascismo* (Bologna: Il Mulino, 1984). For Pombeni, Hitler adopted a strategy of fragmenting the centers of power so that he could still play arbitrating functions and at the same time distance himself in case of mistakes. With Mussolini, instead, there is a tendency, not to decenter, rather to centralize all decisions in his person. In both cases the role of the party was weakened.

123. Speech of March 24, 1924, in *Scritti e discorsi*, vol. IV, p. 65.

124. *Scritti e discorsi*, vol. V, p. 65.

125. Aquarone, op. cit., p. 77.

126. *Scritti e discorsi*, vol. VII, p. 127.

127. *Scritti e discorsi*, vol. VIII, p. 120.

128. In the *Disposizioni* of August 28, 1932, Starace stated: "I forbid in an absolute way that people sing songs or tunes that are not those of the Revolution and that people rhythmically invoke leaders other than the DUCE."

129. Because the party had little or no role in decision-making processes, it also lost its function of mediator between the fascist base and the regime's leadership.

130. Mussolini used his secret police to survey the fascist *gerarchi* (Guido Leto, *OVRA: Fascismo-Antifascismo* [San Rocca Casciano: Cappelli, 1952]).

131. Enrollments were later closed. See Aquarone, op. cit., and De Felice, *Mussolini il fascista*, vol. II, op. cit.

132. Aquarone, op. cit., p. 261.

133. Cited in De Felice, *Mussolini il duce*, vol. I, op. cit., p. 8.

134. Cited in Aquarone, op. cit., pp. 173–174.

135. On this question, see Aquarone, op. cit., pp. 161–162.

136. *Scritti e discorsi*, vol. V, p. 153. In April 1926, he proclaimed: "The Fascist state is the Fascist government, and the Leader of the Fascist government is the Leader of the revolution" (ibid., p. 310).

137. *Scritti e discorsi*, vol. VI, p. 70 (Ascension speech). He then continued: "Is it then a libido of power that holds me? No. . . . It is a duty" (ibid., pp. 70–71).

138. Emil Ludwig, op. cit., p. 131.

139. *Scritti e discorsi*, vol. VIII, p. 256.

140. According to De Felice, Mussolini, from the beginning of his mandate, tried to replace the title of leader of the party with that of Duce of fascism (*Mussolini il fascista*, I, op. cit., p. 439). Robert Michels wrote that with Mussolini the axiom "the Party, it is I" had assumed its maximum development (*First Lectures in Political Sociology*, op. cit., p. 137).

141. Yvon De Begnac, *Palazzo Venezia: Storia di un regime* (Rome: La Rocca, 1950), p. 286.

142. Oswald Spengler, *The Hour of Decision. Part One: Germany and the World.*

Historical Revolution (i.e. Evolution) (New York: Knopf, 1962), trans. Charles Francis Atkinson (first published in English in 1934), pp. 187–188.

143. According to De Begnac, Mussolini believed in predestination, "in a fate that predisposes facts and events and indicates to men the open way to humanity" (op. cit., p. 39). Mussolini himself said: "The sensation of being called to announce a new epoch I had it for the first time when I became close to the group of *La Voce*. . . . Predestination! Something that grasps us and takes possession of us, of our days, without us realizing it, and thus becoming 'destiny:' or with us realizing it and thus becoming 'fate'" (ibid., p. 131). Also see Mussolini's introduction to *Scritti e discorsi*, vol. I, in which he invokes destiny with reference to his own role in Italian history.

144. Ludwig, op. cit., p. 99.

145. "Comment se pense un pouvoir qui se désire absolu? Quel est la fantasmatique dans et par laquelle se rationalize la politique de ce désir? Quel'est l'imagerie de l'absolutisme?" (Louis Marin, "Récit du pouvoir. Pouvoir du récit," *Actes de la recherche en sciences sociales*, 25 [January 1979], p. 28).

146. The prayer was published in *La Tribuna* on July 25, 1927 (cited in Camillo Berneri, *Mussolini: Psicologia di un dittatore* [Milan: Azione Comune, 1966], p. 41). The original credo goes: "We believe in one God, the Father, the Almighty, maker of heaven and earth, of all that is seen and unseen.—We believe in one Lord, Jesus Christ, the only Son of God, eternally begotten of the Father. . . . For us men and for our salvation he came down from heaven: by the power of the Holy Spirit he was born of the Virgin Mary, and became man.—For our sake he was crucified under Pontius Pilate; he suffered, died, and was buried. On the third day he rose again in fulfillment of the Scriptures; he ascended into heaven and is seated at the right hand of the Father. He will come again in glory to judge the living and the dead, and his kingdom will have no end. . . . We believe in one holy catholic and apostolic Church. We acknowledge one baptism for the forgiveness of sins. We look for the resurrection of the dead, and the life of the world to come. Amen."

147. Also see the Balilla organization's credo in George Seldes, *Sawdust Caesar: The Untold History of Mussolini and Fascism* (New York: Harper, 1935), appendix, pp. 409–410.

148. The definition of Mussolini as "envoy of God" was by Cardinal Mercier. See Dino Biondi, op. cit., p. 159.

149. Paolo Ardali, *San Francesco e Mussolini* (Mantova: Paladino, 1926).

150. Cited in Giuseppe Vettori, ed., *Duce & ducetti: Citazioni dall'Italia fascista* (Rome: Newton Compton, 1975), p. 140.

151. On the relation between Church and fascism see Pietro Scoppola, "La Chiesa e il fascismo durante il pontificato di Pio XI," in Alberto Aquarone and Maurizio Vernassa, eds., *Il regime fascista* (Bologna: Il Mulino, 1974).

152. The Pacts were a true success for Mussolini, both at home and abroad. See De Felice, *Mussolini il fascista*, vol. II (Turin, 1968).

153. See, for example, Cardinal Nasalli Rocca of Bologna, who in a 1929 interview to *Avvenire d'Italia* declared that Mussolini had been "the instrument of Providence." Cited in Oreste Del Buono, ed., op. cit., p. 117.

154. Vettori, ed., op. cit., p. 140.

155. *Scritti e discorsi*, vol. VII, p. 13.

156. Ibid., p. 25.

157. Biondi, op. cit., p. 201.

158. *Scritti e discorsi,* vol. VII, p. 25 (speech to the assembly of the regime of March 10, 1929).

159. Cited in Vettori, op. cit., p. 38.

160. *Scritti e discorsi,* vol. III, p. 153.

161. Cited in Del Buono, ed., op. cit., p. 39. The report continued: "[W]ords come out slowly through his semi-closed lips, almost kisses" (ibid).

162. In 1937, in an interview to the United Press, Mussolini described his incredible regimen: "I made of my organism an engine constantly surveyed and controlled that marches with absolute regularity." From *Il Popolo d'Italia* of March 9, now in *Opera Omnia,* vol. XXVIII, p. 136.

163. De Felice, *Mussolini il duce,* vol. I, op. cit., p. 21.

164. Ibid., pp. 21–22.

165. Ibid., p. 20.

166. De Felice explains this attitude with Mussolini's character. He was suspicious, mistrustful, cynical (ibid).

167. Maurice Bédel, *Fascisme An VII* (Paris: Editions de la Nouvelle Revue Française, 1929), p. 10.

168. Cited in Berneri, op. cit., p. 39, from a book of elementary school's essays on Mussolini collected by Dolores Mingozzi as *Mussolini visto dai ragazzi* published in 1928.

169. Del Buono, ed., op. cit., p. 114 (from Mingozzi's book).

170. From *La Domenica del Corriere,* in Del Buono, op. cit., pp. 47–48. In a speech to the Chamber of June 8, 1923, Mussolini told the deputies: "[N]obody must be afraid because I ride horses. . . . if this is due to my youth, this is a divine disease from which we recover every day" (*Scritti e discorsi,* vol. III, p. 153).

171. Ibid. The rose was a constant presence in the early imagery of Mussolini. See Massimo Cardillo, *Il duce in moviola: Politica e divismo nei cinegiornali e documentari 'Luce'* (Bari: Dedalo, 1983), p. 109.

172. See for example *Illustrazione Italiana* of February 17, 1924, p. 184.

173. The postcard market created financial speculations, as in the case of two Florentine men who sued several private and public organizations for reproducing photos of Mussolini of which the two men claimed reproduction rights. See Del Buono, ed., op. cit., p. 311.

174. On aviation see Robert Wohl, *A Passion for Wings: Aviation and the Western Imagination, 1908–1918* (New Haven: Yale University Press, 1994). Also see Peter Fritzsche, *A Nation of Fliers: German Aviation and the Popular Imagination* (Cambridge, Mass.: Harvard University Press, 1992). On Lindbergh also see Modris Eksteins, *Rites of Spring: The Great War and the Birth of the Modern Age* (Boston: Houghton Mifflin, 1989).

175. Paul Virilio, "Futurismo e fascismo," in Serge Fauchereau et al., eds., *Futurismo Futurismi* (Milan: Edizioni Intrapresa, 1986), p. 33.

176. One cannot forget the transoceanic flights of Italo Balbo or De Pinedo, whom Mussolini adopted as a model for the "new Italian man." See *Scritti e discorsi,* vol. V, pp. 114, 197. On the figure of the aviator in fascism, also see George Mosse, "Fascism and the Avant Garde," in *Masses and Man,* op. cit.

177. Mussolini actually defined aviators as leaders. See De Begnac, op. cit., p. 647. Several books were published on Mussolini the aviator. See, for example, Cristoforo Krimer, *Mussolini aviatore* (Siena: Meini, no date); Nello Quilici, *Aviatoria* (Naples: La Nuovissima, 1934); Guido Mattioli, *Mussolini aviatore e la sua opera per l'aviazione* (Rome: L'aviazione, 1939).

178. Cesare Redaelli, *Iniziando Mussolini alle vie del cielo* (Milan: Stabilimento di Arti Grafiche Fratelli Magnano, 1933).

179. Francesco Flora, ed., *Stampa dell'era fascista: Le note di servizio* (Rome, Mondadori, 1945).

180. See *Illustrazione Italiana* of August 19, 1934; March 24, 1935; May 19, 1935; November 1, 1936; January 17, 1937; January 12, 1939.

181. Compare for example Mussolini's attire at his daughter Edda's wedding in 1930 (bourgeois clothes) and at the weddings of his son Vittorio and nephew Vito in 1937 (military uniform). For the 1937 weddings see Archivio Centrale dello Stato, Foto Attivita' del duce, Busta 15.

182. Ludwig, op. cit., p. 50.

183. Berneri gives a portrait of Mussolini that completely discounts Mussolini's image as a courageous man (op. cit.).

184. *The Life of Benito Mussolini,* op. cit., p. 232. Also see Benito Mussolini, *My Autobiography,* op. cit., p. 48. Mussolini writes: "I faced atrocious pain; my suffering was indescribable. I underwent practically all my operations without the aid of an anaesthetic. I had twenty-seven operations in one month; all but two were without anaesthetics."

185. Cited in Paolo Monelli, *Mussolini piccolo borghese* (Milan: Garzanti, 1950), p. 157. The Duce's eyes were often the admired focus of descriptions of his persona.

186. Leo Longanesi, op. cit., pp. 127–128 (note 1). The logic of the event sprouts from a revised version of a superstitious belief. If, while pregnant, a woman craves some food and does not satisfy her desire, her baby will end up carrying a birthmark with the color of the food the mother did not eat. The *fascio* was the official symbol of fascism. See Chapter 3.

187. Cited in Fidia Gambetti, *Gli anni che scottano* (Milan: Mursia, 1967), p. 275.

188. De Begnac, op. cit., p. 652.

189. On fascism and youth see Emilio Gentile, *Le origini dell'ideologia fascista (1918–1925)* (Rome-Bari: Laterza, 1975), pp. 137–140.

190. *Scritti e discorsi,* vol. II, p. 152.

191. *Scritti e discorsi,* vol. III, p. 19.

192. *Scritti e discorsi,* vol. V, p. 340.

193. Beginning in 1924 radio daily broadcasts ended with the hymn *Giovinezza.* Blanc wrote the music for many fascist organizations' official hymns.

194. Philip V. Cannistraro, *La fabbrica del consenso: Fascismo e mass media* (Rome-Bari: Laterza, 1975), p. 80.

195. Ibid., p. 81. This is even more surprising if we consider that fascism encouraged the value of family and aimed at a demographic growth which required continuous births. The regime had even established a tax on bachelorhood.

196. Berneri, op. cit., p. 59.

197. This was Cesare Rossi's opinion (see Biondi, op. cit.). In another episode, which occurred in July 1940, Mussolini invited journalists to witness his "fake"

victory in a tennis game as a show of his youth, dynamism, success (Francesco Flora, op. cit., p. 14). Flora's book reports the orders to the press coming from Mussolini's Ufficio Stampa.

198. See Del Buono, ed., op. cit., p. 243.

199. A. V. Savona and M. L. Straniero, *Canti dell'Italia fascista 1919–1945* (Milan: Mondadori, 1979), p. 145.

200. Margherita Sarfatti, *The Life of Benito Mussolini*, op. cit., p. 230. Also see reports of the doctor treating Mussolini in *Scritti e discorsi*, vol. I, pp. 247–248.

201. "He seemed like San Sebastian, his flesh pierced as with arrows, scarred with wounds and bathed in blood" (Sarfatti, *The Life of Benito Mussolini*, op. cit., p. 230).

202. According to De Felice, in the months immediately following the attempt there was a real "rush" toward fascism (*Mussolini, il fascista*, vol. II, op. cit., p. 150).

203. Vincenzo Rizzo, *Attenti al Duce: Storie minime dell'Italia fascista, 1927–1938* (Florence: Vallecchi, 1981), pp. 5–6. Rizzo's book recounts all real and invented attempts on Mussolini's life.

204. De Felice, *Mussolini il fascista*, vol. II, op. cit., p. 141.

205. *Scritti e discorsi*, vol. V, p. 194.

206. For a similar case concerning Lenin, see Nina Tumarkin, *Lenin Lives! The Lenin Cult in Soviet Russia* (Cambridge, Mass.: Harvard University Press, 1983), where she describes how attempted assassinations of him spurred his cult.

207. For a comparable case see Leo Lowenthal and Norbert Guterman's analysis of the American political agitator and the "magic of survival" (*Prophets of Deceit: A Study of the Techniques of the American Agitator* [Palo Alto: Pacific Books, 1949]). For Lowenthal and Guterman, that belief was connected to a narcissistic personality.

208. *Scritti e discorsi*, vol. V, p. 312.

209. Ibid., p. 313. The next day Mussolini shipped to Tripolitania.

210. Ibid., vol. V, p. 330.

211. According to Gaetano Salvemini, this attempt gave the regime an occasion to criticize France and accuse it of hiding renowned antifascists (*Opere* [Milan, 1961], VI, vol. I, "Scritti sul fascismo," pp. 193–197).

212. *Scritti e discorsi*, vol. V, p. 390.

213. Ibid., p. 390.

214. Michels, in his discussion of political parties, refers to this episode to show Mussolini as a model of "leader of a great party" who has also become "the leader of a great state." Those words from the crowd, according to Michels, "meant to say that there is really no difference between Mussolini the man and Italy the country, and that the death of the one would undoubtedly be followed by the complete ruin of the other" (*First Lectures in Political Sociology*, op. cit., p. 137).

215. A sixteen-year-old, Anteo Zamboni, was the supposed gunman who missed his target during Mussolini's visit in Bologna. He was immediately lynched by the crowd. De Felice considers this attempt "obscure" and hard to explain in full both with reference to the assassins and the instigators (*Mussolini il fascista*, vol. II, op. cit.).

216. *Scritti e discorsi*, vol. V, p. 467.

217. The attempts on Mussolini and the law on capital punishment created a halo around Mussolini. A hysteria about such attempts took place. A special organization of the political police with a capillary set of informers was put in place to de-

tect and unveil plans of crimes against the Duce. Most often the information was invented, so the list of suspected crimes became very long (see Rizzo, op. cit.).

218. See for example Foucault's interpretation of capital executions during the ancien régime, in *Discipline and Punish: The Birth of the Prison* (New York: Vintage, 1979).

219. Ernst Kantorowicz, *The King's Two Bodies: A Study in Medieval Political Theology* (Princeton: Princeton University Press, 1957).

220. Ernst Kantorowicz, "Mysteries of State," *Harvard Theological Review,* vol. 48, no. 1 (January 1955), p. 91.

221. The king of Italy was still a symbolic figure during Mussolini's rule. But he was the king in the tradition of the modern state, and his authority was limited. The regime contributed to the undermining of the king's role. Beginning in December 1928, the Gran Consiglio even controlled the succession to the throne.

222. Cited in Cannistraro, *La fabbrica del consenso,* op. cit., p. 82.

223. Raymond Klibansky, ed., *Benito Mussolini's Memoirs 1942–1943* (New York: Howard Fertig, 1975), trans. Frances Lobb, p. 137. This book was first published in English in 1949 and is a translation of Benito Mussolini's *Il tempo del bastone e della carota,* first published in Italian in 1944.

224. Henri Béraud, *Ce que J'ai vu à Rome* (Paris: Les Editions de France, 1929), p. 39.

225. Ibid., pp. 39, 38.

226. Ibid., p. 37.

227. Teresa Maria Mazzatosta and Claudio Volpi, *L'Italietta fascista (lettere al potere 1936–1943)* (Bologna: Cappelli, 1980), p. 49. The book presents a selection of letters to Mussolini. Direct requests to Mussolini for his photos (autographed, if possible) continuously arrived at the Duce's secretariat. One woman wrote in August 1936 that the photo would be "the most desired gift" for her wedding anniversary. A widow wrote in April 1938: "As an unexpected sun ray I received your photograph" (ibid., pp. 42, 59). For another collection of letters to Mussolini, see Giuseppe Raucci, ed., *Caro duce: Lettere di donne italiane a Mussolini 1922–1943* (Milan: Rizzoli, 1989). Ersilia R. wrote to Mussolini on July 29, 1923, requesting a photo with autograph. She had already filled an album with photos of the Duce cut from magazines and newspapers (ibid., p. 26).

On postcards, see Giuliano Vittori, ed., *C'era una volta il duce: Il regime in cartolina* (Rome: Savelli, 1975), and Enzo Nizza, ed., *Autobiografia del fascismo* (Milan: La Pietra, 1962). On photographs, *Illustrazione Italiana* constitutes a good source; others include Archivio Centrale di Stato, Fototeca, *PNF Ufficio Propaganda, Foto attivita' del duce,* and *Fondo Mostra della Rivoluzione fascista.* A selection of Mussolini's photographs can also be found in De Felice and Goglia, *Mussolini. Il mito,* op. cit.

228. Archivio Centrale dello Stato, PNF, Direttorio, Servizio Amministrativo, 237; Presidenza Consiglio dei Ministri 1937–39, 1.7.2939.

229. The writer Italo Calvino remembers: "You might say that the first twenty years of my life were spent looking at Mussolini's face, since his portrait was hung in every classroom, as it was in every office and public establishment." See Italo Calvino, "The Dictator's Hats," *Stanford Italian Review,* vol. 8, nos. 1/2 (1990), p. 195, trans. Chris Bongie.

230. Berneri, op. cit., p. 40.

231. The Epiphany was a gift-giving festivity that coincided in the Christian calendar with the king's gifts to baby Jesus. Popularly called *Befana*, this festivity was renamed *Befana fascista* when the regime took charge of distributing the gifts.

232. See, for example, Peter Paret, Beth Irwin Lewis, and Paul Paret, *Persuasive Images: Posters of War and Revolution from the Hoover Institution Archives* (Princeton: Princeton University Press, 1992). On the Russian case see Peter Kenez, *The Birth of the Propaganda State: Soviet Methods of Mass Mobilization, 1917–1929* (Cambridge: Cambridge University Press, 1985); Victoria E. Bonnell, "L'immagine della donna nell'iconografia sovietica dalla rivoluzione all'era staliniana," *Storia Contemporanea*, vol. XXII, no. 1 (February 1991), pp. 5–52. Also see Walter Benjamin's impressions in "Moscow Diary," *October*, 35 (Winter 1985), ed. Gary Smith, trans. Richard Sieburth.

233. Béraud, op. cit., p. 24. On graphic and mural writing see Armando Petrucci, "La scrittura tra ideologia e rappresentazione," in *Storia dell'arte italiana*, vol. II (Turin: Einaudi, 1980), p. 91.

234. There is one in Canneto, near Lipari, on the island of Lipari, where many antifascists were sent to *confino*.

235. Vettori lists some of those sentences in a generic and approximate chronological order in *Duce e ducetti*, op. cit., Chapter 3. Some examples: "Obey because you have to obey"; "Who has iron has bread"; "God gave us wheat, our Duce threshes it for us"; "Mussolini is always right"; "Mussolini is never wrong"; "Believe, Obey, Fight."

236. See this introduction, note 56.

237. See Plinio Ciani, *Graffiti del ventennio* (Milan: Sugar, 1975).

238. One also has to take into account the many ephemeral monuments that were built on the occasion of Mussolini's visits around Italy. Some pictures of these monuments are collected in Laura Malvano, *Fascismo e politica dell'immagine* (Turin: Boringhieri, 1988).

239. Béraud, op. cit., p. 40.

240. Ibid., p. 41.

241. *L'Italie fasciste ou l'autre danger* (Paris: Flammarion, 1927), pp. 23–24. On the head of the Duce printed on walls, see Dino Villani, *Storia del manifesto pubblicitario* (Milan: Omnia, 1964), p. 251.

242. The newspaper *La Stampa* wrote of Mussolini in 1932: "We address our thoughts to He who knows everything and sees everything." Needless to say, "He" referred to Mussolini (Biondi, op. cit., p. 242).

243. Photographs from the 1930s are assembled in Nizza, op. cit., and De Felice and Goglia, op. cit.

244. All Mussolini's speeches had to be published on page one. See Cannistraro, *La fabbrica del consenso*, op. cit., p. 81.

245. For an advertisement of the records see Ceserani, *Vetrina del ventennio 1923–1943* (Rome-Bari: Laterza, 1981), photo number 21.

246. See royal decree of February 16, 1939, no. 432, "Caratteristiche dei francobolli commemorativi della proclamazione dell'Impero." Mussolini also appeared in two stamps that were printed to celebrate the Decennial of the fascist revolution.

See royal decree of January 26, 1933, no. 50, "Descrizione tecnica dei francobolli celebrativi del Decennale della marcia su Roma e dell'avvento al potere del fascismo."

247. On radio see Cannistraro, *La fabbrica del consenso,* op. cit., Chapter 5, "La radio"; and Franco Monteleone, *La radio italiana nel periodo fascista: Studi e documenti: 1922–1945* (Venice: Marsilio, 1976). The first speech of the Duce was broadcast on November 4, 1925. His speech of October 10, 1926, was broadcast for the first time all over Italy.

248. The Luce (L'Unione Cinematografica Educativa) was "a government-controlled film agency that produced the Fascist regime's newsreels and documentaries" (Philip Cannistraro, ed., *Historical Dictionary of Fascist Italy,* op, cit., p. 313). The Luce also provided newspapers and magazines with the official photographs of the regime. In 1929 the Luce began to be subordinated directly to Mussolini. See Cannistraro, *La fabbrica del consenso,* op. cit., Chapter 6, "Il cinema."

249. Hitler also constructed his political career on visibility. In his first electoral campaign he visited twelve cities in an eleven-day tour in March 1932. In April 1932 Hitler journeyed by airplane and visited twenty cities in six days (Kershaw, op. cit., pp. 41–42).

250. Prezzolini, "Mussolini oratore ovvero eloquenza e carisma," in Emilio Gentile, ed., *Mussolini e "La Voce,"* op. cit., p. 216.

251. This reference to Mussolini as the Man continued during the regime's years. See Giovanni Gentile, cited in Del Buono, ed., op. cit., pp. 299–300.

252. Prezzolini, op. cit., p. 216.

253. On Mussolini's language also see Augusto Simonini, *Il linguaggio di Mussolini* (Milan: Bompiani, 1978).

254. *Scritti e discorsi,* vol. II, p. 339.

255. See Simonini, op. cit. When he talked, Mussolini used "I" instead of "We." The latter was typical of traditional politicians' style. It is possible that Mussolini was also influenced by the Futurists. See Prezzolini, "Mussolini oratore," op. cit., p. 218.

256. Mussolini told the people of Palermo in a 1924 speech: "And now, Palermitan people, I want to have a dialogue with you. This is both an ancient custom, since the *tribuni* spoke from the *arengo,* and a modern one because it reappeared in Fiume" (*Scritti e discorsi,* vol. IV, p. 118). According to Leso, Mussolini's dialogues were a mystification. Mussolini's questions were never founded on rational argumentation. Rather, they relied on an emotional basis. When the Duce asked: "To whom Italy? To whom Rome? To whom all the victories?"—the answer could only be the standard one: "To us." And when Mussolini asked: "Now, Palermitan people, if Italy asks you and requires from you the necessary discipline, the agreed upon work, devotion to the Fatherland, what do you answer, Palermitan people?"—then the answer was an automatic "Yes" (Erasmo Leso et al., *La lingua italiana e il fascismo* [Bologna: Consorzio Provinciale Pubblica Lettura, 1978], p. 32). Leso analyzes Mussolini's language as religious and founded on faith. Le Bon favored the emotional use of language in politics. See his *The Crowd: A Study of the Popular Mind* (New York: Viking, 1960).

257. *Scritti e discorsi,* vol. II, p. 307. Also see vol. III, pp. 97, 103.

258. Hermann Ellwanger, an admirer of Mussolini, wrote: "Mussolini, thus, had to break not only ancient political principles, but also the political forms and

methods. . . . It would be too easy to substitute an old formula with a new one without bringing in a transformation also in the spiritual and ethical field" (*Sulla lingua di Mussolini* [Milan: Mondadori, 1941], p. 24).

259. See among others *Scritti e discorsi*, vol. V, pp. 221, 282, 339; and vol. VI, p. 229.

260. "The weather, with its Autumn changes, is fascist because it teaches us yet another time to make short speeches, or better to abolish them," Mussolini told war veterans on October 4, 1928 (*Scritti e discorsi*, vol. VI, p. 269). On October 28, 1936, the daily directives to the press stated: "Do not define the words pronounced by the Duce as 'speech.'" See Archivio Centrale dello Stato, Agenzia Stefani, B. 70, fasc. 321/3.

261. *Scritti e discorsi*, vol. V, p. 151.

262. In 1914 Giovanni Zibordi wrote in the *Avanti!*: "His eloquence is one whole thing, I would almost say one piece with his aspect. . . . His eyes and mouth say the same words that he utters" (cited in Berneri, op. cit., p. 50). On November 8, 1921, Ojetti wrote in the *Corriere della sera*: "He underlines every sentence, every affirmation with the appropriate face." Ojetti's article offers a general description of Mussolini's oratorical style.

263. "Sometimes the movement of his mandible and lips is so precise and rigid that it evokes the image of a vise put in action with exact rhythm" (Franco Ciarlantini "Ascoltando il Duce in Augusteo," cited in Simonini, op. cit., p. 196). On Mussolini and his acting in the Luce's newsreels, see Massimo Cardillo, op. cit.

264. As Mussolini told Ludwig: "[T]oday I only said a few words to the *piazza*. Tomorrow millions of people can read them. But those who were down there have a deeper faith in what they heard with their ears, and I could say with their eyes" (Ludwig, op. cit., p. 120).

265. On films in rural areas and mobile cinemas, see Cannistraro, *La fabbrica del consenso*, op. cit., p. 279.

266. Foucault (*Discipline and Punish*, op. cit.) discusses the disciplinary eye that controls people's behavior in social institutions and that is part of the microtechniques of power. For Foucault, power in modern societies consists in anonymous and capillary organization of disciplinary control and does not have a subject. In fascism, however, Mussolini acted as the actual subject of power.

267. Kershaw argues that in 1936 Hitler began to believe more and more in his own myth, as the style and content of his speeches indicate (op. cit., p. 82): "[T]he more he succumbed to the allure of his own Führer cult and came to believe in his own myth, the more his judgment became impaired by faith in his own infallibility, losing his grip on what could and could not be achieved solely through the strength of his 'will'" (p. 264).

CHAPTER 3. THE POLITICS OF SYMBOLS

1. *Scritti e discorsi*, 12 vols. (Milan: Hoepli, 1934–1939), vol. V, p. 164 (speech of October 28, 1925, delivered in Milan).

2. Ibid., pp. 116–117.

3. The aspiration to realize an ideal world under the aegis of a self-proclaimed mission was generally part of the ideological discourse that accompanied the for-

mation of nation-states in Europe at the end of the eighteenth and the beginning of the nineteenth centuries. Both Germany and France, but also England, were at the time advocating the right to pursue a "mission" in the world, an attitude that, as in the case of England, soon showed its imperialistic character. See Federico Chabod, *Storia della politica estera italiana dal 1870 al 1896* (Bari: Laterza, 1965), vol. I.

4. For Cavour, for example, Italy's mission was to reconcile the Church with the question of freedom in the civil world, whereas Quintino Sella looked at science as the new mission of Rome (ibid., pp. 202–203).

5. Vincenzo Gioberti, *Del primato morale e civile degli Italiani* (Naples: C. Batelli e Comp., 1848–1849). According to the historian Chabod, the interpretation of the Italian mission as "supremacy" was not at all surprising in the political climate of nineteenth-century Europe. At the time, a country's invocation of mission could generate two outcomes: on the one hand, the value of "duty" in the notion of "mission" would highlight the end (i.e., humanity) over the means (that is, the nation itself); on the other hand, one could stress in "mission" the meaning of "right," since those in charge of a mission necessarily possess some kind of superior qualities and exceptional characteristics. In the latter conception, and contrary to the first one, the means overcame the end. The fatherland acquired a higher value than humanity, thus opening the way to nationalism (Chabod, op. cit., p. 192).

6. Emilio Gentile, *Il mito dello stato nuovo: Dall'antigiolittismo al fascismo* (Rome-Bari: Laterza, 1982).

7. There were also other opinions on the myth of Rome. They negatively assessed the presence of an old symbol in a nation that should instead look ahead and pursue the values of freedom and progress in its path to modernity. See Chabod's discussion of the question of bringing the capital to Rome. However, these critics, according to Chabod, also opposed reason to fantasy and feelings and did not realize that passions had sustained the struggle for unity (ibid., p. 319).

8. Antonio Gramsci, *Letteratura e vita nazionale* (Rome: Editori Riuniti, 1977), p. 69. The English version can be found in Antonio Gramsci, *Selections from Cultural Writings* (Cambridge, Mass.: Harvard University Press, 1985), p. 201.

9. Fulvio D'Amoja, *La politica estera dell'impero: Storia della politica estera fascista dalla conquista dell'Etiopia all'Anschluss* (Padova: Cedam, 1967), Chapter 1.

10. Mussolini wrote two articles on Gioberti in 1934 that dealt with Italy's "mission." Also see his entry "Fascismo" in *Enciclopedia Italiana*, vol. XIV, 1929–1939, pp. 847–884.

11. *Scritti e discorsi*, vol. II, p. 163.

12. *Opera Omnia*, 36 vols. (Florence: La Fenice, 1951–1963), vol. XIX, pp. 202–203.

13. In an article written for *Il Popolo d'Italia* on May 2, 1922, Mussolini predicted/threatened that in 1923 the May Day festival would be eliminated (*Opera Omnia*, vol. XVIII, pp. 174–175).

14. Ibid., p. 161.

15. Eric Hobsbawm and Terence Ranger argue that all invented traditions "use history as a legitimator of action and cement of group cohesion" (*The Invention of Tradition* [New York: Cambridge University Press, 1983], p. 12).

The myth of Rome has not been comprehensively studied, although there have been several specialized approaches to the subject. For a discussion of scholarly work on the role the myth of Rome played in fascism, see Dino Cofrancesco, "Appunti per un'analisi del mito romano nell'ideologia fascista," *Storia contemporanea*, vol. XI, no. 3 (June 1980), pp. 383–411. For a discussion of the myth of *Romanita'* in Mussolini's Italy, see Emilio Gentile, *Il culto del Littorio: La sacralizzazione della politica nell'Italia fascista* (Rome-Bari: Laterza, 1993), pp. 146–154. Also see Romke Visser, "Fascist Doctrine and the Cult of the Romanità," *Journal of Contemporary History*, vol. 27 (1992), pp. 5–22.

16. According to D'Amoja, Mussolini realized around 1921 that it was necessary "to insist on the links and continuity between fascism's action and Italy's previous history." Therefore, fascism resorted to nationalism and patriotic themes in order to conquer people's sympathies. "By evoking the past, fascism lost the patina of a contingent and negative phenomenon. It was not only a reaction to post-war times and conditions. It rather became the expression of Italy's history in its continuity and development" (op. cit., p. 2). In this operation, fascism completely reinterpreted the history of the Risorgimento and denied its liberal roots. In order to constitute "the presupposition of the fascist revolution," the Risorgimento could not be considered the offspring of the Enlightenment. Rome was its matrix, as Cesare Maria De Vecchi, extraordinary commissar of the National Society for the History of the Risorgimento in 1933, claimed in the statute of the society.

17. *Scritti e discorsi*, vol. II, pp. 277–278 (article "Past and Future" published in *Il Popolo d'Italia*).

18. On fascism's relation to history and the past, see Pier Giorgio Zunino, *L'ideologia del fascismo: Miti, credenze e valori nella stabilizzazione del regime* (Bologna: Il Mulino, 1985).

19. On the general history of Italian stamps, see Federico Zeri, "I francobolli italiani: grafica e ideologia dalle origini al 1948," in *Storia dell'arte italiana* (Turin: Einaudi, 1980), vol. II. According to Zeri, European states between the two wars expressed increasing interest in the style and content of stamps.

20. References to Augustus had a double, ambiguous meaning in fascism: on the one hand, Augustus epitomized the Roman empire; on the other, Christian peace among the peoples (see Cofrancesco, op. cit., p. 395). In his December 1, 1921, speech to the Chamber, Mussolini declared: "[W]e fascists cannot forget that Rome, this small territory, has been once the center, the brain, the heart of the empire. We cannot forget either that in Rome, on this small piece of land, one of history's religious miracles was realized. And an idea that may have destroyed the large force of Rome was assimilated by Rome and converted into the doctrine of its greatness" (*Scritti e discorsi*, vol. II, p. 214).

21. Imperial Rome's archaeology is present in many fascist stamps. See Zeri, op. cit.

22. A revival of classicism and classical studies in Italy took place during the regime. In 1925 an *Istituto di studi romani* was founded and several publications and journals were dedicated to issues connected to Roman history; see Luciano Canfora, *Ideologie del classicismo* (Turin: Einaudi, 1980), and Mariella Cagnetta, *Antichisti e impero fascista* (Bari, 1979). In the field of architecture, monumental and classical styles were privileged by the regime, especially in the 1930s. Arches and columns punctuated the buildings of the Universal Exhibition planned to take place in Rome in 1942. One of the most symbolic projects of the fascist regime, the ex-

hibit was intended as a stable construction, the first of its kind. It testified to the values, principles, and, ultimately, grandeur of Mussolini's Italy in its ideal linkage to the Rome of the past. See Achille Tartaro, ed., *E 42: Utopia e scenario del regime* (Venice: Marsilio, 1987). In general, the regime's classic taste privileged formal perfection and mythical themes, although a mixture of past and future also characterized fascism's classic art, whereas the Rationalists aspired to reach classical effects. See Armando Petrucci, "La scrittura tra ideologia e rappresentazione," in *Storia dell'arte italiana* (Turin: Einaudi, 1980), vol. II.

23. See James Hay, *Popular Film Culture in Fascist Italy: The Passing of the Rex* (Bloomington, 1987); Claudio Carabba, *Il cinema del ventennio nero* (Florence, 1974).

24. The exhibit, which began to be planned in 1932 under the direction of a famous professor of Roman studies, was kept open a whole year, until September 1938. Considerable propaganda efforts encouraged people from all over the country to visit it (Archivio Centrale dello Stato, Segreteria Particolare del Duce, Carteggio Ordinario, 1922–1943, fasc. 135015).

25. Ludovic Naudeau, traveling in Italy in 1926, noted the regime's claims that "all that has been Roman is Italian" (*L'Italie fasciste ou l'autre danger* [Paris: Flammarion, 1927], p. 39).

26. Cofrancesco, op. cit., p. 404. On fascism and social classes in the 1920s, see Jens Petersen, "Elettorato e base sociale del fascismo italiano negli anni venti," *Studi storici*, vol. XVI, no. 3 (July–September 1975); pp. 627–669.

27. Roland Barthes, *Mythologies* (New York: Paladin, 1972). The book was originally published in French in 1957.

28. Philip Cannistraro, ed., *Historical Dictionary of Fascist Italy* (Westport: Greenwood, 1982), p. 205.

29. Local party sections were still called *fasci*.

30. This can perhaps explain the choice of the party's name. Only a few weeks before the decision was made, Mussolini had presented the alternative between *Partito nazionale del lavoro* (National Party of Work) and *Partito fascista del lavoro* (Fascist Party of Work). According to Mussolini, "the word 'work' is necessary, but also the word 'fascist.'" In the end the only word left was *fascista* (Emilio Gentile, *Storia del Partito Fascista [1912–1922]: Movimento e milizia* [Rome-Bari: Laterza, 1989], p. 327).

31. Lynn Hunt, *Politics, Culture, and Class in the French Revolution* (Berkeley: University of California Press, 1984).

32. Loretta Valtz Mannucci, "Aquile e tacchini: iconografie di stato," in Maurizio Vaudagna, ed., *L'estetica della politica* (Rome-Bari: Laterza, 1989).

33. *Scritti e discorsi*, vol. VIII, p. 73. Two years later, in a speech that summarized the regime's work, Mussolini insisted on defining the *fascio* according to his own political vision, again stressing unity, will, and discipline: "The Italian people want to proceed under the sign of the *Littorio*, which means unity, will, discipline" (*Scritti e discorsi*, vol. IX, p. 45 [speech of March 18, 1934 to the regime's assembly]).

34. In 1932 the *Enciclopedia Italiana*, under the entry *fascio*, described the bundle and the ax as "sign and instrument of the magistrate's coercive power which was exercised with the pains of flogging and decapitation. It was the symbol of his *imperium*" (vol. XIV, pp. 846–847).

35. See Emilio Gentile, *Il culto del Littorio*, op. cit., pp. 85–87; and Philip

Cannistraro and Brian Sullivan, *Il Duce's Other Woman* (New York: Morrow, 1993), pp. 304–305.

36. During the Repubblica Sociale Italiana, when Mussolini moved the regime to northern Italy, the design with the ax at the center reemerged in the stamps.

37. Archivio Centrale dello Stato, Partito Nazionale Fascista, *Foglio d'Ordini*, December 20, 1933, no. 17, on medals for athletes. These medals on the one side portrayed the effigy of the Duce; on the other, that of an athlete holding the *fascio*.

38. Archivio Centrale dello Stato, Partito Nazionale Fascista, Direttorio, Uff. Stralcio, *Disposizione* no. 49 of November 17, 1932, which asked that every object given out to children carry a *fascio littorio*.

39. Plinio Ciani, *Graffiti del ventennio* (Milan: Sugarco, 1975), p. 79.

40. Gentile, *Il culto del Littorio*, op. cit., p. 89.

41. On fascist uniforms see Ugo Pericoli, *Le divise del Duce* (Milan: Rizzoli, 1983).

42. Spring was the equivalent of youth, as the fascist hymn went: "Youth, Youth, Spring of Beauty" (Giovinezza, Giovinezza, Primavera di Bellezza).

43. Royal decree-law of October 21, 1923, no. 2451.

44. See Zeri, op. cit. Also, the 1 lira stamp designed by Balla featured an horizontal *fascio*.

45. Royal decree-law of December 12, 1926, no. 2061.

46. Royal decree-law of March 27, 1927, no. 1048.

47. Royal decree-law of April 11, 1929, no. 504.

48. Royal decree-law of August 9, 1929, no. 1517.

49. The same lack of originality and the same omnipresence of the *fascio littorio* characterized another iconographic inheritance of the Roman past that fascism adopted in its imperial days: the Roman eagle. The eagle, which in ancient Rome used to precede the legionnaires, is actually one of the most common political symbols both across time and across nations. The royal eagle characterizes monarchical governments, and it also appears in traditionally republican systems such as the United States. For a history of the eagle's symbolism, see Alain Boureau, *L'Aigle: Chronique politique d'un emblème* (Paris: Editions du Cerf, 1985); and, for the United States, Loretta Valtz Mannucci, "Aquile e tacchini: iconografie di stato," op. cit. During the fascist regime the eagle, although already present in the iconography of the Italian state, enjoyed great prominence, especially in the second half of the 1930s in connection with the conquest of the empire. Small and giant eagles, ephemeral or iron cast, filled the regime's symbolic world, a representation of the imperial force and power of fascism.

50. De Felice considers fascism's reference to the new man the element that distinguishes Italian fascism from National Socialism. Whereas the Nazis' ideal man was the old Aryan who needed to be resuscitated, Mussolini strove to create a really new type (Renzo De Felice, *Intervista sul fascismo* [Rome-Bari: Laterza, 1982]). However, according to Mosse, the new fascist man both in Germany and Italy represented a stereotype that originated in nineteenth-century nationalism. It was part of an antibourgeois rhetoric against the unproductive and talkative intellectuals and tended to establish other bourgeois values, such as order, respectability, honest work, cleanliness, and productivity. Although the vast majority of Nazis believed the ideal German was the ancient Aryan type, the new German man in fact represented the ideal bourgeois, and National Socialism annexed every middle-class virtue that was

under siege in modern times. Certainly, Mosse admits, Italian fascism's new man presented features that were more forward-looking than the German ideal type. But references to the past also characterized Mussolini's vision of the new man and made of it a more ambiguous and ambivalent model of renewal (George Mosse, *Nazism: A Historical and Comparative Analysis of National Socialism. An Interview with Michael A. Ledeen* [New Brunswick: Transaction Books, 1978]).

51. *Scritti e discorsi,* vol. VIII, p. 21.

52. Fascist associations included people of all ages and professions. There were fascist associations of schools; public employees; state employees; railroad and postal services; professionals and artists; and agricultural, commercial, and industrial businesses. Other associations included the Fascist Fallen, Disabled, and Wounded; the National Forest Committee; the National Union of Officers on Leave; the Naval League; the Association of Sailors on Leave; the Nautical Union; the Union of Aeronautics; the National Institute of Fascist Culture; several youth organizations; women fasces, which in 1934 also began to include "rural home-makers"; the Olympics committee; and the Opera Nazionale Dopolavoro (OND, the leisure time association). Academies and colleges for youth were also included.

53. Fascism apparently inherited the black shirt from the Arditi, the special army corp that "daringly" fought during World War I and later joined D'Annunzio in the Fiume enterprise. Ugo Pericoli claims there is no certainty about the color of the Arditi's shirts. According to him, black was a dominant color in Italy, especially in the South (op. cit., p. 4). Black shirts were, however, visible in Fiume, according to Giuseppe Antonio Borgese. See his *Goliath: The March of Fascism* (New York: Viking, 1937), p. 160.

54. In 1926 the basic elements of the official fascist outfit were adopted, and they remained the same until 1943. The uniform included a fez, a black shirt, a black tie, black pants, and a black belt. See Pericoli, op. cit., p. 6.

55. Women changed the color of the shirt to white around 1932 (ibid., p. 15).

56. "[T]he 'black shirt' is not for everyday use and for every occasion. I positively ordered the competent authorities to unfailingly arrest all individuals (isolated or in groups) who improperly wear the black shirt" (*Scritti e discorsi,* vol. IV, p. 352).

57. *Scritti e discorsi,* vol. V, pp. 110–111.

58. See George Seldes, *Sawdust Caesar: The Untold History of Mussolini and Fascism* (New York: Harper, 1935), Appendix 10, p. 408. The commandments were issued by the party secretary, Giovanni Giuriati, in October 1931.

59. See article 3 of the Statute in Mario Missori, *Gerarchie e statuti del P.N.F.: Gran Consiglio, Direttorio Nazionale, Federazioni provinciali: Quadri e biografie* (Rome: Bonacci, 1986), p. 379.

60. Archivio Centrale dello Stato, Partito Nazionale Fascista, Direttorio (Uff. Stralcio), 369.

61. Asvero Gravelli, ed., *Vademecum dello stile fascista* (Rome: Nuova Europa, n.d. but circa 1940), pp. 68, 99. Gravelli compiled the injunctions sent by Starace regarding questions of style. The injunctions I cite from Gravelli's book are the ones missing from the Archivio Centrale dello Stato. See also Archivio Centrale dello Stato, Partito Nazionale Fascista, Direttorio (Uff. Stralcio), 371, Disposizione No. 868.

62. Archivio Centrale dello Stato, Partito Nazionale Fascista, Direttorio (Uff. Stralcio), 371, *Disposizione* no. 757 of March 4.

63. Archivio Centrale dello Stato, Partito Nazionale Fascista, *Foglio di Disposizioni* no. 1240 (January 13, 1939). For the gala uniform, see Pericoli, op. cit., p. 9.

64. Archivio Centrale dello Stato, Partito Nazionale Fascista, *Foglio di Disposizioni* no. 1285 (March 12, 1939).

65. See for instance *Disposizione* no. 309 of October 29, 1934, on badges for party members (all those enrolled in fascist organizations were party members but for the youth). Instructions were given on who, how, and where to wear a badge. Archivio Centrale dello Stato, Partito Nazionale Fascista, Direttorio (Uff. Stralcio), 370.

66. Archivio Centrale dello Stato, Agenzia Stefani, B 70, July 17, 1938 (communication of the Ministry of Popular Culture). Also see Giuseppe Bottai, *Diario*, entry of August 19, 1938, which reports Mussolini's comments on this event: "The employees' uniform is the reform of the bureaucracy. Remember: The cowl does make the monk." Cited in Renzo De Felice, *Mussolini il duce*, vol. II (Turin: Einaudi, 1981), p. 102.

67. Borgese, op. cit., p. 304.

68. Tracy H. Koon, *Believe, Obey, Fight: Political Socialization of Youth in Fascist Italy, 1922–1943* (Chapel Hill: University of North Carolina Press, 1985), p. 66.

69. Ibid., p. 65.

70. Archivio Centrale dello Stato, Agenzia Stefani, B. 70, July 5 (communication of the Ministry of Popular Culture).

71. Archivio Centrale dello Stato, Partito Nazionale Fascista, Direttorio (Uff. Stralcio), 370, no. 577.

72. Archivio Centrale dello Stato, Partito Nazionale Fascista, Direttorio (Uff. Stralcio), 369, no. 34.

73. *Disposizione* of February 27, 1932. See Asvero Gravelli, ed., op. cit., p. 23.

74. Archivio Centrale dello Stato, Partito Nazionale Fascista, Direttorio (Uff. Stralcio), 369, no. 34.

75. Archivio Centrale dello Stato, Partito Nazionale Fascista, Direttorio (Uff. Stralcio), 369, no. 1183.

76. Curiously, only in 1934 did the calendar produced by the party present the new time division beginning from October.

77. A month later, on December 20, 1938, Starace reiterated his ideas about the old New Year celebrations. But he admitted that people who work hard need to have this "traditional recreation." Perhaps Starace received an order from above. Or maybe he realized that since some habits die hard, it was more convenient to show tolerance by patronizing them. Thus, he ordered that "comrade *(camerateschi)* entertainments" be organized in fascist clubs of leisure time (Archivio Centrale dello Stato, Partito Nazionale Fascista, *Foglio di Disposizioni*, no. 1219).

78. Francesco Flora, ed., *Stampa dell'era fascista: Le note di servizio* (Rome: Mondadori, 1945), p. 81.

79. Archivio Centrale dello Stato, Partito Nazionale Fascista, *Foglio di Disposizioni*, no. 1200.

80. See Gravelli, op. cit., for the caricatures and drawings presented to the exhibit.

81. Ibid., p. 93.

82. Ibid., p. 112.

83. Ibid., p. 183.

84. Archivio Centrale dello Stato, Partito Nazionale Fascista, Direttorio (Uff. Stralcio), 371, no. 828.

85. Most of the drawings for the Anti-Bourgeois Exhibit portrayed the bourgeois as fat.

86. Gravelli, op. cit., p. 236.

87. This rule only applied to men.

88. Archivio Centrale dello Stato, Partito Nazionale Fascista, Direttorio (Uff. Stralcio), 371, no. 840 (July 15, 1937).

89. Archivio Centrale dello Stato, Partito Nazionale Fascista, Direttorio (Uff. Stralcio), 371, no. 1039.

90. Archivio Centrale dello Stato, Partito Nazionale Fascista, *Foglio di Disposizioni*, no. 1155 (September 24, 1938).

91. Between members of women groups and fascists the *voi* was recommended.

92. Archivio Centrale dello Stato, Partito Nazionale Fascista, *Foglio di Disposizioni*, no. 983 (February 14, 1938).

93. GIL, Gioventu' Italiana del Littorio, was an umbrella organization of young fascists. In 1939, 7,891,547 youth were enrolled in the several groups headed by GIL. See Pericoli, op. cit., p. 18. Enrollment in the organization was voluntary; however, it was supposed to take place at the same time as a youth's school enrollment.

94. Archivio Centrale dello Stato, Partito Nazionale Fascista, Direttorio (Uff. Stralcio), 371, no. 1046 (April 20, 1938).

95. Oreste Del Buono, ed., *Eja, Eja, Eja, Alalà! La stampa Italiana sotto il fascismo 1919–1943* (Milan: Feltrinelli, 1971), p. 363.

96. Flora, op. cit., pp. 100–101.

97. Del Buono, op. cit., p. 388.

98. Gravelli, op. cit., pp. 286–287.

99. Gentile, *Il culto del Littorio*, op. cit., p. 67.

100. Archivio Centrale dello Stato, Presidenza del Consiglio dei Ministri, 1934–1936, 1.7.6024.

101. Archivio Centrale dello Stato, Partito Nazionale Fascista, Direttorio (Uff. Stralcio), 369, no. 50 (November 20, 1932).

102. Emil Ludwig, *Colloqui con Mussolini* (Milan: Mondadori, 1932), p. 110.

103. According to Borgese, the ancient Romans did not use that gesture as an ordinary salute. He argues instead that the Roman salute was obligatory for slaves (op. cit., p. 159).

104. Gravelli, op. cit., p. 33.

105. Ibid., p. 53.

106. Ibid., p. 80.

107. Archivio Centrale dello Stato, Presidenza del Consiglio dei Ministri, 1934–1936, 1.7.6024.

108. Wasserman's observations were accompanied by visual material: a photographic example of a perfect salute in which the exact trajectory was showed by a straight arrow that followed the straightened arm. The exemplary figure in the photo was Mussolini.

109. Archivio Centrale dello Stato, Partito Nazionale Fascista, Direttorio (Uff. Stralcio), 370, no. 706 (January 2, 1937).

110. Biondi, op. cit., p. 311.

111. See special issue of *Il Ponte*, vol. VIII, no. 10 (October 1952), p. 1397.

112. Flora, op. cit., p. 20.

113. Ibid., p. 19.

114. Archivio Centrale dello Stato, Partito Nazionale Fascista, *Foglio di Disposizioni*, February 4, 1938, *Disposizione* no. 973. The *passo* was adopted on March 1, 1938.

115. *Scritti e discorsi*, vol. II, p. 163.

116. Ibid., pp. 163–164.

117. For this interpretation of the march, see comments of the events in the newspapers of the time. For a list of national festivals during the regime, see law of December 27, 1930, no. 1726.

118. Ludovic Naudeau, op. cit., p. 28.

119. See Mussolini's speech on the march in *Scritti e discorsi,* vol. II, p. 163.

120. From the preface to *Il Gran Consiglio del Fascismo nei primi quindici anni dell'Era Fascista* in Archivio Centrale dello Stato, *Foglio d'Ordini* (July 10, 1938).

121. The *passo romano* was executed with a stretched and rigid leg at the rhythm of 100 steps a minute. The *passo* was 65–70 centimeters long, and one could only proceed 200 meters every three minutes. It was, thus, very tiring (see Pericoli, op. cit. p. 14). Pericoli continues: "In order to execute the *passo romano*, one raised the stretched leg, the tip of the foot forward, until the heel reached 40 centimeters from the ground, forming a corner of 60 degrees. The foot was recalled to the ground, hitting forcefully, while 'the bust and the body had to remain erect and the glance fixed forward.' As the foot touched the ground, one needed to raise immediately the other leg. Consequently, at that moment, the body risked losing balance. To obviate this break-up, men needed to be very close to each other and the arms needed to be still" (ibid).

122. *Opera Omnia*, vol. XXIX, pp. 52–53 (speech of February 1, 1938, introducing the *passo*).

123. Luigi Fontanelli, cited in Dino Biondi, op. cit., p. 308.

124. Professor Sangiorgi wrote an article for *Il Popolo di Roma* of March 29, 1938. Cited in Leo Longanesi, *In piedi e seduti 1919–1943* (Milan: Longanesi, 1980), p. 163.

125. Flora, op. cit., p. 96.

126. Archivio Centrale dello Stato, Partito Nazionale Fascista, *Foglio di Disposizioni* no. 973 (February 4, 1938).

127. Cited in Gentile, *Il culto del Littorio*, op. cit., p. 191.

128. Cited in Yvon De Begnac, *Palazzo Venezia: Storia di un regime* (Rome: La Rocca, 1950), p. 652.

129. On this issue see Daniele Marchesini's discussion of the *Scuola di mistica fascista* in his *La scuola dei gerarchi: Mistica fascista: Storia, problemi, istituzioni* (Milan: Feltrinelli, 1976), p. 131. Also see Dino Grandi's reactions to the *passo romano* in a letter he sent to Mussolini: "I saw these Blackshirts close to; when they marched with the 'passo romano' their eyes sparkled, their lips straightened and hardened, their faces acquired a new expression which was not merely a martial air, but rather the air of satisfied pride with which a hammerer smites and crushes the head of his enemy. Indeed, after the first ten or twelve steps the thudding acquired

a steadily growing power, as the echo of the hammer-blows in the ear of the hammerer himself redoubles their force. In the necessary revolution of our customs which you are making, the 'passo romano' (together with the familiar 'voi' and the uniforms) is and always will be the most potent instrument of Fascist teaching of the young." Cited by Mussolini in his memoirs, in Raymond Klibansky, ed., *Benito Mussolini's Memoirs 1942–1943* (New York: Howard Fertig, 1975), trans. Frances Lobb, pp. 145–146.

130. Klibansky, op. cit., p. 145.

131. Galeazzo Ciano, *Diario (1937–43)* (Milan: Rizzoli, 1980), ed. Renzo De Felice, p. 245 (entry of January 30). (Ciano was minister of foreign affairs from June 10, 1936 to February 8, 1943.) Giuseppe Bottai also criticized the regime for being merely ritualistic, contentless, stylized, and representational. See *Vent'anni e un giorno* (Milan: Garzanti, 1949).

CHAPTER 4. BODILY ECONOMY

1. Benito Mussolini, *Opera Omnia,* 36 vols., (Florence: La Fenice, 1951–1963), vol. XVIII, p. 232.

2. On the ambiguity of the term *borghesia* in Italian politics, see Raffaele Romanelli, "Political Debate, Social History, and the Italian Borghesia: Changing Perspectives in Historical Research," *Journal of Modern History,* vol. 63, nos. 3–4 (December 1991), pp. 717–739.

3. Filippo Tommaso Marinetti, *Teoria e invenzione futurista* (Milan: Mondadori, 1983), ed. with introduction by Luciano De Maria, p. 551.

4. Throughout this chapter I take "mimetism" to mean simulation, as in the chameleon's resemblance to its environment.

5. Yvon De Begnac, *Palazzo Venezia: Storia di un regime* (Rome: La Rocca, 1950), p. 182. Also see Benito Mussolini, *Opera Omnia,* vol. XIV.

6. See *Opera Omnia,* vol. XIV, pp. 230–232 (article "Between the Old and the New *'Navigare necesse,'*" published in *Il Popolo d'Italia* of January 1, 1920).

7. "We do not believe in programs, schemes, saints or apostles. Above all we do not believe in happiness, in salvation, in a promised land" (ibid). Also see Mussolini's article "Illusions and Mystifications. The Leninist Paradise" of November 8, 1919, published in *Il Popolo d'Italia,* now in *Opera Omnia,* vol. XIV, pp. 115–118. During the regime, fascism's anticlericalism was diluted, and Mussolini invoked spiritual values as a justification for upholding the Church: "All creations of the spirit—beginning from the religious ones—come forward as superior, and no one dares to dwell anymore in the position of that anti-clericalism which for many decades has been the favorite occupation of democracy in the western world" ("Where is the World Headed?" in *Gerarchia* [February 25, 1922], now in *Scritti e discorsi,* vol. II, p. 264).

8. See "Dottrina del Fascismo," in *Scritti e discorsi,* 12 vols. (Milan: Hoepli, 1934–1939), vol. VIII, p. 70.

9. Ibid.

10. *Opera Omnia,* vol. XIV, pp. 231–232.

11. On this issue see Augusto Del Noce, "Fascismo come marxismo senza materialismo," in Costanzo Casucci, ed., *Il fascismo: Antologia di scritti critici* (Bologna: Il Mulino, 1982), p. 484.

12. "Dottrina del Fascismo," op. cit., p. 79.

13. "The world is not this material world that appears on the surface, in which man is one individual separated from all others and is governed by a natural law which instinctively leads him to live a life of egoistic and temporary pleasure. The man of Fascism is an individual who is nation and fatherland. It is moral law that links together individuals and generations in a tradition and a mission; that suppresses the instinct of an enclosed life revolving around pleasure to establish in duty a superior life free from the limits of time and space. This is a life in which the individual through self-abnegation, the sacrifice of his particular interests, and death realizes that all spiritual existence in which his human value resides" ("Dottrina del Fascismo," op. cit., p. 68).

14. For an exception, see the work of Victoria de Grazia.

15. Zeev Sternhell, with Mario Sznajder and Maia Asheri, *The Birth of Fascist Ideology: From Cultural Rebellion to Political Revolution* (Princeton: Princeton University Press, 1994).

16. Terry Eagleton, *The Ideology of the Aesthetic* (Oxford: Basil Blackwell, 1990), p. 13.

17. Ibid.

18. Cited in ibid., pp. 197, 199.

19. Cited in ibid., p. 197.

20. Ibid., p. 198.

21. In this context, reason for Marx serves the function of unveiling the contradictions that hamper us from recognizing the political determinants of the good life.

22. Ibid., p. 201, cited from Marx's *Economic and Philosophical Manuscripts*.

23. Ibid., p. 203.

24. Ibid., p. 205.

25. According to Timpanaro, Marxism is not materialistic enough and has failed to emphasize the biological limits of human aspirations to happiness (Sebastiano Timpanaro, "Prassi e materialismo," in *Sul materialismo* [Pisa: Nistri-Lischi, 1970]).

26. Augusto Del Noce, *Il problema dell'ateismo: Il concetto di ateismo e la storia della filosofia come problema* (Bologna, 1964).

27. On this issue see Roy Porter, "History of the Body," in Peter Burke, ed., *New Perspectives on Historical Writing* (Cambridge: Polity Press, 1991).

28. See John Carey, "Revolted by the Masses," *Times Literary Supplement,* January 12–18, 1990, pp. 34–36.

29. Eagleton, op. cit., p. 28.

30. The other option would be to exploit the advantages of aesthetics' tendency to foster extreme subjectivism so to exercise control over political participation and intensify hegemony.

31. Chandra Mukerji, *From Graven Images: Patterns of Modern Materialism* (New York: Columbia University Press, 1983). On consumption and history see John Brewer and Roy Porter, eds., *Consumption and the World of Goods* (London: Routledge, 1993); Lisa Tirsten, "Redefining Consumer Culture: Recent Literature on Consumption and the Bourgeoisie in Western Europe," *Radical History Review,* vol. 57 (1993), pp. 116–159.

32. This revolution was defined as a "democratization of luxury." Michael Miller argues, however, that the expression is misleading, as the beneficiaries of the

commercial revolution before the First World War were the middle classes. See his *The Bon Marché: Bourgeois Culture and the Department Store 1869–1920* (Princeton: Princeton University Press, 1981).

33. Rosalind H. Williams, *Dream Worlds: Mass Consumption in Late Nineteenth-Century France* (Berkeley: University of California Press, 1982), p. 224.

34. See Paul Leroy-Beaulieu's position in Williams, op. cit., pp. 230–231.

35. On the first explanation see Neil McKendrick, John Brewer, and J. H. Plumb, *The Birth of a Consumer Society: The Commercialization of Eighteenth-Century England* (Bloomington: Indiana University Press, 1982). On the second see Colin Campbell, *The Romantic Ethic and the Spirit of Modern Consumerism* (Oxford: Basil Blackwell, 1987).

36. *De la division du travail sociale,* first published in 1893. Also see Williams, op. cit., Chapter 8.

37. Émile Durkheim, *The Elementary Forms of the Religious Life* (London: Allen and Unwin, 1915), first published in French in 1912.

38. See Warren G. Breckman, "Disciplining Consumption: The Debate about Luxury in Wilhelmine Germany, 1890–1914," *Journal of Social History,* vol. 24 (1990/1991), pp. 484–505. Breckman sees the issue of consumption as crucial for an accurate discussion of Germany's attitude toward modernity.

39. Ibid., p. 486.

40. See Daniel Horowitz's discussion in his *The Morality of Spending: Attitudes Toward the Consumer Society in America, 1875–1940* (Baltimore: Johns Hopkins University Press, 1985).

41. On the Lynds' study see Richard Wightman Fox, "Epitaph for Middletown: Robert S. Lynd and the Analysis of Consumer Culture," in Richard Wightman Fox and T. J. Jackson Lears, eds., *The Culture of Consumption: Critical Essays in American History 1880–1980* (New York: Pantheon, 1983).

42. T. J. Jackson Lears, "Mass Culture and its Critics," in *Encyclopedia of American Social History* (New York: Scribners, 1993).

43. "Managing" social desires by offering positive alternatives to mass diversion excited Walter Lippman's fantasy of a "democratic social engineering." He believed the evil of mass consumption could be reversed by exploiting the same principles on which the culture of consumption rested. Thus, the American response to mass culture affirmed the power of experts in guiding people's taste for amusements. Education by a technocratic elite could remedy the enslavement by the commodity to which the popular and middle classes were subjected (ibid.).

44. On national syndicalism see Ferdinando Cordova, *Le origini dei sindacati fascisti, 1918–1926* (Rome-Bari: Laterza, 1974). Also see David D. Roberts, *The Syndicalist Tradition and Italian Fascism* (Chapel Hill: University of North Carolina Press, 1979).

45. The fascists, for example, opposed the strikes of January 1920. See Cordova, op. cit., pp. 25–26.

46. According to Carmen Haider "[i]n the fascist phraseology the word 'corporation' was used for the expression 'national federation of syndicates' up to 1925." See her *Capital and Labor under Fascism* (New York: Columbia University Press, 1930), note 2, p. 53.

47. Cordova, op. cit., p. 55.

48. Haider, op. cit., p. 54.

49. Cordova, op. cit., p. 67.

50. At this time the PNF organized "competence groups" (*gruppi di competenza*) with the goal of developing technical studies of socioeconomic issues.

51. It also changed its name to National Confederation of Fascist Syndicates. See De Felice, *Mussolini il fascista*, vol. II (Turin: Einaudi, 1968), p. 276.

52. On the effects of the pact on fascist syndicalism see Alberto Aquarone, *L'organizzazione dello stato totalitario* (Turin: Einaudi, 1965).

53. On the minimum number of people needed to form an association see Aquarone, op. cit., p. 126.

54. On ideas of corporativism in Germany and France, see Charles Maier, *Recasting Bourgeois Europe: Stabilization in France, Germany, and Italy in the Decade after World War I* (Princeton: Princeton University Press, 1975). Also, Durkheim elaborated some ideas about corporations as occupational associations. See especially *Le socialisme*, first published in 1928 but delivered as lectures beginning in 1896.

55. See Gaetano Salvemini, *Under the Axe of Fascism* (New York: Viking Press, 1936).

56. On the different drafts of the charter, see De Felice, *Mussolini il fascista*, vol. II, op. cit.

57. Aquarone, op. cit., p. 145.

58. See *Scritti e discorsi*, vol. V, p. 86, in which Mussolini talks about the "material and moral election of the masses."

59. The branches of production included commerce, industry, agriculture, banks, air and sea transportation, and internal and ground transportation.

60. On the debates over the establishment of corporations, see G. Lowell Field, *The Syndical and Corporative Institutions of Italian Fascism* (New York: Columbia University Press, 1938).

61. Philip Cannistraro, ed., *Historical Dictionary of Fascist Italy* (Westport: Greenwood, 1982), p. 138.

62. Aquarone, op. cit.

63. Pierluigi Profumieri, "Capitale e lavoro in Italia 1929–1940: una interpretazione economica," in Alberto Aquarone and Maurizio Vernassa, eds., *Il regime fascista* (Bologna: Il Mulino, 1974). According to Cassese, the abstract exaltation of the corporative system through its juridical institutions indeed affected the belief in corporativism's ability to overcome economic quandaries (Sabino Cassese, "Corporazioni e intervento pubblico nell'economia," in ibid).

64. Charles Maier, "The Economics of Fascism and Nazism: Premises and Performance," in Alejandro Foxley, Michael G. McPherson, and Guillermo O'Donnell, eds., *Development, Democracy and the Art of Trespassing: Essays in Honor of Albert O. Hirschman* (Notre Dame: University of Notre Dame Press, 1986).

65. Edward Tannenbaum, *The Fascist Experience: Italian Society and Culture 1922–1945* (New York: Basic Books, 1972), p. 93.

66. See Mussolini's article on fascism and syndicalism in *Scritti e discorsi*, vol. V, p. 86.

67. Mussolini's speech to the Senate, ibid., p. 291. This law was invoked a posteriori as the basis of the corporative system.

68. *Scritti e discorsi,* vol. VI, p. 165.

69. *Scritti e discorsi,* vol. VII, p. 191.

70. An important conference on corporativism took place May 5–8, 1932, in Ferrara. Theorists and politicians debated the essence of fascist corporativism.

71. Speech on syndical law of March 11, 1926, in *Scritti e discorsi,* vol. V, p. 294.

72. Ibid.

73. *Scritti e discorsi,* vol. VIII, p. 72.

74. Representatives of industrialists insisted that fascism follow a realpolitik approach to the economy based on the centrality of industry. Though acknowledging the importance of agriculture in the economy, the industrialists argued that its potential for development was limited, whereas industry as a source of mobile wealth had a natural tendency to expand. The most powerful and most respected states were the industrial states (England and France), for industry constituted an element of dynamism, a manifestation of national prestige (Gino Olivetti, "Capitalismo controllato invece di liberismo," in Casucci, op. cit.).

75. "While socialist syndicalism through class struggle leads to politics with a final program that foresees the suppression of private property and individual initiative, fascist syndicalism, through class collaboration, leads to corporations. Corporations make that collaboration systematic and harmonic by safeguarding property but elevating it to a social function, by respecting individual initiative but within the frame of the Nation's life and economy" (*Scritti e discorsi,* vol. VII, p. 193).

76. Amintore Fanfani, "Declino del capitalismo e significato del corporativismo," in Oreste del Buono, ed., *Eja, Eja, Eja, Alalà! La stampa Italiana sotto il fascismo 1919–1943* (Milan: Feltrinelli, 1971), pp. 223–224.

77. See the entry "Sindacalismo fascista" in *Dizionario di Politica,* vol. IV (Rome, 1940), now in Casucci, op. cit.

78. Ibid., p. 129.

79. Carlo Costamagna, "Stato e corporazioni," in *Dizionario di Politica* (Rome, 1940), now in Casucci, op. cit.

80. On corporativism also see Giuseppe Bottai, *Esperienza corporativa, 1929–1934* (Florence: Vallecchi, 1934).

81. Alfredo Rocco, *Scritti e discorsi politici* (Milan: Giuffré, 1938).

82. "Il corporativismo come liberalismo assoluto e socialismo assoluto," in Casucci, op. cit., p. 148.

83. In his speech of November 14, 1933, to the General Assembly of the National Council of Corporations, Mussolini stated: "It is perfectly conceivable that a national Council of Corporations substitute 'in toto' for the actual Chamber of Deputies: I never liked the Chamber of Deputies. . . . The Chamber of Deputies presupposes a world that we have demolished: it presupposes a plurality of parties, and more often than not the attack of diligence. Ever since we annulled this plurality, the Chamber of Deputies has lost the essential reason for which it was born" (*Scritti e discorsi,* vol. VIII, p. 270).

84. In 1928 Mussolini had already forecast the end of capitalism. See speech of May 7 to the Third National Congress of Fascist Syndicates, *Scritti e discorsi,* vol. VI, pp. 161–166.

85. *Scritti e discorsi,* vol. VIII, pp. 219–222.

86. Ibid., p. 121.

87. Ibid., pp. 257–273.

88. Ibid., p. 259.

89. Ibid. Mussolini condemned the bourgeoisie as a moral category. In 1938, when the polemic against the bourgeoisie became harsher, Mussolini defined the bourgeoisie as a "political-moral category," not as an economic class (*Opera Omnia*, vol. XXIX, p. 187, speech to the Grand Council of October 25).

90. *Scritti e discorsi*, vol. VIII, p. 263.

91. Ibid., p. 264.

92. Ibid., p. 263.

93. *Scritti e discorsi*, vol. IX, p. 20 (speech of January 13, 1934, to the General Assembly of the National Council of Corporations).

94. Many fascists from the conservative-nationalist faction feared the development of industrial capitalism and standardization identified with American Fordism. See Melograni, *Gli industriali e Mussolini: Rapporti tra Confindustria e fascismo dal 1919 al 1929* (Milan: Longanesi, 1972), especially pp. 258–276.

95. Gualberto Gualerni, *Lo Stato industriale in Italia, 1890–1940* (Milan: Etas Libri, 1982), pp. 53–54. Also see Luigi Salvatorelli and Giovanni Mira, *Storia d'Italia nel periodo fascista* (Turin: Einaudi, 1957), pp. 538–542, and Salvemini, op. cit., chapters 11–14. According to Salvatorelli and Mira, the consumption of meat lowered from 22 kilos in 1928 to 18 in 1932; the consumption of sugar went from 9.2 kilos in 1930 to 6.9 in 1932. Also see Cesare Vannutelli, "The Living Standards of Italian Workers, 1929–1939," in Roland Sarti, ed., *The Ax Within: Italian Fascism in Action* (New York: New Viewpoints, 1974).

96. Autarchy implied high import tariffs, import quotas, and embargoes on industrial products. On autarchy, see Shepard B. Clough, *The Economic History of Modern Italy* (New York: Columbia University Press, 1964), and Salvatore La Francesca, *La politica economica del fascismo* (Bari: Laterza, 1972), Chapter II.

97. *Scritti e discorsi*, vol. IX, p. 97.

98. *Scritti e discorsi*, vol. VIII, p. 273.

99. Ibid., p. 271.

100. In his speech of January 13, 1934, to the General Assembly of the National Council of Corporations, Mussolini affirmed that the state represented the consumer, "[t]he anonymous mass which, since it is not organized as consumers in specific organizations, has to be guarded by the organ that represents the collectivity of citizens" (*Scritti e discorsi*, vol. IX, p. 21).

101. Cited in Giovanni Salvemini, op. cit., p. 138.

102. Rachel Bowlby, *Just Looking: Consumer Culture in Dreiser, Gissing, and Zola* (New York: Methuen, 1985).

103. John F. Kasson, *Amusing the Million: Coney Island at the Turn of the Century* (New York: Hill and Wang, 1978); Lewis A. Erenberg, *Steppin' Out: New York Nightlife and the Transformation of American Culture, 1890–1930* (Chicago: University of Chicago Press, 1981); Kathy Peiss, *Cheap Amusements: Working Women and Leisure in Turn-of-the-Century New York* (Philadelphia: Temple, 1986); Stuart Ewen, *Captains of Consciousness: Advertising and the Social Roots of the Consumer Culture* (New York: McGraw Hill, 1976).

104. Kasson, op. cit.

105. William Leach, "Strategists of Display and the Production of Desire" in Simon J. Bonner, ed., *Consuming Visions: Accumulation and Display of Goods in America, 1880–1920* (New York: W.W. Norton and Co., 1989).

106. Other senses, such as touch, were also involved.

107. Leach, op. cit., p. 202. The "satisfaction of desires" was a formula pioneered by the sociologist Lester Ward in his 1903 work *Pure Sociology: A Treatise on the Origin and Spontaneous Development of Society.*

108. Leach, op. cit. Also see his "Transformations in a Culture of Consumption: Women and Department Stores, 1890–1925," *Journal of American History,* vol. 71, no. 2 (September 1984), pp. 319–342.

109. The word did not exist until World War I: "Before 1890 *display* as a term denoting systematic treatment of goods did not exist, nor would it be part of everyday merchandising language until World War I. What display did exist was primitive, as trimmers crowded goods together inside the windows or, weather permitting, piled them up outside on the street" (Leach, "Strategists of Display," op. cit., p. 106).

110. Ibid., p. 109. In a secular manner, which contemptuously challenged established religions, Baum recommended earthly pleasures and the return to a childlike playfulness. In this vein, 1930s display managers conceived their job as recreating daydreaming and childhood fantasies. Store windows enacted fairy tales that defied real life's stresses and strains and solicited deep desires and emotional longings. Store interiors also were reorganized decoratively to this end. Along with hotels, restaurants, and opera houses, they became the stage for beautiful scenarios and imaginary journeys in time and space. Folk wisdom seemed to suggest that people bought hopes, not things (ibid., p. 118).

111. For a French example before World War I, see the case of the Bon Marché in Michael Miller, op. cit., and Rosalind Williams, op. cit.

112. Consumption has been interpreted in its organic meaning of deadly consuming, wasting. See Roy Porter, "Consumption: Disease of the Consumer Society?" in Brewer and Porter, op. cit. Also see Williams, op. cit., chapter 1.

113. Leach, "Strategists of Display," op. cit.

114. See Lary May, *Screening Out the Past: The Birth of Mass Culture and the Motion Picture Industry* (New York: Oxford University Press, 1980).

115. See Peiss, op. cit., and Roy Rosenzweig, *Eight Hours for What We Will: Workers and Leisure in an Industrial City, 1870–1920* (Cambridge: Cambridge University Press, 1983).

116. May, op. cit., p. 38.

117. In 1916 an American study on photoplay by the psychologist Hugo Münsterberg claimed that social order in a democratic society could only be assured by eliminating "forbidden joys—the influx of sensuous elements and expensive luxuries," which inevitably led to a regressive stage of civilization. Although films potentially caused the explosion of sexual desires, Münsterberg believed they could also be used in a reverse trend to reaffirm Victorian values. Because a visual manipulation of the environment conditioned the unconscious, control over film content could help rebuild morality. With the proliferation of nickelodeons, critics of

cinema and vice crusaders resorted to control and regulation in the production of films. Surveillance would affirm moral and cultural standards and promote middle-class virtues: the family character, the refined woman (ibid., pp. 41–42). Although eventually these virtues were accommodated and reinterpreted by a new genera-tion of producers who stressed the new corporate order's values, the reliance on the motion picture and its potential for enlightenment and education helped bring in the film industry as a crucial component of the fast-growing mass culture.

118. Victoria De Grazia, *How Fascism Ruled Women: Italy, 1922–1945* (Berke-ley: University of California Press, 1992).

119. Ibid., p. 81.

120. For an analysis of fashion in relation to the sensual, see Elizabeth Wilson, *Adorned in Dreams: Fashion and Modernity* (London: Virago, 1985).

121. See Thomas Richards's argument in his case study of Victorian England: *The Commodity Culture of Victorian England: Advertising and Spectacle, 1851–1914* (Stanford: Stanford University Press, 1990).

122. See Dino Villani, *Storia del manifesto pubblicitario* (Milan: Omnia, 1964). The first poster of large format was the one for the Italian-American Exhibit in Genoa. See Enzo Cassoni, *Il cartellonismo e l'illustrazione in Italia dal 1875 al 1950* (Rome: Nuova Editrice Spada, 1984), p. 49.

123. For a general history, see Cassoni, op. cit.; Villani, op. cit.; and Dino Villani, *50 anni di pubblicità in Italia* (Milan: L'Ufficio Moderno, 1957). For a history of posters in prefascist Italy, see Giorgio Bocca, ed., *I manifesti italiani fra Belle Époque e fascismo* (Milan: Fabbri, 1971), and Luigi Menegazzi, *Il manifesto italiano 1882/ 1925* (Milan: Electa, 1975).

124. Gian Piero Brunetta, *Storia del cinema italiano, 1895–1945* (Rome: Editori Riuniti, 1979).

125. An important example is the 1912 film *Quo Vadis?* See Elaine Mancini, *Struggles of the Italian Film Industry during Fascism, 1930–1935* (Ann Arbor: UMI Research Press, 1985).

126. Giuliana Bruno, *Streetwalking on a Ruined Map: Cultural Theory and the City Films of Elvira Notari* (Princeton: Princeton University Press, 1993), pp. 97–100. Bruno draws attention to the relation between city films, arcades, and consumption.

127. Ibid., p. 59.

128. Gian Piero Brunetta, *Cinema italiano tra le due guerre: Fascismo e polit-ica cinematografica* (Milan: Mursia, 1975); Riccardo Redi, ed., *Cinema italiano sotto il fascismo* (Venice: Marsilio, 1979).

129. Jean A. Gili, *Stato fascista e cinematografia: Repressione e promozione* (Rome: Bulzoni, 1981).

130. Mancini, op. cit., p. 26.

131. James Hay, *Popular Film Culture in Fascist Italy: The Passing of the Rex* (Bloomington: Indiana University Press, 1987), Appendix A. According to Mancini (op. cit., p. 44), twelve Italian films were produced in 1930. On 1930s fascist films also see Marcia Landy, *Fascism in Film: The Italian Commercial Cinema, 1931–1943* (Princeton: Princeton University Press, 1986); Francesco Savio, *Ma l'amore no: Rea-lismo, formalismo, propaganda e telefoni bianchi nel cinema italiano di regime (1930–1943)* (Milan: Sonzogno, 1975).

132. Mancini, op. cit., p. 58.

133. The first movie poster in Italy appeared in 1911. See Cassese, op. cit., p. 61.

134. Emilio Radius, *Usi e costumi dell'uomo fascista* (Milan: Rizzoli, 1964), p. 88.

135. Radius also says that all theaters, even the worst-looking ones, had a special place on a pedestal for the chairs of the king and queen, a good example of the relation between power and representation (ibid., p. 89).

136. Hay, op. cit., Appendix A.

137. Mancini, op. cit., p. 44.

138. Ibid.

139. Claudio Carabba, *Il cinema del ventennio nero* (Florence: Vallecchi, 1974), p. 17.

140. De Grazia, op. cit., pp. 119, 132. Also see Piero Meldini, ed., *Sposa e madre esemplare: Ideologia e politica della donna e della famiglia durante il fascismo* (Rimini-Florence: Guaraldi, 1975), pp. 126–127. On fascism and film also see Ruth Ben-Ghiat, "Envisioning Modernity: Desire and Discipline in the Italian Fascist Film," in Emily Braun and Philip Cannistraro, eds., *Fascism and Culture: The Visual Arts in Italy, 1919–1945* (Cambridge: Cambridge University Press, forthcoming).

141. Ibid, pp. 132–133.

142. Ludovic Naudeau, *L'Italie fasciste ou l'autre danger* (Paris: Flammarion, 1927), p. 37.

143. On advertisement under fascism and its link to the body, see Karen Pinkus, *Bodily Regimes: Italian Advertising under Fascism* (Minneapolis: University of Minnesota Press, 1995).

144. On publicity graphics in 1930s Italy see Giuseppe Priarone, *Grafica pubblicitaria in Italia negli anni trenta* (Florence: Cantini, 1988). Also see Priarone for a bibliography on graphic arts and posters.

145. De Grazia, op. cit.

146. Guy Debord, *Society of the Spectacle* (Detroit: Black and Red, 1983), first published in French in 1967.

147. Paul Greenhalgh, *Ephemeral Vistas: A History of the Éxpositions Universelles, Great Exhibitions, and World Fairs, 1851–1939* (Manchester: Manchester University Press, 1988), p. 2; Richards, op. cit.; also see Whitney Walton, *France at the Crystal Palace: Bourgeois Taste and Artisan Manufacture in the Nineteenth Century* (Berkeley: University of California Press, 1992).

148. Richards, op. cit., p. 18.

149. In Victorian England these included monarchy and imperialism (ibid).

150. Op. cit., p. 1594. The circulation of national values thus achieved potentially created a homogeneous audience: everyone was the recipient of the message. In this sense, Thomas Richards argues, the invention of a democratic ideology is one of the fundamental elements for the establishment of a consumer culture. The desire for the same objects equalized people, whereas the commodity reigned supreme (Richards, op. cit., p. 81). In Richards' account, the commodity almost constitutes an ideology that supersedes any other representation, be it political or aesthetic. Analyzing the commodity as a semantic system, however, leaves out the issue of the relation between images and desires. Of course, no matter how we choose or what we choose, we will invariably end up choosing commodity, but the act of choosing still has some relevance for the analysis of social relations.

151. Buck-Morss states: "While condemning the contents of modern culture

[fascism] found in the dreaming collective created by consumer capitalism a ready-at-hand receptacle for its own political phantasmagoria" (*The Dialectics of Seeing: Walter Benjamin and the Arcades Project* [Cambridge, Mass.: MIT Press, 1989], p. 312).

152. Victoria De Grazia, *The Culture of Consent: Mass Organization of Leisure in Fascist Italy* (Cambridge: Cambridge University Press, 1981).

153. See Chaper 5.

154. The regime's unified view of folklore, however, was in itself an ideological construction, a historical invention. Italian folklore mainly had a local character and most often was confined to a village or town. The presence of different dialects contributed to this local character and pointed to the existence of cultural variations. Moreover, folklorists' work focused on, and highlighted, regional differences. Fascism, in contrast, strove to eliminate from folklore the elements of national divisiveness. The chairman of the Italian National Committee for popular traditions, Professor Emilio Bodrero, affirmed: "When Fascism asks that we no longer speak of regions in Italy, it is right, because regionalism has been one of the plagues of our history." Two years later Bodrero declared: "The regime had suppressed the word 'region' in every act, document, and declaration, not only because it recalled the memory of a dismembered nation of the past but also because it contained the seeds of division which is entirely contrary to the iron-like concept of national unity of Fascism!" See William E. Simeone, "Fascists and Folklorists in Italy," *Journal of American Folklore*, vol. 91, no. 359 (1977), pp. 546–547, from a speech of 1934. On folklore in Nazi Germany, see Christa Kamenetsky, "Folklore as a Tool in Nazi Germany," *Journal of American Folklore*, vol. 85, no. 337 (1972), pp. 221–235; and "Folktale and Ideology in the Third Reich," *Journal of American Folklore*, vol. 90, no. 358 (1977), pp. 168–178.

155. See De Grazia, *How Fascism Ruled Women*, op. cit.; Luisa Passerini, *Torino operaia e fascismo: Una storia orale* (Bari: Laterza, 1984); and David Horn, *Social Bodies: Science, Reproduction, and Italian Modernity* (Princeton: Princeton University Press, 1994).

156. To be sure, the conceptualization of this divide is in itself problematic. See Jeff Weintraub, "The Theory and Politics of the Public/Private Distinction," paper presented at the American Political Science Association, San Francisco, 1990; and Hanna Pitkin, "Justice: On Relating Private and Public," *Political Theory*, vol. 9, no. 3 (August 1981), pp. 327–352. For a discussion of public and private as applied to the case of Nazi Germany, see Anson Rabinbach, "The Reader, the Popular Novel and the Imperative to Participate: Reflections on Public and Private Experience in the Third Reich," *History and Memory*, vol. 3, no. 2 (Fall/Winter 1991), pp. 5–44.

CHAPTER 5. WAR AND MELODRAMA

1. "Il fascismo e i rurali," in Benito Mussolini, *Scritti e discorsi*, 12 vols. (Milan: Hoepli, 1934–1939), vol. II, pp. 281–290.

2. Ibid., p. 287.

3. "In the assault battalions there were thousands and thousands of peasants. Many of those who participated in the first and second battles of Piave were potentially fascist" (ibid).

4. See Mussolini's speech at the Chamber in *Opera Omnia*, 36 vols. (Florence: La Fenice, 1951–1963), vol. XXI, p. 356.

5. Serpieri left the post in July 1924. In 1929 he became undersecretary for integral land reclamation.

6. On this issue see Adrian Lyttelton, *The Seizure of Power: Fascism in Italy 1919–1929* (New York: Scribner, 1973), p. 350. According to Alessandra Staderini, Serpieri was actually removed from the government because of pressure from southern landowners who opposed his project of transformations. See Staderini, "La politica cerealicola del regime: l'impostazione della battaglia del grano," *Storia contemporanea*, vol. IX, nos. 5–6 (December 1978), p. 1030. On the role of agrarians in fascism and the difference with Nazi Germany, see Gustavo Corni, "La politica agraria del fascismo: un confronto fra Italia e Germania," *Studi Storici*, vol. XXVIII, no. 2 (April–June 1987), pp. 385–421.

7. Staderini, "La politica cerealicola," op. cit.

8. Staderini, "La Federazione Italiana dei Consorzi Agrari (1920–1940)," *Storia Contemporanea*, vol. IX, nos. 5/6 (December 1978), p. 962. The *federazione* (also called Federconsorzi) was a central organization of farmers who united on a local basis in order to purchase the technical means necessary to agricultural work. It mostly represented the middle classes.

9. Alessandra Staderini and Mario Toscano, "La campagna tra realta' e propaganda," in *L'economia italiana tra le due guerre 1919–1939* (Rome: Comune di Roma, 1984), p. 202.

10. Edward Tannenbaum, *The Fascist Experience: Italian Society and Culture 1922–1945* (New York: Basic Books, 1972), p. 95.

11. D. Preti writes: "While the Battle of Wheat had an impact in terms of research for intensifying production in the agrarian areas that were the most developed from the capitalistic point of view, in the agronomically weaker and socially more backward areas of the South it ended up precluding to those areas that were especially poor in organic substances the possibility of wealth that could only come from manure" (cited in Corni, op. cit., p. 407).

12. Valerio Castronovo, "La politica economica del fascismo e il Mezzogiorno," *Studi Storici*, vol. XVII, no. 3 (1976), pp. 25–39.

13. Corni, op. cit., p. 407.

14. Tannenbaum, op. cit., p. 95.

15. Castronovo, op. cit., p. 33. Castronovo argues that fascism's economic politics basically favored the North. On the relation between fascism and economy, see also Paul Corner, "Fascist Agrarian Policy and the Italian Economy in the Interwar Years," in John A. Davies, ed., *Gramsci and Italy's Passive Revolution* (London: Barnes and Noble, 1979).

16. See Cesare Longobardi, *Land-Reclamation in Italy: Rural Revival in the Building of a Nation* (London: P.S. King and Son, Ltd., 1936), p. 40.

17. Staderini, "La politica cerealicola," op. cit., p. 1044.

18. Philip Cannistraro, *La fabbrica del consenso: Fascismo e mass media* (Rome-Bari: Laterza, 1975), p. 278.

19. Maranesi was the president of the Organizzazione Nazionale Combattenti (ONC), an organization founded in 1917 to help the soldiers of World War I readjust to civilian life. See his letter to Mussolini announcing the publication of the Agrarian Collection, Archivio Centrale dello Stato, Segreteria Particolare del Duce, Carteggio Ordinario, 1922–43, fasc. 509.742. The publication of these specialized

collane seems to indicate that the regime's audience was cultivated and educated. The regime in this case addressed agrarian middle classes and not the bulk of the rural population, among whom illiteracy was still rampant.

20. See photos no. 227 and no. 237 for the 1929 event in Archivio Centrale dello Stato, Partito Nazionale Fascista, Fototeca, Ufficio Propaganda, Foto attivita' del Duce, Busta 5. Mussolini presented his plan for *autotreni* at the November 15, 1929, meeting of the Permanent Committee of Wheat. See *Opera Omnia*, vol. XXIV, pp. 167–168.

21. Staderini, "La politica cerealicola," op. cit., p. 1071, note 126.

22. For official photographs see photo no. 1146 for 1929, no. 734 for 1931, and no. 693 for 1932 in Archivio Centrale dello Stato, Partito Nazionale Fascista, Fototeca, Ufficio Propaganda, Foto attività del Duce, Buste 4, 7, 9.

23. Issue of July 11, 1926.

24. Issue of October 24, 1926.

25. See Mussolini's inaugurating speech in *Scritti e discorsi*, vol. VI, pp. 31–36.

26. Archivio Centrale dello Stato, Segreteria Particolare del Duce, Carteggio Ordinario, fasc. 509.828/1.

27. On the reclamation of the Pontine Ager see Riccardo Mariani, *Fascismo e citta' nuove* (Milan: Feltrinelli, 1976), and Diane Ghirardo, *Building New Communities: New Deal America and Fascist Italy* (Princeton: Princeton University Press, 1989).

28. The law of December 24, 1928 (no. 3134) on integral land reclamation stated that it "not only deals with marshlands but it also aims at the intensification of agrarian production in the whole kingdom" (Archivio Centrale dello Stato, La legislazione fascista 1922–1928 [I–VII], Legislatura XXVII, vol. II).

29. Archivio Fotocinematografico, Istituto Nazionale Luce, 1933–391. Also see *Cinegiornale* 1932–1028 (silent) in Archivio Fotocinematografico, Istituto Nazionale Luce.

30. Archivio Centrale dello Stato, Fototeca, Partito Nazionale Fascista, Ufficio Propaganda, Foto attività del Duce, Busta 13, 61359–61677, 61394.

31. Archivio Fotocinematografico, Istituto Nazionale Luce. Also see *Cinegiornali* 1933–317; 1935–707.

32. Staderini, "La politica cerealicola," op. cit. For a different interpretation of the relation between fascism and industry, see Piero Melograni, *Gli industriali e Mussolini: Rapporti tra Confindustria e fascismo dal 1919 al 1929* (Milan: Longanesi, 1972). Melograni argues that fascism did not help the industry.

33. Anna Treves, *Le migrazioni interne nell'Italia fascista: Politica e realta' demografica* (Turin: Einaudi, 1976).

34. On fascism's agrarian politics, also see Giuseppe Tattara, "Cerealicoltura e politica agraria durante il fascismo," in Gianni Toniolo, *L'economia italiana, 1861–1940* (Rome-Bari: Laterza, 1978).

35. Alberto Cadeddu, Stefano Lepre, and Francesca Socrate, "Ristagno e sviluppo nel settore agricolo italiano (1918–1939)," *Quaderni Storici*, nos. 29/30 (May–December 1975), p. 505. Also see Corni, op. cit., and Jon S. Cohen, "La rivalutazione della lira del 1927: uno studio sulla politica economica fascista," in Toniolo, op. cit.

36. Staderini, "La Federazione Italiana dei Consorzi Agrari," op. cit.

37. Corni, op. cit., p. 416.

38. The agricultural issue in the fascist context also needs to be analyzed within a complex set of economic relations both within Italy and in the international arena.

39. Staderini, "La politica cerealicola," op. cit., p. 1071, note 126.

40. *Opera Omnia*, vol. XXIII, p. 343.

41. *Scritti e discorsi*, vol. V, p. 124.

42. *Scritti e discorsi*, vol. VI, p. 262.

43. Ibid., p. 42.

44. Ibid. For other measures the regime took on the matter of reproduction, see David Horn, *Social Bodies: Science, Reproduction, and Italian Modernity* (Princeton: Princeton University Press, 1994).

45. See, among others, *Scritti e discorsi*, vol. VII, pp. 14–15: "People rise when they are numerous" (March 10, 1929). Also see vol. VIII, p. 234: "One needs to be strong first numerically, since if cradles are empty, the nation becomes old and decays" (August 24, 1933). And vol. IX, p. 40: "Irreplaceable condition of supremacy is numerical growth" (March 18, 1934).

A theory on the demographic occupation of territories was developed by the nationalist Enrico Corradini at the Florence Congress of 1910. Corradini turned the question of emigration from a humiliating issue for Italy into a potential element for colonial development, a positive factor in imperialist struggles. After the Libyan war of 1911, which gave Italy her first colonial success, several political groups, also from among the social-democrats, considered Italy's expansion an expression of "healthy imperialism." The conquest of foreign territories was interpreted as an effective answer to the agricultural population's need for expansion, especially those from the South, who were otherwise forced to emigrate. Libya came to be conceived as a "populating colony" (*colonia di popolamento*), and her economic organization was supposed to preserve the agricultural interests of the southerners. See Luigi Goglia and Fabio Grassi, *Il colonialismo italiano da Adua all'impero* (Rome-Bari: Laterza, 1981).

46. *Scritti e discorsi*, vol. VI, pp. 43–44, 45–46.

47. See Mussolini's speech to rural workers of October 26, 1935, in which he affirmed that fascism had sympathy for the 24 million peasants because from them "came and will come the million infantry soldiers, necessary when the moment comes, to defend the legitimate interests of the Nation" (*Scritti e discorsi*, vol. IX, p. 222).

48. In its original German version Korherr's book had been prefaced with an essay by Oswald Spengler.

49. *Opera Omnia*, vol. XXIII, pp. 209–210.

50. Ibid., p. 216.

51. *Scritti e discorsi*, vol. VI, p. 45.

52. *Scritti e discorsi*, vol. V, p. 433.

53. *Opera Omnia*, vol. XXI, p. 356.

54. *Scritti e discorsi*, vol. VI, p. 259.

55. "I prefer those who work hard, straight, a lot, in obedience and, possibly, in silence. To this last category, the true, authentic *rurali* of the Italian Nation belong" (*Scritti e discorsi*, vol. V, p. 430 [October 10, 1926]). He repeated this concept in Polesine on December 15, 1926: "Among all the workers, the most noble and disciplined are the workers of land" (*Scritti e discorsi*, vol. V, p. 474). On December 8, 1929, he

told farmers: "The [rural] army is immense, ordered, disciplined, faithful" (*Scritti e discorsi*, vol. VII, p. 172).

56. Archivio Fotocinematografico, Istituto Nazionale Luce, 1933–312. Mussolini had pronounced the sentence "The war we prefer" in his speech of December 19, 1932, for the foundation of Littoria (*Scritti e discorsi*, vol. VIII, p. 148).

57. Archivio Fotocinematografico, Istituto Nazionale Luce, *Cinegiornale* 1933– 207.

58. The slogan was drawn from Mussolini's speech of December 16, 1934, pronounced for the inauguration of the Province of Littoria in the Pontine Ager. See *Scritti e discorsi*, vol. IX, p. 154. The speech was recorded in the Cinegiornale 1934–595, in Archivio Fotocinematografico, Istituto Nazionale Luce.

59. *Scritti e discorsi*, vol. VI, p. 36.

60. *Scritti e discorsi*, vol. IV, p. 295.

61. *Scritti e discorsi*, vol. III, p. 51 (speech of January 28, 1923, to workers of *Poligrafico*).

62. Ibid., p. 108 (speech at the University of Padova of June 1, 1923).

63. Ibid., p. 135.

64. Mussolini wrote on January 1, 1919: "Imperialism is the eternal and immutable law of life. It is after all the need, desire, will of expansion that every individual, every living and vital people (*popolo*) brings within itself" (*Opera Omnia*, vol. XII, p. 101). Also see Giorgio Rumi, *Alle origini della politica estera fascista (1918–1923)* (Rome-Bari: Laterza, 1968).

65. See "Dottrina del Fascismo," where Mussolini wrote: "One can think of an empire, i.e. a nation that directly or indirectly leads other nations, without the need to conquer one only square kilometer of territory" (*Scritti e discorsi*, vol. VIII, p. 88).

66. Mussolini contrasted the mean economic expansion of the British and the brutal territorial conquests of the Germans to Rome's domination in the Mediterranean, which contributed to world civilization and development (*Scritti e discorsi*, vol. I, p. 374; vol. II, p. 201). In 1932 Mussolini told Ludwig: "I intend the honor of nations in the contribution they gave to the culture of humanity" (Emil Ludwig, *Colloqui con Mussolini* [Milan: Mondadori, 1932], p. 199).

67. *Scritti e discorsi*, vol. I, p. 374.

68. See for example *Scritti e discorsi*, vol. II, pp. 22, 32.

69. Article of April 20, 1919, in *Il Popolo d'Italia*, now in *Opera Omnia*, vol. XIII, p. 72. Also see Giorgio Rumi, "'Revisionismo' fascista ed espansione coloniale (1925–1935)," in Alberto Aquarone and Maurizio Vernassa, eds., *Il regime fascista* (Bologna: Il Mulino, 1974).

70. *Scritti e discorsi*, vol. I, p. 374.

71. Ibid., pp. 374–375.

72. Mussolini's considerations on foreign politics reflected the liberal government's approach to the colonial question, whereas both the fascists and the liberals insisted on Italy's right to a powerful position in the world order, and both affirmed the legitimacy of a poor, proletarian country's claims to expansion. See Goglia and Grassi, op. cit.

73. Northrop Frye, *Anatomy of Criticism: Four Essays* (Princeton: Princeton University Press, 1957). Frye includes melodrama in the romance mode.

74. *Scritti e discorsi,* vol. VI, p. 120 (synthesis on internal and foreign politics to the Ministers' Council, December 15, 1927).

75. For a discussion of fascism's foreign politics and its relation to interior politics, see Jens Petersen, "La politica estera del fascismo come problema storiografico," *Storia Contemporanea,* vol. III, no. 4 (December 1972), pp. 661–705. Petersen, however, tends to underplay the importance of war in fascism's self-definition.

76. *Scritti e discorsi,* vol. V, pp. 190–191.

77. *Scritti e discorsi,* vol. VI, p. 283.

78. On March 24, 1924, the fifth anniversary of the *fasces'* foundation, Mussolini told the Italian mayors convened in Rome: "One does not have the right to believe in humanitarian, peaceful ideologies. They are very beautiful, you see, in theory. They are magnificent, poetic utopias. But the factual reality admonishes us to be vigilant and to consider the ground of foreign politics as a highly mobile ground" (*Scritti e discorsi,* vol. IV, p. 72). A few months later, in a June 4, 1924, speech at the Chamber, Mussolini declared: "But one needs to be vigilant. That is why next to a foreign politics of peace—because only peace can allow us to stand up again—we need to keep ready and efficient all our land, sea and air forces" (ibid., p. 173).

79. Speech of January 29, 1926, at the Chamber of Deputies, in *Scritti e discorsi,* vol. V, p. 259.

80. *Scritti e discorsi,* vol. VI, p. 109.

81. *Scritti e discorsi,* vol. VII, pp. 20–21. (Also see vol. VI, pp. 109, 120, 227, 283.)

82. *Scritti e discorsi,* vol. V, p. 36.

83. *Scritti e discorsi,* vol. VII, p. 200. Six days later, in Florence, Mussolini again attacked those whom he accused of wanting a war against Italy and affirmed: "A powerfully armed fascist Italy will put out her simple alternative: either precious friendship or a very hard hostility" (ibid., p. 206).

84. Ibid., pp. 207–208.

85. Ibid., p. 210.

86. Ibid., p. 211.

87. Ibid., p. 226.

88. Ibid., p. 228.

89. *Scritti e discorsi,* vol. VIII, p. 131.

90. Ibid.

91. Eric Hobsbawm, *The Age of Empire 1875–1914* (New York: Pantheon, 1987).

92. Angelo Del Boca, *Gli italiani in Africa Orientale: Dall'unità alla marcia su Roma* (Rome-Bari: Laterza, 1976). On fascism's rule in the existing colonies, see Denis Mack Smith, *Mussolini's Roman Empire* (New York: Longman, 1976). According to Mack Smith, fascism showed little understanding for indigenous ways of life.

93. For a theory of fascism's imperialism in the 1920s, see Giampiero Carocci, "Appunti sull'imperialismo fascista negli anni '20," in Aquarone and Vernassa, op. cit.; and Renzo De Felice, "Alcune osservazioni sulla politica estera mussoliniana," in ibid.

94. Giorgio Rochat, *Militari e politici nella preparazione della campagna d'Etiopia: Studio e documenti, 1932–1936* (Milan: Franco Angeli, 1971).

95. According to Rochat, the politicians aimed at a colonial war of limited extent; the military planned a war of vast proportions. These internal conflicts created such a situation that in 1934 "fascist Italy prepared a war against Ethiopia, but had

not yet chosen which war" (ibid., p. 95). On the contradictions in Mussolini's foreign politics, see Rumi, "'Revisionismo' fascista e espansione coloniale," op. cit.

96. Rochat, op. cit., p. 39.

97. See Mussolini's memorandum to Badoglio in Rochat, op. cit., pp. 376–379.

98. See Archivio Storico del Ministero degli Affari Esteri, ASMAI II, *La campagna italo-etiopica 1935–36*, pacco 1; and *Rapporti politici: Etiopia*.

99. Ibid., pp. 184 (May 14, 1936).

100. *Scritti e discorsi*, vol. IX, pp. 191–192.

101. On melodrama I follow Peter Brooks, *The Melodramatic Imagination:
Balzac, Henry James, Melodrama, and the Mode of Excess* (New York: Columbia
University Press, 1985). Melodrama, which literally means a drama with music, originally derived from pantomime—a genre played in Paris popular theaters in the second half of the 1700s. This genre, especially in its dialogued form (which began in
the 1780s), almost always featured a "dramatic conflict of clear emblems" accompanied by strong visual images and actions. In the 1800s melodrama developed its
themes and style from this popular tradition and came to be conceived as a drama
of the ordinary.

102. See ibid. Following Northrop Frye's categorization, Brooks argues that melodrama generally operates in the mode of romance.

103. Dissimulation and betrayal are typical of melodrama (ibid., p. 33).

104. *Scritti e discorsi*, vol. IX, pp. 218–220. This speech was aired on the radio
between 6:45 P.M. and 7:10 P.M., and all Italians were supposed to listen to it.

105. Ibid., p. 225 (message for the thirteenth anniversary of the March on Rome,
published in *Foglio d' Ordini* no. 145, on October 27).

106. Ibid.

107. Ibid.

108. Archivio Centrale dello Stato, Partito Nazionale Fascista, *Foglio d'Ordini*,
no. 147.

109. *Scritti e discorsi*, vol. X, pp. 13–14 (December 2, 1935).

110. Ibid., p. 14.

111. Ibid.

112. Ibid., p. 30 (speech to farmers in Pontinia of December 18, 1935).

113. Ibid., p. 35. The appeal, dated February 1, 1936, was published in *Il Popolo
d'Italia*.

114. Ibid., p. 37.

115. Ibid., pp. 40, 41.

116. Ibid., p. 36.

117. Interesting, in this sense, is Mussolini's interview to the *Daily Mail* of May
7, 1936, in which he answered the accusations of planning an invasion of Egypt: "Italy
does not have any, not even a remote, aspiration to Egypt which I consider an independent country, not African, but rather Mediterranean and with which Italy has
been and will always be in very good relations" (ibid., p. 108).

118. *The Italo-Ethiopian Dispute: Abstracts from the Memorandum of the Italian Government to the League of Nations* (Rome: Società Editrice di Novissima,
1935).

119. *Italy and Abyssinia* (Rome: Società Editrice di Novissima, 1936). Lectures
and radio addresses by Italians in America contributed to this goal. See, for exam-

ple, *Italy and World Affairs,* lecture delivered at the Institute of World Affairs at the Ohio Northern University by G. G. D'Anchise, June 1936.

120. *Facts Geneva refuses to See* (Rome: Società Editrice di Novissima, 1935).

121. *Scritti e discorsi,* vol. X, p. 64 (speech to the National Assembly of Corporations of March 23, 1936).

122. Ibid., p. 40. *Ras* were local leaders.

123. Ibid., p. 51 (speech to the National Assembly of Corporations of March 23, 1936).

124. In the article appearing in *Il Popolo d'Italia* of July 31, 1935, Mussolini wrote that the abolition of slavery in Ethiopia was not an objective of the military campaign but a "logical consequence of our politics." "Equally," he affirmed, "the theme of 'civilization' should not be excessively exploited. Also civilization in its double moral and material aspect is not an objective, but will be a consequence of our politics" (*Scritti e discorsi,* vol. IX, pp. 201–202).

125. This narration of the Ethiopian events was also typical of the press. See Mario Isnenghi's study of the *Corriere della Sera* during the Ethiopian campaign, "Il radioso maggio africano del 'Corriere della Sera,'" in *Intellettuali militanti e intellettuali funzionari: Appunti sulla cultura fascista* (Turin: Einaudi, 1979).

126. *Scritti e discorsi,* vol. X, p. 30.

127. Ibid., pp. 63–64.

128. Ibid., p. 20.

129. Ibid., p. 39.

130. Archivio Fotocinematografico, Istituto Nazionale Luce, 1935–783. Mussolini's reference to Tigrai in his article to European students probably took inspiration from the newsreel that dealt with the same episode of the Italians' arrival in Tigrai.

131. See the film documentary *Da Adua ad Axum* in Archivio Fotocinematografico, Istituto Nazionale Luce; and newsreel 1936–894, in which native people welcome the liberators with the Roman salute.

132. *Scritti e discorsi,* vol. X, p. 99.

133. Ibid., p. 100.

134. Ibid., p. 102.

135. Ibid., p. 118.

136. Ibid., p. 159.

137. In an interview to the *Daily Telegraph* of May 28, 1936, he told the reporter that "fascist Italy desires peace and will do everything in her power to keep peace" (ibid., p. 139).

138. Archivio Fotocinematografico, Istituto Nazionale Luce, 1936–856.

139. Archivio Fotocinematografico, Istituto Nazionale Luce, 1936–983. On colonial visions and urbanity, see Krystyna von Henneberg, "Planning the Model Colony: Architecture and Urban Planning in the Making of Fascist Libya, 1922–1943," Ph.D. dissertation, University of California, Berkeley, 1996; and "Tripoli: The Making of Fascist Colonial Capital," in Zeynep Celik, Diane Favro, and Richard Ingersoll, eds., *Streets: Critical Perspectives on Public Space* (Berkeley: University of California Press, 1994).

140. See, for example, newsreel 1937–1211 on the visit of the viceroy Graziani (ibid.).

141. *Scritti e discorsi*, vol. X, p. 168 (speech of December 15, 1936 in Pontinia).

142. Brooks, op. cit., p. 12.

143. Brooks writes that melodrama, as a modern aesthetic form, "starts from and expresses the anxiety brought by a frightening new world in which the traditional patterns of moral order no longer provide the necessary social glue. It plays out the force of that anxiety with the apparent triumph of villainy, and it dissipates it with the eventual victory of virtue. . . . Melodrama . . . strives to find, to articulate, to demonstrate, to 'prove' the existence of a moral universe which, though put into question . . . can be made to assert its presence and its categorical force among men" (ibid., p. 20).

144. See ibid., for a description of melodramatic acting; and Michael Booth, *English Melodrama* (London: H. Jenkins, 1965).

145. Massimo Cardillo, *Il duce in moviola: Politica e divismo nei cinegiornali e documentari "Luce"* (Bari: Dedalo, 1983), p. 142.

146. Ibid., p. 128. On Mussolini's mimicry as "macroscopic," see Giuliano Manacorda in ibid., p. 121. Also see other analyses of Mussolini's acting style in ibid.

147. Gramsci accused "Verdi's music or, rather, the libretti and plots of the plays set to music by Verdi"—of being responsible for what he considered a cultural degradation. Even though at the turn of the century popular theaters and sound films in Italy also presented performances in an operatic style, for Gramsci opera still constituted the most influential element in the process of maintaining a melodramatic conception of life. "[W]ords set to music are more easily recalled, and they become matrices in which thought takes shape out of flux" (Antonio Gramsci, *Selections from Cultural Writings* [Cambridge, Mass.: Harvard University Press, 1985], pp. 377, 378). For Gramsci, opera music in Italy substitutes for the popular novel typical of other countries' popular culture.

148. Carmine Gallone directed several films based on operas. See Francesco Savio, *Ma l'amore no: Realismo, formalismo, propaganda e telefoni bianchi nel cinema italiano di regime (1930–1943)* (Milan: Sonzogno, 1975).

149. On the *carri di tespi* see Mario Corsi, *Il teatro all'aperto in Italia* (Milan-Rome: Rizzoli, 1939), and Emanuela Scarpellini, *Organizzazione teatrale e politica del teatro nell'Italia fascista* (Florence: La Nuova Italia, 1989).

150. Corsi, op. cit., pp. 271–277.

151. Scarpellini, op. cit., p. 198.

152. Ibid., p. 73.

153. Ibid., pp. 255–256. However, in regular theatrical establishments opera was less appreciated than theater.

154. *Scritti e discorsi*, vol. X, pp. 45, 47. A major of the Italian army, Toselli had died at Amba Alagi in December 1895 during Italy's colonial campaign in Africa.

155. Archivio Fotocinematografico, Istituto Nazionale Luce, no. 1937–1094.

156. See the case of the liberal Vittorio Emanuele Orlando, in Luigi Preti, *I miti dell'impero e della razza nell'Italia degli anni '30* (Rome: Opere Nuove, 1965), p. 34.

157. *Scritti e discorsi*, vol. X, p. 29.

158. Cannistraro and Sullivan, *Il Duce's Other Woman* (New York: Morrow, 1993), p. 479.

159. Fascism's power was also demonstrated by the public humiliation of the

occupied nation. Newsreels, newspapers, and magazines showed the submission of the Ethiopian leaders and their public recognition of the regime's authority. See, for example, newsreel 1936–910 in Addis Ababa and 1937–1040 and 1938–1307 in Rome, where the leaders swore faithfulness to the Duce (Archivio Fotocinematografico, Istituto Nazionale Luce).

160. *Scritti e discorsi*, vol. X, p. 31.

161. *Scritti e discorsi*, vol. X, p. 168.

162. On the rhetoric of virility in Italian society before fascism, see Piero Meldini, ed., *Sposa e madre esemplare: Ideologia e politica della donna e della famiglia durante il fascismo* (Rimini-Florence: Guaraldi, 1975). Also the United States's first imperialistic campaigns were connected to the question of virility. See Amy Kaplan, "Romancing the Empire: The Embodiment of American Masculinity in the Popular Historical Novel of the 1890s," *American Literary History*, vol. 2, no. 4 (Winter 1990), pp. 659–690.

163. Piero Melograni, *Rapporti segreti della polizia fascista, 1938–1940* (Rome-Bari: Laterza, 1979). Also see Renzo De Felice, *Mussolini il duce*, vol. II (Turin: Einaudi, 1981).

164. *Scritti e discorsi*, vol. X, p. 169.

165. *Scritti e discorsi*, vol. XII, p. 159.

CONCLUSIONS

1. With this totally Adamitic name Adamo Adami represents, we could say, the ur-prototype of the new fascist man.

2. In his memoirs, Mussolini bitterly recalls that "thousands of portraits of myself were hurled out of the window" after the coup-d'-état of July 24, 1943, which deposed him. See Raymond Klibansky, ed., *Benito Mussolini's Memoirs 1942–1943*, trans. Frances Lobb (New York: Howard Fertig, 1975), p. 97.

3. Luisa Passerini, "L'immagine di Mussolini: specchio dell'immaginario e promessa d'identita,'" *Rivista di Storia Contemporanea*, no. 3 (1986), pp. 322–349.

4. In the 1932 Mostra della Rivoluzione Fascista (Exhibit of the Revolution), "Spirit," according to the plans, constituted one of the four elements that needed to be represented and to dominate the show. In the notes on the exhibit, "Spirit" was connected to sacrifice: "[I]n the part dedicated to the spirit, the Exhibit will represent the spiritual patrimony of the Italian people illuminated by a light of abnegation and sacrifice, the light that has given them their heroic consecration" (Dino Alfieri, *Appunti sul programma della Mostra del Fascismo* [n.p., n.d.]).

5. Emilio Gentile, *Il culto del Littorio: La sacralizzazione della politica nell'Italia fascista* (Rome-Bari: Laterza, 1993).

6. *Leva* was a ritual that marked the passage of young people from youth organizations to the party. It established the youth fascist membership. See Emilio Gentile, "Fascism as Political Religion," *Journal of Contemporary History*, vol. 25, nos. 2/3 (1990), p. 239.

7. Piero Melograni, *Rapporti segreti della polizia fascista, 1938–1940* (Rome-Bari: Laterza, 1979).

8. On consensus in fascism, see Renzo De Felice, *Mussolini il duce*, vol. I (Turin:

Einaudi, 1974); De Felice, *Mussolini il duce*, vol. II (Turin: Einaudi, 1981); Victoria De Grazia, *The Culture of Consent: Mass Organization of Leisure in Fascist Italy* (Cambridge: Cambridge University Press, 1981); De Grazia, *How Fascism Ruled Women: Italy, 1922–1945* (Berkeley: University of California Press, 1992); Alexander De Grand, "Cracks in the Façade: The Failure of Fascist Totalitarianism in Italy (1935–39)," *European History Quarterly*, vol. 21 (1991), pp. 515–535; Jens Petersen, "Elettorato e base sociale del fascismo italiano negli anni venti," *Studi Storici*, no. 3 (July–September 1975), pp. 627–669; and Paul Corner, "I limiti del potere fascista," *Passato e Presente*, vol. 4 (July–December 1983), pp. 167–174.

9. Guillermo O'Donnell, "On the Fruitful Convergences of Hirschman's *Exit, Voice, and Loyalty* and *Shifting Involvements:* Reflections from the Recent Argentine Experience," in Alejandro Foxley, Michael S. McPherson, and Guillermo O'Donnell, eds., *Development, Democracy, and the Art of Trespassing: Essays in Honor of Albert O. Hirschman* (Notre Dame: University of Notre Dame Press, 1986), p. 251.

10. Luisa Passerini, *Fascism in Popular Memory: The Cultural Experience of the Turin Working Class* (Cambridge: Cambridge University Press, 1987), trans. Robert Lumley and Jude Bloomfield.

11. Gianpasquale Santomassimo, "Antifascismo popolare" *Italia contemporanea*, vol. 32, no. 40 (July–September 1980), pp. 39–69.

12. Passerini, *Fascism in Popular Memory*, op. cit., p. 69.

13. David G. Horn, *Social Bodies: Science, Reproduction, and Italian Modernity* (Princeton: Princeton University Press, 1994).

14. The 1926 statute of the party stated that when expelled as a "traitor to the cause," a fascist would have to be banned from political life. In 1929 the statute conceived the ban as more comprehensively embracing the whole of public life. See Gentile, "Fascism as Political Religion," op. cit., p. 236.

15. Horn, op. cit.

16. On this debate see Martin Jay, "'The Aesthetic Ideology' as Ideology; or What Does it Mean to Aestheticize Politics?" *Cultural Critique*, no. 21 (Spring 1992), pp. 41–62.

17. Susan Buck-Morss, "Aesthetics and Anaesthetics: Walter Benjamin's Artwork Essay Reconsidered," *New Formations*, no. 20 (Summer 1993), pp. 123–143, issue on *The Actuality of Walter Benjamin*.

18. Ibid., p. 125.

19. Paul De Man, "Phenomenality and Materiality in Kant," in Gary Shapiro and Alan Sica, eds., *Hermeneutics: Questions and Prospects* (Amherst: University of Massachusetts Press, 1984).

20. Fredric Jameson, "Pleasure: A Political Issue," in Tony Bennett et al., eds., *Formations of Pleasure* (London: Routledge and Kegan Paul, 1983).

21. Terry Eagleton, *The Ideology of the Aesthetic* (Oxford: Basil Blackwell, 1990).

22. On totalitarianism and democracy see Claude Lefort, *Democracy and Political Theory* (Minneapolis: University of Minnesota Press, 1988), trans. David Macey, first published in French in 1986, and *The Political Forms of Modern Society: Bureaucracy, Democracy, Totalitarianism* (Cambridge, Mass.: MIT Press, 1986), ed. with introduction by John Thompson.

23. Jean L. Cohen and Andrew Arato, *Civil Society and Political Theory* (Cam-

bridge, Mass.: MIT Press, 1992). On community see Jean-Luc Nancy, *The Inoperative Community* (Minneapolis: University of Minnesota Press, 1991), ed. Peter Connor, trans. Peter Connor, Lisa Garbus, Michael Holland and Simona Shawney; and Miami Theory Collective, ed., *Community at Loose Ends* (Minneapolis: University of Minnesota Press, 1991).

24. Luisa Passerini, *Fascism in Popular Memory,* op. cit.

Bibliography

MANUSCRIPT SOURCES

A. *Archivio Centrale dello Stato (Rome)*

Agenzia Stefani
Mostra della Rivoluzione Fascista
Partito Nazionale Fascista: Direttorio
Partito Nazionale Fascista: Foglio di Disposizioni
Partito Nazionale Fascista: Foglio d'Ordini
Partito Nazionale Fascista: Ufficio Propaganda, Foto Attivita' del Duce
Presidenza del Consiglio dei Ministri
Segreteria Particolare del Duce. Carteggio Ordinario
Segreteria Particolare del Duce. Carteggio Riservato

B. *Archivio Fotocinematografico Istituto Nazionale Luce (Rome)*
Cinegiornali:
1932 1028; 1030
1933 181; 207; 312; 317; 391
1934 595; 547; 596
1935 707; 732
1936 816; 877; 971; 967; 960; 1000; 983; 888; 1001; 887; 882; 894
1937 1192; 1119; 1103; 1041; 1040; 1094
1938 1307; 1309.

Documentari:
Da Adua ad Axum
Da Dessié ad Addis Abeba
Il Duce inizia la trebbiatura del grano nell'Agro Pontino
Riscatto

C. *Archivio Goglia (Rome)*
D. *Archivio Storico del Ministero degli Affari Esteri (Rome)*

Africa III
Asmai II
Asmai III

E. Library of Congress, Washington, D.C.
Mussolini Speaks!

NEWSPAPERS AND JOURNALS

Critica Fascista
Gazzetta Ufficiale
Gerarchia
Illustrazione Italiana
The New York Times
Il Popolo d'Italia
Variety

BOOKS AND ARTICLES

Adamson, Walter L. *Hegemony and Revolution: A Study of Antonio Gramsci's Political and Cultural Theory*. Berkeley: University of California Press, 1980.
———. "Fascism and Culture: Avant-Gardes and Secular Religion in the Italian Case." *Journal of Contemporary History* 24, no.3 (1989): 411–435.
———. "Modernism and Fascism: The Politics of Culture in Italy, 1903–1922." *American Historical Review* 95, no.2 (April 1990): 359–390.
———. *Avant-Garde Florence: From Modernism to Fascism*. Cambridge, Mass.: Harvard University Press, 1993.
Adler, Franklin H. "Italian Industrialists and Radical Fascism." *Telos*, no. 30 (Winter 1976–1977): 193–201.
Agulhon, Maurice. *Marianne into Battle: Republican Imagery and Symbolism in France, 1789–1880*. Translated by Janet Lloyd. Cambridge: Cambridge University Press, 1981.
Alatri, Paolo. *Lineamenti di storia del pensiero politico*. 2 vols. Messina: La Libra, 1973–1975.
———. *Gabriele D'Annunzio*. Turin: Utet, 1983.
Alfieri, Dino. *Appunti sul programma della Mostra del Fascismo*. N.p., n.d.
Alfieri, Dino, and Luigi Freddi, eds. *Guida alla Mostra della Rivoluzione Fascista*. Florence: Vallecchi, 1933.
———, eds. *Mostra della Rivoluzione Fascista: Guida storica*, I *Decennale della Marcia su Roma*. Rome: Partito Nazionale Fascista, 1933.
Allor, Martin. "Relocating the Site of the Audience." *Critical Studies in Mass Communication*, no. 5 (1988): 217–233.
Apostolidès, Jean-Marie. *Le roi-machine: Spectacle et politique au temps de Louis XIV*. Paris: Editions de Minuit, 1981.
Aquarone, Alberto. *L'organizzazione dello stato totalitario*. Turin: Einaudi, 1965.
Aquarone, Alberto, and Maurizio Vernassa, eds. *Il regime fascista*. Bologna: Il Mulino, 1974.
Arato, Andrew. "The Antinomies of the Neo-Marxian Theory of Culture." *International Journal of Sociology* 7, no.1 (Spring 1977): 4–24.
Ardali, Paolo. *San Francesco e Mussolini*. Mantua: Paladino, 1926.

Arendt, Hannah. *The Origins of Totalitarianism.* New York: Harcourt Brace Jovanovich, 1951.

———. *On Violence.* New York: Harcourt Brace Jovanovich, 1970.

Armellini, Guido. *Le immagini del fascismo nelle arti figurative.* Milan: Fabbri, 1980.

Arvidsson, Claes, and Lars Erik Blomqvist, eds. *Symbols of Power: The Aesthetics of Political Legitimation in the Soviet Union and Eastern Europe.* Stockholm: Almquist and Wiskell International, 1987.

Auerbach, Nina. *Woman and the Demon: The Life of a Victorian Myth.* Cambridge, Mass.: Harvard University Press, 1982.

Balla, Giacomo, and Fortunato Depero. *Ricostruzione futurista dell'universo.* Modena: Fonte d' Abisso, 1989.

Baran, Paul, and Paul Sweezy. *Monopoly Capital: An Essay on the American Economic and Social Order.* New York: Monthly Review Press, 1966.

Barrows, Susanna. *Distorting Mirrors: Visions of the Crowd in Late Nineteenth-Century France.* New Haven: Yale University Press, 1981.

Barthes, Roland. *Mythologies.* Translated by Annette Lavers. New York: Paladin, 1972.

———. *Image, Music, Text.* Translated by Stephen Heath. New York: Hill and Wang, 1977.

Bataille, Georges. *Visions of Excess: Selected Writings, 1927–1939.* Edited and translated by Allan Stoekl. Minneapolis: University of Minnesota Press, 1985.

Bauman, Richard. *Verbal Art as Performance.* Rowley, Mass.: Newbury House Publishers, 1977.

Bedel, Maurice. *Fascisme An VII.* Paris: Editions de la Nouvelle revue française, 1929.

Bellah, Robert N. "Civil Religion in America." *Daedalus* 96, no. 1 (Winter 1967): 1–21.

Beltramelli, Antonio. *L'Uomo nuovo.* (1923) Milan: Mondadori, 1940.

Bendix, Reinhard. "Reflections on Charismatic Leadership." In *Max Weber,* edited by Dennis Wrong. Englewood Cliffs, N.J.: Prentice-Hall, 1970.

Ben-Ghiat, Ruth. "Envisioning Modernity: Desire and Discipline in the Italian Fascist Film." In *Fascism and Culture: The Visual Arts in Italy, 1919–1943,* edited by Emily Braun and Philip Cannistraro. Cambridge: Cambridge University Press, forthcoming.

Benjamin, Walter. *Illuminations.* Edited by Hannah Arendt. Translated by Harry Zohn (1968). New York: Schocken Books, 1973.

———. *Reflections: Essays, Aphorisms, Autobiographical Writings.* Edited by Edmund Jephcott. New York: Harcourt Brace Jovanovich, 1978.

———. "Theories of German Fascism: On the Collection of Essays *War and Warrior.* Edited by Ernst Jünger." *New German Critique,* no. 17 (Spring 1979): 120–128.

———. "Moscow Diary." *October,* no. 35 (Winter 1985).

Bennett, Tony, et al., eds. *Formations of Pleasure.* London: Routledge and Kegan Paul, 1983.

Bentley, Eric, ed. *The Theory of the Modern Stage: An Introduction to Modern Theater and Drama.* New York: Penguin Books, 1968.

Béraud, Henri. *Ce que J'ai vu à Rome.* Paris: Les éditions de France, 1929.

Berezin, Mabel. "The Organization of Political Ideology: Culture, State, and Theater in Fascist Italy." *American Sociological Review* 56 (October 1991): 639–651.

Bergson, Henri. *L'évolution créatrice*. Paris: F. Alcan, 1907.

Berneri, Camillo. *Mussolini: Psicologia di un dittatore*. Milan: Azione Comune, 1966.

Berselli, Aldo. *L'opinione pubblica inglese e l'avvento del fascismo (1919–1925)*. Milan: Franco Angeli, 1971.

Bertone, Gianni. *I figli d'Italia si chiaman Balilla: Come e cosa insegnava la scuola fascista*. Rimini-Florence: Guaraldi, 1975.

Biondi, Dino. *La fabbrica del Duce*. Florence: Vallecchi, 1967.

Bloch, Ernst. *Aesthetics and Politics: Debates between Ernst Bloch, Georg Lukács, Bertolt Brecht, Walter Benjamin, Theodor Adorno*. London: NLB, 1977.

———. *The Utopian Function of Art and Literature: Selected Essays*. Translated by Jack Zipes and Frank Mecklenburg. Cambridge, Mass.: MIT Press, 1988.

Bobbio, Norberto. "L'ideologia del fascismo." In *Il fascismo: Antologia di scritti critici*, edited by Costanzo Casucci. Bologna: Il Mulino, 1982.

Bocca, Giorgio, ed. *I manifesti italiani fra Belle Époque e fascismo*. Milan: Fabbri, 1971.

Bodei, Remo. "Dal Parlamento alla piazza. Rappresentanza emotiva e miti politici nei teorici della psicologia delle folle." *Rivista di storia contemporanea*, no. 3 (1986): 313–321.

Bonnell, Victoria. "L'immagine della donna nell'iconografia sovietica dalla rivoluzione all'era staliniana." *Storia Contemporanea* XXII, no. 1 (February 1991): 5–52.

Bonner, Simon, ed. *Consuming Visions: Accumulation and Display of Goods in America, 1880–1920*. New York: W. W. Norton and Co., 1989.

Booth, Michael R. *English Melodrama*. London: H. Jenkins, 1965.

Borgese, Giuseppe Antonio. *Goliath: The March of Fascism*. New York: Viking, 1937.

Bossaglia, Rossana. *Il Novecento italiano: Storia, documenti, iconografia*. Milan: Feltrinelli, 1979.

Bosworth, R.J.B. *Italy, the Least of Great Powers: Italian Foreign Policy before the First World War*. Cambridge: Cambridge University Press, 1979.

Bottai, Giuseppe. *Esperienza corporativa, 1929–1934*. Florence: Vallecchi, 1934.

———. *Politica fascista delle arti*. Rome: Signorelli, 1940.

———. *Vent'anni e un giorno*. Milan: Garzanti, 1949.

Boureau, Alain. *L'aigle: Chronique politique d'un emblème*. Paris: Editions du Cerf, 1985.

Bowlby, Rachel. *Just Looking: Consumer Culture in Dreiser, Gissing, and Zola*. New York: Methuen, 1985.

Bracher, Karl Dietrich. *The German Dictatorship: The Origins, Structure, and Consequences of National Socialism*. Translated by Jean Steinberg. New York: Praeger Publishers, 1970.

Breckman, Warren. "Disciplining Consumption: The Debate about Luxury in Wilhelmine Germany, 1890–1914." *Journal of Social History*, no. 24 (1990–1991): 484–505.

Brewer, John, and Roy Porter, eds. *Consumption and the World of Goods*. London: Routledge, 1993.

Brooks, Peter. *The Melodramatic Imagination: Balzac, Henry James, Melodrama, and the Mode of Excess*. 1976. Reprint. New York: Columbia University Press, 1985.

Brunetta, Gian Piero. *Intellettuali, cinema e propaganda tra le due guerre.* Bologna: Patron, 1973.

———. *Cinema italiano tra le due guerre: Fascismo e politica cinematografica.* Milan: Mursia, 1975.

———. *Storia del cinema italiano, 1895–1945.* Rome: Editori Riuniti, 1979.

———. "Il sogno a stelle e strisce di Mussolini." In *L'estetica della politica*, edited by Maurizio Vaudagna. Rome-Bari: Laterza, 1989.

Bruno, Giuliana. *Streetwalking on a Ruined Map: Cultural Theory and the City Films of Elvira Notari.* Princeton: Princeton University Press, 1993.

Brustein, William. "The 'Red Menace' and the Rise of Italian Fascism." *American Sociological Review,* no. 56 (October 1991): 652–664.

Buck-Morss, Susan. *The Dialectics of Seeing: Walter Benjamin and the Arcades Project.* Cambridge, Mass.: MIT Press, 1989.

———. "Aesthetics and Anaesthetics: Walter Benjamin's Artwork Reconsidered." *New Formations,* no. 20 (Summer 1993): 123–143.

Bürger, Peter. *Theory of the Avant-Garde.* Translated by Michael Shaw. Minneapolis: University of Minnesota Press, 1984.

Burgwin, James H. *Il revisionismo fascista: La sfida di Mussolini alle grandi potenze nei Balcani e sul Danubio.* Milan: Feltrinelli, 1979.

Burke, Peter, ed. *New Perspectives on Historical Writing.* Cambridge: Polity Press, 1991.

Cadeddu, Alberto, Stefano Lepre, and Francesca Socrate. "Ristagno e sviluppo nel settore agricolo italiano (1918–1939)." *Quaderni storici,* nos. 29/30 (May–December 1975): 497–518.

Cagnetta, Mariella. *Antichisti e impero fascista.* Bari: Dedalo, 1979.

Campbell, Colin. *The Romantic Ethic and the Spirit of Modern Consumerism.* Oxford: Basil Blackwell, 1987.

Canetti, Elias. *Crowds and Power.* Translated by Carol Stewart. New York: Viking, 1966.

Canfora, Luciano. *Ideologie del classicismo.* Turin: Einaudi, 1980.

Cannistraro, Philip V. *La fabbrica del consenso: Fascismo e mass-media.* Rome-Bari: Laterza, 1975.

———, ed. *Historical Dictionary of Fascist Italy.* Westport, Conn.: Greenwood, 1982.

Cannistraro, Philip V., and Brian R. Sullivan. *Il Duce's Other Woman.* New York: Morrow, 1993.

Carabba, Claudio. *Il cinema del ventennio nero.* Florence: Vallecchi, 1974.

Caracciolo, Alberto. *Stato e società civile: Problemi dell'unificazione italiana.* Turin: Einaudi, 1960.

Carchia, Gianni. *La legittimazione dell'arte: Studi sull'intelligibile estetico.* Naples: Guida, 1982.

Cardillo, Massimo. *Il duce in moviola: Politica e divismo nei cinegiornali e documentari "Luce."* Bari: Dedalo, 1983.

Carey, John. "Revolted by the Masses." *Times Literary Supplement,* January 12–18, 1990: 34–36.

Carocci, Giampiero. "Appunti sull'imperialismo fascista degli anni venti." In *Il regime fascista*, edited by Alberto Aquarone and Maurizio Vernassa. Bologna: Il Mulino, 1974.

Casalini, Mario. *Le istituzioni create dallo Stato per l'agricoltura.* Rome: IEMIA, 1937.

Casanova, Eugenio. *I precedenti storici, giuridici ed economici della legge per la bonifica integrale.* Milan: Treves, 1929.

Cassels, Alan. *Fascist Italy.* New York: Thomas Y. Crowell Company, 1968.

Cassese, Sabino. "Corporazioni e intervento pubblico nell'economia." In *Il regime fascista,* edited by Alberto Aquarone and Maurizio Vernassa. Bologna: Il Mulino, 1974.

Cassirer, Ernst. *Symbol, Myth and Culture: Essays and Lectures of Ernst Cassirer, 1935–1945.* Edited by Phillip Verene. New Haven: Yale University Press, 1979.

Cassoni, Enzo. *Il cartellonismo e l'illustrazione in Italia dal 1875 al 1950.* Rome: Nuova Editrice Spada, 1984.

Castronovo, Valerio. *La stampa italiana dall'unità al fascismo.* Bari: Laterza, 1970.

———. "La politica economica del fascismo e il Mezzogiorno." *Studi storici* 17, no. 3 (1976): 25–40.

Casucci, Costanzo, ed. *Il fascismo: Antologia di scritti critici.* Bologna: Il Mulino, 1982.

Ceserani, Gian Paolo. *Vetrina del ventennio 1923–1943.* Rome-Bari: Laterza, 1981.

Chabod, Federico. *L'Italia contemporanea (1918–1948).* Turin: Einaudi, 1961.

———. *Storia della politica estera italiana dal 1870 al 1896.* 1961. Reprint. Bari: Laterza, 1965.

Chiurco, Giorgio Alberto. *Storia della rivoluzione fascista.* 2 vols. Milan: Chiurco, 1972.

Chytry, Joseph. *The Aesthetic State: A Quest in Modern German Thought.* Berkeley: University of California Press, 1989.

Ciani, Plinio. *Graffiti del ventennio.* Milan: SugarCo., 1975.

Ciano, Galeazzo. *Diario, 1937–1943.* Edited by Renzo De Felice. Milan: Rizzoli, 1980.

Clough, Rosa Trillo. *Looking Back at Futurism.* New York: Cocce Press, 1942.

———. *Futurism: The Story of a Modern Art Movement: A New Appraisal.* New York: Philosophical Library, 1961.

Clough, Shepard B. *The Economic History of Modern Italy.* New York: Columbia University Press, 1964.

Cofrancesco, Dino. "Appunti per un'analisi del mito romano nell'ideologia fascista." *Storia contemporanea* 11, no. 3 (June 1980): 383–411.

Cohen, Jean L., and Andrew Arato. *Civil Society and Political Theory.* Cambridge, Mass.: MIT Press, 1992.

Colarizi, Simona, ed. *L'Italia antifascista dal 1922 al 1940: La lotta dei protagonisti.* Rome-Bari: Laterza, 1976.

Cooter, Roger. "The Power of the Body: The Early Nineteenth Century." In *The Natural Order: Historical Studies of Scientific Culture,* edited by Barry Barnes and Steven Shapin. Beverly Hills: Sage Publications, 1979.

Cordova, Ferdinando. *Arditi e legionari dannunziani.* Padova: Marsilio, 1969.

———. *Le origini dei sindacati fascisti, 1918–1926.* Rome-Bari: Laterza, 1974.

Corner, Paul. "Fascist Agrarian Policy and the Italian Economy in the Inter-War Years." In *Gramsci and Italy's Passive Revolution,* edited by John A. Davies. London: Barnes and Noble, 1979.

———. "I limiti del potere fascista." *Passato e Presente,* no. 4 (July–December 1983): 167–174.

Corni, Gustavo. "La politica agraria del fascismo: un confronto fra Italia e Germania." *Studi storici* 28, no. 2 (April–June 1987): 385–422.

Corradini, Enrico. *Discorsi politici (1902–1923).* Florence: Vallecchi, 1923.

Corsi, Mario. *Il teatro all'aperto in Italia.* Milan-Rome: Rizzoli, 1939.

Costamagna, Carlo. "Stato e corporazioni." In *Il fascismo: Antologia di scritti critici,* edited by Costanzo Casucci. Bologna: Il Mulino, 1982.

Crary, Jonathan. "Spectacle, Attention, Counter-Memory." *October,* no. 50 (Fall 1989): 97–107.

Crispolti, Enrico. *Il mito della macchina e altri temi del Futurismo.* Trapani: Celebes, 1969.

———. *La macchina mito futurista.* Rome: Editalia, 1986.

———. *Storia e critica del futurismo.* Rome-Bari: Laterza, 1986.

———. *Il futurismo e la moda: Balla e gli altri.* Venice: Marsilio, 1987.

Croce, Benedetto. *Storia d'Italia dal 1871 al 1915.* 1928. Bari: Laterza, 1966.

Dallmayr, Fred R., and Thomas A. McCarthy, eds. *Understanding and Social Inquiry.* Notre Dame: University of Notre Dame Press, 1977.

D'Amoja, Fulvio. *La politica estera dell'Impero: Storia della politica Estera fascista dalla conquista dell'Etiopia all'Anschluss.* Padova: Cedam, 1967.

D'Annunzio, Gabriele. *La penultima ventura: Scritti e discorsi fiumani.* Edited by Renzo De Felice. Milan: Mondadori, 1974.

———. *Poesie.* Edited by Federico Roncoroni. Milan: Mondadori, 1978.

Danto, Arthur Coleman. *Narration and Knowledge: Including the Integral Text of Analytical Philosophy of History.* New York: Columbia University Press, 1985.

Davis, John A., ed. *Gramsci and Italy's Passive Revolution.* London: Croom Helm, 1979.

De Begnac, Yvon. *Palazzo Venezia: Storia di un regime.* Roma: La Rocca, 1950.

De Bolla, Peter. *The Discourse of the Sublime: Readings in History, Aesthetics and the Subject.* Oxford: Basil Blackwell, 1989.

Debord, Guy. *Society of the Spectacle.* Detroit: Black and Red, 1983.

De Castris, Leone. *Il decadentismo italiano: Svevo, Pirandello, D'Annunzio.* Bari: De Donato, 1974.

De Felice, Renzo. *Mussolini il rivoluzionario.* Turin: Einaudi, 1965.

———. *Mussolini il fascista,* I. Turin: Einaudi, 1966.

———. *Mussolini il fascista,* II. Turin: Einaudi, 1968.

———. "Alcune osservazioni sulla politica estera mussoliniana." In *Il regime fascista,* edited by Alberto Aquarone and Maurizio Vernassa. Bologna: Il Mulino, 1974.

———. *Mussolini il duce,* I. Turin: Einaudi, 1974.

———. *Interpretations of Fascism.* Translated by Brenda Huff Everett. Cambridge, Mass.: Harvard University Press, 1977.

———. *D'Annunzio politico (1918–1938).* Rome-Bari: Laterza, 1978.

———. *Mussolini il duce,* II. Turin: Einaudi, 1981.

———. *Intervista sul fascismo.* Edited by Michael A. Ledeen. Rome-Bari: Laterza, 1982.

———, ed. *Sindacalismo rivoluzionario e fiumanesimo nel carteggio De Ambris-D'Annunzio 1912–1922.* Brescia: Morcelliana, 1966.

———, ed. *Futurismo, cultura e politica.* Turin: Fondazione Giovanni Agnelli, 1988.

De Felice, Renzo, and Luigi Goglia. *Storia fotografica del fascismo*. Rome-Bari: Laterza, 1981.

———. *Mussolini: Il mito*. Rome-Bari: Laterza, 1983.

De Felice, Renzo, and Emilio Mariano, eds. *Carteggio D'Annunzio-Mussolini (1919–1938)*. Milan: Mondadori, 1971.

De Felice, Renzo, Geno Pampaloni, Ettore Paratore, and Mario Praz. *Gabriele D'Annunzio*. Bologna: M. Boni, 1978.

De Grand, Alexander J. *Bottai e la cultura fascista*. Rome-Bari: Laterza, 1978.

———. *The Italian Nationalist Association and the Rise of Fascism in Italy*. Lincoln: University of Nebraska Press, 1978.

———. "Cracks in the Façade: The Failure of Fascist Totalitarianism in Italy (1935/9)." *European History Quarterly* 21 (1991): 515–535.

De Grazia, Victoria. *The Culture of Consent: Mass Organization of Leisure in Fascist Italy*. Cambridge: Cambridge University Press, 1981.

———. *How Fascism Ruled Women: Italy, 1922–1945*. Berkeley: University of California Press, 1992.

Del Boca, Angelo. *Gli Italiani in Africa Orientale: Dall'unità alla marcia su Roma*. Rome-Bari: Laterza, 1976.

Del Buono, Oreste, ed. *Eja, Eja, Eja, Alalà! La stampa italiana sotto il fascismo 1919–1943*. Milan: Feltrinelli, 1971.

Del Noce, Augusto. *Il problema dell'ateismo: Il concetto di ateismo e la storia della filosofia come problema*. 1964. Bologna: Il Mulino, 1970.

———. "Fascismo come marxismo senza materialismo." In *Il fascismo: Antologia di scritti critici*, edited by Costanzo Casucci. Bologna: Il Mulino, 1982.

Delle Piane, Mario. *Gaetano Mosca: Classe politica e liberalismo*. Naples: Edizioni Scientifiche Italiane, 1952.

De Luna, Giovanni. *Benito Mussolini: Soggettivita' e pratica di una dittatura*. Milan: Feltrinelli, 1978.

De Man, Paul. "Phenomenality and Materiality in Kant." In *Hermeneutics: Questions and Prospects*, edited by Gary Shapiro and Alan Sica. Amherst: University of Massachusetts Press, 1984.

De Maria, Luciano, ed. *Per conoscere Marinetti e il futurismo: Un'antologia*. Milan: Mondadori, 1973.

———. "Futurismo, Dada, Surrealismo." *Lettere italiane* 27, no. 4 (October 1975): 381–395.

De Martino, Ernesto. "Intorno a una storia del mondo poplare subalterno." *Società* 5, no. 31 (September 1949): 411–435.

———. *Sud e magia*. Milan: Feltrinelli, 1960.

———. *La terra del rimorso: Contributo a una storia religiosa del Sud*. Milan: Il Saggiatore, 1961.

———. *Mondo popolare e magia in Lucania*. Rome: Basilicata Editrice, 1975.

De Mauro, Tullio. *Storia linguistica dell'Italia unita*. 2 vols. Rome-Bari: Laterza, 1970.

De Michelis, Cesare. *Il futurismo italiano in Russia, 1909–1929*. Bari: De Donato, 1973.

De Rossi, Giulio. *Il partito popolare italiano: Dalle origini al congresso di Napoli*. Rome: La Nuova Cultura, 1920.

Diggins, John P. *Mussolini and Fascism: The View from America.* Princeton: Princeton University Press, 1972.

Dijkstra, Bram. *Idols of Perversity: Fantasies of Feminine Evil in Fin-de-Siècle Culture.* New York: Oxford University Press, 1986.

Di Palma, Giuseppe. "Legitimation from the Top to Civil Society: Politico-Cultural Change in Eastern Europe." *World Politics* 44, no. 1 (October 1991): 49–80.

Dorso, Guido. *La rivoluzione meridionale.* Turin: Einaudi, 1925.

———. *Benito Mussolini alla conquista del potere.* Turin: Einaudi, 1949.

Dumini, Amerigo. *Diciassette colpi.* Milan: Longanesi, 1958.

Durkheim, Émile. *The Elementary Forms of the Religious Life.* Translated by Joseph Ward Swain. London: Allen and Unwin, 1915.

Dyer, Richard. *Stars.* London: BFI Publications, 1979.

E 42: Utopia e scenario del regime. Edited by Achille Tartaro. Venice: Marsilio, 1987.

Eagleton, Terry. *The Ideology of the Aesthetic.* Oxford: Basil Blackwell, 1990.

Eco, Umberto. *La struttura assente: Introduzione alla ricerca semiologica.* Milan: Bompiani, 1968.

Eksteins, Modris. *Rites of Spring: The Great War and the Birth of the Modern Age.* Boston: Houghton Mifflin, 1989.

Elliott, J. H. "Power and Propaganda in the Spain of Philip IV." In *Rites of Power: Symbolism, Ritual, and Politics since the Middle Ages,* edited by Sean Wilentz. Philadelphia: University of Pennsylvania, 1985.

Ellwanger, Hermann. *Sulla lingua di Mussolini.* Milan: Mondadori, 1941.

Erenberg, Lewis A. *Steppin' Out: New York Nightlife and the Transformation of American Culture, 1890–1930.* Chicago: University of Chicago Press, 1981.

Ewen, Stuart. *Captains of Consciousness: Advertising and the Social Roots of the Consumer Culture.* New York: McGraw Hill, 1976.

Facts Geneva Refuses to See. Rome: Società Editrice di Novissima, 1935.

Falasca-Zamponi, Simonetta. "The Aesthetics of Politics: Symbol, Power and Narrative in Mussolini's Fascist Italy." *Theory, Culture & Society* 9, no. 4 (November 1992): 75–91.

Faye, Jean-Pierre. *Théorie du récit: Introduction aux "langages totalitaires."* Critique de la raison, l'économie narrative. Paris: Hermann, 1972.

Ferrara, Alessandro. "Autonomy and Authenticity." Ph.D. dissertation. University of California, Berkeley, 1984.

Ferry, Luc. *Homo aestheticus: L'invention du goût à l'age démocratique.* Paris: Grasset, 1990.

Fest, Joachim C. *Hitler.* Translated by Richard Winston and Clara Winston. New York: Harcourt Brace Jovanovich, 1974.

Field, G. Lowell. *The Syndical and Corporative Institutions of Italian Fascism.* New York: Columbia University Press, 1938.

Fiore, Tommaso. *Un popolo di formiche: Lettere pugliesi a Piero Gobetti.* Bari: Laterza, 1951.

Fisher, Philip. "Appearing and Disappearing in Public: Social Space in Late Nineteenth-Century Literature and Culture." In *Reconstructing American Literary History,* edited by Sacvan Bercovitch. Cambridge, Mass.: Harvard University Press, 1986.

Flora, Francesco, ed. *Stampa dell'era fascista: Le note di servizio.* Rome: Mondadori, 1945.

Forgacs, David. *Italian Culture in the Industrial Era, 1880–1980: Cultural Industries, Politics, and the Public.* Manchester: Manchester University Press, 1990.

Foscanelli, Umberto. *D'Annunzio e il fascismo.* Milan: Audace, n.d.

Foucault, Michel. *Birth of the Clinic.* Translated by A. M. Sheridan Smith. New York: Vintage, 1973.

———. *The History of Sexuality.* Translated by Robert Hurley. New York: Pantheon Books, 1978.

———. *Discipline and Punish: The Birth of the Prison.* Translated by Alan Sheridan. New York: Vintage, 1979.

———. *Power/Knowledge. Selected Interviews and Other Writings 1972–1977.* Edited by Colin Gordon. Translated by Colin Gordon, Leo Marshall, John Mepham, and Kate Soper. New York: Pantheon Books, 1980.

Fox, Richard Wightman, and T. J. Jackson Lears, eds. *The Culture of Consumption: Critical Essays in American History 1880–1980.* New York: Pantheon Books, 1983.

Fraser, Nancy. "Foucault on Modern Power: Empirical Insights and Normative Confusions." *Praxis International* 6, no. 3 (October 1981): 272–286.

Friedländer, Saul. *Reflections of Nazism: An Essay on Kitsch and Death.* Translated by Thomas Weyr. New York: Harper and Row, 1984.

Friedrich, Carl J., and Zbigniew K. Brzezinski. *Totalitarian Dictatorship and Autocracy.* Cambridge, Mass.: Harvard University Press, 1956.

Frisby, David. *Fragments of Modernity: Theories of Modernity in the Work of Simmel, Kracauer and Benjamin.* Cambridge: Polity Press, 1985.

Fritzsche, K. Peter. *A Nation of Fliers: German Aviation and the Popular Imagination.* Cambridge, Mass.: Harvard University Press, 1992.

Frye, Northrop. *Anatomy of Criticism: Four Essays.* Princeton: Princeton University Press, 1957.

Furet, François. *Interpreting the French Revolution.* Translated by Elborg Forster. Cambridge: Cambridge University Press, 1981.

Fussell, Paul. *The Great War and Modern Memory.* New York: Oxford University Press, 1975.

Galli, Giorgio. "Il fascismo e la violenza come strumento di azione politica." In *Il fascismo: Antologia di scritti critici,* edited by Costanzo Casucci. Bologna: Il Mulino, 1982.

Gambetti, Fidia. *Gli anni che scottano.* Milan: Mursia, 1967.

Gay, Peter. *Weimar Culture: The Outsider as Insider.* New York: Harper and Row, 1968.

Geertz, Clifford. "Centers, Kings, and Charisma: Reflections on the Symbolics of Power." In *Culture and Its Creators: Essays in Honor of Edward Shils,* edited by Joseph Ben-David and Terry N. Clark. Chicago: University of Chicago Press, 1977.

———. *Negara: The Theater State in Nineteenth-Century Bali.* Princeton: Princeton University Press, 1980.

Geiger, Roger L. "Democracy and the Crowd: The Social History of an Idea in France and Italy, 1880–1914." *Societas* 7, no. 1 (Winter 1977): 47–71.

Gentile, Emilio. *"La Voce" e l'età giolittiana.* Milan: Pan, 1972.

———. *Le origini dell'ideologia fascista (1918–1925)*. Rome-Bari: Laterza, 1975.

———. *Il mito dello stato nuovo: Dall'antigiolittismo al fascismo*. Rome-Bari: Laterza, 1982.

———. *Storia del Partito Fascista (1919–1922): Movimento e milizia*. Rome-Bari: Laterza, 1989.

———. "Fascism as Political Religion." *Journal of Contemporary History* 25, nos. 2/3 (1990): 229–251.

———. *Il culto del Littorio: La sacralizzazione della politica nell'Italia fascista*. Rome-Bari: Laterza, 1993.

———, ed. *Mussolini e "La Voce."* Florence: Sansoni, 1976.

Gentile, Giovanni. *Origini e dottrina del fascismo*. Rome: Libreria del Littorio, 1929.

Gerra, Ferdinando. *L'impresa di Fiume nelle parole e nell'azione di Gabriele D'Annunzio*. Milan: Longanesi, 1966.

Ghirardo, Diane Yvonne. *Building New Communities: New Deal America and Fascist Italy*. Princeton: Princeton University Press, 1989.

Gili, Jean A. *Stato fascista e cinematografia: Repressione e promozione*. Rome: Bulzoni, 1981.

———. *L'Italie de Mussolini et son cinéma*. Paris: H. Veyrier, 1985.

Gioberti, Vincenzo. *Del primato morale e civile degli italiani*. Naples: C. Batelli e Comp., 1848–1849.

Gli Annitrenta. Arte e cultura in Italia. Milan: Mazzotta, 1982.

Goglia, Luigi. *Storia fotografica dell'impero fascista, 1935–1941*. Rome-Bari: Laterza, 1985.

Goglia, Luigi, and Fabio Grassi, eds. *Il colonialismo italiano da Adua all'impero*. Rome-Bari: Laterza, 1981.

Goldberg, Jonathan. *James I and the Politics of Literature: Jonson, Shakespeare, Donne, and their Contemporaries*. Baltimore: Johns Hopkins University Press, 1983.

Goldfarb, Jeffrey C. *Beyond Glasnost: The Post-Totalitarian Mind*. Chicago: University of Chicago Press, 1989.

Golomshtok, Igor. *Totalitarian Art: In the Soviet Union, the Third Reich, Fascist Italy and the People's Republic of China*. New York: Icon Editions, 1990.

Golsan, Richard J., ed. *Fascism, Aesthetics, and Culture*. Hanover: University Press of New England, 1992.

Gombrich, Ernst Hans. *Symbolic Images*. Oxford: Phaidon, 1978.

Gramsci, Antonio. *Letteratura e vita nazionale*. 1950. Rome: Editori Riuniti, 1977.

———. *Passato e presente*. Turin: Einaudi, 1951.

———. *Selections from the Prison Notebooks*. Edited and translated by Quintin Hoare and Geoffrey Nowell Smith. New York: International Publishers, 1971.

———. *Selections from Cultural Writings*. Edited by David Forgacs and Geoffrey Nowell Smith. Translated by William Boelhower. Cambridge, Mass.: Harvard University Press, 1985.

Gravelli, Asvero. *Vademecum dello stile fascista*. Rome: Nuova Europa, [1940?].

Greenblatt, Stephen. "Invisible Bullets: Renaissance Authority and its Subversion." *Glyph*, no. 8 (1981): 40–61.

Greenhalgh, Paul. *Ephemeral Vistas: A History of the Éxpositions Universelles, Great Exhibitions, and World's Fairs, 1851–1939*. Manchester: Manchester University Press, 1988.

Gregor, A. James. *Interpretations of Fascism*. Morristown, N.J.: General Learning Press, 1974.

Griffin, Roger. *The Nature of Fascism*. New York: St. Martin's, 1991.

Groys, Boris. *Lo stalinismo ovvero l'opera d'arte totale*. Milan: Garzanti, 1992.

Gualerni, Gualberto. *Lo stato industriale in Italia, 1890–1940*. Milan: Etas Libri, 1982.

Habermas, Jürgen. "Hannah Arendt's Communications Concept of Power." *Social Research* 44, no. 1 (Spring 1977): 3–24.

———. "The Entwinment of Myth and Enlightenment." *New German Critique*, no. 26 (Spring–Summer 1982): 13–30.

———. "Modernity—An Incomplete Project." In *The Anti-Aesthetic: Essays on Post-Modern Culture*, edited by Hal Foster. Post Townsend, Washington: Bay Press, 1983.

———. "The French Path to Postmodernity: Bataille between Eroticism and General Economics." *New German Critique*, no. 33 (Fall 1984): 79–102.

———. *The Theory of Communicative Action*. 2 vols. Translated by Thomas McCarthy. Boston: Beacon Press, 1984–1987.

———. *The Structural Transformation of the Public Sphere: An Inquiry into a Category of Bourgeois Society*. Translated by Thomas Burger. Cambridge, Mass: MIT Press, 1989.

Haider, Carmen. *Capital and Labor under Fascism*. New York: Columbia University Press, 1930.

Hall, Stuart. "Culture, the Media and the 'Ideological Effect.'" In *Mass Communication and Society*, edited by James Curran, Michael Gurevitch, and Janet Woollacott. London: Edward Arnold in association with the Open University Press, 1977.

Hamilton, Alastair. *The Appeal of Fascism: A Study of Intellectuals and Fascism, 1919–1945*. New York: Macmillan, 1971.

Harvey, David. *The Condition of Postmodernity: An Enquiry into the Origins of Cultural Change*. Oxford: Basil Blackwell, 1989.

Hay, James. *Popular Film Culture in Fascist Italy: The Passing of the Rex*. Bloomington: Indiana University Press, 1987.

Herf, Jeffrey. *Reactionary Modernism: Technology, Culture and Politics in Weimar and the Third Reich*. Cambridge: Cambridge University Press, 1984.

Hillach, Ansgar. "The Aesthetics of Politics." *New German Critique*, no. 17 (Spring 1979): 99–119.

Hobsbawm, Eric. *The Age of Empire 1875–1914*. New York: Pantheon Books, 1987.

Hobsbawm, Eric, and Terence Ranger, eds. *The Invention of Tradition*. New York: Cambridge University Press, 1983.

Horn, David G. *Social Bodies: Science, Reproduction, and Italian Modernity*. Princeton: Princeton University Press, 1994.

Horowitz, Daniel. *The Morality of Spending: Attitudes Toward the Consumer Society in America, 1875–1940*. Baltimore: Johns Hopkins University Press, 1985.

Huet, Marie-Hélène. *Rehearsing the Revolution: The Staging of Marat's Death, 1793–1797*. Translated by Robert Hurley. Berkeley: University of California Press, 1982.

Hulten, Pontus, ed. *Futurism and Futurisms—Futurismo e Futurismi*. New York: Abbeview Press, 1986.

Hunt, Lynn. *Politics, Culture, and Class in the French Revolution.* Berkeley: University of California Press, 1984.

Huyssen, Andreas. *After the Great Divide: Modernism, Mass Culture, Postmodernism.* Bloomington: Indiana University Press, 1986.

Isnenghi, Mario. *Il mito della grande guerra da Marinetti a Malaparte.* Bari: Laterza, 1970.

———. "Valori popolari e valori 'ufficiali' nella mentalità del soldato fra le due guerre." *Quaderni storici,* no. 38 (1978): 701–709.

———. *L'educazione dell'italiano: Il fascismo e l'organizzazione della cultura.* Bologna: Cappelli, 1979.

———. *Intellettuali militanti e intellettuali funzionari: Appunti sulla cultura fascista.* Turin: Einaudi, 1979.

The Italo-Ethiopian Dispute: Abstracts from the Memorandum of the Italian Government to the League of Nations. Rome: Società Editrice di Novissima, 1935.

Italy and Abyssinia. Rome: Società Editrice di Novissima, 1936.

Jackson Lears, T. J. *No Place of Grace: Anti-Modernism and the Transformation of American Culture 1880–1920.* New York: Pantheon, 1981.

———. "Mass Culture and Its Critics." In *Encyclopedia of American Social History.* New York: Scribner, 1993.

Jameson, Fredric. *Fables of Aggression: Windham Lewis, the Modernist as Fascist.* Berkeley: University of California Press, 1981.

———. "Pleasure: A Political Issue. In *Formations of Pleasure,* edited by Tony Bennett et al. London: Routledge and Kegan Paul, 1983.

Jay, Martin. "Should Intellectual History Take a Linguistic Turn? Reflections on the Habermas-Gadamer Debate." In *Modern European Intellectual History: Reappraisals and New Perspectives,* edited by Dominick LaCapra and Steven L. Kaplan. Ithaca: Cornell University Press, 1982.

———. "'The Aesthetic Ideology' as Ideology; Or What Does It Mean to Aestheticize Politics?" *Cultural Critique,* no. 21 (Spring 1992): 41–62.

———. *Downcast Eyes: The Denigration of Vision in Twentieth-Century French Thought.* Berkeley: University of California Press, 1993.

———. "Experience Without a Subject: Walter Benjamin and the Novel." *New Formations,* no. 20 (Summer 1993): 145–156.

Jemolo, Arturo Carlo. *Chiesa e Stato in Italia negli ultimi cento anni.* Turin: Einaudi, 1949.

Jennings, J. R. *Georges Sorel: The Character and Development of His Thought.* New York: St. Martin's Press, 1985.

Joll, James. *Intellectuals in Politics: Three Biographical Essays.* London: Weidenfeld and Nicolson, 1960.

Jones, Larry Eugene. "The Dying Middle: Weimar Germany and the Fragmentation of Bourgeois Politics." *Central European History* 5, no. 1 (1972): 23–55.

Jünger, Ernst. "Le soldat du travail." *Recherches,* nos. 32/33 (September 1978): 35–53.

Kamenetsky, Christa. "Folklore as a Tool in Nazi Germany." *Journal of American Folklore* 85, no. 337 (1972): 221–235.

———. "Folktale and Ideology in the Third Reich." *Journal of American Folklore* 90, no. 358 (1977): 168–178.

Kantorowicz, Ernst Hartwig. "Mysteries of State." *Harvard Theological Review* 48, no. 1 (January 1955): 65–91.

——. *The King's Two Bodies: A Study in Medieval Political Theology.* Princeton: Princeton University Press, 1957.

Kaplan, Alice Jaeger. *Reproductions of Banality: Fascism, Literature, and French Intellectual Life.* Minneapolis: University of Minnesota Press, 1986.

Kaplan, Amy. "Romancing the Empire: The Embodiment of American Masculinity in the Popular Historical Novel of the 1890s." *American Literary History* 2, no. 4 (Winter 1990): 659–690.

Kasson, John F. *Amusing the Million: Coney Island at the Turn of the Century.* New York: Hill and Wang, 1978.

Keane, John, ed. *Civil Society and the State: New European Perspectives.* London: Verso, 1988.

Kelikian, Alice A. *Town and Country under Fascism: The Transformation of Brescia, 1915–1926.* Oxford: Clarendon Press, 1986.

Kenez, Peter. *The Birth of the Propaganda State: Soviet Methods of Mass Mobilization, 1917–1929.* Cambridge: Cambridge University Press, 1985.

Kern, Stephen. *The Culture of Time and Space 1880–1918.* Cambridge, Mass.: Harvard University Press, 1983.

Kershaw, Ian. *The 'Hitler Myth': Image and Reality in the Third Reich.* Oxford: Clarendon Press, 1987.

Kertzer, David I. *Ritual, Politics, and Power.* New Haven: Yale University Press, 1988.

Kinser, Bill, and Neil Kleinman. *The Dream That Was No More a Dream: A Search for Aesthetic Reality in Germany, 1890–1945.* New York: Harper and Row, 1969.

Klibansky, Raymond, ed. *Benito Mussolini's Memoirs 1942–1943.* Translated by Frances Lobb. New York: Howard Fertig, 1975.

Klinger, Cornelia. "The Concept of the Sublime and the Beautiful in Kant and Lyotard." *Constellations* 2, no. 2 (October 1995): 207–223.

Knei-Paz, Baruch. *The Social and Political Thought of Leon Trotsky.* Oxford: Clarendon Press, 1978.

Koon, Tracy H. *Believe, Obey, Fight: Political Socialization of Youth in Fascist Italy, 1922–1943.* Chapel Hill: University of North Carolina Press, 1985.

Kracauer, Siegfried. *The Mass Ornament.* Translated, edited and with an introduction by Thomas Y. Levin. Cambridge, Mass.: Harvard University Press, 1995.

Krimer, Cristoforo. *Mussolini aviatore.* Siena: Meini, n.d.

LaCapra, Dominick. *Soundings in Critical Theory.* Ithaca: Cornell University Press, 1989.

LaCapra, Dominick, and Steven L. Kaplan, eds. *Modern European Intellectual History: Reappraisals and New Perspectives.* Ithaca: Cornell University Press, 1982.

Lacoue-Labarthe, Philippe, and Jean-Luc Nancy. *The Literary Absolute: The Theory of Literature in German Romanticism.* Translated by Philip Barnard and Cheryl Lester. Albany, N.Y.: State University of New York Press, 1988.

——. *Il mito nazi.* Genova: Il Melangolo, 1992.

La Francesca, Salvatore. *La politica economica del fascismo.* Bari: Laterza, 1972.

Landy, Marcia. *Fascism in Film: The Italian Commercial Cinema, 1931–1943.* Princeton: Princeton University Press, 1986.

Laqueur, Walter, ed. *Fascism: A Reader's Guide.* Berkeley: University of California Press, 1976.

Laqueur, Walter, and George Mosse, eds. *1914: The Coming of the First World War.* New York: Harper and Row, 1966.

Laura, Ernesto G. *Immagine del fascismo: Come nacque, come conquistò l'Italia, chi lo aiuto, 'come finí,' attraverso fotografie e documenti originali.* Milan: Longanesi, 1973.

Leach, William. "Transformations in a Culture of Consumption: Women and Department Stores, 1890–1925." *Journal of American History* 71, no. 2 (September 1984): 319–342.

———. "Strategists of Display and the Production of Desire." In *Consuming Visions: Accumulation and Display of Goods in America, 1880–1920,* edited by Simon Bonner. New York: W. W. Norton and Co., 1989.

Le Bon, Gustave. *The Crowd: A Study of the Popular Mind.* New York: Viking, 1960.

Ledeen, Michael A. *The First Duce: D'Annunzio at Fiume.* Baltimore: Johns Hopkins University Press, 1977.

Lefort, Claude. *The Political Forms of Modern Society: Bureaucracy, Democracy, Totalitarianism.* Edited by John Thompson. Cambridge: MIT Press, 1986.

———. *Democracy and Political Theory.* Minneapolis: University of Minnesota Press, 1988.

Le Rider, Jacques. *Modernité viennoise et crise de l'identité.* Paris: Presses Universitaires de France, 1990.

Leso, Erasmo. "Aspetti della lingua del fascismo." In *Storia linguistica dell'Italia del Novecento. Atti del V Convegno Internazionale di Studi, Roma 1–2 giugno 1971.* Rome: Bulzoni, 1973.

Leso, Erasmo, Michele Cortelazzo, Ivano Paccagnella, and Fabio Foresti. *La lingua italiana e il fascismo.* Bologna: Consorzio provinciale pubblica lettura, 1978.

Leto, Guido. *OVRA: Fascismo-Antifascismo.* Rocca San Casciano: Cappelli, 1952.

Linz, Juan. "An Authoritarian Regime: Spain." In *Cleavages, Ideologies and Party Systems: Contributions to Comparative Political Sociology,* vol. 3 of *Transactions of the Westmark Society,* edited by Erik Allardt, and Yrjo Littunen. Helsinki: Academic Bookstore Distributor, 1964.

Lista, Giovanni. *Arte e politica: Il futurismo di sinistra in Italia.* Milan: Multhipla, 1980.

———. *Le livre futuriste: De la libération du mot au poème tactile.* Modena: Panini, 1984.

———. *Futurism.* New York: Universe Books, 1986.

Lloyd, David. "Arnold, Ferguson, Schiller: Aesthetic Culture and the Politics of Aesthetics." *Cultural Critique* 1, no. 2 (Spring 1986).

Longanesi, Leo. *In piedi e seduti 1919–1943.* Milan: Longanesi, 1980.

Longobardi, Cesare. *Land-Reclamation in Italy: Rural Revival in the Building of a Nation.* London: P. S. King and Son Ltd., 1936.

Lowenthal, Leo. *Literature, Popular Culture, and Society.* Palo Alto: Pacific Books, 1961.

———. "German Popular Biographies: Culture's Bargain Counter." In *The Critical Spirit: Essays in Honor of Herbert Marcuse,* edited by Kurt Wolff and Barrington Moore, Jr. Boston: Beacon Press, 1967.

Lowenthal, Leo, and Norbert Guterman. *Prophets of Deceit: A Study of the Techniques of the American Agitator.* Palo Alto: Pacific Books, 1949.

Ludwig, Emil. *Colloqui con Mussolini.* Milan: Mondadori, 1932.

Lukes, Steven. *Power: A Radical View.* London: Macmillan, 1974.

———. *Essays in Social Theory.* London: Macmillan, 1977.

Lunn, Eugene. *Marxism and Modernism: An Historical Study of Lukács, Brecht, Benjamin, and Adorno.* Berkeley: University of California Press, 1982.

Lussu, Emilio. *Marcia su Roma e dintorni.* Turin: Einaudi, 1965.

Lyttelton, Adrian. *The Seizure of Power: Fascism in Italy 1919–1929.* New York: Scribner, 1973.

———. "Fascismo e violenza: conflitto sociale e azione politica nel primo dopoguerra." *Storia contemporanea* 13, no. 6 (December 1982): 965–983.

Mack Smith, Denis. *Mussolini's Roman Empire.* New York: Longman, 1976.

Maier, Charles S. *Recasting Bourgeois Europe: Stabilization in France, Germany, and Italy in the Decade after World War I.* Princeton: Princeton University Press, 1975.

———. "The Economics of Fascism and Nazism: Premises and Performance." In *Development, Democracy, and the Art of Trespassing: Essays in Honor of Albert O. Hirschman,* edited by Alejandro Foxley, Richard McPherson, and Guillermo O' Donnell. Notre Dame: University of Notre Dame Press, 1986.

———, ed. *Changing Boundaries of the Political: Essays on the Evolving Balance between the State and Society, Public and Private in Europe.* Cambridge: Cambridge University Press, 1987.

Malvano, Laura. *Fascismo e politica dell'immagine.* Turin: Boringhieri, 1988.

Mancini, Elaine. *Struggles of the Italian Film Industry during Fascism, 1930–1935.* Ann Arbor: UMI Research Press, 1985.

Mangoni, Luisa. *L'interventismo della cultura: Intellettuali e riviste del fascismo.* Rome-Bari: Laterza, 1974.

Mann, Thomas. *Reflections of a Nonpolitical Man.* Translated by Walter D. Morris. New York: F. Ungar, 1983.

Marabini Moevs, Maria Teresa. *Gabriele D'Annunzio e le estetiche della fine del secolo.* L'Aquila: L. U. Japadre, 1976.

Marchesini, Daniele. *La scuola dei gerarchi: Mistica fascista: storie, problemi, istituzioni.* Milan: Feltrinelli, 1976.

Marcuse, Herbert. *Negations: Essays in Critical Theory.* Translated by Jeremy J. Shapiro. Boston: Beacon Press, 1968.

Mariani, Riccardo. *Fascismo e città nuove.* Milan: Feltrinelli, 1976.

———, ed. *Latina: Storia di una città.* Florence: Alinari, 1982.

Marin, Louis. "La description de l'image." *Communications,* no. 15 (1970): 186–210.

———. "Récit du pouvoir. Pouvoir du récit." *Actes de la recherche en sciences sociales* 25 (January 1979): 23–43.

———. *Portrait of the King.* Translated by Martha M. Houle. Minneapolis: University of Minnesota Press, 1987.

———. "The Narrative Trap: The Conquest of Power." In *Ideological Representation and Power in Social Relations,* edited by Mike Gane. London: Routledge, 1989.

Marinetti, Filippo Tommaso. *I manifesti del futurismo.* Florence: Edizioni di "Lacerba," 1914.

————. *Les mots en liberté futuristes*. Milan: Edizioni Futuriste di "Poesia," 1919.

————. *Futurismo e fascismo*. Foligno: Campitelli, 1924.

————. *Teoria e invenzione futurista*. Edited by Luciano De Maria. Milan: Mondadori, 1968.

————. *Marinetti: Selected Writings*. Edited by R. W. Flint. Translated by R. W. Flint and Arthur Coppotelli. New York: Farrar, Straus and Giroux, 1971.

Marinetti, Filippo Tommaso, and Fillia. *La cucina futurista*. Milan: Sonzogno, 1986.

Martin, Marianne W. *Futurist Art and Theory 1909–1915*. Oxford: Clarendon Press, 1968.

Mason, T. W. "The Primacy of Politics: Politics and Economics in National Socialist Germany." In *The Nature of Fascism*, edited by S. J. Woolf. New York: Random House, 1968.

Matteotti, Giacomo. *Scritti e discorsi*. Parma: Guanda, 1974.

Mattioli, Guido. *Mussolini aviatore e la sua opera per l'aviazione*. Rome: L'Aviazione, 1939.

May, Lary. *Screening Out the Past: The Birth of Mass Culture and the Motion Picture Industry*. New York: Oxford University Press, 1980.

Mazzatosta, Teresa Maria, and Claudio Volpi, eds. *L'Italietta fascista (lettere al potere 1936–1943)*. Bologna: Cappelli, 1980.

McKendrick, Neil, John Brewer, and J. H. Plumb. *The Birth of a Consumer Society: The Commercialization of Eighteenth-Century England*. Bloomington: Indiana University Press, 1982.

Megaro, Gaudens. *Mussolini in the Making*. London: Allen and Unwin, 1938.

Meldini, Piero, ed. *Sposa e madre esemplare: Ideologia e politica della donna e della famiglia durante il fascismo*. Rimini-Florence: Guaraldi, 1975.

Melograni, Piero. *Storia politica della grande guerra, 1915/1918*. Bari: Laterza, 1969.

————. *Gli industriali e Mussolini: Rapporti tra Confindustria e fascismo dal 1919 al 1929*. Milan: Longanesi, 1972.

————. "The Cult of the Duce in Mussolini's Italy." *Journal of Contemporary History* 11, no. 4 (October 1976): 221–237.

————. *Rapporti segreti della polizia fascista, 1938–1940*. Rome-Bari: Laterza, 1979.

Menarini, Alberto. *Ai margini della lingua*. Florence: Sansoni, 1947.

Menegazzi, Luigi. *Il manifesto italiano 1882/1925*. Milan: Electa, 1975.

Metz, Christian. *The Imaginary Signifier: Psychoanalysis and the Cinema*. Translated by Celia Britton, Annwyl Williams, Ben Brewster, and Alfred Guzzetti. Bloomington: Indiana University Press, 1982.

Miami Theory Collective, ed. *Community at Loose Ends*. Minneapolis: University of Minnesota Press, 1991.

Michels, Robert. *First Lectures in Political Sociology*. Translated by Alfred De Grazia. Minneapolis: University of Minnesota Press, 1949.

————. *Political Parties: A Sociological Study of the Oligarchical Tendencies of Modern Democracy*. Translated by Eden and Cedar Paul. New York: Collier Books, 1962.

Milfull, John, ed. *The Attractions of Fascism: Social Psychology and Aesthetics of the "Triumph of the Right."* New York: Berg, 1990.

Miller, Michael B. *The Bon Marché: Bourgeois Culture and the Department Store, 1869–1920*. Princeton: Princeton University Press, 1981.

Milza, Pierre. *Le fascisme italien et la presse française (1920–1940)*. Bruxelles: Complexe, 1987.

Missiroli, Mario. *La politica estera di Mussolini 1922–38*. Milan, 1939.

Missori, Mario. *Gerarchie e statuti del P.N.F.: Gran consiglio, Direttorio nazionale, Federazioni provinciali: Quadri e biografie*. Rome: Bonacci, 1986.

Mitzman, Arthur. *The Iron Cage: An Historical Interpretation of Max Weber*. New York: Knopf, 1969.

Mola, Aldo Alessandro. *L'imperialismo italiano: La politica estera dall'Unità al fascismo*. Rome: Editori Riuniti, 1980.

Mommsen, Wolfgang. "Max Weber's Political Sociology and His Philosophy of World History." In *Max Weber*, edited by Dennis Wrong. Englewood Cliffs, N.J.: Prentice-Hall, 1970.

Monelli, Paolo. *Mussolini, piccolo borghese*. Milan: Garzanti, 1950.

Monteleone, Franco. *La radio italiana nel periodo fascista: Studio e documenti: 1922–1945*. Venice: Marsilio, 1976.

Moore, Barrington, Jr. *Political Power and Social Theory: Six Studies*. Cambridge, Mass.: Harvard University Press, 1958.

Morin, Edgar. *Le cinéma; ou, l'homme imaginaire, essai d'anthropologie*. Paris: Éditions de Minuit, 1956.

Mosse, George L. *The Nationalization of the Masses: Political Symbolism and Mass Movements in Germany from the Napoleonic Wars through the Third Reich*. New York: Howard Fertig, 1975.

———. *Nazism: A Historical and Comparative Analysis of National Socialism*. New Brunswick, 1978.

———. *Masses and Man: Nationalist and Fascist Perceptions of Reality*. New York: Transaction Books, 1980.

———. *Nationalism and Sexuality: Respectability and Abnormal Sexuality in Modern Europe*. New York: Howard Fertig, 1985.

———. "The Political Culture of Italian Futurism: A General Perspective." *Journal of Contemporary History* 25, nos. 2/3 (1990): 253–268.

Mouffe, Chantal, ed. *Gramsci and Marxist Theory*. London: Routledge and Kegan Paul, 1979.

Mukerji, Chandra. *From Graven Images: Patterns of Modern Materialism*. New York: Columbia University Press, 1983.

Murphy, Peter. "Between Romanticism and Republicanism: The Political Theory of Claude Lefort." Review of *The Political Forms of Modern Society: Bureaucracy, Democracy, Totalitarianism*, by Claude Lefort. *Thesis Eleven*, no. 23 (1989): 131–142.

Mussolini, Benito. *My Autobiography*. London: Hutchinson and Co., 1928.

———. "Fascismo." *Enciclopedia Italiana di scienze, lettere ed arti*. Vol. 14. Rome: Istituto Giovanni Treccani, 1929–1939.

———. *Scritti e discorsi di Benito Mussolini*. 12 vols. Milan: Hoepli, 1934–1939.

———. *Opera Omnia*. 36 vols. Edited by Edoardo Susmel and Duilio Susmel. Florence: La Fenice, 1951–1963.

Nancy, Jean-Luc. *The Inoperative Community*. Edited by Peter Connor. Translated by Peter Connor, Lisa Garbus, Michael Holland, and Simona Sawhney. Minneapolis: University of Minnesota Press, 1991.

Nanni, Torquato. *Benito Mussolini.* Florence: Libreria della Voce, 1915.

Naudeau, Ludovic. *L'Italie fasciste ou l'autre danger.* Paris: Flammarion, 1927.

Nello, Paolo. *L'avanguardismo giovanile dalle origini al fascismo.* Rome-Bari: Laterza, 1978.

Neumann, Franz. *Behemoth: The Structure and Practice of National Socialism 1933–1944.* 1944. New York: Harper and Row, 1966.

Nichols, Bill. *Ideology and the Image: Social Representation in the Cinema and Other Media.* Bloomington: Indiana University Press, 1981.

Nizza, Enzo, ed. *Autobiografia del fascismo.* Milan: La Pietra, 1962.

Nolte, Ernst. *Three Faces of Fascism: Action Française, Italian Fascism, National Socialism.* Translated by Leila Vennewitz. New York: Holt, Rinehart and Winston, 1965.

Novelletto, Arnaldo, ed. *L'Italia nella psicoanalisi.* Rome: Istituto della Enciclopedia Italiana, 1989.

Nye, Robert A. *The Origins of Crowd Psychology: Gustave Le Bon and the Crisis of Mass Democracy in the Third Republic.* London: Sage Publications, 1975.

O'Donnell, Guillermo. "On the Fruitful Convergences of Hirschman's *Exit, Voice and Loyalty* and *Shifting Involvements:* Reflections from the Recent Argentine Experience." In *Development, Democracy, and the Art of Trespassing: Essays in Honor of Albert O. Hirshman,* edited by Alexandro Foxley, Michael S. McPherson, and Guillermo O'Donnell. Notre Dame: University of Notre Dame Press, 1986.

O'Donnell, Guillermo, and Philippe Schmitter, eds. *Transitions from Authoritarian Rule: Tentative Conclusions about Uncertain Democracies.* Baltimore: Johns Hopkins University Press, 1986.

Olivetti, Gino. "Capitalismo controllato invece di liberismo." In *Il fascismo: Antologia di scritti critici,* edited by Costanzo Casucci. Bologna: Il Mulino, 1982.

Oppenheim, Janet. *"Shattered Nerves": Doctors, Patients, and Depression in Victorian England.* New York: Oxford University Press, 1991.

Orgel, Stephen. *The Illusion of Power: Political Theater in the English Renaissance.* Berkeley: University of California Press, 1975.

Orsolini Cencelli, Valentino. *Le Paludi Pontine nella preistoria, nel mito, nella leggenda, nella storia, nella letteratura, nell'arte e nella scienza.* Rome: Opera Nazionale per i Combattenti, 1934.

Ozouf, Mona. *Festivals and the French Revolution.* Translated by Alan Sheridan. Cambridge, Mass.: Harvard University Press, 1988.

Paetzoldt, Heinz. "Walter Benjamin's Theory of the End of Art." *International Journal of Sociology* 7, no. 1 (Spring 1977): 25–75.

Panofsky, Erwin. *Studies in Iconology: Humanistic Themes in the Art of the Renaissance.* New York: Oxford University Press, 1939.

Panunzio, Sergio. "Sindacalismo fascista." In *Il fascismo: Antologia di scritti critici,* edited by Costanzo Casucci. Bologna: Il Mulino, 1982.

Papa, Emilio R. *Storia di due manifesti: Il fascismo e la cultura italiana. Con un saggio di Francesco Flora.* Milan: Feltrinelli, 1958.

Paret, Peter, Beth Irwin Lewis, and Paul Paret. *Persuasive Images: Posters of War and Revolution from the Hoover Institution Archives.* Princeton: Princeton University Press, 1992.

Passerini, Luisa. *Torino operaia e fascismo: Una storia orale.* Bari: Laterza, 1984.

———. "L'Immagine di Mussolini: specchio dell'immaginario e promessa d'identità." *Rivista di storia contemporanea,* no. 3 (1986): 322–349.

———. *Fascism in Popular Memory: The Cultural Experience of the Turin Working Class.* Translated by Robert Lumley and Jude Bloomfield. Cambridge: Cambridge University Press, 1987.

———. *Mussolini immaginario: Storia di una biografia 1915–1939.* Rome-Bari: Laterza, 1991.

Peiss, Kathy. *Cheap Amusements: Working Women and Leisure in Turn-of-the-Century New York.* Philadelphia: Temple, 1986.

Perfetti, Francesco. *Il sindacalismo fascista.* Vol. 1, *Dalle origini alla vigilia dello stato corporativo (1919–1930).* Rome: Bonacci, 1988.

Pericoli, Ugo. *Le divise del Duce.* Milan: Rizzoli, 1983.

Perloff, Marjorie. *The Futurist Moment: Avant-Garde, Avant-Guerre, and the Language of Rupture.* Chicago: University of Chicago Press, 1986.

Petersen, Jens. "La politica estera del fascismo come problema storiografico." *Storia contemporanea* 3, no. 4 (December 1972): 661–705.

———. "Elettorato e base sociale del fascismo italiano negli anni venti." *Studi storici* XVI, no. 3 (July–September 1975): 654–660.

———. "La nascita del concetto di 'Stato totalitario' in Italia." *Annali dell'Istituto storico italo-germanico in Trento* 1 (1975): 143–168.

———. "Il problema della violenza nel fascismo italiano." *Storia contemporanea* 13, no. 6 (December 1982): 985–1008.

Petracchi, Giorgio. *La Russia rivoluzionaria nella politica italiana: Le relazioni Italo-Sovietiche 1917–25.* Rome-Bari: Laterza, 1982.

Petri, Omero. *L'italiano nuovissimo (il Messia).* Turin: Bocca, 1928.

Petrucci, Armando. "La scrittura tra ideologia e rappresentazione." In *Storia dell'arte italiana.* Vol. 2, *Grafica e immagine.* Turin: Einaudi, 1980.

Pinkus, Karen. *Bodily Regimes: Italian Advertising under Fascism.* Minneapolis: University of Minnesota Press, 1975.

Pitkin, Hanna. "Justice: On Relating Private and Public." *Political Theory* 9, no. 3 (August 1981): 327–352.

Poggioli, Renato. *The Theory of the Avant-Garde.* Translated by Gerald Fitzgerald. Cambridge, Mass.: Harvard University Press, 1968.

Policastro, Guglielmo. *Homo novus.* Catania: Minerva, 1923.

Pombeni, Paolo. *Demagogia e tirannide: Uno studio sulla forma-partito del fascismo.* Bologna: Il Mulino, 1984.

Porter, Roy. "History of the Body." In *New Perspectives in Historical Writing,* edited by Peter Burke. Cambridge: Polity Press, 1991.

———. "Consumption: Disease of the Consumer Society?" In *Consumption and the World of Goods,* edited by John Brewer and Roy Porter. London: Routledge, 1993.

Praz, Mario. *The Romantic Agony.* Translated by Angus Davidson. London: Oxford University Press, 1933.

Preti, Luigi. *I miti dell'impero e della razza nell'Italia degli anni trenta.* Rome: Opere Nuove, 1965.

Prezzolini, Giuseppe. "Benito Mussolini." In *Mussolini e "La Voce,"* edited by Emilio Gentile. Florence: Sansoni, 1976.

———. "Mussolini oratore ovvero eloquenza e carisma." In *Mussolini e "La Voce,"* edited by Emilio Gentile. Florence: Sansoni, 1976.

Priarone, Giuseppe. *Grafica pubblicitaria in Italia negli anni trenta.* Florence: Cantini, 1988.

Profumieri, Pierluigi. "Capitale e lavoro in Italia, 1929–1940: Una interpretazione economica." In *Il regime fascista,* edited by Alberto Aquarone and Maurizio Vernassa. Bologna: Il Mulino, 1974.

Propp, Vladimir I. *Theory and History of Folklore.* Translated by Ariadna Y. Martin, Richard P. Martin, et al. Minneapolis: University of Minnesota Press, 1984.

Pye, Christopher. "The Sovereign, the Theater, and the Kingdome of Darknesse: Hobbes and the Spectacle of Power." *Representations,* no. 8 (Fall 1984): 85–106.

Quilici, Nello. *Aviatoria.* Naples: La Nuovissima, 1934.

Rabinbach, Anson G. "Toward a Marxist Theory of Fascism and National Socialism: A Report on Developments in West Germany." *New German Critique,* no. 3 (Fall 1974): 127–153.

———. "The Aesthetics of Production in the Third Reich." *Journal of Contemporary History* 11, no. 4 (1976): 43–74.

———. *The Human Motor: Energy, Fatigue, and the Origins of Modernity.* New York: Basic Books, 1990.

———. "The Reader, the Popular Novel and the Imperative to Participate: Reflections on Public and Private Experience in the Third Reich." *History and Memory* 3, no. 2 (Fall/Winter 1991): 5–44.

Radius, Emilio. *Usi e costumi dell'uomo fascista.* Milan: Rizzoli, 1964.

Radway, Janice A. *Reading the Romance: Women, Patriarchy, and Popular Literature.* Chapel Hill: University of North Carolina Press, 1984.

Raucci, Giuseppe, ed. *Caro Duce: Lettere di donne italiane a Mussolini 1922–1943.* Milan: Rizzoli, 1989.

Redaelli, Cesare. *Iniziando Mussolini alle vie del cielo.* Milan: Stabilimento di Arti Grafiche Fratelli Magnani, 1933.

Redi, Riccardo, ed. *Cinema italiano sotto il fascismo.* Venice: Marsilio, 1979.

Repaci, Antonino. *La Marcia su Roma: Nuova edizione riveduta e accresciuta con altri documenti inediti.* Milan: Rizzoli, 1972.

Rhodes, Anthony Richard Ewart. *The Poet as Superman: A Life of Gabriele D'Annunzio.* London: Weidenfeld and Nicolson, 1959.

Richards, Thomas. *The Commodity Culture of Victorian England: Advertising and Spectacle, 1851–1914.* Stanford: Stanford University Press, 1990.

Ricoeur, Paul. "The Model of the Text: Meaningful Action Considered as a Text." In *Understanding and Social Inquiry,* edited by Fred R. Dallmayr and Thomas A. McCarthy. Notre Dame: University of Notre Dame Press, 1977.

Rizzo, Vincenzo. *Attenti al Duce: Storie minime dell'Italia fascista, 1927–1938.* Florence: Vallecchi, 1981.

Roberts, David D. *The Syndicalist Tradition and Italian Fascism.* Chapel Hill: University of North Carolina Press 1979.

Rocco, Alfredo. *Scritti e discorsi politici.* Milan: Giuffré, 1938.

Rochat, Giorgio. *Militari e politici nella preparazione della campagna d' Etiopia: Studio e documenti, 1932–1936.* Milan: Franco Angeli, 1971.

Rogin, Michael Paul. "Max Weber and Woodrow Wilson: The Iron Cage in Germany and America." *Polity* 3, no. 4 (Summer 1971): 557–575.

Romanelli, Raffaele. "Political Debate, Social History, and the Italian *Borghesia:* Changing Perspectives in Historical Research." *Journal of Modern History* 63 (December 1991): 717–739.

Romano, Sergio. "Sorel e Mussolini." *Storia contemporanea* 15, no. 1 (February 1984): 123–131.

Rosenzweig, Roy. *Eight Hours for What We Will: Workers and Leisure in an Industrial City 1870–1920.* Cambridge: Cambridge University Press, 1983.

Rossi, Cesare, ed. *Il delitto Matteotti nei procedimenti giudiziari e nelle polemiche giornalistiche.* Milan: Ceschina, 1965.

Rowe, William, and Vivian Schelling. *Memory and Modernity: Popular Culture in Latin America.* London: Verso, 1991.

Ruiz, Teofilo F. "Unsacred Monarchy: The Kings of Castile in the Late Middle Ages." In *Rites of Power: Symbolism, Ritual, and Politics since the Middle Ages,* edited by Sean Wilentz. Philadelphia: University of Pennsylvania Press, 1985.

Rumi, Giorgio. *Alle origini della politica estera fascista (1918–1923).* Rome-Bari: Laterza, 1968.

———. "'Revisionismo' fascista ed espansione coloniale (1925–1935)." In *Il regime fascista,* edited by Alberto Aquarone and Maurizio Vernassa. Bologna: Il Mulino, 1974.

Salaris, Claudia. *Le futuriste: Donne e letterature d'avanguardia in Italia (1909– 1944).* Milan: Edizioni delle Donne, 1982.

———. *Storia del futurismo: Libri, giornali, manifesti.* Rome: Editori Riuniti, 1985.

———. *Il futurismo e la pubblicità: Dalla pubblicità dell'arte all'arte della pubblicità.* Milan: Lupetti, 1986.

Salomone, William A. *Italian Democracy in the Making: The Political Scene in the Giolittian Era, 1900–1914.* Philadelphia: University of Pennsylvania Press, 1945.

Salvatorelli Luigi, and Giovanni Mira. *Storia del fascismo: L'Italia dal 1919 al 1945.* Rome: Edizioni di Novissima, 1952.

———. *Storia d'Italia nel periodo fascista.* Turin: Einaudi, 1957.

Salvemini, Gaetano. *Il ministro della malavita.* Rome, 1919.

———. *The Fascist Dictatorship in Italy.* New York: Holt, 1927.

———. *Under the Axe of Fascism.* New York: Viking, 1936.

———. *Scritti sul fascismo.* Milan: Feltrinelli, 1961.

Santarelli, Enzo. "Guerra d'Etiopia, imperialismo e terzo mondo." *Movimento di liberazione in Italia,* no. 97 (1969): 35–51.

Santomassimo, Gian Pasquale. "Antifascismo popolare." *Italia contemporanea* 32, no. 40 (July–September 1980): 39–69.

Sapori, Francesco. *L'arte e il Duce, con 130 illustrazioni fuori testo.* Milan: Mondadori, 1932.

Sarfatti, Margherita Grassini. *The Life of Benito Mussolini.* London: Thornton Butterworth, 1925.

———. *Dux.* Milan: Mondadori, 1926, 1934.

Sarti, Roland. *Fascism and the Industrial Leadership in Italy, 1919–1940: A Study in the Expansion of Private Power under Fascism*. Berkeley: University of California Press, 1971.

————, ed. *The Ax Within: Italian Fascism in Action*. New York: New Viewpoints, 1974.

Savio, Francesco. *Ma l'amore no: Realismo, formalismo, propaganda e telefoni bianchi nel cinema italiano di regime (1930–1943)*. Milan: Sonzogno, 1975.

Savona, A. V., and M. L. Straniero, eds. *Canti dell'Italia fascista (1919–45)*. Milan: Mondadori, 1979.

Scarpellini, Emanuela. *Organizzazione teatrale e politica del teatro nell'Italia fascista*. Florence: La Nuova Italia, 1989.

Schmitt, Carl. *The Concept of the Political*. Translated by George Schwab. New Brunswick, N.J.: Rutgers University Press, 1976.

————. *The Crisis of Parliamentary Democracy*. Translated by Ellen Kennedy. Cambridge, Mass.: MIT Press, 1985.

————. *Political Theology: Four Chapters on the Concept of Sovereignty*. Translated by George Schwab. Cambridge, Mass.: MIT Press, 1985.

Schnapp, Jeffrey. "Epic Demonstrations: Fascist Modernity and the 1932 Exhibition of the Fascist Revolution." In *Fascism, Aesthetics, and Culture*, edited by Richard J. Golsan. Hanover: University Press of New England, 1992.

————. "18 BL: Fascist Mass Spectacle." *Representations*, no. 43 (Summer 1993): 89–125.

Schorske, Carl E. *Fin-de-siècle Vienna: Politics and Culture*. New York: Knopf, 1980.

Schudson, Michael. "The New Validation of Popular Culture: Sense and Sentimentality in Academia." *Critical Studies in Mass Communication*, no. 4 (1987): 51–68.

————. "How Culture Works: Perspectives from Media Studies on the Efficacy of Symbols." *Theory and Society* 2, no. 18 (1989): 153–180.

Scoppola, Pietro. "La Chiesa e il fascismo durante il pontificato di Pio XI." In *Il regime fascista*, edited by Alberto Aquarone and Maurizio Vernassa. Bologna: Il Mulino, 1974.

Seldes, George. *Sawdust Caesar: The Untold History of Mussolini and Fascism*. New York: Harper, 1935.

Serafin, Tullio, and Alceo Toni. *Stile, tradizioni e convenzioni del melodramma italiano del Settecento e dell'Ottocento*. Milan: Ricordi, 1958–64.

Serpieri, Arrigo. *Il compito dell'agronomo nella bonifica integrale*. Rome, 1930.

————. *La legge sulla bonifica integrale nel primo anno di applicazione*. Rome: Istituto Poligrafico di stato, 1931.

————. *La legislazione sulla bonifica*. Rome, 1948.

Shapiro, Gary, and Alan Sica, eds. *Hermeneutics: Questions and Prospects*. Amherst: University of Massachusetts Press, 1984.

Shils, Edward Albert. "Charisma." In *International Encyclopedia of the Social Sciences*. New York: Macmillan, 1968.

————. *Center and Periphery: Essays in Macrosociology*. Chicago: University of Chicago Press, 1975.

Simeone, William E. "Fascists and Folklorists in Italy." *Journal of American Folklore* 91, no. 359: 443–558.

Simmel, Georg. *The Conflict in Modern Culture and Other Essays*. Translated by K. Peter Etzkorn. New York: Teachers College Press, 1968.

Simonini, Augusto. *Il linguaggio di Mussolini*. Milan: Bompiani, 1978.

Sontag, Susan. *Under the Sign of Saturn*. New York: Farrar, Straus and Giroux, 1980.

Sorel, Georges. *Reflections on Violence*. Translated by T. E. Hulme. London: Allen and Unwin, 1916.

Spackman, Barbara. "The Fascist Rhetoric of Virility." *Stanford Italian Review* 8, nos. 1–2 (1990): 81–101.

Spengler, Oswald. *The Hour of Decision, Part One: Germany and World*. Translated by Charles Francis Atkinson. 1934. New York: Knopf, 1962.

Spinosa, Antonio. *Starace*. Milan: Rizzoli, 1981.

Spirito, Ugo. *Il corporativismo: Dall'economia liberale al Corporativismo, i fondamenti della economia corporativa, capitalismo e Corporativismo*. Florence: Sansoni, 1970.

———. "Il capitalismo come liberalismo assoluto a socialismo assoluto." In *Il fascismo: Antologia di scritti critici*, edited by Costanzo Casucci. Bologna: Il Mulino, 1982.

Spiro, Herbert J. "Totalitarianism." In *Encyclopedia of the Social Sciences*. New York: Macmillan, 1968.

Spriano, Paolo. *Torino operaia nella grande guerra (1914–1918)*. Turin: Einaudi, 1960.

———. *The Occupation of the Factories: Italy 1920*. Translated by Gwyn A. Williams. London: Pluto Press, 1975.

Staderini, Alessandra. "La Federazione Italiana dei Consorzi Agrari (1920–1940)." *Storia contemporanea* 9, nos. 5/6 (December 1978): 951–1025.

———. "La politica cerealicola del regime: l'impostazione della battaglia del grano." *Storia contemporanea* 9, nos. 5/6 (December 1978): 1027–1079.

Staderini, Alessandra, and Mario Toscano. "La campagna tra realtà e propaganda." In *L'economia italiana tra le due guerre 1919–1939*. Rome: Comune di Roma, 1984.

Starobinski, Jean. *Jean-Jacques Rousseau: Transparency and Obstruction*. Translated by Arthur Goldhammer. Chicago: University of Chicago Press, 1988.

Stern, Fritz. "The Political Consequences of the Unpolitical German." *History, A Meridian Periodical*, no. 3 (September 1960): 104–134.

———. *The Politics of Cultural Despair: A Study in the Rise of the Germanic Ideology*. Berkeley: University of California Press, 1961.

Stern, Joseph Peter. *Hitler: The Führer and the People*. Berkeley: University of California Press, 1975.

Sternhell, Zeev, Mario Sznajder, and Maia Asheri. *The Birth of Fascist Ideology: From Cultural Rebellion to Political Revolution*. Translated by David Maisel. Princeton: Princeton University Press, 1994.

Stollman, Rainer. "Fascist Politics as a Total Work of Art: Tendencies of the Aesthetization of Political Life in National Socialism." *New German Critique*, no. 14 (Spring 1978): 41–60.

Stone, Marla. "Staging Fascism: The Exhibition of the Fascist Revolution." *Journal of Contemporary History* 28 (1993): 215–243.

Stromberg, Roland N. *Redemption by War: The Intellectuals and 1914*. Lawrence: Regents Press of Kansas, 1982.

Strong, Roy C. *Art and Power: Renaissance Festivals, 1450–1650*. Berkeley: University of California Press, 1984.

Stuart Hughes, H. *Consciousness and Society: The Reorientation of European Social Thought 1890–1930.* New York: Vintage, 1958.

Susman, Warren I. *Culture as History: The Transformation of American Society in the Twentieth Century.* New York: Pantheon, 1984.

Tager, Michael. "Myth and Politics in Sorel and Barthes." *Journal of the History of Ideas* 47, no. 4 (October–December 1986): 625–639.

Talmon, Jacob Leib. *The Rise of Totalitarian Democracy.* Boston: Beacon Press, 1952.

Tannenbaum, Edward R. *The Fascist Experience: Italian Society and Culture 1922–1945.* New York: Basic Books, 1972.

Tasca, Angelo. *The Rise of Italian Fascism, 1918–1922.* London: Methuen, 1938.

Tassinari, Giuseppe. *Ten Years of Integral Land-Reclamation under the Mussolini Act.* Faenza: Fratelli Lega, 1939.

Tattara, Giuseppe. "Cerealicoltura e politica agraria durante il fascismo." In *L'economia italiana, 1861–1940,* edited by Gianno Toniolo. Rome-Bari: Laterza, 1978.

Theweleit, Klaus. *Male Fantasies.* 2 vols. Translated by Stephen Conway. Minneapolis: University of Minnesota Press, 1987–1989.

Tiersten, Lisa. "Redefining Consumer Culture: Recent Literature on Consumption and the Bourgeoisie in Western Europe." *Radical History Review,* no. 57 (1993): 116–159.

Timpanaro, Sebastiano. *Sul materialismo.* Pisa: Nistri-Lischi, 1970.

Toniolo, Gianni. *L'economia italiana, 1861–1940.* Rome-Bari: Laterza, 1978.

Treves, Anna. *Le migrazioni interne nell'Italia fascista: Politica e realtà demografica.* Turin: Einaudi, 1976.

Tulis, Jeffrey K. *The Rhetorical Presidency.* Princeton: Princeton University Press, 1987.

Tumarkin, Nina. *Lenin Lives! The Lenin Cult in Soviet Russia.* Cambridge, Mass.: Harvard University Press, 1983.

Vajda, Mihaly. *Fascism as a Mass Movement.* New York: St. Martin's, 1976.

Valeri, Nino. *Da Giolitti a Mussolini: Momenti della crisi del liberalismo.* Florence: Parenti, 1957.

———. *D'Annunzio davanti al fascismo, con documenti inediti.* Florence: Le Monnier, 1963.

Valtz Mannucci, Loretta. "Aquile e tacchini: iconografie di stato." In *L'estetica della politica,* edited by Maurizio Vaudagna. Rome-Bari: Laterza, 1989.

Vannutelli, Cesare. "The Living Standards of Italian Workers, 1929–1939." In *The Ax Within: Italian Fascism in Action,* edited by Roland Sarti. New York: New Viewpoints, 1974.

Vettori, Giuseppe, ed. *Duce & ducetti: Citazioni dall'Italia fascista.* Rome: Newton Compton, 1975.

Villani, Dino. *50 anni di pubblicità in Italia.* Milan: L'Ufficio Moderno, 1957.

———. *Storia del manifesto pubblicitario.* Milan: Omnia, 1964.

Virilio, Paul. "Futurismo e fascismo." In *Futurismo Futurismi,* edited by Serge Fauchereau, Antonio Porta, and Claudia Salaris. Milan: Edizioni Intrapresa, 1986.

Visser, Romke. "Fascist Doctrine and the Cult of the Romanità." *Journal of Contemporary History* 27 (1992): 5–22.

Vittori, Giuliano, ed. *C'era una volta il duce: Il regime in cartolina.* Rome: Savelli, 1975.

Vivarelli, Roberto. *Il dopoguerra in Italia e l'avvento del fascismo (1918–1922)*. Naples: Istituto Italiano per gli Studi Storici, 1967.

Von Geldern, James R. *Bolshevik Festivals, 1917–1920*. Berkeley: University of California Press, 1993.

Von Henneberg, Krystyna. "Tripoli: The Making of Fascist Colonial Capital." In *Streets: Critical Perspectives on Public Space*, edited by Zeynep Celik, Diane Favro, and Richard Ingersoll. Berkeley: University of California Press, 1994.

———. "Planning the Model Colony: Architecture and Urban Planning in the Making of Italian Fascist Libya, 1922–1943." Ph.D. dissertation. University of California, Berkeley, 1996.

Von Hofmannstahl, Hugo. *Selected Essays*. Edited by Mary E. Gilbert. Oxford: Basil Blackwell, 1955.

Wagner-Pacifici, Robin Erica. *The Moro Morality Play: Terrorism as Social Drama*. Chicago: University of Chicago Press, 1986.

Waite, Robert George Leeson. *Vanguard of Nazism: The Free Corps Movement in Post-War Germany, 1918–1923*. Cambridge, Mass.: Harvard University Press, 1952.

Walton, Whitney. *France at the Crystal Palace: Bourgeois Taste and Artisan Manufacture in the Nineteenth Century*. Berkeley: University of California Press, 1992.

Weber, Eugene. *France: Fin de Siècle*. Cambridge, Mass.: Belknap Press, 1986.

Weber, Max. *From Max Weber: Essays in Sociology*. Edited and translated by H. H. Gerth and C. Wright Mills. 1946. New York: Oxford University Press, 1980.

———. *Economy and Society: An Outline of Interpretive Sociology*. 2 vols. Edited by Guenther Roth and Claus Wittich. Berkeley: University of California Press, 1978.

Webster, Richard A. *The Cross and the Fasces: Christian Democracy and Fascism in Italy*. Stanford: Stanford University Press, 1960.

Weintraub, Jeff. "The Theory and Politics of the Public/Private Distinction." Paper presented at the American Political Science Association, San Francisco, 1990.

White, Hayden V. *The Content of the Form: Narrative Discourse and Historical Representation*. Baltimore: Johns Hopkins University Press, 1987.

Whitebook, Joel. "Hypostatizing Thanatos: Lacan's Analysis of the Ego." *Constellations* 1, no. 2 (October 1994): 214–230.

Wilentz, Sean, ed. *Rites of Power: Symbolism, Ritual, and Politics since the Middle Ages*. Philadelphia: University of Pennsylvania Press, 1985.

Williams, Rosalind H. *Dream Worlds: Mass Consumption in Late Nineteenth-Century France*. Berkeley: University of California Press, 1982.

Willis, Paul, and Philip Corrigan. "Orders of Experience: Working Class Cultural Forms." *Social Text*, no. 7 (Spring–Summer 1983): 85–103.

Willis, Paul E. *Learning to Labour: How Working Class Kids Get Working Class Jobs*. Farnborough, U.K.: Saxon House, 1977.

Wilson, Elizabeth. *Adorned in Dreams: Fashion and Modernity*. London: Virago, 1985.

Wohl, Robert. *The Generation of 1914*. Cambridge, Mass.: Harvard University Press, 1979.

————. *A Passion for Wings: Aviation and the Western Imagination, 1908–1918.* New Haven: Yale University Press, 1994.

Wolin, Richard. *Walter Benjamin: An Aesthetic of Redemption.* New York: Columbia University Press, 1982.

————. "Foucault's Aesthetic Decisionism." *Telos,* no. 67 (Spring 1986): 71–86.

Woolf, S. J., ed. *The Nature of Fascism.* New York: Random House, 1968.

Zangrandi, Ruggero. *Il lungo viaggio attraverso il fascismo: Contributo alla storia di una generazione.* Milan: Feltrinelli, 1962.

Zanotti-Karp, Angela. "Elite Theory and Ideology." *Social Research* 37, no. 2 (Summer 1970): 275–295.

Zeri, Federico. "I francobolli italiani: Grafica e ideologia dalle origini al 1948." In *Storia dell'arte italiana,* vol. 2, *Grafica e immagine.* Turin: Einaudi, 1980.

Zunino, Piergiorgio. *L'ideologia del fascismo: Miti, credenze e valori nella stabilizzazione del regime.* Bologna: Il Mulino, 1985.

Photograph Credits

Figure 1:   Reprinted with permission of *Variety*, Inc.

Figure 2:   From Dino Biondi, *La fabbrica del Duce* (Florence: Vallecchi, 1967).

Figure 3:   From Renzo De Felice and Luigi Goglia, *Mussolini: Il mito* (Rome-Bari: Laterza, 1983).

Figure 4:   From Renzo De Felice and Luigi Goglia, *Storia fotografica del fascismo* (Rome-Bari: Laterza, 1982).

Figure 5:   From *Gli Annitrenta: Arte e cultura in Italia* (Milan: Mazzotta, 1982).

Figure 6:   From Renzo De Felice and Luigi Goglia, *Storia fotografica del fascismo* (Rome-Bari: Laterza, 1982).

Figure 7:   From Dino Biondi, *La fabbrica del Duce* (Florence: Vallecchi, 1967).

Figure 8:   From *Storia d'Italia*. Annali 2. *L'immagine fotografica, 1845–1945*, by Carlo Bertelli and Giulio Bollati (Turin: Einaudi, 1979), volume 2.

Figure 9:   From *Storia d'Italia*. Annali 2. *L'immagine fotografica, 1845–1945*, by Carlo Bertelli and Giulio Bollati (Turin: Einaudi, 1979), volume 2.

Figure 10:   From Renzo De Felice and Luigi Goglia, *Mussolini: Il mito* (Rome-Bari: Laterza, 1983).

Figure 11:   From Plinio Ciani, *Graffiti del Ventennio* (Milan: SugarCo., 1975).

Figure 12:   From Renzo De Felice and Luigi Goglia, *Storia fotografica del fascismo* (Rome-Bari: Laterza, 1982).

Figure 13:   From Fidia Gambetti, *Gli anni che scottano* (Milan: Mursia, 1967).

Figure 14:   From Asvero Gravelli, ed., *Vademecum dello stile fascista* (Rome: Nuova Europa, [1940]).

Figure 15:   From Teresa Maria Mazzatosta and Claudio Volpi, *L'Italietta fascista (Lettere al potere, 1936–1943)* (Bologna: Cappelli, 1980).

Figure 16:   From Asvero Gravelli, ed., *Vademecum dello stile fascista* (Rome: Nuova Europa, [1940]).

Figure 17:   Copyright 1934 by N. Tim Gidal.

Figure 18:   From Cesare Longobardi, *Land-Reclamation in Italy: Rural Revival in the Building of a Nation* (London: P. S. King and Son Ltd., 1936).

Figure 19:   From Enzo Nizza, ed., *Autobiografia del fascismo* (Milan: La Pietra, 1962).

Figure 20:   From Giuliano Vittori, ed., *C'era una volta il duce: Il regime in cartolina* (Rome: Savelli, 1975).

Figure 21:   From Enzo Nizza, ed., *Autobiografia del fascismo* (Milan: La Pietra, 1962).

Index

Addis Ababa, 176, 177
Adowa, 167, 179
aesthetics: and anaesthetics, 12, 192; and
   art, 10–12; Benjamin, on politics and,
   9–10; and the body, 11, 12; Borgese,
   on fascist politics and, 8; and decisionism, 204–205n9; etymological
   meaning of, 11; and fascism, 8–10,
   39–40, 117–118, 188, 192–193; and
   harmony, 28; Nazi Germany's politics and, 8; and politics, 8–10, 192–
   194; Simmel on, 28; and totalitarianism, 27–28; Weber on religion and,
   200n46
Amba Alagi, 179
Amendola, Giovanni, 27
Anti-Bourgeois Exhibit, 105
Antieuropa, 107
Apollonio, Mario, 115
Aquarone, Alberto, 62
Ardali, Paolo (father), 65
Arditi, 34, 72
art for art's sake, 9, 10, 13, 117, 187; and
   autonomy of art, 9, 11
Austin, J. L., 3
Autarchic Exhibit of the Italian Mineral,
   105
autarchy, 138, 150
autogenesis, 11; Buck-Morss on, 24–25;
   in fascism, 8, 13, 67, 88
Avanti!, 34, 35

Balla, Giacomo, 99
Barthes, Roland, 94
Basso, Lelio, 27
Battle of Wheat, 150–155; Competition
   for the Victory of Wheat, 152; and
   demographic growth, 158–162; failure of the, 154; Mussolini as propa-

gandist for the, 152–153; and the
   reclamation of the Pontine Ager,
   153; and the symbolism of bread,
   155–162; and war, 160–162
Baum, Frank, 140–141
beautiful, the, and the sublime,
   11–12
Beavan, Margaret, 53
Befana fascista, 79, 97, 234n231
Beltramelli, Antonio, and biography of
   Mussolini, 50
Benjamin, Walter, 8, 14, 187; on aesthetic
   politics and fascism, 9–10, 25; on
   aesthetic politics and war, 9, 39; on
   aura, 9; on concentration and distraction, 199n42; on experience
   and sensory alienation, 12, 201n56
Béraud, Henri: on imitators of Mussolini, 82; on Mussolini's omnipresence, 78, 79–80, 82
Bergson, Henri, 30
Berneri, Camillo, 73
Bidou, Henri, 51
biographies, and personality, 47
Birth of Rome, 91–92, 113, 115
black shirt, 241n53, 241n56; rules on
   the, 101–104; as symbol of fascism,
   101, 103
Black Shirts, 64, 65, 101, 149, 176, 182;
   and the March on Rome, 1–2
Blanc, Giuseppe, 72
blood: fascism's rhetoric of, 33, 35–38,
   167; origins of the mystique of,
   195n6
Bonomi, Ivanoe, 48, 85
Borgese, Giuseppe Antonio, 8
Boselli, Paolo, 48
Briand, Aristide, 20
Brooks, Peter, 177

Compositor: Integrated Composition Systems
Text: 10/13 Aldus
Display: Syntax
Printer and binder: Thomson-Shore, Inc.